CULTURAL HERITAGE LAW AND POLICY

Series Editors

PROFESSOR FRANCESCO FRANCIONI

Emeritus Professor at the European University Institute, Florence

PROFESSOR ANA VRDOLJAK

UNESCO Chair of International Law and Cultural Heritage and Professor of Law at the University of Technology, Sydney

International Heritage Law for Communities

CULTURAL HERITAGE LAW AND POLICY

The aim of this series is to publish significant and original research on and scholarly analysis of all aspects of cultural heritage law through the lens of international law, private international law, and comparative law. The series is wide in scope, traversing disciplines, regions, and viewpoints. Topics given particular prominence are those which, while of interest to academic lawyers, have significant bearing on policymaking and current public discourse on the interaction between art, heritage, and the law.

International Heritage Law for Communities

Exclusion and Re-Imagination

LUCAS LIXINSKI

OXFORD
UNIVERSITY PRESS

OXFORD
UNIVERSITY PRESS

Great Clarendon Street, Oxford, OX2 6DP,
United Kingdom

Oxford University Press is a department of the University of Oxford.
It furthers the University's objective of excellence in research, scholarship,
and education by publishing worldwide. Oxford is a registered trade mark of
Oxford University Press in the UK and in certain other countries

First Edition published in 2019

Impression: 1

Published in the United States of America by Oxford University Press
198 Madison Avenue, New York, NY 10016, United States of America

British Library Cataloguing in Publication Data
Data available

Library of Congress Control Number: 2018967782

ISBN 978–0–19–884330–6

Printed and bound by
CPI Group (UK) Ltd, Croydon, CR0 4YY

To Darragh
partner, friend, home

Series Editors' Preface

States' dominance in the definition and in the operation of contemporary international law remains a received wisdom in the halls of international and regional organizations, offices of departments of foreign affairs, and classrooms of universities, worldwide. This trait has been particularly marked in respect of the legal protection of cultural heritage. It informs the leading multilateral treaties in the field—from those covering armed conflict to World Heritage, and from regulating the trade in cultural objects to safeguarding intangible heritage. This bias is understandable.

If states are an artifice, then the creation, protection, and promotion of the *national* cultural identity and patrimony has been foundational and fundamental to its acceptance by its citizenry. It is no coincidence then that the way protection of cultural heritage has been articulated internationally is driven first and foremost by this preoccupation. It is a bias which is replicated in related areas of international law covering culture and cultural heritage including human rights, international humanitarian law, international criminal law, international economic law and development law, and intellectual property and environmental law.

Yet this was never the whole picture. At a time in international law and human relations that has uncovered the unsustainability of long-held principles and systems, this edifice of state dominance is being challenged in multi-faceted ways, from human rights, the protection of the environment, the safeguarding of cultural heritage. These challenges have always been present. However, our moment is significant in their intensity and proliferation.

Lixinski's focus on the role of 'communities' in contemporary cultural heritage law brings us to the epicentre of this phenomenon. Minorities and Indigenous peoples have been recognized by international law as possessing their own distinct ethnic, cultural, religious, and linguistic identities and which attract legal rights for their protection and promotion. Recognition of these rights belies the very notion of a monolithic, national cultural identity. Much of this drive is propelled by human rights law. Significantly, contemporary understanding of 'community' has moved beyond groups defined by ethnic, cultural, or religious identity to cover children, elder people, women, gender and sexual orientation, people with disabilities, migrants and refugees, and workers. There is also growing acknowledgement that people can identify with multiple communities and such identities can be fluid and competing in nature. This book provides us with a rich, broad approach and thoughtful analysis of the implications of this phenomenon for the legal protection of cultural heritage today. The current legal frameworks, the priorities they promote and inequities that they sublimate are found wanting. In particular, the opening up of the state to cultural claims advanced by people, groups, and communities remains hampered by the traditional notions of sovereignty and of 'national culture' which underscore the still dominant role of states in relevant international organizations. By focussing on this tension, Lixinski's clear-eyed examination offers a way forward. He recognizes that in challenging the central tenets of the edifice created by states, communities enable a means of redefining and renewing international cultural heritage law and international law more broadly.

Francesco Francioni and
Ana Filipa Vrdoljak
December 2018

Acknowledgements

I am incredibly thankful to a number of people, anonymous and otherwise, as well as institutions, for this book. I am thankful to the Faculty of Law at UNSW Sydney, for being a fantastic intellectual home where this project could be brewed, and for their funding for much of this work through an Early Career Research Grant at the initial stages of this project in 2012, and also for a Law School Research Fellowship in 2016 that gave me precious writing time. Their Early Career Grant allowed me to undertake research at the UNESCO Archives which was key to shaping this book. I am also very thankful to the staff at the UNESCO Archives in Paris for their generosity.

I am grateful, too, to Kathy Bowrey, who has been my mentor at UNSW since my first day at the university, and continues to offer honest and constructive insights into my research. I thank many of my colleagues, whose input at various Law Staff seminars, and also one-on-one conversations over lunch or randomly in the hallway, proved useful to clarify ideas and identify new avenues of inquiry. Too many to list, I instead thank them as a group in an extremely collegial environment. Ana Vrdoljak and Francesco Francioni also provided insightful feedback to an earlier version of this manuscript and helped sharpen my core argument.

I would also like to thank the many audiences who have generously and anonymously given me feedback when I presented several parts of this book at different conferences. I am thankful to audiences in Adelaide, Amsterdam, Cambridge (UK), Cambridge (Massachusetts), Canberra, Doha, Durham, Florence, Lund, New Delhi, New York, Oslo, Ravenna, Sydney, Trondheim, Vienna, Warsaw, Washington, DC, and Wollongong. My students in Sydney, Sherbrooke, Santiago, Porto Alegre, Geneva, and Bogotá have also been incredibly receptive and responsive audiences, to whom I am grateful not only for the input, but also for the energy with which they have injected me to pursue this project. And the following very talented (former) students, whom I met and had the privilege of mentoring in the Philip C. Jessup International Law Moot Court Competition, provided me with research assistance for different chapters: Sean Cameron, Matthew Kingsland, and Camila Zúñiga. All errors and omissions, of course, remain my own.

A special thanks is also due to the Oxford University Press team behind the production of this book: Merel Alstein, Jack McNichol, Francesco Francioni, and Ana Vrdoljak. The two anonymous reviewers of the manuscript also gave me valuable feedback.

Finally, I thank my partner, Darragh, to whom this book is dedicated, and the many friends I was lucky to make and keep along the way.

Contents

Table of Cases

For the benefit of digital users, indexed terms that span two pages (e.g., 52–53) may, on occasion, appear on only one of those pages.

INTERNATIONAL

DOMESTIC

Table of Legislation

INTERNATIONAL SOFT LAW INSTRUMENTS

DOMESTIC LEGISLATION

List of Abbreviations

AHD	Authorized Heritage Discourse
ARSIWA	Articles on the Responsibility of States for Internationally Wrongful Acts
CBD	Convention on Biological Diversity
CH	cultural heritage
EC	European Communities
ECCC	Extraordinary Chambers in the Courts of Cambodia
GATS	General Agreement on Trade in Services
GATT	General Agreement on Tarrifs and Trade
ICC	International Criminal Court
ICCROM	International Centre for the Study of the Preservation and Restoration of Cultural Property
ICH	intangible cultural heritage
ICHC	Convention for the Safeguarding of the Intangible Cultural Heritage
ICJ	International Court of Justice
ICL	international criminal law
ICOMOS	International Council on Monuments and Sites
ICSID	International Centre for the Settlement of Investment Disputes
ICTY	International Criminal Tribunal for the former Yugoslavia
IHL	international humanitarian law
IP	intellectual property
IUCN	International Union for Conservation of Nature
NGO	non-governmental organization
OUV	outstanding universal value
TK	traditional knowledge
TRIPS	Agreement on Trade-Related Aspects of Intellectual Property Rights
UCH	underwater cultural heritage
UCHC	Convention on the Protection of the Underwater Cultural Heritage
UN	United Nations
UNEP	United Nations Environment Programme
UNESCO	United Nations Educational, Scientific, and Cultural Organization
UNWTO	World Tourism Organization
WCED	World Commission on Environment and Development
WHC	World Heritage Convention
WHIPCOE	World Heritage Indigenous Peoples Council of Experts
WIPO	World Intellectual Property Organization
WTO	World Trade Organization

1

Introduction

I argue in this book that the five key treaties for the protection of different types of heritage under the United Nations Educational, Scientific and Cultural Organization (UNESCO) have, by design or in their implementation, effectively prevented local communities, who bear the brunt of the costs associated with international heritage protection, from having a say in how their heritage is managed. The exclusion of local communities often alienates them not only from international decision-making processes, but also from their cultural heritage, ultimately meaning that systems put in place for the protection of cultural heritage contribute to their disappearance in the long term. This book adds to existing literature by looking at these UNESCO treaties not as isolated regimes (which is the common practice in the field) but rather as belonging to a discursive continuum on cultural heritage. In doing so, the book focuses on themes that cut across the relevant UNESCO regimes, rather than on the regimes themselves. It uses this mechanism to highlight the shortcomings of UNESCO treaties, and how choices made in drafting the relevant treaties have continuing and potentially negative impacts on how we think about and safeguard heritage. My intention in this book is not to question the wisdom of the drafters of the multiple treaties, but rather to understand the compromises made at the time, and thereby question the continuing validity of some of the mechanisms in international heritage law.

In the past few years, the spotlight has fallen on UNESCO for its actions in the field of cultural heritage protection. The conflict in Syria and Iraq, as well as the civil war in Mali, have brought into evidence the importance of cultural heritage internationally; as a symbol of our shared humanity, an attack on cultural heritage meant a denunciation of an entire cosmopolitan project, and, as such, heritage came under attack in conflicts led by fundamentalist groups.

One result of these attacks on heritage was that legal tools meant to prevent and punish those actions came under close scrutiny. An effect of this scrutiny has been to highlight the diversity of regimes that have been created under the aegis of UNESCO over the past seven decades to protect different types of heritage. These regimes do not always communicate with one another, and that can lead to mismatches in addressing complex situations like the conflict in Syria and Iraq, for instance, where at least three different UNESCO treaties are triggered: the 1954 Hague Convention for the protection of heritage in wartime,[1] because we are dealing with a conflict; the 1970 Convention on movable cultural heritage,[2] because of the extensive looting of museums and archaeological sites, at least partly to finance the conflict on the side of the insurgents; and the 1972 World Heritage Convention (WHC),[3] because many of the sites attacked for propaganda value, like the ancient city of Palmyra, are on the World Heritage List.

Beyond issues of effectiveness of individual regimes, the conflict in Syria and Iraq has also emphasized the need for coordination among the several treaties, which have for the most part acted separately from one another since their creation. UNESCO has now gone to great lengths to create better coordination mechanisms,[4] and I am hopeful these efforts will bear fruit.

These actions, centred on the language of international campaigns, echo efforts in the 1950s and 1960s around cultural heritage that put UNESCO on the proverbial map, like the Aswan Dam campaign in Egypt and Sudan, and the responses to the flooding of Venice and Florence.[5] The Syria and Iraq heritage campaign, if it may be called that, also underscores the fraught connection between heritage and peace: more specifically, peace narratives are hardly ever directly woven into heritage listings or other UNESCO heritage mechanisms,[6] and that omission hinders the potential for heritage to advance the peace mandate given to it by the UNESCO Constitution.[7] And, from the point of view of international law, the situations in Syria, Iraq, and Mali showcase the shortcomings of implementation of international heritage law, in at least two ways.

The first way is apparent: there is a need to analyse synergies, convergences and conflicts among different specialized regimes of international law for the protection of cultural heritage under UNESCO. The majority of the literature that has attempted to tackle the field of international heritage law to date has focused on each

[1] Convention for the Protection of Cultural Property in the Event of Armed Conflict with Regulations for the Execution of the Convention 1954 (adopted 14 May 1954, entered into force 7 August 1956) 249 UNTS 240 (1954 Hague Convention).

[2] Convention on the Means of Prohibiting and Preventing the Illicit Import, Export and Transfer of Ownership of Cultural Property 1970 (adopted 14 November 1970, entered into force 24 April 1972) 823 UNTS 231 (1970 Convention).

[3] Convention concerning the Protection of the World Cultural and Natural Heritage 1972 (adopted 23 November 1972, entered into force 15 December 1975) 1037 UNTS 151 (WHC).

[4] See e.g. UNESCO, *UNESCO reiterates call for unity and coordination to protect Syrian Cultural Heritage*, available at <http://whc.unesco.org/en/news/1475> (accessed 27 October 2017); and UNESCO, *International Coordination Committee for the Safeguarding of the Cultural Heritage of Iraq*, available at <http://whc.unesco.org/en/activities/181/> (accessed 27 October 2017). See also Lostal, Marina, *International Cultural Heritage Law in Armed Conflict: Case-Studies of Syria, Libya, Mali, the Invasion of Iraq, and the Buddhas of Bamiyan* (Cambridge University Press, 2017).

[5] For a history, which details how '[n]ational interests routinely trumped internationalist efforts', see Meskell, Lynn, *A Future in Ruins: UNESCO, World Heritage, and the Dream of Peace* (Oxford University Press, 2018), 28–58 (quote at 41).

[6] Except for dissonant/difficult/negative heritage. On this connection, see generally Lixinski, Lucas, 'Cultural Heritage Law and Transitional Justice: Lessons from South Africa', *International Journal of Transitional Justice* 9(2) (2015), 278–96.

[7] I am grateful to Gabriele D'amico for this insight. On the different versions of peace in the original UNESCO mandate, see Laves, Walter H. C. and Thomson, Charles A., *UNESCO: Purpose, Progress, Prospects* (Indiana University Press, 1957), 29–30.

regime or type of heritage in isolation. In doing so, these works, however valuable in their own right, also have blind spots, in failing to critically examine how international heritage law can operate as a whole, as opposed to in its sub-niches.[8] As UNESCO has developed new and more sophisticated approaches for the protection of cultural heritage, the regimes have multiplied and overlaps have become evident. This plurality has now become a significant problem in itself, impacting upon the effectiveness of the regimes.

Secondly, these regimes still rely on a particular state-centric version of international law, in which substate actors are largely ignored. At most, one can speak of an object-centric version of heritage law,[9] but that assumes a certain intrinsic value to heritage that is inconsistent with its political uses. Not only does this mismatch fly in the face of an effective 'human dimension' of international heritage law,[10] but it also means that ultimately these regimes are less effective. If local communities, who live with, in, or around heritage and in many respects practice and keep alive this very heritage, are disengaged from legal governance projects, inevitably they will be disengaged from the heritage itself, and legal structures put in place to ensure the existence of heritage for future generations will in fact be at least partly responsible for the disappearance of said heritage.

This book focuses on the challenge of participation in the governance of important cultural resources. More specifically, it investigates the possibilities of promotion of community-based governance of cultural heritage. As cultural heritage is regulated by international law, communities who live with the heritage and keep it alive tend to be excluded from management processes.

Heritage law is an important vehicle for identity and the protection of the built and natural environment. According to the UNESCO Constitution, it is responsible for creating national cohesiveness, intercultural understanding, and world peace. It is also an important driver of economic development, be it through tourism or the use of the knowledge associated with heritage practices. Although UNESCO has accomplished many great things in the field of international heritage safeguarding,[11] the protection of these resources is also undermined because UNESCO, in creating a specialized toolset for dealing with heritage, has gradually moved heritage concerns away from the people who interact with it on a daily basis. These people, or communities, are responsible for conserving the heritage that exists around them on a daily basis, and for keeping the cultural connections between people and physical heritage alive. These connections are what makes heritage meaningful, and more than 'an old

[8] I am in fact deeply indebted to these works. See e.g. Blake, Janet, *International Cultural Heritage Law* (Oxford University Press, 2015); Forrest, Craig, *International Law and the Protection of Cultural Heritage* (Routledge, 2010); Nafziger, James A. R., and Scovazzi, Tullio (eds), *The Cultural Heritage of Mankind* (Martinus Nijhoff, 2008).

[9] Fechner, Frank C., 'The Fundamental Aims of Cultural Property Law', *International Journal of Cultural Property* 7(2) (1998), 376–94, 379.

[10] Francioni, Francesco, 'The Human Dimension of International Cultural Heritage Law: An Introduction', *European Journal of International Law* 22(1) (2011), 9–16 (even though he suggests heritage does have intrinsic value).

[11] Lixinski, Lucas, '*Luci e Ombre*: The Bright and Dark Sides of International Heritage Law', *Italian Yearbook of International Law* 22 (2012), 133–53. See also generally Chapter 8.

building', or 'a beautiful site'. The importance of local communities' connection to heritage cannot be underestimated.

Internationally, communities have been involved in the early implementation of the UNESCO culture mandate, which includes cultural heritage protection. However, as the organization evolved, communities were gradually excluded from governance processes, and heritage management became the domain of experts, as is discussed in Chapter 3.

By shedding light on the unintended consequences of UNESCO treaties, the book also maps how UNESCO defines its own powers in the field, and how the convergence of stakeholders such as states, heritage experts, museum communities, and private parties authorizes and exploits heritage for purposes that often do not correspond with the objectives of people who create and live with or around cultural heritage that has gained international recognition. A principled choice in defence of communities is not uncontroversial, and has for instance been charged with effectively frustrating multiculturalism, which is one of the objectives of heritage safeguarding in international law.[12] But I maintain that communities, as the basic stakeholders, should be at the centre of decisions affecting their heritage, as opposed to the current situation of exclusion from those processes.

In many respects, this book is also an attempt at promoting a critically engaged international heritage law, which challenges the conservation paradigm under which heritage is usually thought of, defined, and protected (discussed in what follows). In doing this, I also seek to promote a reengagement between heritage lawyers and heritage scholars and professionals in other disciplines—an engagement which has waned, and needs to be recovered if the possibilities of the law as a language of emancipation are to be tapped into. In addition to the reigning conservation paradigm, other obstacles that need to be tackled to pave the way for greater critical engagement are the state-centric nature of heritage, and the operation of the public/private distinction with respect to heritage law.

One of the key issues that needs to be considered a priori is the nature of culture in relation to basic principles of international law. International law is based on state-centrism, which comes a long way in alienating communities from their heritage and allowing culture to in some respects become a proxy for state sovereignty (as discussed in Chapter 2), and in the name of subsidiarity, which is a general principle of international law[13] and applicable particularly in regulatory attempts related to cultural matters.[14] Also importantly, international law in many respects

[12] Fishman, Joseph P., 'Locating the International Interest in Intranational Cultural Heritage Disputes', *The Yale Journal of International Law* 35 (2010), 347–404, 352.

[13] Carozza, Paolo G., 'Subsidiarity as a Structural Principle of International Human Rights Law', *American Journal of International Law* 97 (2003) 38–79.

[14] Fechner (n 9) 380. But see Anglin, Raechel, 'The World Heritage List: Bridging the Cultural Property Nationalism–Internationalism Divide', *Yale Journal of Law & the Humanities* 20(2) (2008), 241–75, 242–3 (arguing that certain mechanisms of international heritage law can bridge nationalism and internationalism, even if the author does not include communities in her analysis, and focuses on states and UNESCO as the only stakeholders); and Francioni, Francesco, 'Beyond State Sovereignty: The Protection of Cultural Heritage as a Shared Interest of Humanity', *Michigan Journal of International Law* 25 (2003–4), 1209–28, 1210 (arguing that international heritage law in fact helps promote a move beyond state sovereignty).

conditions heritage as being territorial. But the mapping of heritage onto territory is problematic, in that it reinforces a certain static version of culture that, while in line with international law's contingencies and voluntarism, shapes heritage as territorial without taking into account that territory as a legal-political construct is not static in the same way as territory as a geological reality. More specifically, international heritage law ends up defining as Iraqi, for instance, the heritage of Mesopotamia, and as Canadian the heritage of Indigenous inhabitants of North America. Territory also focuses on statehood, and not on people, as Westphalian international law glosses over communities.[15] And even more contemporary forms of international law are increasingly territorialized as they pay more attention to the local, according to some.[16]

Territory, as a sovereignty trope, shares many of its effects with the public/private distinction,[17] reinforcing for instance a separation between domestic and international law that neglects the role of domestic law, and particularly alternative dispute resolution, with respect to heritage.[18] The public/private distinction is also key to bear in mind when thinking critically about international heritage law. More specifically, heritage in many respects is 'structured by the push and pull between the private nature of property and the public nature of culture',[19] which affects not only legal regimes, but also fundamentally what counts as law or heritage. As Kuzmarov argues, 'the tension between the public and the private spheres arises out of the fact that within leading political theories culture is the purview of the state, while property is the purview of everything else—nonstate actors, such as corporations, individuals, and civil society'.[20]

Communities are usually pushed into the private, and therefore rendered invisible; likewise, private regulation that affects the possibilities of heritage is largely neglected by international heritage law, and the important historical impact of private lawmaking (sometimes even in questioning the boundaries between legal and illegal) is missed.[21] Private actions are largely deemed to be apolitical, a separation

[15] This problematic relationship with territory can also be illustrated through the lenses of regionalism as a tool for the construction of shared cohesion and peace. For instance, the fluidity of Eastern European borders until the mid-twentieth century favours a common Eastern European identity. However, heritage projects in the region, while a number of them try to foster shared identity, are still invariably articulated in the language of nationalism, or, at the very least, administratively fall under the authority of one national government. That is the case particularly with the restitution of cultural objects, where movable heritage is returned to fixed (or quasi-fixed) territory. I am grateful to Eva Manikowska for this insight. On regionalism in international heritage law, see Blake (n 8) 313–36.

[16] Eslava, Luis, *Local Space, Global Life: The Everyday Operation of International Law and Development* (Cambridge University Press, 2015), 262.

[17] See e.g. Francioni, Francesco, 'Public and Private in the International Protection of Global Cultural Goods', *The European Journal of International Law* 23(3) (2012), 719–30.

[18] For instance, see Goodman, Simon, *The Orpheus Clock: The Search for My Family's Art Treasures Stolen by the Nazis* (Scribe, 2015).

[19] Kuzmarov, Betina, 'The Coherence of the Concept of Cultural Property: A Critical Examination', *International Journal of Cultural Property* 20 (2013), 233–56, 235.

[20] Ibid.

[21] On this history in general, and particularly with respect to antiquities, see Harvey, Simon, *Smuggling: Seven Centuries of Contraband* (Reaktion Books, 2016), particularly 193–207.

that cannot be justified historically or normatively.[22] In fact, smuggling, as a form of illegality in the private, has always been political, and has geopolitical dimensions that map onto empire.[23] The impact of the public/private dichotomy is thus particularly important in assessing the role of self-regulation, which is central in defining the conservation paradigm (see later in this chapter), and also in understanding the economic dynamics of heritage and their relationship to the law (Chapter 5).

This dichotomy between the public and the private also depends, as far as the law is concerned, on the type of heritage. Movable heritage lends itself much more easily to being engaged by private international law,[24] as does intangible cultural heritage (particularly in its intellectual property aspects).[25] But a full engagement with private international law on this matter is beyond the scope of this book, and the lesson to be drawn here refers more fundamentally to the ability of the conceptual private to obscure relationships and create blind spots that ultimately harm certain stakeholders and ways of regulating heritage.

In the next section, I will set up the relationships between law and non-law in heritage safeguarding, as a means to establish the way in which this book operates, and its overall approach. Section 1.2 then engages with the conservation paradigm present in international heritage law, which I seek to debunk in this book. A note on terminology follows in Section 1.3, as it is important to elucidate some of the terms used in this book upfront, particularly my usage of 'heritage', instead of 'cultural heritage', and the definition of 'community'. The final section presents the structure of the book, and the questions guiding each of the chapters.

1.1 Relationships between Law and Non-Law in Heritage Safeguarding[26]

Understanding these relationships reengages communities by moving beyond basic analytical categories of the law (which, as indicated, are inadequate) and closer to the needs and values of heritage practitioners. The relationships between heritage law and heritage studies are certainly not straightforward, and different approaches to the law and to heritage in general tend to define the scope of the possible interactions. These relationships are contingent on the politics of the field: more orthodox approaches to a field will invite orthodox law, whereas heterodox approaches—in their critique of the colonizing effects of the law—are more resistant to the law,

[22] Muir Watt, Horatia, 'Private International Law beyond the Schism', *Transnational Legal Theory* 2(3) (2011), 347–427.

[23] Harvey (n 21) 10.

[24] See e.g. Roodt, Christa, *Private International Law, Art and Cultural Heritage* (Edward Elgar, 2015).

[25] See e.g. de Miguel Asensio, Pedro A., 'Transnational Contracts Concerning the Commercial Exploitation of Intangible Cultural Heritage', in Tullio Scovazzi, Benedetta Ubertazzi, and Lauso Zagato (eds), *Il patrimonio culturale intangibile nelle sue diverse dimensioni* (Giuffrè Editore, 2012), 93–126.

[26] This section is largely based on Lixinski, Lucas, 'Between Orthodoxy and Heterodoxy: the Troubled Relationships between Heritage Studies and Heritage Law', *International Journal of Heritage Studies* 21(3) (2015), 203–14.

and sometimes reject it, not properly considering heterodox possibilities within the law. But understanding these relationships is essential if international heritage law seeks to promote greater engagement with, and have more influence on, the ways in which heritage is understood and managed. Further, since heritage uses a language of management that is closely related to the language contained in treaties under UNESCO, the heritage lawyer needs to have a clearer sense of how their role is perceived outside the legal discipline, and how their interpretation of legal matters raised by UNESCO treaties can have an actual impact on heritage.

This book, even though it relies consistently on heritage studies (and management) literature, can be read as primarily making an intervention in law, and, more specifically, international law. But it is an intervention that I also hope will help people in heritage studies and management grapple with the law more openly and consistently, at least to the extent the law shapes a fair amount of their practice, even if indirectly. In helping articulate these connections between heritage law on one hand and heritage studies and management on the other, I highlight the space and means through which community aspirations can be articulated. By exposing blind spots and dark sides, I also point at the twilight in which the fragile flowers of community-centred heritage governance, to paraphrase Lévi-Strauss, can grow.[27]

International heritage law is closely connected to knowledge produced outside of the legal field, for two main reasons. First, classically seen, heritage is a highly technical field, meaning it requires understanding and application of concepts such as authenticity, integrity, and conservation. Those are what I call orthodox approaches to heritage. Second, critically understood, heritage is a means through which identity is formed, contested, and negotiated. And identity forms, conforms, and destroys polities, thereby forming an integral part of wider political processes. I call these heterodox approaches to heritage, because they challenge assumptions about the 'goodness' of heritage, and consider heritage beyond an end in itself.

From an orthodox perspective, there are three main ways in which the field of heritage studies refers to the law. The first one is through passing (and sometimes incorrect) mentions of international instruments. The heritage studies scholar will acknowledge the existence of the relevant law, but will not distinguish it technically between a binding and a non-binding instrument, simply treating it as a legal discursive thread among many others that lends authority to an argument about what a heritage expert ought to do in their professional practice. One example is the treatment of the ICOMOS (Venice) Charter of 1964 on the same level as the World Heritage Convention[28] or as if it were binding international law and could be 'breached',[29] while it is in fact a charter signed by experts, and not states, and it has little or no status as international law. It is only a binding instrument (such as a Convention adopted under UNESCO, but not Declarations under it) that imposes

[27] Lévi-Strauss, Claude, *Anthropologie structurale deux* (Plon, 1973), 300.

[28] Labadi, Sophia, 'World Heritage, Authenticity and Post-Authenticity', in Sophia Labadi and Colin Long (eds), *Heritage and Globalisation* (Routledge, 2010), 66–84, 67–8.

[29] Harrison, Rodney, 'The Politics of Heritage', in Rodney Harrison (ed.), *Understanding the Politics of Heritage* (Manchester University Press, 2010), 154–96, 172.

legally valid obligations upon states; all other instruments contribute to discursive threads, but are not in themselves hard law, and should, I would suggest, be accorded different weights.[30]

A second way heritage studies treats the law is to think of law as one source among many. Swenson has suggested to that effect that 'debates about legislation help scrutinizing the prevalence of "heritage-consciousness", but it would be reductive to draw a direct link between legal provisions, or even support for a Bill, and the intensity of love for "heritage"'.[31] Similarly, in a collection of essays about heritage methods, Soderland has referred to the law—in adding an additional layer of multidisciplinarity—as a relevant historical source for understanding the context in which heritage is institutionalized and protected at a certain point in time.[32] Soderland's is a useful insight in that it understands the historical contingencies of the law and the heritage process. More specifically, by admitting that the law is a useful source for identifying the sociopolitical moment in which heritage priorities and strategies were decided upon, it opens the door for reassessing those decisions with respect to the values and uses of heritage. However, it is also a very limited insight, as it instrumentalizes the law and reduces it to the level of only a document to be read, as opposed to a tool to be wielded. More specifically, she suggests that 'the law provides a lens through which a historiographical heritage is brought to the forefront, and in turn through which the phenomenon of heritage can be historicized'.[33]

Finally, orthodox approaches within heritage studies often think of heritage precisely as 'an object defined through a set of institutional practices, such as those defined by law and regulation'.[34] In this way, the law is part of the normative bounds within which heritage can be created, enacted, and protected. Carman and Sørensen also state that the law played an important role in the professionalization and export of heritage practices, leading to mismatches between the traditional owners of heritage and its institutional guardians.[35] In this sense, the law is seen as the instrument that will give direction to the aspirations of heritage studies, even if it has in the past done so at the expense of communities (which can be part of the problem with the law in heterodox heritage studies, discussed in what follows).

From the disciplinary perspective of the law, it seems that (orthodox) legal scholars writing in international heritage law by and large do not engage with heritage studies. In some cases, the law will reject outright heritage studies considerations. For instance, in the *Temple of Preah Vihear* case the International Court of Justice

[30] But see discussion of the conservation paradigm in Section 1.2 of this chapter.

[31] Swenson, Astrid, 'The Law's Delay? Preservation Legislation in France, Germany and England, 1970–1994', in Melanie Hall (ed.), *Towards World Heritage: International Origins of the Preservation Movement 1870–1930* (Ashgate, 2011), 139–54, 141.

[32] Soderland, Hilary A., 'The History of Heritage: A Method in Analyzing Legislative Historiography', in Marie-Louise Stig Sørensen and John Carman (eds), *Heritage Studies: Methods and Approaches* (Routledge, 2009), 55–84.

[33] Ibid., 79.

[34] Carman, John and Sørensen, Marie-Louise Stig, 'Heritage Studies: An Outline', in Marie-Louise Stig Sørensen and John Carman (eds), *Heritage Studies: Methods and Approaches* (Routledge, 2009), 11–28, 12.

[35] Ibid., 16–17.

(ICJ) said that '[t]he Parties have also relied on other arguments of a physical, historical, religious and archaeological character, but the Court is unable to regard them as legally decisive'.[36] That is mostly because the ICJ decided to focus on the boundary set in the 1904 Treaty, but it is also telling of the little weight that orthodox law gives to heritage considerations. It reflects how deferential orthodox law is to those decisions made by (also orthodox) heritage studies experts, by portraying the law as separate from those considerations. If the law is separate from heritage studies considerations, then the law works simply as a venue in which heritage studies validates itself, but not one where heritage studies can be challenged. In other words, the law here only serves to protect heritage studies and management processes, and to enable and promote mechanisms for heritage protection. The latter, for instance, are mechanisms like the World Heritage lists and the Intangible Heritage lists (discussed in detail in Chapter 7) as means for awareness-raising about the importance of heritage for its own sake, which also end up facilitating the appropriation of heritage by nominating states, often to the detriment of communities from whom this heritage stems and who could otherwise make a valid claim for use of their heritage as a means to contest state authority and control.[37]

The prevailing assumption, it seems, is that those substantive decisions requiring the input of heritage studies work have been done in the drafting and setting up of regimes. For instance, one must consider the work on the development and subsequent implementation of the 1972 World Heritage Convention, where experts were vital for the establishment of the regime, and are still heavily involved in its implementation and enforcement.[38] That is a sort of interaction that happens in practice but is often neglected in scholarship. The same can be said about the 2001 Convention on the Protection of the Underwater Cultural Heritage (UCHC)[39] and the 2003 Convention for the Safeguarding of the Intangible Cultural Heritage (ICHC), which was drafted by a group of experts from both heritage law and cultural heritage management.[40] Many early studies of intangible cultural heritage in law, however, largely neglected that instrument, or the 1989 Recommendation that preceded it, focusing rather on issues such as intellectual property protection.[41] The ICHC's effect is to exclude whatever little there is about community involvement as

[36] *Case Concerning the Temple of Preah Vihear* (Cambodia v. Thailand). Merits. Judgment of 15 June 1962. ICJ Reports 1962, p. 6. Lixinski, Lucas, Bordin, Fernando Lusa, and Schmitz, Maite de Souza, 'Identity Beyond Borders: International Cultural Heritage Law and the Temple of Preah Vihear Dispute', *ILSA Quarterly* 20(1) (2011), 30–7.

[37] Lixinski, Lucas, 'Selecting Heritage: The Interplay of Art, Politics and Identity', *European Journal of International Law* 22(1) (2011), 81–100.

[38] Francioni, Francesco (ed), *The 1972 World Heritage Convention: A Commentary*. (Oxford University Press, 2008).

[39] O'Keefe, Patrick J., '"Commercial Exploitation": Its Prohibition in the UNESCO Convention on Protection of the Underwater Cultural Heritage 2001 and Other Instruments', *Art, Antiquity & Law* 18(2) (2013), 129–48.

[40] Kuruk, Paul, 'Cultural Heritage, Traditional Knowledge and Indigenous Rights: An Analysis of the Convention for the Safeguarding of Intangible Cultural Heritage', *Macquarie Journal of International and Comparative Environmental Law* 1(1) (2004), 111–34.

[41] For a review of the literature, see Lixinski, Lucas, *Intangible Cultural Heritage in International Law* (Oxford University Press, 2013).

a matter of international concern, by, as we discuss in Chapter 3, relegating communities to the national level only.

After a regime has been drafted, it is up to the lawyer simply to describe it, and to ensure that the processes set up then by heritage studies experts are functioning and enforceable. It is not for the lawyer, it seems, to question those decisions, to the same extent that heritage work on the ground is fundamentally different from drafting international conventions.[42] This doctrinal approach—in which the law acts as the humble servant or the deferential enforcer of a series of heritage studies and management considerations made in the past—is problematic as it prevents the law from keeping up with changes to the field of heritage, and, even in more legal theoretical work, leads to generalizations about practices within heritage management and studies, such as the case with Merryman's classic essay on 'internationalism' in cultural heritage, where he describes the activities of heritage in broad terms, as simply what individual art and antiquities dealers or museums do, without reference to the political engagements at stake, which clearly have an influence on how the law is shaped.[43] The effect on communities is exclusionary, since the initial choices made in the drafting of regimes are never really revisited in this understanding of the law.

The third way the law relates to heritage studies is by acting as its 'ultimate arbiter'. In this scenario, lawyers do take into account considerations outside the law, but they act as the ultimate arbiters of all matters and sometimes encroach into the domain of heritage studies. It is a positive approach to the extent that it promotes active engagement between the two disciplines. However, because the legally trained professional—in a conventional reading of the law, the judge—is the one making the decision that is relevant to the (thus narrowly construed) law, the law is the ultimate arbiter of heritage. This view is particularly present in the area of restitution of cultural objects, which is where most of the judicialization of heritage law has happened. The work of heritage studies is instrumentalized in order to serve the law. This is the view espoused by Leiboff, in an article about the underappreciated role of art experts in legal disputes involving art. She argues that '[w]hile law is unable to trust its judgment about the artistic and cultural, it will still make art experts and institution[s] subject to the overriding truth of the law'.[44] Law lacks an effective way to connect to the cultural dimension in the way its material form connects to the intangible values, identity, or status.[45] Law does, in this context, precisely what Smith charges the Authorized Heritage Discourse (AHD) with doing—closing the time and space in which creative work (or, in our case, heritage) develops.[46] Here, the law has the potential to include communities, but it seems that instead the law replaces itself as the prevailing form of expertise, over

[42] Prott, Lyndel V., 'UNESCO International Framework for the Protection of the Cultural Heritage', in James A. R. Nafziger and Ann M. Nicgorski (eds), *Cultural Heritage Issues: The Legacy of Conquest, Colonization and Commerce* (Martinus Nijhoff, 2009), 257–85.

[43] Merryman, John Henry, 'Cultural Property Internationalism', *International Journal of Cultural Property* 12(1) (2005), 11–39.

[44] Leiboff, Marett, 'Clashing Things', *Griffith Law Review* 10(2) (2001), 294–316, 294.

[45] Ibid., 296.

[46] Smith, Laurajane, *Uses of Heritage* (Routledge, 2006).

that of heritage managers, but not necessarily paying much attention to the competing expertise of communities (which the law sees itself as naturally representing, often unaware of how law is itself an entrenched system of expertise with its own vocabulary and exclusionary effects).

Much of heritage discourse seems to be 'couched in, or ornamented with, legal arguments'.[47] Even though the limitations of legal argument (or legal semiotics) have been widely discussed within heterodox legal circles,[48] by and large classic legal argument is still relied on by heritage studies scholars. Such scholars seemingly hope to draw institutional backing (or even simply institutionalization) from the reliance on legal arguments (and they succeed in the effort). Heterodox heritage law (and international law more generally) has surely shifted away from relying only upon itself and its own actors for the resolution of legal problems, and has instead integrated broader concerns and stakeholders that had previously been neglected. It can thus include communities by renegotiating the parameters of law and legal practice, which includes its participants.

Heterodox (or critical) heritage studies, on the other hand, represents the move away from understanding heritage as an assemblage of artefacts, monuments, sites, and manifestations disconnected from social and political contexts, and towards a contextual understanding of heritage as a discourse.

> Being critical in heritage studies simply means 'thinking about' heritage: why do we value particular objects, places and practices from the past more than others? How does heritage function within society? If we memorialize some aspects of heritage, what other aspects might we forget in the process?[49]

This critical move results, at least to some extent, in an open challenge of the law. While there is work in heterodox heritage studies that attempts to bring about changes in the law (or in policy, that feeds into law), heterodox heritage studies can be defined as 'a position that aims to ... open up the field of enquiry to recognise and explore definitions, uses and ideas of heritage that sit outside ... the International charters, conventions and other treaties that tend work to transmit and reinforce the AHD ...'.[50] To the extent that the law 'normalizes' and 'authorizes' a series of practices around heritage that heterodox heritage studies has taken upon itself to question and challenge, heritage is understood in terms of a discourse, and the law is a part of the discourse that needs to be challenged. Communities can play a role in this challenge (and often do).

Of course, this view also means that law can be deemed irrelevant to heritage studies, instead of rejected. Heritage work that engages with definitions of heritage

[47] Audi, Alan, 'A Semiotics of Cultural Property Argument', *International Journal of Cultural Property* 14 (2007), 131–67, 131.

[48] Kennedy, Duncan, 'Form and Substance in Private Law Adjudication', *Harvard Law Review* 89 (1976), 1685–778; and Kennedy, Duncan, 'A Semiotics of Legal Argument', *Syracuse Law Review* 42 (1991), 75–116.

[49] Harrison, Rodney and Likman, Audrey, 'Critical Approaches to Heritage', in Rodney Harrison (ed.), *Understanding the Politics of Heritage* (Manchester University Press, 2010), 48–80, 75.

[50] Smith, Laurajane, 'Editorial', *International Journal of Heritage Studies* 18(6) (2012), 533–40, 538.

that have met no legal recognition (say, uses and definitions of heritage by Indigenous groups in countries where their customary law is not recognized by the country's settler legal system) is one instance of valid heritage work that does not directly engage with the law. The community then bypasses legal engagement and resists being defined by a legal system that shows it animosity.

More so than in other fields, debates about the restitution of cultural heritage are held using the language of the law.[51] It is a problematic statement, in that it generalizes the field of heritage studies and tries to make the law constitutive of all understandings of heritage (and the practices of the field). But it speaks to a concern about non-lawyers freely using legal considerations, with the unintended consequence of perpetuating orthodox legal discourses, as non-lawyers are not trained to perceive (and critique) the inherent contradictions and power structures of legal discourse in the area.[52] In a way, then, legal arguments about restitution still rely heavily on notions that put museums (colonizers) in opposition with traditional owners of artefacts (colonized), perpetuating a strand of discourse that heterodox heritage studies has been trying to come to terms with, while engaging communities.

Heterodox heritage studies seems to ignore the process of normalizing international law on cultural heritage in this area, which seems to have become a primary concern of the law.[53] As a result, heterodox heritage studies alienates and rejects—by and large—the law. This is because the law, as heterodox heritage studies understands it, does little in the way of promoting the emancipation of victims of colonialism. While this problem is also part of heterodox heritage studies' critique of other disciplines, like archaeology and anthropology, it is an important part of the critique of heritage law, and one that underscores the exclusion of communities, a central premise of this book's normative project.

The implication is that heterodox heritage law is faced with an existential challenge because it wishes to rely on heterodox heritage studies that largely resists the possibility of engaging with the law. All that heterodox heritage law can do is attack orthodox heritage law from within the disciplinary boundaries of the law, or level a general charge against the lack of politicization of heritage law.[54] This lack of engagement with more sophisticated heritage concerns is a problem for heterodox heritage studies, to the extent that it fails to engage heterodox heritage law, which could otherwise serve as an ally in pursuing heterodox heritage studies goals. The downside to this approach is that it does not favour open engagement with heterodox heritage studies, which would help advance the heterodox heritage law critique. Because the heterodox fields (heritage studies and heritage law) contest their orthodox equivalents in fairly similar

[51] Audi (n 47). [52] Ibid.

[53] Hall, Melanie, 'Introduction', in Melanie Hall (ed.), *Towards World Heritage: International Origins of the Preservation Movement 1870–1930* (Ashgate, 2011), 1–19.

[54] Shyllon, Folarin, 'Cultural Heritage Legislation and Management in Nigeria', *International Journal of Cultural Property* 5(2) (1996), 235–68.

terms (the use of the fields as enablers and perpetuators of unequal power dynamics, primarily), it is deplorable that they do not work together, particularly in that this work also converges in identifying and correcting imbalances against excluded actors like communities.

If law is to work as a facilitator of heterodox heritage studies agendas, heterodox heritage studies should be willing to look into the agenda of heterodox heritage law, and think of this incipient approach as a potential ally. Many of the goals of the agendas of both fields are common. The manifesto of the Association of Critical Heritage Studies is perhaps the best place to look for the agenda of heterodox heritage studies. The manifesto identifies said agenda as being primarily about 'question[ing] the conservative cultural and economic power relations that outdated understandings of heritage seem to underpin and invite the active participation of people and communities who to date have been marginalised in the creation and management of "heritage"'.[55] Similarly, heterodox (international) law in general aims at questioning power relations ingrained in traditional understandings of the legal system and the oscillation between politics and idealism in the making and implementation of international law,[56] the role of experts in the creation and implementation of the law,[57] and the marginalization of actors in the international legal process,[58] which would come to include communities.[59] There is a fair amount of synergy in these agendas, and both fields would greatly benefit from open engagement with each other. More specifically, heterodox heritage studies could benefit from heterodox heritage law's quality as 'law', as being able to articulate claims and agendas in the vocabulary of power and institutions, which can contribute greatly to the realization of heterodox heritage studies' agendas. Conversely, international heritage law can greatly benefit from heterodox heritage studies' insights into how heritage is created, and the power relations underlying heritage safeguarding mechanisms. Communities benefit from being able to tap into the law to challenge and disrupt power relations, and ultimately promote a shift towards community power over heritage.

But what is the conservation paradigm under which international heritage law, whether orthodox or heterodox, operates? The next section engages with this paradigm in more detail, and particularly the notion of authenticity within it. It shows how the paradigm reinforces and is reinforced by the troubled relations between law and non-law, having the same result of excluding communities and putting up obstacles to make it hard for them to (re)claim their own heritage.

[55] Available at http://www.criticalheritagestudies.org/history/ (accessed 26 October 2018).

[56] Koskenniemi, Martti, *From Apology to Utopia: The Structure of International Legal Argument* (Cambridge University Press, 2006).

[57] Kennedy, David, *Of War and Law* (Princeton University Press, 2006); and Kennedy, David, *A World of Struggle: How Power, Law and Expertise Shape Global Political Economy* (Princeton University Press, 2016).

[58] Orford, Anne (ed.), *International Law and Its Others* (Cambridge University Press, 2006).

[59] Chimni, B. S., *International Law and World Order: A Critique of Contemporary Approaches* (Cambridge University Press, 2nd edn 2017), 547.

1.2 The Conservation Paradigm

As indicated earlier, the key argument of the book is that international law prevents communities from having access to decision-making processes about their heritage. That exclusion happens usually for the benefit of states, buying into a state-centric and territorial logic of international law, but it also means that states work with significant input from one class of non-state actors: experts. Experts by and large seem to drive the rules, and international law in most instances seems to play the role of humble servant of heritage practices, meaning it enforces a certain way of thinking about cultural heritage without actually understanding what those practices are or entail, and particularly what they mean for the different stakeholders.

The objective of this section is to introduce what I call in this book the conservation paradigm. Admittedly, there is a significant amount of nuance in the practice under this paradigm, which this section (or even an entire book) could not hope to adequately accommodate. But I believe a version of this paradigm, however simplified, needs to be put forth, if anything to provide a clearer indication of what my argument in the book is couched against, particularly in the difficulties of communities' engagement with heritage practices.

In order to discuss the conservation paradigm, I will rely on the International Council of Monuments and Sites (ICOMOS), one of the leading international expert organizations in the field. I do so because ICOMOS provides us with a fairly standardized vocabulary of heritage practice, and, as a deeply influential organization around the world, its documents affect the majority of heritage practice.[60] Also, given its status before UNESCO, and close cooperation with UNESCO and a number of heritage treaties, its views are closely intertwined with the way international law in the field was drafted and is currently implemented (discussed in more detail in Chapter 3 in particular).

Before getting to the key ICOMOS texts defining the heritage paradigm, one more caveat: there is a significant difference in approaches within ICOMOS. Discussions with ICOMOS personnel indicate that there is a divide between 'international' ICOMOS, which is the global and most influential part of the organization, and 'Australian' ICOMOS, which, while still affiliated, has more specific ideas as to what the conservation paradigm means. I will discuss them both in turn, and, while acknowledging the influence of the Australian ICOMOS version of the paradigm particularly in South East Asia and the Pacific, it is my understanding that the international ICOMOS version is the one with the broader reach, and so it is the one I refer to when speaking of the conservation paradigm.

The key ICOMOS instrument, which sets out the basic features of the conservation paradigm, is the Venice Charter[61]. This instrument does not define its terms

[60] For some scholarly guidance, see generally Corsane, Gerard (ed.), *Heritage, Museums and Galleries: An Introductory Reader* (Routledge, 2005).

[61] International Charter for the Conservation and Restoration of Monuments and Sites (The Venice Charter 1964).

directly, but it implies that conservation is the maintenance of a monument on a permanent basis,[62] and that it implies preserving its setting. The Venice Charter states that scientific methods are key to the way heritage is protected, through conservation and restoration.[63] It makes some allowance for social uses of heritage (as it facilitates conservation), but only to the extent that the layout or decoration of the building are not in any way changed.[64] Heritage is therefore made into a frozen snapshot of the past, and changes are only allowed in rigidly set out circumstances.

With respect to restoration, the Venice Charter specifies that it is a 'highly specialized operation', the goal of which is to 'preserve and reveal the aesthetic and historic value of the monument and is based on respect for original material and authentic documents'.[65] Adaptive reuse of heritage, for instance, is in principle ruled out, but seemingly only when there is no other viable alternative, and 'any extra work which is *indispensable* must be distinct from the architectural composition and must bear a contemporary stamp'.[66] Restoration, like conservation, is reliant on science primarily, and sees the protection of heritage as an end in itself, giving heritage intrinsic value.

A number of other charters have come out of the ICOMOS General Assembly since the Venice Charter, referring to specific heritage conservation challenges such as historic gardens,[67] historic towns,[68] underwater heritage,[69] timber structures,[70] wall paintings,[71] and industrial heritage[72]. These charters have added important elements that for instance require communities to be consulted in the formulation of the interpretation of a heritage site (but not necessarily its governance).[73] The

62 Ibid., Article 4. 63 Ibid., Article 2. 64 Ibid., Article 5.

65 Ibid., Article 9. 66 Ibid., emphasis added.

67 Historic Gardens (the Florence Charter 1981), at http://www.icomos.org/images/DOCUMENTS/Charters/gardens_e.pdf.

68 Charter for the Conservation of Historic Towns and Urban Areas (the Washington Charter 1987), at http://www.icomos.org/images/DOCUMENTS/Charters/towns_e.pdf

69 Charter on the Protection and Management of the Underwater Cultural Heritage (1996), at http://www.icomos.org/images/DOCUMENTS/Charters/underwater_e.pdf.

70 Principles for the Preservation of Historic Timber Structures (1999), at http://www.icomos.org/images/DOCUMENTS/Charters/wood_e.pdf.

71 ICOMOS Principles for the Preservation and Conservation-Restoration of Wall Paintings (2003), at http://www.icomos.org/images/DOCUMENTS/Charters/wallpaintings_e.pdf.

72 ICOMOS Charter on the Interpretation and Presentation of Cultural Heritage Sites (2008), at http://www.icomos.org/images/DOCUMENTS/Charters/GA2011_ICOMOS_TICCIH_joint_principles_EN_FR_final_20120110.pdf.

73 See e.g. the ICOMOS Charter for the Interpretation and Presentation of Cultural Heritage Sites (2008), at http://www.icomos.org/images/DOCUMENTS/Charters/interpretation_e.pdf.

> Principle 6: Inclusiveness. The Interpretation and Presentation of cultural heritage sites must be the result of meaningful collaboration between heritage professionals, host and associated communities, and other stakeholders. 1. The multidisciplinary expertise of scholars, community members, conservation experts, governmental authorities, site managers and interpreters, tourism operators, and other professionals should be integrated in the formulation of interpretation and presentation programmes. 2. The traditional rights, responsibilities, and interests of property owners and host and associated communities should be noted and respected in the planning of site interpretation and presentation programmes. 3. Plans for expansion or revision of interpretation and presentation programmes should be open for public comment and involvement. It is the right and responsibility of all to make their opinions and perspectives known. 4. Because the question of intellectual property and traditional

exclusion of communities in many ways results in them seeing their customary rights and practices being restricted by conservation practices without appropriate compensation, leading to a resentment of heritage practices.[74] But the Venice Charter is still referred to in these instruments as the key foundational document and basis for the ethos of ICOMOS and its activities, and has never been revised.

The Venice Charter has been influential in UNESCO activity in the area, not only because ICOMOS became an important participant in the activities of the UNESCO culture sector for many heritage treaties, but also because its views on scientific approaches to heritage were endorsed in the negotiation of multiple heritage treaties. As early as 1958, the Head of the then Museums and Monuments Division of UNESCO praised the input of experts in heritage governance, and as an integral part of the early implementation of this Division's mandate.[75] Later statements in the context of the drafting of standard-setting instruments (which led to the World Heritage Convention) actually supported the inclusion of communities as key to the protection of heritage,[76] but relied on experts primarily for the 'presentation' of said heritage, and its translation to the outside world. Experts were considered to be better placed to 'evaluate the material conditions necessary to ensure that monuments shall be protected and respected'.[77] This report also hailed the Venice Charter as 'a basic document of great importance',[78] an view reiterated by other participants who incorporated many of the Venice Charter precepts in other drafting history of the World Heritage Convention.[79]

Differently from the Venice Charter, in 1979 Australian ICOMOS, one of the National Committees of the organization, approved its Burra Charter. The Burra Charter's original iteration sets out the relationship with the Venice Charter as 'following it closely', but it also says that 'Australia ICOMOS will press it [the Burra Charter] forward as a model for the revision of the Venice Charter'.[80] Notably, these

cultural rights is especially relevant to the interpretation process and its expression in various communication media (such as on-site multimedia presentations, digital media, and printed materials), legal ownership and right to use images, texts, and other interpretive materials should be discussed, clarified, and agreed in the planning process.

[74] Brumann, Christophe and Berliner, David, 'Introduction. UNESCO World Heritage—Grounded?', in Christophe Brumann and David Berliner (eds), *World Heritage on the Ground—Ethnographic Perspectives* (Berghahn, 2016), 1–34, 23.

[75] van der Haagen, J. K., 'The Part Played by UNESCO in the Preservation of the Cultural Heritage of Mankind and in the Development of Museums', speech delivered at an Archaeological Congress organized by the League of Arab States. WS/018.68, January 1958.

[76] d'Ossat, G De Angelis, 'The Scientific Concepts on Which the Protection and Presentation of Monuments and Sites is Based', paper presented at the Meeting of Experts to co-ordinate with a view to their international adoption, the principles and scientific, technical and legal criteria which would make is [sic] possible to establish an effective system for the protection of monuments and sites (January 1968). SXC/CS/27/3, para. 8.

[77] Ibid., para. 14. [78] Ibid., para. 20.

[79] See e.g. Zachwatowicz, J., *Scientific and Technical Rules for Protection Operations*, report presented at the Meeting of Experts to co-ordinate with a view to their international adoption, the principles and scientific, technical and legal criteria which would make it possible to establish an effective system for the protection of monuments and sites. SHC/CS/27/4, of 31 January 1968, para. 23.

[80] Saunders, David, *Chairman's message about the new Guidelines*, attached to The Australia ICOMOS *Guidelines for the Conservation of Places of Cultural Significance* ('Burra Charter') (1979).

references to the relationship between the Burra and Venice charters have been excluded from subsequent versions of the Burra Charter, lending credence to the idea of a division in the approaches by different parts of the organization. The Burra Charter has been revised a number of times since, with minor revisions in 1981, 1988, a more substantive revision in 1999, and another minor revision in 2013.

The Burra Charter, even if different in spirit from the Venice Charter, is useful in that it more clearly defines the terms of the conservation paradigm (conservation, maintenance, preservation, and restoration).[81] But, unlike its global counterpart, the Burra Charter is much more invested in the participation of communities,[82] and in understanding the relationship with heritage safeguarding as one requiring nuanced analysis of social and intangible values associated with heritage. Also importantly, particularly in its latest iteration, the Burra Charter is much more accommodating to change as an integral part of the relationship people have with heritage, and the idea that heritage will inevitably change. That said, it adopts a somewhat cryptic formula that defines conservation as requiring 'a cautious approach of changing as much as necessary but as little as possible'.[83] In other words, the conservation paradigm is open to change, but only one that is justified by the higher imperative of maintaining cultural ties to a heritage place. This formula challenges the conservation paradigm by making an allowance for change at all, but is cautious in what kind of change is permissible.

Also key to the Burra Charter's take on the conservation paradigm is the idea that multiple interpretations of or narratives around heritage are permissible at the same time (even if the Burra Charter itself requires that the narrative of a heritage place be presented succinctly, which creates the risk of conflicting accounts being written out of the summary).[84] It also states that the statement of cultural significance of heritage should be periodically reviewed,[85] which again challenges the idea of heritage as having static values that are connected to a specific past. But one must keep in mind that the Burra Charter, however progressive, is not the dominant heritage paradigm; instead, the Venice Charter, in its interpretation by international ICOMOS, should be taken as the dominant one.

The ICOMOS charters (Venice and Burra), while not technically legally binding international instruments, are deeply influential. The confusion as to their character among heritage practitioners evidences their perceived influence (the fact that they are drafted to look and read like legal instruments does not help either). And yet, as far as lawyers, and particularly international lawyers, are concerned, those documents are seldom, if ever, factored into an analysis of international heritage law. There is thus a disconnect between law and non-law in the implementation of the conservation paradigm, and, while it is impossible to give either of these two

[81] The Burra Charter: The Australia ICOMOS Charter for Places of Cultural Significance, 2013. Article 1.

[82] Ibid., Article 12. [83] Ibid., Article 3.1.

[84] Guidelines to the Burra Charter: Cultural Significance (1999), Article 3.4; see also Practice Note: Understanding and assessing cultural significance (Version 1: November 2013), attached to the 2013 version of the Burra Charter, at 5.

[85] Burra Charter (n 81) Article 26.4.

charters the full weight of binding international law, at the very least they should be treated as a form of self-regulation or industry standards, and given the weight that other forms of private lawmaking receive in transnational law scholarship and practice. But, in practice, they disappear into the invisible private, discussed earlier. The effect on communities is that the Burra Charter's positive language eludes the law. Overall, practice excluding communities goes unchallenged by law's emancipatory promise (which therefore goes unfulfilled). Further, and most importantly, because they (and particularly the Venice Charter) define the conservation paradigm under which international heritage law is interpreted on the ground, they need to be taken more seriously, and engaged with if international heritage law is to be more effective.

The scientificism of the conservation paradigm, particularly in the unrevised Venice Charter, is very much historically contingent, if not in its origins then at least in its perpetuation. More specifically, this conservation paradigm's emphasis on scientific methods and expert rule is a product of a Cold War environment in which the engagement of local communities (or any sort of communities), an important part of UNESCO's beginnings,[86] was seen as too political, and paralysed by the bipolarity of international relations. UNESCO's early activities in the field of culture comprised facilitating direct communications with and among artists and heritage managers, but that practice was eventually replaced by more concerted standard-setting.[87] Even if UNESCO was originally created to be the soul to the United Nations' body,[88] the Cold War had a deep influence in UNESCO's activities from a fairly early stage, not only in sidelining much of its activity,[89] but also in enshrining a certain way of thinking about its mandate as less political, which was necessary to set even small programmes in motion.[90]

The conservation paradigm, therefore, is a means of thinking about heritage that privileges scientific ways of engaging with or displaying heritage. It means preservation of heritage in its original form,[91] and assumes that heritage is a product of the past that needs to be kept in that position lest a sense of loss is experienced,[92] for the appreciation of present and future generations. It ultimately defines heritage and selects it as 'showcased history', alienating communities by failing to acknowledge 'contiguous histories that are underinterpreted [sic]'.[93]

In doing so, the conservation paradigm defines heritage along similar lines of the Authorized Heritage Discourse (AHD), discussed in more detail in Chapter 3. For now, it suffices to say that the AHD, as defined by Laurajane Smith, is the idea that

> there is . . . a hegemonic discourse about heritage, which acts to constitute the way we think, talk and write about heritage. The 'heritage' discourse . . . naturalizes the practice of rounding

86 Laves and Thomson (n 7) 17. 87 Ibid., 106–33. 88 Ibid., 3.

89 Ibid., 310–11.

90 Pearson, Christopher E. M., *Designing UNESCO: Art, Architecture and International Politics at Mid-Century* (Ashgate, 2010), 52–6. For an alternative, and more optimistic, version of the history of UNESCO with respect to heritage, see Droit, Roger-Pol, *Humanity in the Making: Overview of the Intellectual History of UNESCO 1945–2005* (UNESCO Publishing, 2005), 131–49.

91 Fechner (n 9) 382. 92 Brumann and Berliner (n 74) 17.

93 Bell, Jonathan S., 'The Politics of Preservation: Privileging One Heritage over Another', *International Journal of Cultural Property* 20 (2013), 431–50, 432.

up the usual suspects to conserve and 'pass on' to future generations, and in so doing ... validates a set of practices and performances, which populates both popular and expert constructions of 'heritage' and undermines alternative and subaltern ideas about 'heritage'.[94]

The AHD assumes the prevalence of expert opinion, which, coupled with the 'breathless bureaucratic machinery' of some bodies under UNESCO overseeing international heritage regimes,[95] leads to a reinforcement of the conservation paradigm.

By and large, this conservation paradigm has been under attack. In many respects, the focus of heritage safeguarding has shifted tremendously since the Venice Charter,[96] particularly through the Nara Document on Authenticity, discussed later, which pushes forward a more culturally sensitive (and even relativist, according to some) take on heritage.[97] It now involves less scientificism, and more involvement of people, and the functions of heritage over its mere existence,[98] as the Burra Charter and its evolution evidence. Part of this move has been triggered by movements like Public Archaeology (also known as Community Archaeology),[99] which by and large challenge the prevailing assumptions about heritage conservation and use.[100] These are valuable movements but they are mostly based domestically, and have so far eluded the international arena, which is the focus of this book. At any rate, I discuss the role of heritage experts in the conservation paradigm, and challenges thereto, in more detail in Chapter 3.

But it is important to remark that even this move to a more 'values-based approach' to the conservation paradigm is not without its critics, who insist that even this approach still focuses too much on the built 'fabric' of heritage, and neglects intangible values (a criticism denied in Burra Charter policy documents).[101] Admittedly, an approach based entirely on the intangible values of heritage,[102] which sees all of heritage as intangible,[103] would be more inclusive of communities. However, the values-based version of the conservation paradigm espoused by this book takes into account intangibility as a central feature of heritage law, and a way to reimagine the system of heritage law, and thus satisfies, in my view, the critique of values-based approaches.

[94] Smith, *Uses of Heritage* (n 46) 11. [95] Brumann and Berliner (n 74) 1.

[96] de la Torre, Marta, 'Values and Heritage Conservation', *Heritage & Society* 60(2) (2013), 155–66, 155.

[97] Ibid., 159.

[98] Loulanski, Tolina, 'Revising the Concept for Cultural Heritage: The Argument for a Functional Approach', *International Journal of Cultural Property* 13 (2006), 207–33, 207.

[99] For a summary, see Kersel, Morag and Chesson, Meredith, 'Not the Usual Suspects. New Directions in Community Archaeology' (2011) 11(4) *SAA Record*, 43–6. Lynn Meskell also suggests that archaeology was essentially divorced from heritage at the UNESCO level, with archaeologists being used only 'as technocrats and consultants in the intergovernmental and preservationist sphere. Archaeology had become the helpmate of heritage'. Meskell, *A Future in Ruins* (n 5) 23.

[100] See e.g. Coombe, Rosemary J. and Weiss, Lidsaw M., 'Neoliberalism, Heritage Regimes, and Cultural Rights', in Lynn Meskell (ed.), *Global Heritage: A Reader* (Wiley-Blackwell, 2015), 43–69, 49.

[101] Poulos, Ioannis, 'Moving Beyond a Values-Based Approach to Heritage Conservation', *Conservation and Management of Archaeological Sites* 12(2) (2010), 170–85, 172. Cf. ICOMOS Australia, *Practice Note: The Burra Charter and Archaeological Practice* (2013).

[102] Ibid., 178. [103] Smith, *Uses of Heritage* (n 46) 56.

An important part of the conservation paradigm, as indicated, is the notion of authenticity, which, much like the broader conservation paradigm, has changed over time.[104] But I focus now on the paradigm and concept of authenticity enshrined under UNESCO. Authenticity in many respects sets the standard against which heritage is measured and valued, and becomes a coalescing force around which value is attributed to heritage.[105] Authenticity has been referred to as a 'superstition',[106] but one that is craved, and more culture-specific than it is portrayed by the objective veneer of the conservation paradigm.[107]

However, the law on cultural heritage, particularly international heritage law, has always taken authenticity as being outside of its purview, something to be decided upon by other heritage professionals with greater expertise. But, when it comes to (judicial) dispute settlement, a quintessentially legal function, legal professionals can be (and are) called upon to adjudicate authenticity of heritage, which works as a trigger to determine a series of rights and obligations of parties with respect to heritage.

The concept of authenticity, tied to the conservation paradigm, appears first in the 1964 Venice Charter discussed earlier. In this Charter, the concept of authenticity appears both in the Preamble and in Article 8 (the latter dealing with restoration). The Preamble's reference suggests that the entire spirit of ICOMOS and of the heritage preservation movement is somehow oriented towards promoting a notion of authenticity, which, as Stovel suggests, is inherited from the North American heritage conservation model.[108]

UNESCO treaties do not define authenticity, and in fact do not even mention it consistently. But the 1994 Nara Document on Authenticity fills the gap. The Nara Document was prepared by a group of forty-five experts from twenty-seven different countries under the auspices of ICOMOS, with a view to provide guidelines for the assessment of authenticity. The document defines authenticity as

> the essential qualifying factor concerning values. The understanding of authenticity plays a fundamental role in all scientific studies of the cultural heritage, in conservation and restoration planning, as well as within the inscription procedures used for the World Heritage Convention *and other* cultural heritage inventories.[109]

Notably, subsequent UNESCO instruments have not made reference to authenticity, neither in their texts nor in guidelines or directives for their

[104] See e.g. Worsley, Lucy, 'Changing Notions of Authenticity: Presenting a Castle Over Four Centuries', *International Journal of Heritage Studies* 10(2) (2004), 129–49.

[105] This discussion draws on Lixinski, Lucas, 'A Tale of Two Heritages: Claims of Ownership over Intangible Cultural Heritage and the Myth of "Authenticity" ', *Transnational Dispute Management* 11(2) (2014).

[106] Eggert, Paul, *Securing the Past: Conservation in Art, Architecture and Literature* (Cambridge University Press, 2009), 62.

[107] Ibid., 74.

[108] Stovel, Herb, 'Effective Use of Authenticity and Integrity as world Heritage Qualifying Conditions', *City & Time* 2(3) (2007), 21–36, 23.

[109] Nara Document on Authenticity, WHC-94/CONF.003/INF.008 (adopted 6 November 1994), para. 10 (emphasis added).

implementation. This absence would suggest that, on some level, the idea of authenticity has been abandoned. However, it is ingrained in the conservation paradigm through ICOMOS texts, which are used by and relied upon by heritage managers and practitioners on the ground, and therefore influential if not on the law, at least on its implementation. The effect on communities is that the operation of heritage law hinges on giving meaning to a notion of authenticity, and that communities are not recognized by the law as having the ability to provide just such meaning.

Further, and perhaps most importantly, the WHC, which relies on authenticity for the assessment of World Heritage sites,[110] is still the central instrument of the international heritage system, and heritage professionals everywhere still take the conceptual framework erected under that instrument as a means to design and implement general policies with respect to heritage. Authenticity is thus still used across the board not only with respect to monuments and sites (the mandate of ICOMOS, the organization that imbued the concept into UNESCO law), but also other types of heritage outside the purview of UNESCO.

A claim of 'authenticity' of heritage carries with it a series of rights to the one who controls the 'authentic' manifestation of heritage. In the context of tangible heritage, these problematic aspects of authenticity have not been particularly evident, because of the connection of the heritage to territory, and its delimited boundaries. However, when it comes to intangible heritage in particular, because such heritage is not restricted to a territory, and can travel great distances, it becomes apparent that a claim for authenticity allows one state or group to assert pride and control over its own heritage at the expense of everyone else. And, if two peoples practice the same heritage, to make any such assertion of 'authenticity', particularly at the international level, means to denigrate the competing heritage. The effect on communities is that they become pawns in political games played by their states, in which a community's experience of heritage is packaged and pitted against another community's, in order to determine whose experience is more 'authentic'.

Authenticity, therefore, as an integral part of the conservation paradigm, plays a key function in asserting value over heritage. It is in many respects the linchpin of how heritage value is produced, and central to the operation of the legal system around culture. A more community-oriented version of international heritage law needs to be more mindful of the work the conservation paradigm and authenticity do, especially inasmuch as they create value and direct control over heritage. To eliminate authenticity would beckon its replacement with another trope for assigning value and control, so the answer may not necessarily lie there; rather, it may be that communities need to be able to assert authenticity in their own terms, while being mindful of the need for authenticity to be non-exclusive, and couched on representativeness instead.

[110] Operational Guidelines for the Implementation of the World Heritage Convention, paras 78–95.

1.3 A Note on Terminology

This book, as in the title, usually avoids the distinction of 'cultural heritage' and 'natural heritage'. Admittedly, cultural heritage is the majority of the field I examine. 'Natural heritage' is usually thought of as belonging to the field of environmental law, which leads to some confusion as to whether international heritage law is a field of international law in its own right, or a subset of international environmental law,[111] a confusion that, as argued in Chapter 5, is unconstructive. Further, natural heritage is mentioned as an autonomous category only as part of the World Heritage Convention, but, as Chapters 2 and 6 will show, it also appears more than usually assumed.

There are at least four reasons why I avoid this distinction. First, in many respects, all heritage is considered as such because of a cultural connection humans feel to a place or site, regardless of whether it is composed of natural or human-made elements. Thus, the distinction between cultural and natural heritage focuses more on the constitutive elements of heritage, instead of on the work it does, and it perpetuates the conservation paradigm this book criticizes. Second, the distinction between nature and culture creates the classification confusion of the field, mentioned in the previous paragraph. Third, and more centrally, the influence of natural heritage, and the way we think about it particularly in the context of the conservation paradigm, is far more pervasive when discussing cultural heritage than usually assumed. The distinction between cultural and natural heritage obscures that influence of nature on culture, and vice-versa, and is thus one the blind spots this book sets out to shed light on. And fourth, even though I am biased in that most of my work to date has been on cultural heritage, I believe many of the arguments in this book beyond the specific chapter on the environment (Chapter 5) apply to both cultural and natural heritage. Hence, in this book I prefer the blanket term 'heritage'.

Further, I refer to 'heritage', instead of 'property', even though I question in the next chapter the usefulness of the move from property to heritage, and partly advocate for a return to the property terminology. The reasons for that are twofold. First, the field has defined itself for the most part around the concept of heritage, scholars and practitioners in the United States being a notable exception in still referring primarily to 'cultural property' (in addition to military lawyers and other International humanitarian law scholars and practitioners, who only focus on one regime). Second, as Chapter 2 shows, I ultimately adopt a somewhat conciliatory approach, embracing the focus on certain values that heritage promotes. Therefore, heritage in this book is meant to be not only both natural and cultural, but also a banner behind which a field is defined, with certain values assigned to its focus of study.

[111] See for instance Boer, Ben and Wiffen, Graeme, *Heritage Law in Australia* (Oxford University Press, 2006), 8.

Finally, a brief note is needed on what I mean in this book by 'community'. This notion, and particularly its colonial load, will be discussed in further detail in Chapter 3, but for now it is important to remark on two elements of the meaning I seek to attribute to 'community' in this book. The first element is that 'community' defies precise definition from the outside, particularly because of the colonial history of the term's deployment. Second, 'community' in heritage studies has come to be defined relationally, that is, connected to the heritage as an interest that binds the group, rather than being defined elsewhere and then having heritage attached to it. So, for present purposes, and in this book in general, by 'community' I mean the groups that live in, with, or around heritage sites and artefacts, and generally (but particularly with respect to intangible heritage) the groups that create and attribute value to heritage by virtue of heritage's importance to their identity. While I discuss further the idea that myriad values can be attributed to heritage, and they speak directly to the uses of heritage beyond the conservation paradigm, the importance to identity is a common element in how any heritage community is constituted and engages with its culture, in my view.

1.4 The Book's Structure

The rest of this book is divided into eight chapters, which can be roughly grouped into three parts: scope, application, and redefinition. Chapters 2–4 engage with the scope of application of the field of international heritage law (subject matter, *ratione personae*, and temporal—or the what, the who, and the when), as a means to place the community in the broader field of international heritage law, not only as an actor, but also with respect to other fundamental building blocks. Chapters 5–7 engage with matters that, while cutting through, or even essential parts of, international heritage treaties, are seldom analysed across the range of treaties under UNESCO, and, because of this lack of analysis, create blind spots which allow for communities to be excluded (or the present where and the how). And chapters 8–9 build on the insights of the previous parts to present a version of a new, more critically engaged field of international heritage law (or the future where and how).

Chapter 2 focuses on the multiple definitions of 'heritage' in UNESCO instruments, and particularly on their relationships to the idea of 'property', and whether and to what extent either concept better serves communities and other local stakeholders. It examines the drafting history of the key UNESCO treaties in the area, to identify the role of communities and other stakeholders in the definitions, as well as the political compromises made. After examining the drafting history of the treaty definitions, the chapter reexamines the move from 'cultural property' to 'cultural heritage', an important part of the elevation of the field to one overseeing international public goods. The aspirations of 'heritage' are in many respects better suited to the cosmopolitan aspirations of UNESCO than those of 'property' (in particular the specific meaning of property highlighted in the treaties, which works as a proxy for state sovereignty). But I argue in this chapter that this shift has had unintended consequences, key among which is the exclusion of communities, because they need to negotiate domestic frameworks that still largely rely on property, and are ultimately excluded from international processes. The field would do well to revisit the idea of 'property', but, as the chapter discusses, a specific understanding of property that goes against conventional wisdom based on property as the ultimate bastion of individual liberty.

Chapter 3 looks at the actors and stakeholders in the field of international heritage law. It focuses a significant amount of energy on the roles of states and experts, and on identifying the key actors with a seat at the international table, before looking at museums, collectors, and other corporate actors, and the elusive 'community', which is at the centre of this book's project. The chapter argues that community, while ambiguous and laden with colonial legacies, is still a concept worth trying to define and use.

Chapter 4 looks at the way international heritage law applies across time, and the different influences that the relationship between international heritage law and time on one hand, and how communities relate to their heritage over time on the other, have on community engagement with heritage management and law. Often enough relying on time as a means to define heritage, international heritage law has in many respects a difficult relationship with Chronos. From the age of heritage down to the non-retroactivity of treaties which essentially resets the clock on a number of heritage disputes and injustices, the temporal application of international heritage law plays a significant role in shaping what is permissible heritage, and how the law addresses heritage. After exploring some of these tensions, the chapter uses genocide's relationship to cultural heritage as a means to examine how heritage plays roles before, during, and after major events, in ways that the law does not always capture constructively. I argue in this chapter that a fuller engagement with the potentials of heritage and its impact on society can only be possible through more integrated constructions of the multiple heritage regimes, and communities having a key role in their implementation and oversight.

Chapter 5 introduces the second major part of this book, looking at the application of international heritage law. But, instead of focusing immediately on matters that are internal to international heritage treaties, this part starts with an area that is largely excluded from, or even antithetical to, international heritage law. More specifically, this chapter focuses on the ways in which the economics of heritage are engaged (or disengaged) by international heritage treaties, and what these intersections have to say about the avenues through which communities themselves can engage with the law and economics of heritage. The common assumption is that economic uses of heritage cheapen what is otherwise unique and special culture. Therefore, the economics of heritage end up either made illegal, or ignored. The result backfires: the market does not stop interacting with cultural heritage, it is just that its regulation moves to other fora, which are less sympathetic to culture and its special character. In the process, communities are once again disengaged and excluded from controlling their heritage, which often has harmful effects on the heritage itself. The chapter also looks at the literature on heritage economics and the contribution it can make to heritage law, as well as the connection between heritage and development, particularly from the standpoint of communities. This chapter, like Chapter 4, uses examples external to international heritage law to make a case about the limitations and blind spots of the network of treaties under UNESCO, ultimately arguing for clearer engagement between international heritage law and economic matters.

Related to the notion of heritage as development explored in Chapter 5, Chapter 6 focuses on the relationship between heritage and sustainable development, and, more broadly, the environment. It highlights in particular the effects that the environment and sustainable development have on the place of communities in how we think about heritage conservation and safeguarding. The chapter also shows how 'natural' heritage has a much more pervasive impact on how we think of heritage in international law, and the conservation paradigm more specifically. The chapter discusses the implications of sustainability for heritage safeguarding; how environmental considerations, while in and of themselves positive and desirable, can also have the effect of excluding community stakeholders, ultimately compromising their ability to promote sustainable safeguarding of heritage, and, in more extreme cases, the very existence of the heritage they set out to protect. The chapter thus argues that sustainable development, in the heritage context, needs to take communities into account more seriously, if it is to effectively pursue its goals.

Chapter 7 concludes the second major part of the book and tackles head-on issues of application that are at the forefront of international heritage treaties. The chapter looks at tools inherent to international heritage treaties such as listing, international funds, and cooperation mechanisms, and the ways communities can (or, more often, cannot) rely on them. It also considers how, once compared across treaties, they share certain commonalities and differences that are revealing about the way international heritage law as a body of rules operates, particularly vis-à-vis communities. The chapter then examines the somewhat elusive matter of enforcement of international heritage law, which is for the most part reliant on non-specific fora, and sometimes other treaties altogether, to translate heritage goals into the language of those other instruments. While there are potential shortcomings with this reality, it is also true that the filtering that is a consequence of this movement can have beneficial effects on the inclusion of communities as a central part of heritage processes, as a recent international criminal law judgment shows. Lastly, the chapter engages briefly with the matter of domestic implementation as yet another process of translation of international heritage law in other contexts.

The third part of this book, focuses on a reassessment or even redefinition of the field. It is mostly composed of Chapter 8, which uses the insights gained from previous chapters to outline the bright and dark sides of international heritage law, particularly as seen from the perspective of communities' engagement with their own heritage and with the legal structures surrounding heritage. This chapter argues that, while there have been tremendous achievements in the field of international heritage law under UNESCO's tutelage, each one of these achievements has brought with it unintended consequences, which we need to be mindful of if we are to continue constructive engagement with the field. This chapter, while setting these bright and dark sides in pairs, should not be read as creating dualities, but rather as dialectically bridging concepts, and showing cause and effect: every bright side casts a shadow, which needs our attention.

As the concluding chapter of the book, Chapter 9 pulls together the many strings of argument, so as to provide elements for a more community-centred international heritage law, which, I argue, is ultimately an improved and more sustained way of safeguarding heritage for present and future generations, therefore better fulfilling UNESCO's ambitions of promoting peace through heritage and culture.

2

Definitions: From Cultural Property to Cultural Heritage (and Back?)

In order to critically assess the impact of international heritage law on communities, a first step is to unpack the very definition of heritage, and legal discourses around it. I unpack heritage in this chapter as a means of understanding whether and how communities are positioned with respect to cultural heritage on a definitional level, the input of communities in defining and attributing value to heritage, and how claims around heritage are staked out through definitions. This chapter traces the evolution of the notion of 'cultural heritage' in the different UNESCO instruments as an attempt to more clearly understand how international law has conceived of culture as a proxy for sovereignty, and 'heritage of [hu]mankind' as a banner of cosmopolitanism. Cultural heritage is a notion where these two apparently conflicting views of international law and their roles must be negotiated.

I argue in this chapter that the move from cultural property to heritage, while it enhanced many of the values of cultural heritage—and particularly its connection to intangible cultural processes rather than tangible buildings, monuments, and artefacts—has also had the (unintended) consequence of disassociating communities from heritage they live with or around, and for whose survival they are necessary. As a result, a return to a specific way of conceptualizing property may be needed, at least in some respects.

This chapter offers a genealogy of the concept of 'cultural heritage' in international heritage law as a means to showcase how debates over sovereignty and cosmopolitanism have played out since midway through the twentieth century inside a UN Specialized Agency. Additionally, I attribute part of the disconnect between communities and their heritage promoted by the law to one between domestic and international: while international legal discourse, and cosmopolitanism with it, has embraced the notion of heritage, domestic law still relies heavily on the category of property as a means to implement international legal obligations with respect to heritage. So, while the language of heritage in international law has introduced key values into the way we think about culture, domestically the language of property seems to be impervious to or deny those aspirations. The effect of this mismatch is once again to exclude communities from controlling their own culture.

This chapter will assess the way the multiple treaties under UNESCO have defined cultural heritage, and the values attached to those definitions. I will also rely on primary sources and scholarly work around the history of UNESCO,[1] and, on the international law front, work on the definition of cultural heritage in international law, and the shift from cultural 'property' to cultural 'heritage'.[2] The purpose of using these sources is to paint a clearer picture of how heritage is defined by international law across the spectrum of UNESCO instruments, and to ultimately show how there is ambiguity at the centre of the field, which 'may at times lead to contradictory positions and unintended outcomes'.[3]

By rejecting 'property', international heritage law also rejects an important yardstick that connects the values articulated in the international (beautifully contained in the word 'heritage') to the needs of people on the ground. In search of a replacement yardstick, international heritage law defers to sovereignty as a basic principle of international law. The effects of this deference are alienation, and ultimately the reinforcement of the Authorized Heritage Discourse (AHD) and the conservation paradigm.

Further, the back and forth between heritage and property also shows a largely lost narrative of the engagement between a legal (property) and a non-legal (heritage) concept and category. The embracing of the term heritage in latter treaties is a victory for non-lawyers in the field, but it also means less legal certainty, and a further divorce between law and non-law in the safeguarding of cultural heritage, as legal processes where enforcement is clearer, like domestic law, still rely on the legal and better circumscribed category of property over heritage.

If property is still used domestically, particularly locally, in heritage management, it is a category worthy of exploration. The continued use of property in domestic law to refer to, define, and manage cultural heritage may be read as meaning that international law's aspirations have failed, and the terminology disconnect creates a way to ignore the values of the international. That said, this chapter also revisits the meanings of property, and its functions in the law. I do so to show that 'cultural property' is not necessarily the ultimate commodification of heritage and its subordination to neoliberal economics that are just as, and probably even more, exclusionary than the shield created by the term 'heritage'.

This chapter proceeds as follows: Section 2.1 revisits the shift from cultural property to cultural heritage through the lenses of the key UNESCO treaties and their

[1] This historical scholarship includes Pearson, Christopher E. M., *Designing UNESCO: Art, Architecture and International Politics at Mid-Century* (Ashgate, 2010).

[2] The main works in this respect are Francioni, Francesco, 'A Dynamic Evolution of Concept and Scope: From Cultural Property to Cultural Heritage', in Abdulqawi A. Yusuf (ed.), *Standard-setting in UNESCO: Normative Action in Education, Science and Culture* (Martinus Nijhoff, 2007), 221–36; Blake, Janet, 'On Defining the Cultural Heritage', *International and Comparative Law Quarterly* 49 (2000), 61–85; Prott, Lyndel V. and O'Keefe, Patrick J., '"Cultural Heritage" or "Cultural Property"?', *International Journal of Cultural Property* 1 (1992), 307–20; Bendix, Regina, 'Héritage et patrimoine: de leurs proximités sémantiques et de leurs implications', in Chiara Bortolotto (ed.), *Le patrimoine culturel immaterial: Enjeux d'une nouvelle catégorie* (Éditions de la Maison des sciences de l'homme, 2011), 99–121; and Francioni, Francesco, 'Cultural Property, International Law', *Max Planck Encyclopedia of Public International Law* (Oxford University Press, 2008). For a pre-Second World War evolution of the idea of cultural property in international law, see generally Vrdoljak, Ana Filipa, *International Law: Museums and the Return of Cultural Objects* (Cambridge University Press, 2006).

[3] Blake, 'On Defining the Cultural Heritage' (n 2) 85.

drafting history. Section 2.2 focuses on the exclusionary effects of the discourses around the category of cultural heritage, in order to set up the shift back to property in Section 2.3.

2.1 Treaty Histories and Definitions

While a number of instruments predated the creation of UNESCO,[4] this chapter, much like this entire book, focuses on the five key treaties under the aegis of this organization. Roger O'Keefe has suggested that the definition in the Hague Convention and its Protocol need to be taken in isolation from other UNESCO treaties, since each one of the treaties has a specific object and purpose.[5] I respectfully disagree. Even if I accepted the premise that different definitions are deployed for the different objects and purposes of different treaties, at its highest I could put this argument to mean that the definitions of treaties drafted specifically for different *types* of cultural heritage (underwater, intangible, movable, etc.) would be fundamentally different. The Hague Convention and protocols, however, refer not to a type of cultural heritage, but to cultural heritage in a specific anomalous context (wartime). Nevertheless, what I propose to do in this section is to look at definitions across the treaties as a means to distil principles underlying the way international heritage law defines cultural heritage and the values associated with it.

The Preamble to the 1954 Hague Convention is the first formal legal usage in the English language of the term 'heritage' in the context of cultural protection.[6] Similarly, the preamble also speaks of the protection of culture of 'peoples', and of '[hu]mankind', thereby intentionally enshrining a cosmopolitan spirit that is meant to be dissociated from state sovereignty, and referring to anthropological knowledge that gives cultures to peoples, rather than nation states.[7] That said, the definition in the actual text of the 1954 Hague Convention, in Article 1, speaks of cultural 'property'.[8]

[4] For an overview, see Graham, Gael M., 'Protection and Reversion of Cultural Property: Issues of Definition and Justification', *The International Lawyer* 21(3) (1987), 755–93, 756–66.

[5] O'Keefe, Roger, *The Protection of Cultural Property in Armed Conflict* (Cambridge University Press, 2006), 102 and 248.

[6] Ibid., 95. [7] Ibid.

[8] Convention for the Protection of Cultural Property in the Event of Armed Conflict with Regulations for the Execution of the Convention 1954 (adopted 14 May 1954, entered into force 7 August 1956) 249 UNTS 240 (1954 Hague Convention or Hague Convention):

> Article 1. Definition of cultural property. For the purposes of the present Convention, the term 'cultural property' shall cover, irrespective of origin or ownership: (a) movable or immovable property of great importance to the cultural heritage of every people, such as monuments of architecture, art or history, whether religious or secular; archaeological sites; groups of buildings which, as a whole, are of historical or artistic interest; works of art; manuscripts, books and other objects of artistic, historical or archaeological interest; as well as scientific collections and important collections of books or archives or of reproductions of the property defined above; (b) buildings whose main and effective purpose is to preserve or exhibit the movable cultural property defined in sub-paragraph (a) such as museums, large libraries and depositories of archives, and refuges intended to shelter, in the event of armed conflict,

The drafters of the Hague Convention thought that the Hague Rules of 1907 were overambitious in their definition of protected (cultural) property, and therefore aimed at providing a more realistic definition that would actually be able to protect at least some cultural heritage during conflict. By narrowing down the definition, they reasoned, it would be possible to give more protection to whatever fell under said definition.[9] Ultimately, though, it seems that even this narrowing of the definition has been unsuccessful, in light of military practice, and is still considered ambiguous.[10]

The narrowing of the category meant that suggestions by specific states of additions to the definition, which would in retrospect have helped the coordination with subsequent UNESCO treaties, went unheeded. The United States asked for the inclusion of religious monuments and natural sites.[11] Japan also suggested that natural sites be added to the definition, because they are 'considered sources of culture of sentiments for the people', as well as important sources for scientific research.[12] A similar nod to scientific research was made by Vietnam, who suggested scientific research centres be included in the definition.[13] Israel suggested that mounds where artefacts are found and libraries (the latter separately from Article 1.b) should also be included in the definition of the Hague Convention.[14]

Even if the definition contained in the Hague Convention is 'for the purposes of the present Convention', and its subsequent protocols, it has inevitably been influential in subsequent discourses around the definition of cultural heritage. Therefore, it deserves close attention.

The key language that needs interpreting in the Hague Convention for our present purposes is that of 'great importance to the cultural heritage of every people',[15] because it attributes value to heritage, and also because 'every people' connects heritage to specific stakeholders. The ambiguity of the term 'every people' is resolved in favour of interpreting it as the heritage 'of each respective people', at least if one takes into account the Hague Convention's preamble, an interpretation supported by state reports on the implementation of the treaty, and by key scholars like Roger O'Keefe.[16] In practice, the effect of this interpretation is that the Hague Convention's definition is open to a certain sense of representativeness (and potentially an open avenue for communities), or at least that it relies on the discretion and competence of each state party to identify the heritage within its own territory that is worthy of protection.[17] The fact that it is states that have the ability to identify heritage challenges to a certain extent the people-centric (as opposed to

the movable cultural property defined in sub-paragraph (a); (c) centers containing a large amount of cultural property as defined in sub-paragraphs (a) and (b), to be known as 'centers containing monuments'.

[9] O'Keefe (n 5) 101. [10] Ibid., 110.

[11] Intergovernmental Conference on the Protection of Cultural Property in the Event of Armed Conflict, *Observations concerning the Draft Convention for the Protection of Cultural Property in the Event of Armed Conflict*. The Hague, 21 April–12 May 1954. CBC/4 (15 February 1954), page 10.

[12] Ibid., page 9. [13] Ibid., page 19. [14] Ibid., page 7.

[15] 1954 Hague Convention (n 8), Article 1.a. [16] O'Keefe (n 5) 103–4.

[17] Ibid., 105–6.

state-centric) aspirations of the preamble, much in the way that the language on 'property' in the operative part of the treaty challenges the idea of 'heritage' in the preamble. One of the possible effects of this reliance on states to define cultural heritage in the context of armed conflict, for instance, is that states can refuse to define as heritage worthy of protection the heritage of minorities or armed groups in the context of non-international armed conflicts (a matter discussed in more detail in Chapter 4).

With respect to the relationship between the 1954 Hague Convention and the conservation paradigm, one of the important innovations of the Convention in relation to previous (pre-UNESCO) international heritage law is the protection of 'groups of buildings', in Article 1.a (language which was added very late in the negotiating process).[18] This innovation reflected a move in preservationism that sought to (re)contextualize cultural heritage and focus not only on isolated buildings, but on larger architectural fabrics. This language was opposed by a number of states during the negotiations, and passed by a fairly narrow margin.[19] However close the vote was, it is important to highlight that, as early as the Hague Convention, there is a move towards context in international heritage law that challenges intrinsic value in favour of relational values, even if it is still one predicated on built fabric, as opposed to living social connections.

The 1999 Second Protocol to the Hague Convention was an opportunity to revisit many of the tensions around the definition of 'cultural property' in the 1954 treaty, and in doing so accommodate best practice and (then) current knowledge in the field. The initial report behind the drafting of the Second Protocol noted the imprecision of the definition in the 1954 Hague Convention, as well as divergences from other UNESCO treaties that had been adopted up until that moment.[20] In fact, the original report urged that the definitions of the 1970 Convention (for movable heritage) and the World Heritage Convention (WHC) (for immovable heritage) be incorporated.[21] During negotiation of the Second Protocol, proposals were made to change the definition of heritage in order to update and expand it. There was even consideration of the possibility of including natural heritage (therefore, the environment) under the purview of the Second Protocol. This change was rejected, however, because natural heritage was deemed to have too many peculiarities that would make it incompatible with the cultural heritage regime.[22] Even a general updating of the concept of heritage was rejected because of the need that the Second Protocol be seen as closely aligned with rather than replacing the Hague Convention.[23]

Ultimately, in spite of the cries for redefinition, the wording in the Hague Convention was taken as acceptable by the participants in the meeting of experts,

[18] For instance, the 26 February 1954 draft did not include this language.
[19] O'Keefe (n 5) 102–3. [20] Ibid., 248.
[21] Toman, Jiří, *Cultural Property in War: Improvement in Protection—Commentary on the 1999 Second Protocol to the Hague Convention of 1954 for the Protection of Cultural Property in the Event of Armed Conflict* (UNESCO Publishing, 2009), 50.
[22] Ibid. [23] Ibid.

and the question was not reopened.[24] As a result, the Second Protocol merely incorporates by reference the definition in the 1954 treaty.[25] But the Second Protocol did consider the relationship to the WHC and the definition therein in some more detail. Already under the Hague Convention, over time, the idea of 'great importance' in its text had been interpreted by a number of states as equating with the notion of 'Outstanding Universal Value' (OUV) in the World Heritage Convention, discussed in this section.[26] That said, the drafters of the Second Protocol ultimately rejected that only those sites on the World Heritage List were worthy of protection under the Hague Convention system, and said that property that lacked OUV, but still had national or local importance, also fell under the general scope of application of the system.

However, when it comes to the enhanced protection system under the Second Protocol, the relationship to OUV is more pronounced.[27] The Second Protocol creates a new List of Cultural Property under Enhanced Protection. The system is modelled, for the most part, on the 1972 WHC.[28] Although the notion of simply incorporating cultural heritage on the World Heritage List into the Enhanced Protection List was rejected (partly because of the difference in the definition of 'heritage' between the two instruments, which affects their scope of application), the presence of cultural heritage on the World Heritage List serves as a powerful guide to the 'greatest importance for humanity' threshold.[29] In fact, according to the guidelines implementing the Second Protocol, there is a presumption that heritage on the World Heritage List meets the criteria for enhanced protection.[30] Listing is addressed in more detail in Chapter 7, but it is important to highlight here the push

[24] I Diplomatic Conference on the Second Protocol to the Hague Convention for the Protection of Cultural Property in the Event of Armed Conflict. The Hague, 15–26 March 1999. *Summary Report.* Paris, June 1999, para. 47. See also O'Keefe (n 5) 248.

[25] Second Protocol to the Hague Convention of 1954 for the Protection of Cultural Property in the Event of Armed Conflict (adopted 26 March 1999, entered into force 9 March 2004) 2253 UNTS 172 (Hague Protocol II): 'Article 1 Definitions. For the purposes of this Protocol: [. . .] b. "cultural property" means cultural property as defined in Article 1 of the Convention [. . .].'

[26] O'Keefe (n 5) 108.

[27] See Lixinski, Lucas, 'Environment and War: Lessons from Cultural Heritage Law', in Rosemary Rayfuse (ed.), *War and the Environment: New Approaches to Protecting the Environment in Relation to Armed Conflict* (Martinus Nijhoff, 2014), 157–77.

[28] Convention concerning the Protection of the World Cultural and Natural Heritage 1972 (adopted 23 November 1972, entered into force 15 December 1975) 1037 UNTS 151 (WHC). Henckaerts, Jean-Marie, 'New Rules for the Protection of Cultural Property in Armed Conflict: The Significance of the Second Protocol to the 1954 Hague Convention for the Protection of Cultural Property in the Event of Armed Conflict', in María Teresa Dutli (ed.), *Protection of Cultural Property in the Event of Armed Conflict* (International Committee of the Red Cross, 2002), 27–55, 43. UNESCO in 1993 even invited states to submit items of the World Heritage List for consideration for inscription in the Special Protection List. No nominations resulted from this effort. See Hladík, Jan, 'UNESCO's Activities for the Implementation and Promotion of the 1954 Hague Convention for the Protection of Cultural Property in the Event of Armed Conflict and its two Protocols', in María Teresa Dutli (ed.), *Protection of Cultural Property in the Event of Armed Conflict* (International Committee of the Red Cross, 2002), 57–77, 66.

[29] Toman (n 21) 188.

[30] Guidelines for the Implementation of the 1999 Second Protocol to the Hague Convention of 1954 for the Protection of Cultural Property in the Event of an Armed Conflict (adopted March 2012), Guideline 36.

for closer coordination among UNESCO instruments, and the ultimately missed opportunity that could have created more transparency within UNESCO.

In some respects, the Hague Convention and its Second Protocol could have been a window into how the field of international heritage law had evolved over forty-five years, particularly in respect to the definition of cultural heritage. But the opportunity to revise the definition was missed, illustrating that there are dissonances between definitions authorized at a certain point in time, reflecting values of each period, and influencing subsequent practice and innovation with respect to heritage. The law's resistance to change makes it even more important that a genealogy of the definition of heritage be undertaken to highlight the mismatches between those definitions and contemporary practice of and aspirations towards cultural heritage.

The 1970 Convention uses the 'cultural property' terminology as well, in its fairly extensive definition.[31] This convention was preceded by a 1964 Recommendation, which contained a definition of cultural property that the 1970 treaty built upon.[32] The drafting history of the 1964 Recommendation follows in the footsteps of the Hague Convention, while noting domestic practice in the implementation of the Hague Convention and general domestic law, which was either more prescriptive than the Hague treaty (e.g. by applying an

[31] Convention on the Means of Prohibiting and Preventing the Illicit Import, Export and Transfer of Ownership of Cultural Property 1970 (adopted 14 November 1970, entered into force 24 April 1972) 823 UNTS 231 (1970 Convention):

> Article 1. For the purposes of this Convention, the term 'cultural property' means property which, on religious or secular grounds, is specifically designated by each State as being of importance for archaeology, prehistory, history, literature, art or science and which belongs to the following categories: (a) Rare collections and specimens of fauna, flora, minerals and anatomy, and objects of palaeontological interest; (b) property relating to history, including the history of science and technology and military and social history, to the life of national leaders, thinkers, scientists and artist and to events of national importance; (c) products of archaeological excavations (including regular and clandestine) or of archaeological discoveries; (d) elements of artistic or historical monuments or archaeological sites which have been dismembered; (e) antiquities more than one hundred years old, such as inscriptions, coins and engraved seals; (f) objects of ethnological interest; (g) property of artistic interest, such as: (i) pictures, paintings and drawings produced entirely by hand on any support and in any material (excluding industrial designs and manufactured articles decorated by hand); (ii) original works of statuary art and sculpture in any material; (iii) original engravings, prints and lithographs; (iv) original artistic assemblages and montages in any material; (h) rare manuscripts and incunabula, old books, documents and publications of special interest (historical, artistic, scientific, literary, etc.) singly or in collections; (i) postage, revenue and similar stamps, singly or in collections; (j) archives, including sound, photographic and cinematographic archives; (k) articles of furniture more than one hundred years old and old musical instruments.

[32] Recommendation on the Means of Prohibiting and Preventing the Illicit Export, Import and Transfer of Ownership of Cultural Property (adopted 19 November 1964):

> I. Definition. 1. For the purpose of this recommendation, the term 'cultural property' means movable and immovable property of great importance to the cultural heritage of a country, such as works of art and architecture, manuscripts, books and other property of artistic, historical or archaeological interest, ethnological documents, type specimens of flora and fauna, scientific collections and important collections of books and archives, including musical archives. 2. Each Member State should adopt whatever criteria it deems most suitable for defining which items of cultural property within its territory should receive the protection envisaged in this recommendation by reason of their great importance.

age threshold), or less so (e.g. by having a broader definition).[33] The drafting also points out to the International Customs Convention, and the categories in it.[34] It seems in fact that the International Customs Convention, and the influence of the International Customs Union during the drafting of the 1970 Convention, have been decisive in shaping this specific instrument, particularly as a number of states had adopted the International Customs Convention, and thereby already incorporated that terminology in their domestic laws.[35] Thus, the practicalities of law enforcement seem to be a more important driver in the definition of heritage in the 1970 Convention than underlying issues about the role and place of cultural heritage, at least on the surface. Procedural expediency seems to replace due consideration of heritage and its role, and the perspectives of state law enforcement agents are paramount to other views.

While the customs definition was useful, there was also a concerted effort to not rely entirely on it, at least initially, nor on the Hague Convention definition. That reluctance left drafters with domestic law, of which the most frequent definitional criterion seemed to be age.[36] Subsequent negotiations revisited this issue, and introduced a time criterion that had to do not with the age of the object, but rather a cut-off on the date of production (1920 was suggested).[37] And, as with the Hague Convention, there is a fairly wide margin of discretion for each state to determine whether the objects are 'of particular importance', in accordance with their own rules.[38] This discretion was opposed by countries like Japan, who argued that this allowance would create inconsistencies in the definition, and ultimately compromise the effectiveness of the instrument.[39]

For the movable heritage category, though, this nationalistic impulse is more easily understandable, given the 1970 Convention's commitment to attempt to return property to newly decolonized countries, shared at least in part by the preceding Recommendation. Hence, there are clear nationalistic undertones, rather than the (frustrated) cosmopolitan aspirations of the Hague Convention. But the cosmopolitan spirit makes an appearance in the 1970 Convention definition as a limitation to the state's power to determine 'importance'. So, while for the Hague

[33] *Technical and Legal Aspects of the Preparation of International Regulations to Prevent the Illicit Import, Export and Sale of Cultural Property*, UNESCO/CUA/115, of 14 April 1962, 5–6.

[34] Ibid., 6.

[35] Reading this history from the perspective of US–Mexico bilateral cooperation in the area of illicit trafficking, see Nafziger, James A. R., 'The 1970 UNESCO Convention: Insights, Circumspections, and Outlooks', in Jorge A. Sánchez Cordero (ed.), *La Convención de la UNESCO de 1970: Sus Nuevos Desafíos* (2014) 211–28, 211–18.

[36] *Technical and Legal Aspects* (n 33) 8.

[37] Means of Prohibiting the Illicit Import, Export and Sale of Cultural Property. Preliminary Report prepared in accordance with Article 10.1 of the Rule of Procedure concerning the recommendations to Member States and International Conventions covered by the terms of Article IV, paragraph 4, of the Constitution. UNESCO/CUA/123, 15 July 1963, page 6.

[38] Ibid., 7.

[39] Means of Prohibiting the Illicit Import, Export and Sale of Cultural Property. Preliminary Report prepared in accordance with Article 10.1 of the Rule of Procedure concerning the recommendations to Member States and International Conventions covered by the terms of Article IV, paragraph 4, of the Constitution. UNESCO/CUA/123, 15 July 1963. Annex I—Replies to circular letter CL/1667 and document UNESCO/CUA/123, received from Member States by 10 February 1964, page 10.

Convention the notion of 'importance' means full discretion for the state party (and is thus nationalistic), in the 1970 Convention it is a limit on the same discretion, in order to enable a market in antiquities (and is therefore cosmopolitan). Note that the key players here seem to be just states (of different 'types', yes, but states nonetheless), and that they act as the proxies for their populations, in line with the Westphalian paradigm of international law.

With respect to the precision needed for a definition, the United Kingdom delegate called the difficulties in the definition 'insuperable',[40] while the United States delegation said the idea of cultural objects was 'so vague as to defy definition'.[41] In response, the UNESCO Secretariat skirted these objections simply by saying they did not refer to specific wording in the draft's language, and restated their criteria around 'importance' and the ability left to each state to define their own heritage for the purposes of the Recommendation.[42] UNESCO thus asserted and expanded its authority by sidestepping states and falling back on experts as a 'neutral' source of legitimacy.

After the adoption of the Recommendation in 1964, UNESCO moved to preparing what became the 1970 Convention. In the drafting, it was highlighted that its purpose would be to protect the cultural heritage of peoples, as opposed to the cultural heritage of humankind.[43] The process of revising and expanding the definition for the 1970 Convention took into account again the language of the International Customs Convention, alongside other instruments like the Hague Convention, the agreements on the end of occupation in West Germany, and the 1964 Recommendation, while distinguishing the objectives of those instruments from those of the 1970 Convention.[44] For instance, the 1970 definition sought to eliminate the 'great importance' threshold, while maintaining the need for designation by individual states.[45] The result here is to keep the nationalistic impulse, while eliminating the cosmopolitan check on it. The International Customs Union, as an observer at the diplomatic conference, restated the importance of its own definition, given its wide acceptance by states at the time.[46]

[40] Ibid., 22. [41] Ibid., 23–4.

[42] Means of Prohibiting the Illicit Import, Export and Sale of Cultural Property. Preliminary Report prepared in accordance with Article 10.1 of the Rule of Procedure concerning the recommendations to Member States and International Conventions covered by the terms of Article IV, paragraph 4, of the Constitution. UNESCO/CUA/123, 15 July 1963. Annex II—Secretariat's Response, pages 2–3. See also Draft Report of the Special Committee of Governmental Experts to prepare a draft Recommendation on means of prohibiting and preventing the illicit export, import and sale of cultural property, 13–24 April 1964. IEIS/DR/91, 24 April 1964, para. 18.

[43] Means of prohibiting and preventing the illicit import, export and transfer of ownership of cultural property—Preliminary report prepared in compliance with Article 10.1 of the Rules of Procedure concerning Recommendations to Member States and International Conventions covered by the terms of Article IV, paragraph 4, of the Constitution. SHC/MD/3, 8 August 1969, para. 10.

[44] Ibid., paras 21–26. [45] Ibid., para. 28.

[46] UNESCO General Conference, 16th Session. Item 19 of the Provisional Agenda—Draft convention on the means of prohibiting and preventing the illicit import, export and transfer of ownership of cultural property, 16 C/17, 13 July 1970. Annex II—Report of the Special Committee of Governmental Experts to examine the draft convention on the means of prohibiting and preventing the illicit import, export and transfer of ownership of cultural property, para. 12.

The delegates at the diplomatic conference in 1970 stressed the need for a precise definition, while at the same time highlighting that the 1970 Convention should steer away from dealing with domestic property law.[47] So, even though the reliance on domestic law has been crucial in the definition, the use of language seems to be where the influence ends, as domestic property law is off limits to the treaty. A disconnect between domestic and international law is thereby created. To facilitate law enforcement, the definition left as little subjectivity as possible in the assessment of cultural heritage, and it closely followed the language of the International Customs Convention.[48]

After the 1970 Convention, another Recommendation was approved, more broadly on the 'protection of movable cultural property'. The 1978 Recommendation contains yet another definition of cultural heritage,[49] which in many respects expands upon the 1970 Convention. This new definition includes, for instance, items of applied arts, mummies, the product of underwater excavations, and photographic and film archives. In light of the broadening of the definition, and at the suggestion of East Germany, a coda was added to the definition, again deferring to states on the definition, but implying each state should adopt criteria to classify and define their own heritage.[50] The need for definition is once again reinforced, presumably for the

[47] Ibid., paras 17–18. [48] Ibid., para. 20.

[49] Recommendation for the Protection of Movable Cultural Property (adopted 28 November 1978):

> I. Definitions. 1. For the purposes of this Recommendation: (a) 'movable cultural property' shall be taken to mean all movable objects which are the expression and testimony of human creation or of the evolution of nature and which are of archaeological, historical, artistic, scientific or technical value and interest, including items in the following categories: (i) products of archaeological exploration and excavations conducted on land and under water; (ii) antiquities such as tools, pottery, inscriptions, coins, seals, jewellery, weapons and funerary remains, including mummies; (iii) items resulting from the dismemberment of historical monuments; (iv) material of anthropological and ethnological interest; (v) items relating to history, including the history of science and technology and military and social history, to the life of peoples and national leaders, thinkers, scientists and artists and to events of national importance; (vi) items of artistic interest, such as: paintings and drawings, produced entirely by hand on any support and in any material (excluding industrial designs and manufactured articles decorated by hand); original prints, and posters and photographs, as the media for original creativity; original artistic assemblages and montages in any material; works of statuary art and sculpture in any material; works of applied art in such materials as glass, ceramics, metal, wood, etc.; (vii) manuscripts and incunabula, codices, books, documents or publications of special interest; (viii) items of numismatic (medals and coins) and philatelic interest; (ix) archives, including textual records, maps and other cartographic materials, photographs, cinematographic films, sound recordings and machine-readable records; (x) items of furniture, tapestries, carpets, dress and musical instruments; (xi) zoological, botanical and geological specimens; [...] 2. Each Member State should adopt whatever criteria it deems most suitable for defining the items of movable cultural property within its territory which should be given the protection envisaged in this Recommendation by reason of their archaeological, historical, artistic, scientific or technical value.

[50] International Instruments on the Prevention and Coverage of Risks to Movable Cultural Property. Final report prepared under Article 10.3 of the Rules of Procedure concerning Recommendations to Member States and International Conventions covered by the terms of Article IV, paragraph 4, of the Constitution. CC-78/WS/9, 20 March 1978. Annex I—Analytical study of the general observations and comments made by Member States on the preliminary report and the first draft recommendation (Document CC-77/WS/45), para. 25.

purposes of law enforcement, and turned into an 'objective' assessment into which political actors like communities would have no stake.

Subsequent practice under the 1970 Convention, particularly under the 'Intergovernmental Committee for Promoting the Return of Cultural Property to its Countries of Origin or its Restitution in case of Illicit Appropriation', has engaged with these definitions again. The engagement of this Committee has in particular emphasized the need for a broad definition of heritage that not only shifts the focus away from objects (which was the early emphasis of the Committee) and towards other forms of cultural expression, including movable, immovable, tangible, and intangible cultural heritage, but also highlights Indigenous heritage in particular.[51] The Indigenous rights discourse, in fact, has helped shift international attention from 'property' towards heritage, by connecting heritage to identity and religious and spiritual values.[52] In this particular, subsequent practice has at least attempted to overcome the exclusion of communities under the guise of 'neutrality', and has reinjected some of the postcolonial and emancipatory spirit into the treaty.

Therefore, while the 1954 Hague Convention definition stems from a broader cosmopolitan commitment to the heritage of humankind, the definition of heritage with respect to movable heritage, anchored by the 1970 treaty, seems to be based on domestic law, including customs regulations. These two treaties thus showcase different tensions with respect to cultural heritage and its objectives. But they also present similar gaps, such as the virtual exclusion of nature from the definitions of heritage (in spite of attempts by multiple states, particularly in the Hague Convention drafting). This gap is remedied by the World Heritage Convention, which again reassesses the definition of heritage for the purposes of international law, and this time refers to it for the first time as 'heritage' in the main text of the treaty.

The WHC expands the realm of international heritage law in many significant ways. For one, it is the first international instrument to comprehensively deal with the status of immovable heritage in peacetime.[53] Secondly, it bridges the gap between culture and nature in ways that the Hague Convention and the 1970 Convention failed to do (which will be explored in some detail in Chapter 6). In bridging the gap between culture and nature, though, the WHC still relies on some degree of separation as far as the concept of heritage is concerned, containing separate articles for cultural and natural heritage.[54] Communities, particularly traditional ones, where

[51] Vrdoljak (n 2) 213–14. [52] Ibid., 270.

[53] In fact, the Operational Guidelines to the Convention are very explicit in that only immovable heritage can be considered, stating that 'nominations of immovable heritage which are likely to become movable will not be considered'. Operational Guidelines for the Implementation of the World Heritage Convention (2015), para. 48.

[54] WHC:

> I. Definitions of the cultural and the natural heritage:
> Article 1. For the purposes of this Convention, the following shall be considered as 'cultural heritage': *monuments*: architectural works, works of monumental sculpture and painting, elements or structures of an archaeological nature, inscriptions, cave dwellings and combinations of features, which are of outstanding universal value from the point of view of history, art or science; *groups of buildings*: groups of separate or connected buildings which, because

the separation is more porous, end up excluded in the early years, in favour of a certain expert-driven scientificism.

The definition of heritage contained in the WHC responds to a specific vision of the conservation paradigm discussed in Chapter 1. In fact, the early pushes for what became the WHC emphasized the need for appropriate technical criteria for the conservation of monumental heritage.[55] It is worth highlighting that the WHC has evolved tremendously in its practice, and that includes expanding the definition of heritage,[56] in a 'dynamic reinterpretation of the concept'.[57] Of course, the treaty itself has not changed, but the Operational Guidelines to the WHC have, in order to accommodate evolving notions of heritage and its worth, which have attempted to move away from elitist notions of heritage to things that are closer to human beings (and therefore community-centric and intangible heritage).[58] One of the effects of this evolution is to shift away from heritage itself, and towards the values attributed to it. While that movement is observable as well in the heritage studies literature, there is a legal-mechanical reason behind it: under the WHC, the definition of cultural heritage (or natural heritage, for that matter) cannot be amended, save for great efforts;[59] however, OUV, which is a characteristic of all groups of cultural and natural heritage in the WHC, is not defined in the WHC, in spite of concern by the drafters on this matter[60]—rather, it is for the Operational Guidelines to define this value;[61] as the Guidelines can be more easily amended or changed, it has been the way in which the definition of heritage, and the conservation paradigm under it, has evolved. Therefore, the evolution of the notion of heritage under the WHC has happened around the edges, rather than centrally. To be sure, there is only so far that a change to criteria can go, as the main definition in the treaty still limits the

of their architecture, their homogeneity or their place in the landscape, are of outstanding universal value from the point of view of history, art or science; *sites*: works of man or the combined works of nature and of man, and areas including archaeological sites which are of outstanding universal value from the historical, aesthetic, ethnological or anthropological points of view.

Article 2. For the purposes of this Convention, the following shall be considered as 'natural heritage': *natural features* consisting of physical and biological formations or groups of such formations, which are of outstanding universal value from the aesthetic or scientific point of view; *geological and physiographical formations* and precisely delineated areas which constitute the habitat of threatened species of animals and plants of outstanding universal value from the point of view of science or conservation; *natural sites* or precisely delineated natural areas of outstanding universal value from the point of view of science, conservation or natural beauty.

55 Yusuf, Abdulqawi A., 'Article 1—Definition of Cultural Heritage', in Francesco Francioni and Federico Lenzerini (eds), *The 1972 World Heritage Convention: A Commentary* (Oxford University Press, 2008), 23–50, 24.

56 Ibid, 29.

57 Francioni, 'A Dynamic Evolution of Concept and Scope' (n 2) 230.

58 Cameron, Christina and Rössler, Mechtild, *Many Voices, One Vision: The Early Years of the World Heritage Convention* (Ashgate, 2013), 240.

59 The amendment procedure is in Article 37 of the WHC.

60 UNESCO General Conference, Draft Convention for the Protection of the World Cultural and Natural Heritage and Draft Recommendation Concerning the Protection, at National Level, of the Cultural and Natural Heritage (15 June 1972), 17 C/18, para. 14.

61 Operational Guidelines for the Implementation of the World Heritage Convention (2015), paras 49–53.

possibilities for World Heritage and the conservation paradigm under it. After all, changing the criteria against which one can value and protect heritage does not necessarily challenge the core of the definition.[62]

Early proposals for the WHC did not mention the term 'heritage', and focused instead only on certain cultural categories, without an umbrella term. They focused on monuments and groups of buildings for the most part (or monuments and sites, which would have included nature),[63] drawing a comparison between those and 'centers containing monuments' in the Hague Convention definition.[64] That said, at the time the science branch of UNESCO was working on a draft for the protection of natural sites, which was to be submitted to the 1972 Stockholm Conference (United Nations Conference on the Human Environment), a landmark event in international environmentalism. The science and culture arms of UNESCO then decided to merge the two drafts, and that exacerbated the scientificism around heritage, but also paved the way for the umbrella term 'heritage' being for the first time enshrined in the main text of a UNESCO cultural treaty (as opposed to the preamble).[65]

The influence of the nascent environmental movement, of course, goes beyond introducing the term 'heritage' to the main text of the treaty (even if that contribution cannot be underestimated). The category of natural heritage itself is a contribution to how we think about heritage more generally, and the available models for its protection (discussed in more detail in Chapter 7). To be more specific, the introduction of the category of natural heritage was the way in for the United States national parks model to be at the forefront of proposals for the structure of what became the WHC.[66]

The definition of natural heritage, like the one for cultural heritage, relies on OUV quite substantially. Further, and differently from cultural heritage, natural heritage also relies on the linkage with science (all three categories of natural heritage) for its definition, as well as conservation (categories 2 and 3) and aesthetics (categories 1 and 3).[67] As is discussed further in Chapter 6, this connection to science raises the stakes of natural heritage, and helps reinforce a certain view of the conservation paradigm that inevitably spills over to cultural heritage as well. So, in spite of the relative underrepresentation of natural heritage on the World Heritage

[62] For a more optimistic view on this evolution, as well as a detailed account of how it happened, see Yusuf (n 55) 31–40.

[63] d'Ossat, G. De Angelis, 'The Scientific Concepts on Which the Protection and Presentation of Monuments and Sites is Based', paper presented at the Meeting of Experts to co-ordinate with a view to their international adoption, the principles and scientific, technical and legal criteria which would make is [sic] possible to establish an effective system for the protection of monuments and sites (January 1968). SXC/CS/27/3, paras 15–17.

[64] UNESCO Executive Board, *Possible International Instrument for the Protection of Monuments and Sites of Universal Value* (22 April 1970), 84 EX/14, paras 41–42.

[65] Yusuf (n 55) 26.

[66] Redgwell, Catherine, 'Article 2—Definition of Natural Heritage', in Francesco Francioni and Federico Lenzerini (eds), *The 1972 World Heritage Convention: A Commentary* (Oxford University Press, 2008), 63–84, 64.

[67] Ibid., 66.

List (a phenomenon that may also have to do with the finiteness of nature, whereas culture keeps flourishing),[68] natural heritage has been greatly influential on the way we define and think about cultural heritage. And that influence is felt in the creation of a mixed type of heritage under the WHC.

The introduction of the category of cultural landscapes, as under Article 1 of the WHC,[69] has been a significant evolution. That said, it has also created some confusion, being accused of imprecision, and of muddying the separation between cultural and natural heritage that the drafters implemented.[70] This category has stranded cultural heritage in the text of the WHC, and natural heritage in earlier iterations of the Operational Guidelines.[71] A response to this muddying of the categories has been the merger of the criteria for OUV into a single set in 2003 (as opposed to the historically separate sets for cultural and natural heritage).[72] The effect of this merger of the concepts is a further approximation between culture and nature in the very definition of World Heritage, which also brings World Heritage closer to the reality of many (particularly traditional) communities that live in, around, or otherwise with heritage.

While the WHC embraces the language of 'heritage', the language of property does not quite go away, either. After all, World Heritage Sites are still largely referred to as 'properties'. Immediately after the WHC defines cultural and natural heritage, for instance, it refers to this heritage as 'properties' in the territory of a state, which need defining for protection purposes.[73] Taken at its best, the return to the terminology of property implies that heritage, for legal protection purposes, needs to be defined and constrained, a point which I have argued elsewhere relates to the commodification of cultural heritage.[74] But needing to define and constrain heritage can also mean divorcing it from its practitioners, and the changes those stakeholders may want to make to heritage sites. Therefore, the return to property in the World Heritage Convention, to the extent it is property of the state party, is a means to define heritage, to exercise control over it. But the control is handed over to the state, essentially dealing a blow to the cosmopolitan spirit that the WHC otherwise embodies. In spite of its best intentions, the WHC system falls short of being the 'kind of global heritage commons' that was once envisioned, and needs to work through its states parties as 'the operative arms that UNESCO or the [World Heritage] Committee itself lacks'.[75]

68 Ibid., 83. 69 Operational Guidelines, para. 47.

70 Cameron and Rössler (n 58) 70.

71 As discussed by Whitby-Last, K., 'Article 1: Cultural Landscapes', in Francesco Francioni and Federico Lenzerini (eds), *The 1972 World Heritage Convention: A Commentary* (Oxford University Press, 2008), 51–63, 52–3.

72 Cameron and Rössler (n 58) 97.

73 WHC, Article 3: 'It is for each State Party to this Convention to identify and delineate the different *properties* situated on its territory mentioned in Articles 1 and 2 above' (emphasis added).

74 Lucas Lixinski, *Intangible Cultural Heritage in International Law* (Oxford University Press, 2013), 14–18.

75 Brumann, Christophe and Berliner, David, 'Introduction. UNESCO World Heritage—Grounded?', in Christophe Brumann and David Berliner (eds), *World Heritage on the Ground—Ethnographic Perspectives* (Berghahn, 2016), 1–34, 9.

In the drafting of the WHC, then UNESCO Director-General René Maheu attempted to reconcile this tension between internationalism and nationalism with respect to World Heritage. In the opening of a meeting of the committee of experts drafting the WHC, Mr Maheu said that the revised draft of the WHC was 'based on the principle that the cultural and natural heritage belongs to [hu]mankind as a whole, which means that it lies outside the proprietorship of States while remaining within the framework of their sovereignty'.[76] This idea seems to redefine the use of 'property' for the purposes of the WHC, meaning not the body of property law domestically, but reinforcing the notion that 'property' is just a means to delimit heritage. In fact, the body of property law, even though key in the domestic implementation of the WHC, is largely avoided by the treaty. That manoeuvre does not mean that in actuality World Heritage sites avoid the legal categorization and association with property that comes with the status: these sites are still very much property in practice,[77] in spite of the WHC's best efforts to avoid the economics of heritage (of which property rights are a big aspect, and as is discussed in Chapter 5).

The definition of cultural heritage in the WHC has been influential in subsequent instruments. It has helped the Underwater Cultural Heritage Convention (UCHC), for instance, in raising awareness of the existence of underwater cultural heritage, and helping merge maritime World Heritage (often natural) with underwater cultural artefacts.[78] And, for the Intangible Cultural Heritage Convention (ICHC), the WHC's definition and its evolution helped take the relational definition of heritage (which was the result of the evolution of the definition in the WHC through the criteria for assessment of OUV, as discussed) even further.[79] But, before getting to the relational aspects of heritage and the shift in the conservation paradigm ostensibly promoted by the ICHC, it is necessary to look in more detail at the definition of underwater cultural heritage in the UCHC.

The UCHC is the first treaty to make a clean break with the terminology of 'cultural property', based on the idea of using the treaty to create an international protective system rather than a means to allocate title and rights to underwater heritage (which could have implications for how sovereignty was construed in those areas).[80] The UCHC in some respects reinforces the historical conservation paradigm in the origins of the WHC, which can be attributed to a resurgence of reliance on expert rule, as discussed in Chapter 3. Its definition of underwater heritage focuses on cultural remains of a certain age.[81] This period oscillated in the drafting between

[76] Address by Mr René Maheu, Director-General of the United Nations Educational, Scientific and Cultural Organization (UNESCO), at the opening of the meeting of the Special Committee of Governmental Experts to prepare a draft Convention and a draft Recommendation to Member States concerning the protection of monuments, groups of buildings and sites (4 April 1972) (emphasis in the original).

[77] Brumann and Berliner (n 75) 19. [78] Yusuf (n 55) 43–4. [79] Ibid., 41–3.

[80] Francioni, 'A Dynamic Evolution of Concept and Scope' (n 2) 232.

[81] Convention on the Protection of the Underwater Cultural Heritage 2001 (adopted 2 November 2001, entered into force 2 January 2009) 2562 UNTS 3 (UCHC):

> Article 1—Definitions. For the purposes of this Convention:
> 1. (a) 'Underwater cultural heritage' means all traces of human existence having a cultural, historical or archaeological character which have been partially or totally under water,

50 and 100 years, and a compromise at some point was put forward that the time limit be 100 years, but allowing states to consider certain objects submerged for less than 100 years as underwater cultural heritage.[82] The Argentinean delegation, for instance, supported this latter view.[83] Chapter 4 engages with the matter of time with respect to cultural heritage, and for our current purposes I will focus on the definition in the UCHC and its history, particularly in relation to the concept of property.

The drafting of the UCHC underlines that the main body of materials covered by the treaty are not just shipwrecks, but also artefacts linked to them.[84] Discussions during the drafting considered whether underwater landscapes should be included in the definition in addition to objects of archaeological interest, but, in the view of the drafters, underwater landscapes would likely fall under state jurisdiction, and thus outside the jurisdictional scope of the UCHC.[85] Further, landscapes would require coordination with the World Heritage Convention, which was seen as undesirable in this respect.[86] Likewise, the notion of palaeontological underwater artefacts was ultimately excluded from the definition for being part of the UNCLOS regime,[87] thus enshrining a separation between nature and culture that reverts the trend started in the Hague Convention, and ultimately crystallized in the WHC text. The South Korean and Tunisian delegations opposed this exclusion, and insisted on the inclusion of landscapes, and a narrower definition of warships (discussed shortly).[88] This may have been a missed opportunity to engage with

periodically or continuously, for at least 100 years such as: (i) sites, structures, buildings, artefacts and human remains, together with their archaeological and natural context; (ii) vessels, aircraft, other vehicles or any part thereof, their cargo or other contents, together with their archaeological and natural context; and (iii) objects of prehistoric character. (b) Pipelines and cables placed on the seabed shall not be considered as underwater cultural heritage. (c) Installations other than pipelines and cables, placed on the seabed and still in use, shall not be considered as underwater cultural heritage. [. . .]

[82] Report of the meeting of governmental experts on the draft convention for the protection of the underwater cultural heritage (29 June–2 July 1998). CLT-98/CONF.202/7, para. 9.

[83] Third Meeting of Governmental Experts to consider the draft Convention on the Protection of the Underwater Cultural Heritage. Synoptic Report of comments on the Draft Convention on the Protection of the Underwater Cultural Heritage made by Member States of UNESCO (April 2000). CLT-2000/CONF.201/3, 3.

[84] UNESCO Executive Board, Feasibility Study for the drafting of a new instrument for the protection of the underwater cultural heritage (23 March 1995). 146 EX/27, paras 4–5.

[85] UNESCO General Conference, Report by the Director-General on action taken concerning the desirability of preparing an international instrument for the protection of the underwater cultural heritage (5 August 1997). Annex I—Summary report of the meeting of experts for the protection of underwater cultural heritage (22–24 May 1996). 29 C/22, para. 9.

[86] Strati, Anastasia, *Draft Convention on the Protection of Underwater Cultural Heritage—A Commentary prepared for UNESCO* (CLT-99/WS/8, April 1999), 16.

[87] Report of the fourth meeting of governmental experts on the draft Convention on the protection of the underwater cultural heritage (26 March–6 April 2001). CLT-2001/CONF.203/INF.3, 6–7.

[88] UNESCO General Conference, Report by the Director-General on action taken concerning the desirability of preparing an international instrument for the protection of the underwater cultural heritage (5 August 1997). Annex II—Observations by states on the report of the meeting of experts jointly organized by UNESCO, the United Nations Law of the Sea Office of Legal Affairs and the International Maritime Organization. 29 C/22, Views of the Republic of Korea, paras 2–3, Views of Tunisia, paras 2–3.

intangible aspects of underwater cultural heritage, as well as with natural aspects. In fact, the UCHC stresses that underwater heritage must have 'a cultural, historical or archaeological character', a criterion added at a relatively late stage in the negotiations.[89]

Instead, states stressed the importance of a clear definition for matters of legal certainty,[90] which is a common theme in the history of treaty definitions. This push for precision in the definition came mostly from the practice of common law countries, who traditionally take a selective approach to heritage, in opposition to the expansionist and protectionist take of civil law countries.[91] But in spite of the push for a narrow, legally precise definition, the UCHC incorporated far more than just shipwrecks and artefacts associated with shipwrecks; but the definition was not as broad as it could have been, in a concerted effort to exclude areas within a state's sovereign jurisdiction.[92] The reference to aircraft, for instance, is an innovation of the UCHC vis-à-vis other international and regional initiatives covering underwater heritage, and the UCHC in general ends up referring to all traces of human existence, in line with the Council of Europe's Valetta Convention on the matter.[93] Likewise, qualitative criteria were excluded from the UCHC, which is one of the reasons behind UK opposition, namely the existence of too many shipwrecks under its jurisdiction, and the undesirability of extending legal protection under the UCHC to all of them.[94] The lack of a qualitative criterion in the definition affects the protection mechanisms, and is one of the reasons why the UCHC is the only UNESCO treaty that does not contain a list, as is discussed in Chapter 7. It also has the potential to democratize heritage in favour of communities, but, as will be discussed in the next chapter, that is not possible under the UCHC for other reasons (primarily its reliance on expert rule).

While the drafting of the definition was deemed a difficult and somewhat controversial process,[95] there seemed to be agreement in that warships should be excluded, as a means of protecting state sovereignty.[96] Coupled with the exclusion of underwater landscapes, the exclusion of warships can be read as meaning that the space for cosmopolitanism in the definition of heritage for the UCHC was carved only in the negative, after fully protecting state sovereignty. The protection of sovereignty as a key element of the definition of UCH was deemed by many states, such as Canada, to be central to the process.[97]

[89] Dromgoole, Sarah, *Underwater Cultural Heritage and International Law* (Cambridge University Press, 2013), 91.

[90] UNESCO General Conference, Report by the Director-General on action taken concerning the desirability of preparing an international instrument for the protection of the underwater cultural heritage (5 August 1997). Annex I—Summary report of the meeting of experts for the protection of underwater cultural heritage (22–24 May 1996). 29 C/22, para. 13. See also Strati (n 86) 15.

[91] Dromgoole (n 89) 92. [92] Ibid., 66–7. [93] Ibid., 87. [94] Ibid., 93.

[95] UNESCO General Conference, Report by the Director-General on action taken concerning the desirability of preparing an international instrument for the protection of the underwater cultural heritage (5 August 1997). Annex I—Summary report of the meeting of experts for the protection of underwater cultural heritage (22–24 May 1996). 29 C/22, para. 21.

[96] Ibid., paras 22–26.

[97] UNESCO General Conference, Report by the Director-General on action taken concerning the desirability of preparing an international instrument for the protection of the underwater cultural heritage (5 August 1997). Annex II—Observations by states on the report of the meeting of experts jointly

The same exclusion of state sovereignty, like in other UNESCO treaties, meant the exclusion of the domestic law of property.[98] Drafters for instance decided that consideration of 'abandonment' of underwater heritage (akin to the abandonment of property in domestic property law) created a division between lawyers and archaeologists, and was also incompatible with the domestic law of several member states, particularly in Latin America. A definition of abandonment was included in one of the drafts of the UCHC, which would affect ownership questions indirectly.[99]

Ultimately, though, drafters considered that the question of title should not be dealt with at all by the UCHC,[100] including the matter of abandonment. This pragmatic compromise allowed the UCHC to stay in line with its predecessor in deterring the question to state sovereignty and enabled the inclusion of warships within the scope of the convention, facilitating the negotiation process as a whole.[101] The drafting history does suggest, however, that the exclusion of ownership matters from the UCHC means that 'all underwater cultural heritage should be protected, regardless of ownership. In other words, the owner of a wreck may use it, but only with the consent of and according to the conditions established by the competent authorities'.[102] Effectively, this choice means that the UCHC attempts to clearly subordinate domestic property law to the requirements of cultural heritage protection, while at the same time fully doing away with the 'property' terminology that had been deployed by preceding treaties. The reasons for the elimination of property in this context are connected to the nature of UCH as falling outside territorial jurisdiction, unlike other heritage treaties, whose scope is primarily territorial, thus reinforcing the idea that property is a proxy for sovereignty in international heritage treaties. But it still means an important step away from state property as a form of control over heritage, which is only partly replicated in the Intangible Cultural Heritage Convention.

I have written on the definition of ICH elsewhere,[103] but it is necessary to highlight specific elements of the ICHC definition[104] in comparison with other definitions

organized by UNESCO, the United Nations Law of the Sea Office of Legal Affairs and the International Maritime Organization. 29 C/22, Views of Canada, para. 2.

[98] On ownership with respect to UCH generally, see Dromgoole (n 89) 96–119.

[99] Strati (n 86) 16–17.

[100] Report of the meeting of governmental experts on the draft convention for the protection of the underwater cultural heritage (29 June–2 July 1998). CLT-98/CONF.202/7, paras 12–13.

[101] Dromgoole (n 89) 117.

[102] Strati (n 86) 17.

[103] Lixinski (n 74) 7–10 and 34–6.

[104] Convention for Safeguarding of the Intangible Cultural Heritage 2003 (adopted 17 October 2003, entered into force 20 April 2006) 2368 UNTS 3 (ICHC):

> Article 2—Definitions. For the purposes of this Convention, 1. The 'intangible cultural heritage' means the practices, representations, expressions, knowledge, skills—as well as the instruments, objects, artefacts and cultural spaces associated therewith—that communities, groups and, in some cases, individuals recognize as part of their cultural heritage. This intangible cultural heritage, transmitted from generation to generation, is constantly recreated by communities and groups in response to their environment, their interaction with nature and their history, and provides them with a sense of identity and continuity, thus promoting respect for cultural diversity and human creativity. For the purposes of this Convention, consideration will be given solely to such intangible cultural heritage as is compatible with existing international human rights instruments, as well as with the requirements of mutual

in the relevant UNESCO treaties. Many expressions have been used in the past to describe intangible heritage, including 'folklore', 'traditional cultural expressions', 'Indigenous culture', and 'traditional or popular culture', among many others.[105] While 'intangible cultural heritage' is a term that can be criticized (for creating an apparent opposition to tangible heritage, for instance), it is the one for which it was possible to find consensus when drafting the ICH Convention. That said, the choice of the term 'intangible cultural heritage' has been criticized by some scholars. The term makes sense within the administrative logic of UNESCO, precisely because of its opposition to tangible cultural heritage, which was addressed in other UNESCO instruments. However, to conceive of this type of heritage as 'intangible' in theory weakens its worth, rendering it disconnected and conveying the impression that its existence is ethereal or irrelevant. Further, the term 'intangible heritage' arguably weakens the status of traditional culture in legal practice, and can lessen the possibilities of protection.[106] Considering this treaty is the one most open to community governance (as discussed in the next chapter), and that intangible heritage in general is central to community initiatives around heritage, this criticism is not a fatal blow.

The discussion on the definition of what became ICH as being in opposition to physical heritage has a long history at UNESCO. A 1984 study, for instance, engages with definition of 'non-physical heritage'.[107] It outlines the following four elements to a definition of non-physical heritage, popular traditions, or folklore: (1) collective and spontaneous participation by the community; (2) 'impersonal or anonymous origin'; (3) non-commercial and oral transmission; and (4) intergenerational structure.[108] These four elements can still be seen in the ICHC, and the idea of community participation is particularly important in challenging the conservation paradigm. The idea of impersonal origin serves to eschew property in the domain of ICH.[109] The idea of links to the community was reinforced in the early developments of the programme that was the basis for the ICHC, making 'a critical, inseparable linkage to the social life of the community' and essential part of the definition of non-physical heritage.[110]

respect among communities, groups and individuals, and of sustainable development. 2. The 'intangible cultural heritage', as defined in paragraph 1 above, is manifested inter alia in the following domains: (a) oral traditions and expressions, including language as a vehicle of the intangible cultural heritage; (b) performing arts; (c) social practices, rituals and festive events; (d) knowledge and practices concerning nature and the universe; (e) traditional craftsmanship. [. . .]

[105] UNESCO, *International Round Table: 'Intangible Cultural Heritage—Working Definitions'*, meeting held in Turin, Italy on 14–17 March 2001.

[106] McCann, Anthony et al., 'The 1989 Recommendation Ten Years On: Towards a Critical Analysis', in Peter Seitel (ed.), *Safeguarding Traditional Culture: A Global Assessment* (Smithsonian Institution, 2001), 57–64, 60.

[107] Dunaway, David K., 'The World's Non-Physical Heritage', paper prepared for the Consultation of Experts to Define the Non-Physical Heritage (27–30 November 1984). CLT-84/CONF.603/COL (1 September 1984).

[108] Ibid., 8. [109] Ibid., 9.

[110] Final Report of the Meeting of Experts to Draw Up a Future Programme Concerning the Non-Physical Heritage. CLT-84/CONF.603/COL.2, 31 May 1985, 2.

Language was 'unanimously considered' part of non-physical heritage,[111] but the ICHC later made language less central, as a means to defer to sovereignty.[112] Therefore, even if best knowledge in the area suggests that language should be part of the definition of heritage in the ICHC, (domestic) politics changes the status of language. In this way, the cosmopolitan aspiration of the ICHC, particularly with respect to ethnic groups and their possible emancipation through culture, gives way to a compromise that protects the sovereignty of states.

As to whether non-physical heritage should be defined in the negative (i.e. in opposition to physical heritage), the 1984 report said that this approach 'violates the unitary nature of a worldview which produces both material and non-material representations: this broad usage incorporates "the totality of the creative genius of a society", into non-physical heritage: all culture, in fact'.[113] This early report therefore already incorporates a holistic view of the definition of what became ICH, and one that strives to be all-encompassing vis-à-vis other types of heritage. The same view is espoused by Janet Blake in her report that served as the basis for the negotiation of the ICHC, even if she admonishes that focusing too much on intangible in opposition to tangible reinforces Eurocentrism with respect to tangible heritage, rather than challenging it.[114]

One of the predecessors to the ICHC, the 1989 Recommendation on the Safeguarding of Traditional Culture and Folklore, used the term folklore. The definition of folklore given by the Recommendation[115] was useful in making communities a central part of the definition.[116] However, it was argued that the definition was too product oriented (and therefore dependent upon physical means), overlooking the fact that the real object of protection was the social practices and cultural contexts from which the products derived (therefore, intangible heritage as an independent type of heritage).[117] It was also felt by some communities that it was ultimately demeaning, and needed to be revised.[118]

[111] Ibid., 3. [112] As discussed in Lixinski (n 74). [113] Dunaway (n 107) 10.

[114] Blake, Janet, *Developing a New Standard-Setting Instrument for the Safeguarding of Intangible Cultural Heritage: Elements for Consideration* (UNESCO Publishing, 2001), 8–9.

[115] Recommendation on the Safeguarding of Traditional Culture and Folklore (1989):

> A. Definition of folklore. For purposes of this Recommendation: Folklore (or traditional and popular culture) is the totality of tradition-based creations of a cultural community, expressed by a group or individuals and recognized as reflecting the expectations of a community in so far as they reflect its cultural and social identity; its standards and values are transmitted orally, by imitation or by other means. Its forms are, among others, language, literature, music, dance, games, mythology, rituals, customs, handicrafts, architecture and other arts.

[116] Blake, *Developing* (n 114) 10.

[117] See Munjeri, Dawson, 'Following the Length and Breadth of the Roots: Some Dimensions of Intangible Heritage', in Laurajane Smith and Natsuko Akagawa (eds), *Intangible Heritage* (Routledge, 2009), 207–42, 217; and Aikawa-Faure, Noriko, 'From the Proclamation of Masterpieces to the *Convention for the Safeguarding of Intangible Cultural Heritage*', in Laurajane Smith and Natsuko Agakawa (eds) *Intangible Heritage* (Routledge, 2009), 1–44, 21.

[118] UNESCO Executive Board, Report on the preliminary study on the advisability of regulating internationally, through a new standard-setting instrument, the protection of traditional culture and folklore. 161 EX/15, 16 May 2001, para. 25.

Another predecessor, the Masterpieces of the Oral and Intangible Heritage of Humanity programme, moved the definition closer to the current one, but engaged with it indirectly as well through selection criteria, much like the WHC did in using its Operational Guidelines, as discussed. Two main selection criteria were set for this programme: universal value as a general cultural criterion, and organizational criteria. The latter included the participation of the communities concerned with that particular manifestation of ICH in its protection.[119] The exact meaning of 'outstanding universal value' when it came to intangible heritage, however, was questioned by several states during the first meeting of the jury to select these masterpieces, in 2001. The jury responded by offering three criteria for defining the value of ICH: (1) outstanding value to the custodial community and for cultural diversity; (2) being a long-lived practice; and (3) specific creation linked to a specific cultural space.[120]

ICH seemed to be the best option for the new treaty, though, despite criticism. 'Folklore' was a term already charged with the product-oriented connotations of the 1989 Recommendation, as well as being perceived to imply banality within sacred traditions, ways of life, and cultural identity generally.[121] 'Treasures', on the other hand, was seen as being too paternalistic (and too oriented towards a 'westernized' conception of heritage modelled after the WHC). Further, 'oral heritage' was considered too narrow in scope,[122] while 'traditional culture' seemed to ignore the fact that ICH is about living cultures being constantly recreated.[123]

During the drafting of what became the ICHC, Francesco Francioni, Chair of the drafting meeting held in Turin (2001), presented a comprehensive report on issues that should be taken into account when drafting a definition of ICH, which had by then become a high priority for UNESCO.[124] The report outlined the possibility of legally protecting 'non-material' goods using the example of intellectual property (IP) rights, but also drawing a line distinguishing between ICH and IP, in that IP focuses on the end product of the creative process, whereas ICH is the process itself. One important definitional issue in the ICHC is the idea that ICH refers not to the cultural objects, but rather to the social and cultural processes of which these objects are but the products. This was an important change of focus that happened gradually in heritage studies, and one that was decisively pushed into the ICHC by the Organization of African Unity (later replaced by the African Union), alongside the

[119] Aikawa-Faure (n 117) 18. [120] Ibid., 32.

[121] Blake, Janet, *Commentary on the UNESCO 2003 Convention on the Safeguarding of the Intangible Cultural Heritage* (Institute for Art and Law, 2006), 22 and 32. But see Telesetsky, Anastasia and Nafziger, James A. R., 'Toward a Broader Concept of the Intangible Cultural Heritage', *Transnational Dispute Management* 11(2) (2014), 1–16, 2 (arguing that the definition in the ICHC may not have been successful in breaking with the negative charge of the idea of 'folklore' after all).

[122] Aikawa-Faure (n 117) 27.

[123] Kurin, Richard, 'Safeguarding Intangible Cultural Heritage: Key Factors in Implementing the 2003 Convention', *International Journal of Intangible Heritage* 2 (2007), 10–20, 12.

[124] UNESCO, Address by Mr Koïchiro Matsuura, Director-General of the United Nations Educational, Scientific and Cultural Organization (UNESCO), on the occasion of the International Round Table: '*Intangible Cultural Heritage: Working Definitions*'. DG/2001/33, 14 March 2001.

group of experts responsible for the initial drafting of the ICHC.[125] This change of focus also has a positive effect on communities.

The 2001 report then outlined definitions of cultural heritage in existing international instruments, concluding that elements could be drawn from all these definitions that would be relevant for the formulation of a legal definition of intangible heritage, such as its significance, the importance of a broad definition with a non-exclusive typology, criteria that could be operationalized by the organ eventually in charge of administering the ICHC, and the fact that intangible heritage should focus on the 'internal' cultural manifestations, and not on the products. A definition was proposed, and much of it made it into the final instrument.[126]

What exactly falls under the definition of 'intangible cultural heritage', however, was the object of much debate during the meeting of the Restricted Drafting Group in 2002. Three difficulties were identified: (1) that any such category of intangible heritage would be too broad; (2) conversely, that a list would run the risk of being too specific and restrictive; and (3) that it would be necessary to harmonize the different views of states with respect to their perceptions of what ICH is. The (eventually adopted) flexible approach was identified as being necessary, taking into account UNESCO Member States' views on the topic, but at the same time avoiding overlaps with the mandates of other international organizations (most notably the WIPO and the WTO), while attending to the concerns of experts and facilitating legal protection.[127] Ultimately, the definition seems to have taken these factors into account, by weaving an open definition, with a non-exhaustive list of examples, and avoiding using examples from the area of IP law (out of respect for the division of work with the WIPO, but also with the consequence of autonomizing intangible heritage beyond the domains of IP).

Intangible heritage, like Indigenous heritage, must be seen as holistic.[128] This holistic understanding is both dependent on and independent of tangible heritage. To be more accurate, the ICHC makes several tangible elements dependent on the intangible expressions from which they derive, and not the other way around. In other words, it protects objects because they derive from a larger cultural practice, and not vice versa, which would be the traditional response of museums, for instance, in protecting the objects themselves and hoping, perhaps, to indirectly protect the culture behind them.

Further, the ICHC definition includes the precedence of group rights in the context of intangible heritage (since the rights belong primarily to the community, and only 'in some cases' to individuals), which is key in rearticulating the stakeholders in international heritage law, as is discussed in Chapter 3. For our present purposes,

[125] Aikawa-Faure (n 117) 23.

[126] UNESCO, *International Round Table: 'Intangible Cultural Heritage—Working Definitions'*, meeting held in Turin, Italy on 14–17 March 2001.

[127] UNESCO, *Preparation of a preliminary draft International Convention on the Intangible Cultural Heritage, Meeting of the 'Restricted Drafting Group' (RDG) in Paris, 20–22 March 2002—Outline Work Plan*, paras 30–1.

[128] Kearney, Amanda, 'Intangible Cultural Heritage: Global Awareness and Local Interest', in Laurajane Smith and Natsuko Akagawa (eds), *Intangible Heritage* (Routledge, 2009), 209–26, 217.

it suffices to say that the ICHC's definition at least nominally gives the control over ICH to communities, rather than states. However, as the following chapter discusses, ultimately the control still rests with the state, so this step in the evolution of definitions, much like the move from property to heritage, is one that does not go particularly far in practice, even if it opens a precedent that may be taken up again in the future.

Besides, the ICHC definition clearly sets a limit on what can be protected culture, by giving importance to universalist conceptions of human rights. The ICHC affirms that those cultural practices that are incompatible with internationally recognized human rights do not fall within its scope of application. Examining a human rights exception to the ICHC falls outside the scope of this chapter,[129] but it is still important in that ICH ends up defined against the normative standards of a separate area of law, and one which is not particularly friendly towards communities.[130]

We have seen so far that definitions in UNESCO treaties have strived for specificity, for the sake of legal certainty, and for the most part have still adopted fairly broad definitions. The ICHC is no different in that the definition is very broad, but this wide reach is necessary in such a comprehensive area of law, which tries to bring together interests which can at times be incompatible.

Moreover, the ICH definition is 'forward-looking', in the sense that it protects manifestations of heritage necessary for the continuation of a certain community. Heritage studies have traditionally looked at heritage as escapist and 'backward-looking',[131] primarily because of their connection to tangible heritage and archaeology, where the object necessarily predated its discovery, turning these objects into sites for the exploration of 'lost' history. However, it is important to notice the shift in discourse when it comes to the safeguarding of intangible heritage, which aims at defending living cultures. This shift helps unsettle the conservation paradigm discussed in Chapter 1, and particularly the scientificism enshrined so centrally in treaties like the WHC and the UCHC. It also has effects on communities by including them in thinking about whether heritage is in fact 'living'.

The definition of the ICHC stresses that '[t]his intangible cultural heritage [. . .] provides [the communities] with a sense of identity [. . .]'. It is precisely *because* intangible cultural heritage provides a sense of identity that it is worthy of protection. Heritage connects each person to the community they stem from, and creates a sense of shared experience, and thus identity. Protecting this shared identity, and, ultimately, a shared humanity, is perhaps the most important goal behind heritage safeguarding.

The definition of ICH is multifaceted and complex, and looks at heritage as an integral part (rather than a product) of a living culture, and an essential part of the

[129] But see Lixinski (n 27) 172–3.

[130] Lixinski, Lucas, 'Heritage for Whom? Individuals' and Communities' Roles in International Cultural Heritage Law', in Federico Lenzerini and Ana Filipa Vrdoljak (eds), *International Law for Common Goods—Normative Perspectives on Human Rights, Culture and Nature* (Hart, 2014), 193–213.

[131] Lumley, Robert, 'The Debate on Heritage Reviewed', in Gerard Corsane (ed.), *Heritage Museums and Galleries: An Introductory Reader* (Routledge, 2005), 15–25, 17.

maintenance of this culture through time. In doing so, it seems to accommodate a more cosmopolitan engagement with heritage and its control (ultimately betrayed by its implementation mechanisms, as discussed here in Chapters 3 and 7), and it avoids the matter of property beyond state control by deferring it to a different regime, that of IP rights.[132] Lastly, it is important to note that the definition in the ICHC, unlike the one in the WHC, has so far not been challenged in the implementation of the treaty. The Operational Directives for the Implementation of the ICHC do not make any considerations about the ways in which heritage is to be assessed against any criteria, beyond indicating that ICH should fall under the definition in Article 2 of the ICHC.[133]

The analysis of these five treaties and their definitions of heritage suggests a few commonalities, and also key differences. On the commonalities, key themes emerge like the tension between nationalism and internationalism or cosmopolitanism, and the engagement with nature or natural features associated with heritage. On the differences, one can see for instance differences in the engagement with the conservation paradigm, which has a substantial impact on whether and how communities are taken into account in the practice of international heritage treaties, particularly in making assessments as to whether heritage is worth safeguarding. But the most important difference is the progressive abandonment from one treaty to the next of the terminology of property, either in relation to property law as an area of domestic law, or as a stand-in for state sovereignty and control. This shift has significant impacts on how communities can (or cannot) control their own heritage on the ground. Whether this shift is reflected in the literature engaging with the two categories, and what the literature means when it speaks of 'property' in this context, is the subject of the next section, which also discusses in more detail the exclusionary effects vis-à-vis communities of the tension between property and heritage.

2.2 Discourses and Exclusion

The history of the key UNESCO treaties reveals that the category of 'property' is a fairly resilient one. It was only the UCHC that made a decisive break with it, and, even then, only because it was meant to address heritage normally outside a state's sovereignty. The drafting history also reveals that property does not usually mean the common usage of property as a private law category of ownership, which was left for the *domaine réservé* of states. For the most part, property is a proxy for state sovereignty, a means to balance the cosmopolitan spirit embodied in the idea of heritage since the 1954 Hague Convention. One must not forget that treaties are products of their time, and that in this respect protection of sovereignty was in line with the state of international law in the Cold War era,[134] a state of affairs which, as discussed in

[132] For a discussion, see Lixinski, *Intangible Cultural Heritage* (n 74) 175–204.

[133] Operational Directives for the Implementation of the Convention for the Safeguarding of the Convention for the Safeguarding of the Intangible Cultural Heritage (2016), para. I.1.1.

[134] Blake, 'On Defining the Cultural Heritage' (n 2) 62.

the next chapter, saw communities as a politically charged term, and therefore one that could not be part of the diplomatic and international legal vocabulary, lest it suffer the paralysis brought by the capitalist/communist divide in the period.

Francesco Francioni suggests that the idea of 'cultural property' is a direct result of the creation of UNESCO, and a means to differentiate cultural property (which fell under the purview and standard-setting action of the organization) from other types of protected property in time of conflict (such as schools and hospitals).[135] That view, which may suggest that administrative convenience lies at the root of the creation of the category of cultural property (subsequently evolved into heritage), calls into question efforts to dissociate heritage from property in contemporary discourse. But Francioni also admonishes that the use of the term property should not be read as meaning something different from a concern with the cultural value of heritage, and that UNESCO practice in this area has shown 'remarkable continuity'.[136]

The usual narrative[137] suggests that developments in the field reached a point at which the values attached to property needed to be modified in order for other social goals to be secured. It involved a change not in the content of what was protected, but in how the question of protection was approached, and one that could in theory accommodate multicultural groups within the same state.[138] While 'property' as a legal category offers certain advantages, as it is often viewed as a near-absolute bundle of rights once conferred, its use implied the setting up of a social policy to protect the possessor of the cultural object. This approach, however, came into conflict with the fundamental goal of heritage protection, as there was a shift from protecting individual interests to protecting the interests of society in the preservation of cultural goods.[139] Moreover, property was generally too narrow a concept to 'cover all evidence of human life that we are trying to preserve'.[140] It was perceived by heritage experts outside the law that the law needed to catch up with their usage of heritage as the umbrella term.[141] In fact, heritage seems to be a term imported into the law from anthropology and archaeology,[142] underscoring the importance of clearer relationships between law and non-law in this area, as discussed in Chapter 1.

The law had evolved to deem the value to be protected by norms to be present and future generations, or society as a whole, rather than the particular possessor of a certain object.[143] This idea of protecting the interests of future generations gradually led to a change in terminology, and the term 'cultural heritage' began to be used in the English-language literature. Relatedly, cultural heritage was seen as a non-renewable resource like the environment or mineral resources.[144]

135 Francioni, 'Cultural Property, International Law' (n 2) para. 1.

136 Francioni, 'A Dynamic Evolution of Concept and Scope' (n 2) 235.

137 Which I have myself used; see Lixinski, *Intangible Cultural Heritage* (n 74) 5–7.

138 Graham (n 4) 776.

139 Prott and O'Keefe (n 2) 309.

140 Ibid., 307.

141 Ibid., 319.

142 Blake, 'On Defining the Cultural Heritage' (n 2) 63. Cf. Craig Forrest, *International Law and the Protection of Cultural Heritage* (Routledge, 2010), 1 ('The ascendancy of the notion of cultural heritage owes much to the law.').

143 Prott and O'Keefe (n 2) 309.

144 Blake, 'On Defining the Cultural Heritage' (n 2) 69.

In this respect, cultural heritage ends up tied with the notion of 'common heritage of [hu]mankind',[145] which is defined by five characteristics: universal, intergenerational, non-economic, scientific, and free from sovereign control.[146] The narrative of heritage as an interest of humankind helps drive cosmopolitanism, and the idea, enshrined in the UNESCO Constitution, of heritage as a conduit for mutual understanding among peoples and lasting peace, which had earlier historical antecedents.[147] Therefore, the connection of heritage to a universal discourse of commonality has helped divorce economics from heritage, and reinforce the interests of the scientific community (at the expense of communities). It is only sovereignty that has remained with respect to heritage, at least translated as 'respect [to] the special interests of the State of origin'.[148]

As to the shift in international legal discourse from 'property' to 'heritage', it is largely seen as meaning an acceptance that the protection of heritage goes beyond the protection of the actual sites, objects, and artefacts;[149] instead, what is to be protected is the relationship between these sites, objects, and artefacts and human beings,[150] with a view towards intergenerational safeguarding of culture.[151] In this sense, what is protected is precisely the element of intangibility behind all heritage, even if the competing social goals of heritage and property still subsist, and need to be balanced.[152] This focus on the relationships implies the articulation of the idea that cultural heritage belongs to the whole of humankind, and must be protected to favour those communities more connected to it, as opposed to the individuals in possession of the items. It is thus meant to create an opening for community-centric heritage governance.

A critique of the use of the term 'property' goes beyond criticizing the ultimate value to be protected. After all, in one way or another, the protection of objects is one of the aims of property law, the difference being that property law does not question who is to benefit from such protection. It protects the interests of the possessor. For the purposes of the critique outlined here, it may well be said that the owner (of heritage as property) is society as a whole, and thus 'cultural property' would still work as a concept. At least that seems to be the version espoused in the international treaties, of property as a proxy for state sovereignty, and closing the door on communities.

Several scholars, particularly in the field of legal anthropology, have raised the point that 'property' is a 'Western' concept, which does not necessarily address the

[145] Francioni, 'A Dynamic Evolution of Concept and Scope' (n 2) 235.

[146] Joyner, Christopher C., 'Legal Implications of the Concept of the Common Heritage of Mankind', *International and Comparative Law Quarterly* 35 (1986), 190–9.

[147] Forrest (n 142) 11–13.

[148] Blake, 'On Defining the Cultural Heritage' (n 2) 71–2.

[149] Bendix (n 2).

[150] This shift was also mirrored in general debates about property law. Property has shifted from being a legal protection of an object (or the exclusive rights of the owner to its property in relation to non-owners) to the relationship between non-owners and the property, to the extent some rights can also be granted to non-owners. For a discussion and reconceptualization of property law, see generally Kennedy, David, 'Some Caution about Property Rights as a Recipe for Economic Development', *Accounting, Economics and Law* 1 (2011), 1–62.

[151] Janet Blake, *International Cultural Heritage Law* (Oxford University Press, 2015), 8–9.

[152] Prott and O'Keefe (n 2) 309.

needs of all peoples. There are several examples of societies that do not recognize 'property' as a social possibility; rather than owning something, individuals belonging to these societies believe that they are owned by the environment around them, which is in certain cases nothing short of the embodiment of the deities that they worship. It seems natural that a religion does not allow one to own one's object of worship, lest the reason for it (namely, that you worship some entity mightier than you) would cease to exist. If everything around me is a deity, and I cannot own a deity, I do not own anything.[153] This argument is closely related to the critique that using the term 'property' implies a commodification of cultural aspects of life, which should not be treated as goods in the marketplace.[154] Further, the use of the term 'property' also reinforces the idea that cultural values can be captured and frozen.[155]

It is worth noting that, as indicated in the previous section, Indigenous rights advocates pushed for heritage instead of property in the negotiations of the 1970 Convention. That move coincided with a specific moment in Indigenous rights advocacy, which is still observable in many contexts today, in which the international is seen as an alternative to the oppressive domestic, and proposed an 'at times subversive view of the cultural heritage'.[156] It also aligned with the idea, espoused by many Indigenous peoples, that they do not own the land; rather, the land owns them.[157] Therefore, embracing a cosmopolitan notion of heritage, instead of a domestic version of property, was appropriate. That is so especially considering how domestic property law had until then (and still does in many jurisdictions) largely prevented Indigenous peoples from gaining full property title to their lands, and, consequently, their heritage.[158] In many respects, then, Indigenous international claims against the state could be covertly translated as claims about heritage, and an interest in international control over culture. But, as Karen Engle has shown, translating Indigenous culture (and therefore their claims) as heritage is in effect the weakest form of Indigenous rights advocacy, far weaker than property.[159] It seems that it was the case simply that property was not available as an avenue, either domestically or internationally. Hence, the attempt to rely on the category of heritage has the positive effect of opening the international to communities, but what is behind that curtain is far weaker than the mere difficult domestic category of property.

The use of the term 'property' in the context of the protection of cultural heritage is, in the end, associated with things whose value transcends their physical existence. One compelling example of this is that one of the fundamental aspects of property as a right, *ius abutendi*, cannot be exercised when dealing with cultural

[153] A real-life example is given by Prott and O'Keefe (n 2) 310 (mentioning a famous Australian domestic case, *Milirrpum v Nabalco Pty Ltd*).

[154] Blake, 'On Defining the Cultural Heritage' (n 2) 65–6.

[155] Laurajane Smith, *Uses of Heritage* (Routledge, 2006), 101.

[156] Blake, 'On Defining the Cultural Heritage' (n 2) 75.

[157] Prott and O'Keefe (n 2) 310.

[158] For a discussion of this international movement, with a particular focus on the Americas, see generally Engle, Karen, *The Elusive Promise of Indigenous Development: Culture, Rights, Strategy* (Duke University Press, 2010).

[159] Ibid.

goods. *Ius abutendi* is the faculty that the owner of a thing has to destroy the object; this is rather difficult to accept when speaking of cultural heritage.[160] Further, even if this objection could be overcome, certain categories of cultural heritage seem to escape property (the discussion between IP and ICH comes to mind),[161] and heritage acts as a unifying concept for cultural attributes, rather than economic or proprietary ones.[162] Communities end up stuck with culture, and lack access to economics and the political power that comes with it.

In several English-language jurisdictions, implementing international heritage law means having resort to domestic law categories of property, as there is not always a clear domestic law equivalent to the international concept of heritage.[163] In federal countries like Australia, the situation is particularly acute, as the implementation of international heritage law is a federal prerogative, but property law (and private law more generally, including trusts[164] and contracts as an often preferred method of negotiating the interests of public authorities and private owners)[165] is the competence of subfederal entities (states and territories, in Australia). We thus end up with two sets of background legal orders: a federal background legal order, made of specific implementing legislation, and broader background norms (for instance, administrative law, but also export control laws)[166] that need to be triggered; and at the local level, private property law comes into play.[167] In unitary countries, the tension is only between the bodies of law, as opposed to the levels of jurisdiction, which makes the resolution of conflicts potentially easier, but nonetheless challenging, as different concepts need to be translated across different bodies of law.

All of these are tensions largely sidestepped by international heritage law, as the previous section demonstrated, for understandable reasons. But this avoidance has ultimately counterproductive effects on how international obligations are brought to fruition, and how heritage is conceptualized at the domestic level. It also means that communities close to heritage, because they are not present at international fora, are left with domestic law that cannot capture the same values as the international legal system. At its best, this mismatch causes confusion and sends conflicting messages; at its worst, it has the effect of further divorcing communities from their heritage as it is understood and conceptualized internationally. States, in

160 Prott and O'Keefe (n 2) 310. See also Sax, Joseph L., *Playing Darts with a Rembrandt: Public and Private Interests in Cultural Treasures* (University of Michigan Press, 1999).

161 See e.g. Lixinski, Lucas and Buckingham, Louise, 'Propertization, Safeguarding and the Cultural Commons: The Turf Wars of Intangible Cultural Heritage and Traditional Cultural Expressions', in Valentina Vadi and Bruno de Witte (eds), *Culture and International Economic Law* (Routledge, 2015), 160–74.

162 Prott and O'Keefe (n 2) 313.

163 For instance, with reference to Australia, see Boer, Ben and Wiffen, Graeme, *Heritage Law in Australia* (Oxford University Press, 2006), 72.

164 Ibid., 252. Note that trusts are a construct of Islamic legal systems that was imported into the common law, but do not exist as such in the civil law.

165 Boer and Wiffen (n 163) 212.

166 Gilman, Derek, *The Idea of Cultural Heritage* (Cambridge University Press, 2010), 141–55 (comparing Australia, the United Kingdom, and the United States).

167 Ibid., 179.

implementing their international legal obligations, end up enforcing this separation between communities and heritage at the conceptual level, with trickle-down effects to other forms of heritage law and policy. This problem of domestic implementation is even further amplified when going into linguistic domains that require not only the international-to-domestic (and in some cases federal-to-local) translation, but also a language one.

Even if international law has relied on domestic traditions in the drafting of the key treaties, as indicated above, there are still problems of translating these instruments back into domestic law, which are only compounded by linguistic/legal-cultural matters. The terms used to refer to cultural property or cultural heritage across different languages vary quite significantly, and, in trying to find accurate yet appropriate translations, the otherwise ostensibly uniform, expert-driven discourse of cultural heritage tends to get modified in its interactions with the broader categories of domestic law triggered by the simple act of identifying an appropriate legal term in the native tongue.[168]

But beyond implementation dynamics (revisited in Chapter 7), the move in legal discourse from property to heritage can be read as a reconceptualization of the conservation paradigm in three different respects: a move from monuments to people; a move from objects to functions; and a move 'from preservation per se to purposeful preservation, sustainable use and development'.[169] The third move in particular still relies heavily on input from outside the law, except that the input can be widened to include not only archaeologists and anthropologists (responsible for the initial shift from property to heritage and deeply influential in the negotiation of definitions in international treaties,[170] as mentioned) who enshrined the AHD and a version of the conservation paradigm. Economists can also be brought on board, particularly if preservation as a tool of development is to be considered (as is discussed in Chapter 5).[171] This move thus has the potential to bring community governance to the forefront of development. The fact it does not is a testament to the resilience of Westphalian categories (and their further entrenchment under the guise of community governance)[172] and to how the creation of new categories does not necessarily resolve the problem; a new category hides the problem, and generates a blind spot which, in this case, has deep effects on communities.

Likewise, the use of 'cultural heritage' as a legal concept is not free from difficulties. One of the problems that the use of the concept poses derives from it having been imported from other disciplines without incorporating the necessary theoretical background of these disciplines, such as anthropology or cultural studies, which are critical of international legal definitions of culture for focusing too much on

[168] Frigo, Manlio, 'Cultural Property v Cultural Heritage: A "Battle of Concepts" in International Law?', *International Review of the Red Cross* 86(854) (2004), 367–78, 370; and Loulanski, Tolina, 'Revising the Concept for Cultural Heritage: The Argument for a Functional Approach', *International Journal of Cultural Property* 13 (2006), 207–33, 219.

[169] Loulanski (n 168) 207.

[170] Forrest (n 142) 21–2.

[171] Loulanski (n 168) 219.

[172] Eslava, Luis, *Local Space, Global Life: The Everyday Operation of International Law and Development* (Cambridge University Press, 2015), 262.

culture as a product/commodity, or as a practice.[173] This transplantation has led to 'cultural heritage' being one of the most problematic legal concepts dealt with today.[174] For instance, it still relies heavily on the notion of property to propel a conservation instinct that prevents heritage from changing or evolving, and in fact commodifies it in potentially destructive ways.[175] In addition, the fact that 'heritage' as a legal concept tries to embrace features such as national patrimony, regional and ethnic legacies, and a commonly shared global heritage is also part of the challenge, as these features often translate into incompatible aims.[176] Communities end up caught in the crossfire, as agencyless witnesses to and pawns in the manipulation of their heritage.

All things considered, the concept of 'heritage' is important because of its capacity to include notions beyond economics and ownership that are typical of property. Most importantly, it allows us to think of heritage as a 'cultural process', which can help us think of it as by turns experience, identity, intangibility, memory and remembering, performance, place, and even dissonance.[177] Property can in fact freeze the process by enshrining the material form of heritage, as far as heritage scholars are concerned.[178]

That said, economics and ownership as control are important for communities if they are to be included in decision-making about their heritage. It gives them the leverage they need to be part of heritage management processes. Without property title or some other version of control, there is absolutely no reason for communities' views to be considered. In fact, their views may be seen as challenging the cosmopolitan spirit of heritage as a universal language, which is not always nor necessarily the case (as discussed in more detail in Chapter 8).

Heritage internationalism, therefore, and the move to the concept of 'heritage' it embodies, has the effect of creating disincentives for the inclusion of certain stakeholders. Instead, it privileges others that can speak the uniform language of cultural heritage, which tend to be states and experts (as discussed in Chapter 3). Further, as discussed in Chapter 1, the move towards heritage disengages the private of 'property' by privileging the public of 'heritage', thereby creating another means that facilitates, or at least has the unintended consequence of facilitating, the exclusion of communities and other substate actors.[179]

Nevertheless, the shift from property to heritage does not mean that property goes away. Rather, property still applies to several aspects of cultural heritage, depending

173 Ahmed, Mohsen Al Attar, Aylwin, Nicole S., and Coombe, Rosemary J., 'Indigenous Cultural Heritage Rights in International Human Rights Law', in Catherine Bell and Robert Patterson (eds), *Protection of First Nations' Cultural Heritage: Laws, Policy and Reform* (University of British Columbia Press, 2009), 311–42, 330.

174 Blake, 'On Defining the Cultural Heritage' (n 2) 63.

175 Lowenthal, David, 'Why Sanctions Seldom Work: Reflections on Cultural Property Internationalism', *International Journal of Cultural Property* 12 (2005), 393–423, 396–7.

176 Blake, 'On Defining the Cultural Heritage', cit., 64 (citing Lowenthal, David, *The Heritage Crusade and the Spoils of History* (Cambridge University Press, 1998), 227).

177 Smith (n 155) 44–8.

178 Ibid., 83.

179 Kuzmarov, Betina, 'The Coherence of the Concept of Cultural Property: A Critical Examination', *International Journal of Cultural Property* 20 (2013), 233–56, 235.

on how heritage is framed domestically or internationally. A coherent system that takes into account the needs of culture and heritage, and the social goals behind the idea of cultural heritage, is needed, and so far, does not exist.[180] But, by not acknowledging the continuing influence of categories of property,

> we con ourselves into heritage hypocrisy. Personal selfishness is seldom confessed, mostly self-concealed. National avarice is rebuked, tribal self-interest justified as cultural survival and global equity. Few are willing to admit the reality that [. . .] cultural property [. . .] is valued precisely because it *is* private, *our own*, not somebody else's.[181]

In other words, hiding the category of property (either in the private, or in the background) has the key effect of disguising the politics of heritage and compromising its legal articulation and safeguarding. It also makes it much more difficult to contest the pre-approved or authorized boundaries of what is permissible when it comes to heritage, often to the prejudice of those who have been initially excluded in the shift from property to heritage, like communities.

Academic discourse around the definition of cultural heritage, and the evolution from property to heritage, seems to take a different position as to what property means in the cultural sense, and legal scholars in particular (who seem to be the bulk of those concerned with this question) think of property as the private law category that was excluded from treaties. The effect of this usage of property is twofold: first, it takes international heritage law discourses in directions that were not originally part of the legal framework; second, it helps integrate the domestic into the ways in which we think about cultural heritage globally.

These two intertwined effects ultimately produce a positive outcome in integrating property, but ultimately, the majority of the scholarship denounces property in favour of heritage as the reigning concept, and in the end the effect of integrating the domestic dimensions, which are key for the implementation of international heritage law (discussed in more detail in Chapter 7), tends to be missed. In the process, communities' control over their heritage, which is only properly articulated in domestic law, is further pushed into the background, in favour of a more universal discourse around heritage that serves the needs of an expert-driven conservation paradigm (as discussed in Chapters 1 and 3). The next section examines what it would mean to reconsider property in the cultural context, and whether a version of property as a legal category could in fact do some of the work that has been excluded from international heritage law, particularly with respect to communities.

2.3 Rethinking Property

The concept of property, with its legal load, seems to be a possibility worth exploring when it comes to redefining cultural heritage in a way that is more conducive to the inclusion of communities in the management of and control over heritage. But

[180] Prott and O'Keefe (n 2) 312.

[181] Lowenthal, 'Why Sanctions Seldom Work' (n 175) 401 (original emphasis).

what version of property law is needed is not as clear-cut as one might think. On one extreme there is the view that cultural heritage 'is, in most ways, just like ordinary property, and existing laws and practices that govern the treatment of ordinary property should apply to cultural property'.[182] On the other, there is the view that cultural heritage is a special kind of property, and needs specific regulation.[183] At stake here is a claim to the morality of cultural heritage, and the values attributed to it. But the question that remains underexplored is what the law of property in this context should look like. While the version of cultural heritage as ordinary property seems to suppose (neo)liberal economics as the basis for libertarian property law (focused on individual liberties), that should not be a given. Much discussion about the foundations of property, whether related to heritage or not, implies social responsibilities attached to ownership, and this section explores what this version of property could do for cultural heritage.

Property has traditionally been construed, at least in the common law world, using Blackstone's 'sole and despotic dominion' formula, which is not too different from Roman law categories influential in civil law countries, and on which Blackstone himself relied. A more nuanced view sees property as exclusion instead; as a means to reengage formal rigidity with respect to property.[184] But even this view misses the contingencies of how property is conceptualized and engaged, and also misses the idea of property as an umbrella for a set of plural institutions, that can embrace pluralistic values.[185]

The notion of property has been used at times to imply absolute power, and at other times to mean no protection for individual rights at all. It therefore has variable power,[186] a notion often missed in debates about property in the cultural context. Cultural heritage helps destabilize prior understandings of the binary of power/non-power of property.[187] In other words, property is usually defined in a way that can be so simplified it is distorted; cultural heritage as a concept can help displace the distortion.[188]

The work that heritage can do in reimagining property is not unique to heritage, and can be done by other purposive engagements with property and its protective characteristics.[189] As Hanoch Dagan has suggested: 'because property allocates claim to various scarce resources in society, property must be about distribution, as well as about our conceptions of community and social responsibility'.[190] Further, heritage can help as a reminder that property is not only exclusionary, but also inclusionary, as a number of property institutions can 'facilitate important spheres of human interaction and flourishing'.[191] Inclusionary manifestations of property are

[182] Posner, Eric A., 'The International Protection of Cultural Property: Some Skeptical Observations', *Chicago Public Law and Legal Theory Working Paper No. 141* (2006), available at <http://ssrn.com/abstract_id=946778>.

[183] See for instance Sax, *Playing Darts with a Rembrandt* (n 160) and discussion in what follows here.

[184] Dagan, Hanoch, *Property Values and Institutions* (Oxford University Press, 2011), xi.

[185] Ibid.

[186] Underkuffler, Laura S., *The Idea of Property: Its Meaning and Power* (Oxford University Press, 2003), viii.

[187] Ibid., ix.

[188] Prott and O'Keefe (n 2) 310–11.

[189] Dagan (n 184) xiii.

[190] Ibid., 3.

[191] Ibid., xiii.

just as intrinsic to property as exclusion, and should not be seen as limitations.[192] Cultural heritage is among these, assuming the correctness of the proposition that heritage is an essential binding element of human society.

The connection between property and the idea of rights has been explored in depth by Laura Underkuffler.[193] She argues that even though rights have a protective power, and property can be considered to fall in this category, in property the range of situations where the protective power fails is much wider, and there are compelling reasons why property should lack 'the presumptive power traditionally associated with rights'.[194]

Underkuffler identifies three traditional conceptions of property: (1) property as things (which misses the relational qualities of property); (2) property as a fundamental right (which does not account for the specificities of property vis-à-vis other types of rights); and (3) property as limited rights in or to things (the version to which she subscribes).[195] This third version is what she also terms an 'operative' version of property, in which limitations to the idea of property as the protection of an individual liberty sphere intersect with tensions that are settled via incorporating said tensions into the very concept of property.[196] This mechanism does away with the presumptive power of property over competing public interests, as the core values underlying the defence of property are of the same kind as those in competition with it.[197] In other words, ownership is the source of its own restrictions.[198] Cultural heritage, in this view, is an integral part of property, and not set in opposition to it.[199] But it is property with built-in limitations to accommodate public interests. Therefore, international heritage law would do well to accommodate property as more than a proxy for state sovereignty (even if I acknowledge the political difficulties of trying to harmonize domestic private law, but more on that in what follows). Communities would benefit in this instance by being able to frame their claims in relation to a public interest that now works with them (since it is in the public interest to protect heritage), as opposed to seeing communities' (traditionally conceptualized) private law property title to heritage in opposition to heritage's public values.

In order to explain the resilience of the idea of property as rights, van der Walt has argued that the rules and practices that entrench and protect property insulate themselves against change 'through the security- and stability-seeking tendency of tradition and legal culture', which includes stability and security concerns associated with rights doctrines more generally.[200] These notions can get in the way of reformist attempts to favour 'weak and marginalized' populations.[201] In this way, attempts to conciliate between private and public interests may not be sufficient, and a reconsideration of the rights-based property paradigm may be needed.[202] A rethinking of property requires acknowledging that 'these features of the rights paradigm, in both the civil law and the common law traditions, are based on socio-political and

[192] Ibid., 38. [193] Underkuffler (n 186). [194] Ibid., 5. [195] Ibid., 30.
[196] Ibid., 52. [197] Ibid., 75.
[198] van der Walt, A. J., *Property in the Margins* (Hart, 2009), 31. [199] Ibid., 110–16.
[200] Ibid., viii. [201] Ibid., ix. [202] Ibid., 14–15.

socio-economic assumptions and rhetoric about the role of property in individual lives and in society, rather than purely on legal tradition or doctrine'.[203] Property is ordered and conflicts are adjudicated in a way that favours existing rights and the status quo in acontextual and backwards-looking ways. And, while there are some variations to it, only a few of these challenge the fundamentals of this reading of property.[204]

This insight fits well in the context of cultural heritage, in which the concept of 'property' has been essentialized by non-legal stakeholders (particularly anthropological and archaeological experts) to the point where no productive engagement with the notion of property is possible within cultural heritage law. The most that seems possible is to get to the point of thinking of public interests with respect to culture as part of the bundle of property, as suggested earlier. But that does not necessarily give marginalized communities the control over their culture that they might desire, as the public interest is usually translated into the conservation paradigm, which at best gives only conditional control to communities over their heritage, by not allowing radical transformation of the heritage, or even more fundamental challenges to the heritage narratives built into the heritage, which inevitably change over time.

Part of the impulse to defend the status quo in property law is that it is centred on the assumption that having property is the rule, and not having it is an abnormality. Therefore, property law works to maintain control, rather than help marginalized groups gain access to property in the first place. This assumption helps normalize the status of subaltern groups,[205] which can be particularly damning to many traditional communities connected to heritage. The fact that the notion of heritage has been read as stripping property away in favour of the greater good (embodied by the state or the international community) means that these communities now face an uphill battle to (re)gain control over their heritage.

Further, property, inasmuch as it is associated with domestic law, poses difficulties in presenting a unified discourse, as property law is largely considered to be fragmented, at least across the major legal traditions,[206] and also in some respects across countries belonging to the same traditions.[207] Hence, to appropriately tackle the notion of property requires integrating insights from several different legal traditions, beyond international law. Domestic law has influenced international law, and vice-versa. It is useful therefore to trace how domestic property law has historically accommodated the idea of concern for public goods, particularly cultural public goods. Importantly, as Joseph Sax suggested, there is a mismatch between intellectual and physical property. While for intellectual property there is more willingness to secure and protect a robust public interest, conventional wisdom with respect to physical property relies on the exclusionary view that the theorists discussed here have debunked.[208] The greater willingness to embrace a public interest with respect to intangibles can help cultural heritage, especially as it moves away from things

[203] Ibid., 28. [204] Ibid., 31–2. [205] Ibid., 232.
[206] Prott and O'Keefe (n 2) 315. [207] Ibid., 317
[208] Sax, *Playing Darts with a Rembrandt* (n 160) 3.

and towards cultural connections and intangible practices (in essence, intangible heritage). But, even focusing only on tangible heritage, Sax also demonstrates how, historically, the privileging of private property rights has not actually been as central as often suggested, and there is a case to be made for safeguarding property over cultural heritage in a way that makes allowance for public interests.

Joseph Sax argues that heritage was formulated first as a public concern and subject of public discourse in late eighteenth-century revolutionary France.[209] More specifically, a member of the French revolutionary government, Henri Grégoire, was asked to produce reports on a proposal to destroy Latin inscriptions on monuments (deemed unrevolutionary). In his reports, he engaged with the matter, but also thought it necessary to answer a preliminary question, of why nations seek to protect monuments.[210] He thus became the first person to propose preservation as a public duty, based on Enlightenment and French revolutionary values. He asserted that liberty can only be realized through the flourishing of creative energies, which is dependent on tolerance for difference, as well as 'the pursuit of knowledge and repudiation of ignorance'.[211] He thus introduced notions of 'common property' and 'common heritage', and articulated a sense of property that went beyond its narrow economic sense,[212] and attached a sense of duty to the property over cultural artefacts. In fact, the people would recover their property by having items moved out of private collections and into museums.[213] Therefore, property here acquires a much broader sense, one that is not only economic and exclusionary, but also attached to national identity and even politics. In this sense, property, at least with respect to monuments and cultural artefacts, attracts duties towards the broader community, which was embodied by the state in revolutionary France.

Ultimately, Sax argues that the community at large has a stake in certain objects because they embody ideas or information of public interest. Those objects bring together public and private interests, suggesting that unqualified protection of property is neither appropriate nor desirable, for both legal and ethical reasons.[214] In addition to his work on France, he also refers to examples in a number of common law jurisdictions, including the important United States case about the preservation of Grand Central Terminal in New York City.[215] Analysing these cases across a range of jurisdictions and involving a number of cultural activities beyond heritage (such as presidential archives and contemporary art), Sax ultimately demonstrates that there is agreement with the proposition that not only heritage should be thought of as an integral part of the concept of property, but culture more broadly. For our purposes, though, we will focus on cultural heritage, and rely on this broadening of the finding to other cultural activities simply as support for the proposition that

[209] Sax, Joseph L., 'Heritage Preservation as a Public Duty: The Abbé Grégoire and the Origins of an Idea', *Michigan Law Review* 88(5) (1990), 1142–69, 1143.

[210] Ibid.,1143–4.

[211] Ibid., 1155.

[212] For an articulation of this connection particularly in the French legal tradition, see Xifaras, Mikhail, *La Propriété: Etude de Philosophie du Droit* (Presses Universitaires de France, 2004).

[213] Sax (n 209) 1158.

[214] Sax, *Playing Darts with a Rembrandt* (n 160) 9–10.

[215] Ibid., 55–9.

cultural heritage law does not operate in a vacuum (an idea subsequent chapters of this book will return to).

In the common law, property can also be defined in a way that incorporates the interests of the public or community at large. As a matter of political theory that has been deeply influential in the common law world, the usual characterization of property is the Lockean idea of it being the guarantor of private liberty. But it is also, according to Locke, the means to enter the public sphere.[216] Hannah Arendt, for instance, focuses on property on the basis of its relationship with public participation.[217]

Of course, pushed too far, property title in favour of communities and other traditional owners of heritage can also lead to an absurd situation in which the state is still required to protect heritage, but cannot inquire about what it is, where it came from, nor where it is headed.[218] Or it can lead to the approach of a number of market nations, who apply blanket ownership to cultural heritage in a way that, at least when it comes to artefacts, renders the laws virtually unenforceable, and therefore self-defeating.[219] State property for cultural heritage, like the French revolutionary model inspired by Grégoire and still largely in place, resolves the issue of control and ownership in a way that simplifies the matter of implementation of international legal obligations, but at the same time it creates no incentive (and arguably creates a number of disincentives) for the enforcement of heritage protection, and for communities to seek to continue engaging with the heritage in question.

The Scottish model, for instance, highlights the shortcomings of a blanket model, particularly as compared to the rest of Britain (England and Wales).[220] Scotland espouses a blanket ownership law which, while on the surface a stronger form of protection, misses non-legal policy approaches, such as the policing of sites and comprehensive reporting systems.[221] The lesson from Scotland, which applies to a number of domestic jurisdictions, is that reliance on state property alone, or excessive burdens towards a public sphere other than the one immediately connected to the heritage in question, can be counterproductive.

A question that remains unresolved in this discussion of property law, which is largely based on theoretical accounts and domestic legal experiences, is the role of international law. After all, as the drafting history of UNESCO treaties has shown, property as property law was intentionally avoided by UNESCO treaties, given the difficulties of reconciling domestic approaches. So, even if agreement could be reached on a theoretical basis, the actual practice of property law suggests there are irreconcilable rifts that prevent the uniformization of property law to an extent sufficient to allow its interaction with heritage treaties.

But contemporary surveys of international law with respect to property suggest agreement is possible. John Sprankling has suggested that modern international

216 Kuzmarov (n 179) 239. 217 Ibid., 241.

218 Lowenthal, 'Why Sanctions Seldom Work' (n 175) 400.

219 Fincham, Derek, 'A Coordinated Legal and Policy Approach to Undiscovered Antiquities: Adapting the Cultural Heritage Policy of England and Wales to Other Nations of Origin', *International Journal of Cultural Property* 15 (2008), 347–70, 351.

220 For the full comparison, see ibid. 221 Ibid., 363.

law directly or indirectly creates property rights, protects property rights stemming from domestic law, coordinates property rights arising from domestic law, restricts property rights with a domestic origin, and even prohibits the creation of certain property rights in domestic law.[222] Therefore, there seems to be a sufficient body of international property law, based on pure international law or derived from municipal law (as 'general principles of law', in the sense of a source of international law under the Statute of the International Court of Justice, Article 38.1.c)[223] to displace the historical assertion about the impossibility of international heritage law engaging with the theme of property rights.

The fact that significant parts of property law can largely be characterized as general principles of law, and therefore applicable as part of international law in the interpretation of international heritage law treaties, does not necessarily provide the answer to all the challenges posed in this chapter. For one, it still does not fully address the matter of international heritage treaties having purposefully excluded property law, instead using property as a proxy for state sovereignty. The incorporation of property as property law into heritage treaties can create tensions about regime interaction that need mediating.

Further, it is unclear to what extent international lawyers in general, and international heritage lawyers in particular, are able to think of property law as more than property as exclusion, and skirt the essentialized version of property that 'reinforces a culture of alienation that underplays the significance of belonging to a community'.[224] International (heritage) law, with its cosmopolitan aspirations, may in fact be better placed than most other law to engage with this communitarian and inclusionary spirit, which can have trickle-down benefits in the implementation of international heritage law, undoing the domestic/international mismatch discussed here in a productive way. But international heritage law needs to prioritize property when it discusses heritage, instead of treating property (and the economic effects that come with it, discussed in Chapter 5) as the enemy. The economic aspects of property, to be sure, belong more easily with the notion of property as exclusion, in that this version of property 'commodifies both our citizenship and our membership in local communities'.[225] But, as discussed, there are other emancipatory effects of property, which international heritage law would do well to embrace, even if it chooses to keep resisting the economics of heritage. The effect on communities would be significant, as property as inclusionary and communitarian necessarily caters for the centrality of the role of non-state actors, particularly collective ones, in controlling resources, including cultural heritage.

At a minimum, therefore, property cannot be understood without the incorporation of public goods, in a purposive interpretation. It operates through institutions, and is closely connected in many respects to freedom of contract.[226] But it is also often tied to a rights binary, which sees public interests, including heritage specifically, as an integral part of property. Therefore, the divorce between heritage and

[222] Sprankling, John G., *The International Law of Property* (Oxford University Press, 2014), 41.
[223] Ibid., 203. [224] Dagan(n 184) 45. [225] Ibid. [226] Ibid., 34.

property, executed in international law for pragmatic reasons, cannot be sustained in the application of international heritage law.

Taken a step further, the notion of property as rights still fails to fully incorporate marginalized groups like the communities that I argue throughout this book need to be incorporated into heritage governance at all levels. But that is only because its contingencies are missed, and in fact *dis*missed as belonging to a reified legal tradition, instead of being part of the anthropological and archaeological discourse that informs not only the conservation paradigm but the making of international heritage law more generally. Therefore, a manoeuvre that insulates property from the sphere of the main forces behind international heritage law results in further underappreciation of what property, or at least certain versions of property, can do for heritage and, more importantly, heritage holders.

That international law has for pragmatic reasons avoided delving into matters of property law could once have been justified, but that no longer seems to be a strong explanation. As general principles of law around property have coalesced, the divide among the large legal families has been bridged. Therefore, international heritage law can engage with property as more than a proxy for state sovereignty, and rather as a language of power and distribution, or outright transformation, that can benefit heritage indirectly by benefitting communities, and also directly simply as a part of the core of property law.

Historical discourses about how cultural heritage gets intermingled with property may have helped pave the way for heritage as a sovereign prerogative, particularly in revolutionary France, but, read in their context, these discourses can also be taken as simply elevating cultural heritage as favouring the community connected to it, regardless of whether that community is the state or a differently configured entity. Therefore, the definition of heritage, allied with the version of property espoused here, can go further than a heritage that is set as being in opposition to, or transcending, property. It is time to recover these narratives about the role of heritage vis-à-vis property, and of the concept of property more generally, as a means to give more effectiveness to the concept of heritage as it has been transformed over time, and particularly its current iteration, which is more centred on communities as a central part of the definition, value, and safeguarding of this public good. Only then will the cosmopolitan values embraced by international heritage law and UNESCO in particular really be advanced.

The UNESCO engagement with the notion of heritage, and the transformation of cultural property into cultural heritage that the organization has promoted, has admittedly had negative and exclusionary effects. But it is also important in its aspirations to conceptually thinking of heritage beyond sovereignty. The road has been long, but advances have been made in detaching at least some aspects of heritage from states, and reverting to other actors that more closely map onto the ideals of UNESCO of promoting enduring peace through cultural understanding. Therefore, while property has a key role to play—and I have argued that the abandonment of the notion of property has had negative consequences and should be revisited—the aspirational values of the UNESCO definitions of heritage in fact reinforce the versions of property advocated here, and across all major legal systems.

UNESCO has played a key role in introducing aspirational values around heritage, and these values must be embraced and strengthened in order to assist in the interpretation of property in the terms proposed here.

But the definition of cultural heritage (or cultural property) is only part of the much larger puzzle of international heritage law. Now that we understand the concept that holds the field together, it is important to understand who the actors in this field are, and how they wield (or fail to wield) this concept. A mapping of these stakeholders is the objective of the next chapter.

3

Stakeholders in International Heritage Law

In mapping out the field, it is important to understand the players involved, in spite of the field's tendency to focus on methods and subjects of cultural safeguarding rather than inquiring into those doing the safeguarding.[1] To be sure, under public international law, states are the primary (and only, in a strict formalist view) addressees of international heritage law. However, international heritage instruments are meant to shape the conduct not only of states, but of a plethora of actors involved in cultural heritage matters.

As far as this book is concerned, local communities are a key stakeholder. As I argue throughout this book, though, they are also ignored or neglected by various international cultural heritage law instruments. This chapter aims at understanding the many roles of different actors, in juxtaposition to the place of communities and other local actors. It is argued here that there is an oligopoly when it comes to decision-making in heritage matters, with the state at the helm, and closely followed by expert organizations. Other non-state actors tend to pit themselves against one or both of these stakeholders. Communities, however, do not enjoy that luxury. They do not have the institutional structures museums can rely on, nor the economic resources corporate actors enjoy. Communities also do not have international human rights law as an avenue of recourse, given its limited recognition of group rights.[2] As a result, they seemingly would need to rely on the state for the defence of their interests. But it is not in most states' interests to do that, at least not before UNESCO.

This chapter is structured as follows: Section 3.1 places the state in international heritage law, with a view to outlining core obligations that would lead to international state responsibility (which would be a key incentive for state compliance with international heritage treaties). Section 3.2 focuses on the role of expert organizations, largely relying on my previous work on the matter.[3] Section 3.3 examines

[1] Paterson, Robert K. and Telesetsky, Anastasia, 'Heritage Inc.: A Mini-Symposium on Heritage Protection and Private Actors. Held at the Faculty of Law, University of British Columbia, Vancouver, Canada, 16 March 2012', *International Journal of Cultural Property* 19 (2012), 549–71, 549.

[2] Lixinski, Lucas, 'Heritage for Whom? Individuals' and Communities' Roles in International Cultural Heritage Law', in Federico Lenzerini and Ana Filipa Vrdoljak (eds), *International Law for Common Goods—Normative Perspectives on Human Rights, Culture and Nature* (Hart, 2014), 193–213. But see recent developments in the Inter-American Court of Human Rights, in which the Court stated that Indigenous communities are entitled to the recognition of their legal personality as communities. See the case of the *Kaliña and Lokono Peoples v Suriname* (Merits, Reparations and Costs) Inter-American Court of Human Rights Series C No. 309 (25 November 2015).

[3] Lixinski, Lucas, 'International Cultural Heritage Regimes, International Law and the Politics of Expertise', *International Journal of Cultural Property* 20(4) (2013), 407–29.

the role of museums, and particularly the current liberal defence of the universal museum. Section 3.4 investigates the roles of private actors, particularly collectors and corporations. After mapping all these actors, Section 3.5 engages with the elusive concept of 'community' in cultural heritage, and the potentials and pitfalls of this notion, alongside its colonial baggage. In spite of the difficulties in definition, we should not default to other, more easily defined stakeholders. As the chapter shows, the 'community' can be largely defined through its ability to constructively occupy the blind spots in other stakeholders' fields of action. But a negative definition is a definition nonetheless, and it plays an important role in reconceptualizing the field.

3.1 States

States are the primary addressees of international heritage law, under the sovereignty- and territoriality-based logic discussed in Chapters 1 and 2. Therefore, it is important to map out the key roles that states play in the field of international heritage law, and a useful way to understand states' roles is to map out their legal obligations that may trigger international legal responsibility.[4] After all, the risk of international responsibility is a key incentive for the performance of international obligations (alongside reputational costs).

In that respect, heritage treaties create obligations that are mostly imposed on states for internal consumption, thus attempting to replace domestic norms with the treaties' rules. This displacement helps create a more uniform language for heritage governance, as discussed in more detail in Chapter 7. But, for all the work UNESCO instruments do to shape disparate domestic practices, they still for the most part leave the ultimate control over heritage and its meanings to states, as Chapter 2 discussed. There is very little in UNESCO instruments that points to states' direct obligations towards their peers in international lawmaking, that is, other states.

In the aftermath of the Second World War, norms created for the return of Nazi-looted antiquities and other cultural artefacts were deemed so progressive in their approach to state responsibility that they would constitute a new principle of international law.[5] Following the war, UNESCO was created, and since then the body of international heritage law has evolved greatly, but not necessarily with respect to state responsibility. Many speak of *erga omnes* obligations vis-à-vis cultural heritage, or at least of a shift from negative obligations (not to destroy)

[4] For a fuller exploration of these issues, see Lixinski, Lucas and Tzevelekos, Vassilis, 'The Strained, Elusive and Wide-Ranging Relationship between International Cultural Heritage Law and the Law of State Responsibility: From Collective Enforcement to Concurrent Responsibility', in Alessandro Chechi and Marc-Andre Renold (eds), *Cultural Heritage Law and Ethics: Mapping Recent Developments* (Schulthess, 2017) 7–43.

[5] Vrdoljak, Ana Filipa, *International Law, Museums and the Return of Cultural Objects* (Cambridge University Press, 2006), 145.

to positive obligations (to protect and safeguard).[6] A plethora of norms have developed under the aegis of UNESCO and other international organizations, both of hard and soft law. These outline a series of obligations that states undertake to protect heritage.

But these instruments by and large only determine obligations that states have towards their own heritage that has been added to international inventories, or towards the maintenance of an international system of safeguarding. There is relatively little in these instruments that speaks to state obligations towards heritage that is not within their territory, or that is affected by non-state actors. And, even if state responsibility is triggered, there is a lingering question as to whether its legal regime is helpful, since a factual scenario in which state responsibility is triggered in the context of heritage would in most cases imply the destruction of the heritage, which is often conceived of as an 'irreparable loss'.[7]

Modern warfare, deep seabed exploitation, and other activities increasingly affect cultural heritage deemed of international importance by UNESCO and states alike. But it is unclear whether the existing primary norms are sufficient to satisfy the second prong needed to trigger state responsibility, that of a 'breach of an international legal obligation'.[8]

UNESCO instruments for the safeguarding of cultural heritage as a rule proclaim the importance of heritage for all of humanity, using lofty language to the effect that 'damage to cultural property belonging to any people whatsoever means damage to the cultural heritage of all [hu]mankind'.[9] But what hard obligations are actually set out in these instruments with respect to the heritage of others?

The Hague Convention of 1954, on the protection of cultural heritage in wartime, determines that states have the obligation to protect heritage in their own territories and in the territories of other state parties during wartime.[10] But this treaty only applies during times of declared conflict, and particularly inter-state conflicts.[11] With respect to non-international armed conflicts, the Hague Convention optimistically declares that all parties to a conflict are bound, as a minimum, to the obligations of

[6] Francioni, Francesco, 'Au-delà des traités: l'émergence d'un nouveau droit coutumier pour la protection du patrimoine culturel', *Revue Internationale de Droit International Public* 111 (2007) 19–41; Francioni, Francesco, 'Beyond State Sovereignty: The Protection of Cultural Heritage as a Shared Interest of Humanity', *Michigan Journal of International Law* 25 (2003–4) 1209–28; and Graham, Gael M., 'Protection and Reversion of Cultural Property: Issues of Definition and Justification', *The International Lawyer* 21(3) (1987) 755–93, 756.

[7] Carducci, Guido, 'Articles 4–7', in Francesco Francioni (ed.), *The 1972 World Heritage Convention: A Commentary* (Oxford University Press, 2008), 103–45, 144–5.

[8] International Law Commission, Articles on Responsibility of States for Internationally Wrongful Acts, November 2001, Supplement No. 10 (A/56/10), chp.IV.E.1 (ARSIWA), Article 2.b.

[9] Convention for the Protection of Cultural Property in the Event of Armed Conflict with Regulations for the Execution of the Convention 1954 (adopted 14 May 1954, entered into force 7 August 1956) 249 UNTS 240 (1954 Hague Convention), Preamble. See also e.g. the Recommendation concerning the International Exchange of Cultural Property (26 November 1976), at para. 2: 'all cultural property forms part of the common cultural heritage of mankind and that every State has a responsibility in this respect, not only towards its own nationals but also towards the international community as a whole'.

[10] Hague Convention, Article 4.1.

[11] Hague Convention, Article 18.

respect in Article 4.[12] But, in reality, the enforcement of this provision has been very difficult in terms of state responsibility.

The 1970 Convention, on movable cultural heritage, was created with state responsibility in mind—or, more specifically, with reparations for internationally wrongful acts as one of its drivers. The harm of colonization and conquest, and the consequent taking of cultural artefacts from colonial areas, was seen as an internationally wrongful act that could be remedied in the aftermath of decolonization. This logic, opposed by former colonial powers, was ultimately excluded from the language of the treaty, but it still permeates its spirit.[13] In terms of what remained in the treaty from its original spirit, the 1970 Convention requires states to create domestic law prohibiting the export of cultural property,[14] but that obligation is something that state only owes itself, so as to prevent objects leaving its territory. The only obligation the ratifying state owes other states is to prevent the import of cultural objects coming from churches and museums of other ratifying states (after the entry into force of the treaty), and to engage in diplomatic negotiations for the return of objects illicitly imported into their territory.[15] There is also an obligation to criminalize or impose administrative sanctions against the illegal import, export, and transfer of ownership of these artefacts.[16] Finally, Article 9 of the treaty creates an obligation for affected states to cooperate in measures to remedy the pillage of cultural artefacts from one state, as long as said state determines who the affected states are, and calls them to collaborate.[17] Presumably, other states would be affected by the failure to impose import controls (legislative or administrative), and that is the type of obligation that would be enforceable for the purposes of state responsibility. But it is an obligation of means, and not results, that is subject to the due diligence regime.

The World Heritage Convention (WHC) places heritage under its aegis squarely within the territorial state's sovereignty,[18] even if it does recognize that states have a duty to cooperate in the protection of world heritage in other states as well.[19] But this duty of cooperation is defined as assisting the territorial state in its efforts to conserve and identify its heritage.[20] The key provision in the WHC for this chapter's purposes is Article 6.3, which provides that states parties will not take deliberate measures against world heritage situated in the territory of other parties.[21] It has been argued that these provisions, and particularly Article 6.3, create obligations that apply to and among states parties, and can engender state responsibility.[22] But the WHC is still unclear in its application to non-state actors, for instance, and the

[12] Hague Convention, Article 19. [13] Vrdoljak (n 5) 206.

[14] Convention on the Means of Prohibiting and Preventing the Illicit Import, Export and Transfer of Ownership of Cultural Property 1970 (adopted 14 November 1970, entered into force 24 April 1972) 823 UNTS 231 (1970 Convention), Article 6.

[15] 1970 Convention, Article 7.b. [16] 1970 Convention, Article 8.

[17] 1970 Convention, Article 9.

[18] Convention concerning the Protection of the World Cultural and Natural Heritage 1972 (adopted 23 November 1972, entered into force 15 December 1975) 1037 UNTS 151 (WHC), Article 4.

[19] WHC, Article 6.1. [20] WHC, Article 7. [21] WHC, Article 6.3.

[22] Carducci (n 7) 127.

way state responsibility relates to said obligations. There are also concerns about the applicability of these norms to non-parties, thus calling into question the possibility of the WHC norms creating *erga omnes* obligations. It also does not create clear obligations for states with respect to cultural heritage that has not been identified or listed for the purposes of the WHC.

The Underwater Cultural Heritage Convention (UCHC) determines its obligations around the interests of 'humanity', providing that states shall protect underwater heritage 'for the benefit of humanity',[23] as well as take measures 'individually or jointly' to protect underwater heritage.[24] Because of the nature of underwater heritage, which is often in waters beyond the national jurisdiction of any one state, and also where overlapping jurisdiction often applies (e.g. the flag state and the territorial state in the case of a Spanish wreck discovered in US waters), it seems to be a regime more open to considering issues of concurrent responsibility.[25]

Relatedly, the UCHC also articulates specific obligations for states not to allow the entry into their territory of underwater heritage items,[26] or the use of a state's territory or facilities for activities incompatible with the UCHC by states and non-state actors alike.[27] In fact, the UCHC clearly directs a state to regulating the conduct of private actors under its jurisdiction, or flying its flag.[28] In this treaty, it is the deterritorialized nature of the heritage that allows for this type of obligation (but the thirty-year evolution of the field since the WHC may also be a factor to be considered). Thus, certain domains of heritage seem to lend themselves to creating primary obligations owed to other states, as opposed to simply the undefined 'international community'.

The Intangible Cultural Heritage Convention (ICHC) contains no provisions that create obligations one state would owe another, or the international community. It restricts itself to creating obligations upon a state to inventory and list intangible cultural heritage (ICH) within its own territory, and to cooperate with the international safeguarding system. This return to sovereignty, especially in the aftermath of the UCHC, can be explained in two ways. One way is to think of ICH as by definition more territorial than underwater heritage, but that explanation does not hold water, to the extent that ICH is not attached to land and territory in the way that, for instance, World Heritage is. In fact, much intangible heritage is common to multiple cultures, and that has sometimes led to tensions and disputes between different states claiming the same intangible heritage.[29] The more likely explanation is that, because intangible heritage was seen as too politically volatile during the drafting of the treaty, states created stronger sovereignty safeguards than in other

[23] Convention on the Protection of the Underwater Cultural Heritage 2001 (adopted 2 November 2001, entered into force 2 January 2009) 2562 UNTS 3 (UCHC), Article 2.3.

[24] UCHC, Article 2.4.

[25] For a detailed articulation of these issues, see Dromgoole, Sarah, *Underwater Cultural Heritage and International Law* (Cambridge University Press, 2013).

[26] UCHC, Article 14. [27] UCHC, Article 15. [28] UCHC, Article 16.

[29] Lixinski, Lucas, 'A Tale of Two Heritages: Claims of Ownership over Intangible Cultural Heritage and the Myth of "Authenticity"', *Transnational Dispute Management* 11(2) (2014).

domains of cultural heritage, and excluded (intentionally or not) the possibility of owing obligations to other states.[30]

What this survey of the different regimes under UNESCO shows is that most of the obligations undertaken under the relevant treaties are obligations a state owes itself, or the 'international community' as a whole. Very few obligations are actually owed to identifiable other states, which calls into question the usefulness of these treaties to create obligations that can trigger state responsibility. But some domains make certain levels of this type of obligation possible, because of the very nature of the heritage (such as underwater heritage). Others impose fairly discrete obligations of means and due diligence. The community here is hidden in this duality of nationalism and internationalism or cosmopolitanism, discussed in further detail in Chapter 2. Therefore, by focusing on states the law reinforces this duality, and hides the community. The articulation of heritage outside the law tells a different story, which is another reason for relying on non-legal insights, as discussed in Chapter 1.

Therefore, if there are clear instruments to safeguard heritage, but they frame their safeguarding within the exclusive domain of a state's sovereignty (except for a few situations), there is no incentive in international heritage law for communities to be engaged, particularly if they could challenge a state's monopoly, or even the state itself. But that is not to say international heritage law does not include any non-state actors. To the contrary, there is a group of non-state actors that is at the forefront of international heritage law, and has been key in its drafting and implementation. They occupy this space by translating community aspirations into the language of governance, at least on the surface. But, in so doing, they effectively exclude communities in the short term, losing sight of their aspirations in the long term.

3.2 Expert Organizations

This section (and the chapter and book in general) requires an important caveat. When discussing 'experts', I do not mean any specific or individual expert. I do not mean to launch an attack on the work of thousands of well-meaning experts engaged in the safeguarding of cultural heritage. Rather, I am focused here on the way the possibilities of action for these experts are shaped by the rules of the expert organizations within which they operate, and the dominant conservation paradigm that feeds into and is augmented by these organizations' institutional cultures. I wish to make an argument that looks at the role of experts not as individuals, but as members of a group with respect to cultural heritage. This argument will allow for a clearer examination of the broader contours of their practice, and how said practice affects communities in particular. But the terms 'experts' and 'expert organizations' will be used interchangeably here, referring to the latter.

[30] For a critique of the sovereignty safeguards, see Lixinski, Lucas, 'Selecting Heritage: The Interplay of Art, Politics and Identity', *European Journal of International Law* 22(1) (2011), 81–100.

The idea that (academic) experts are no longer as a rule imprisoned in their ivory towers is more or less commonplace today. Relevant for the context of heritage, experts in the humanities in particular concede that they engage in the practice of governmentality.[31] An important element of being an expert is to engage with society, to provide avenues for policymaking, to have an 'impact'. But there is a remaining question as to who is served by that expert engagement, and the extent to which, potentially, experts engaged in 'reality' can be seen even to enter post-national lawmaking in lieu of other non-state actors.

Identifying the 'expert' is of course a challenge in itself. In the context of organizations like the Council of Europe, an 'expert' is essentially anyone who is an external contractor.[32] If we think of the expert as an 'outsider' still, then naturally that actor can put themselves in a disinterested position, and see themselves as not contributing to one or another project. But in effect the expert, at least in anthropology (which is closely connected to heritage management) can be seen as defining their professional identity 'in relations of dependency and competition' which replicate colonial patterns, whether in a situation of formal colonialism or in relations between Indigenous peoples and the white settler population.[33] The way expert knowledge is used is revealing of the limitations of such a notion.

In terms of the contribution of expert knowledge to policymaking by political actors, Christina Boswell has suggested that expert knowledge plays a crucial role in policymaking and political arguments, but that role is not a direct contribution to policy. Rather, it consists of what she refers to as 'symbolic uses', either legitimizing or substantiating political arguments. In the former case, an organization simply bolsters its claim to jurisdiction by using expert argument to enhance its epistemic authority. In the latter, organizations use expert knowledge only to the extent it substantiates their positions to begin with.[34]

Boswell's argument focuses on uses of expert knowledge for domestic law- and policy-making, but I suggest her findings can also apply to international and post-national contexts. More specifically, it would seem that experts, even if they do not work towards protecting their own interests as a class and effectively represent community interests, are still not likely to be given credence by law- and policy-makers

[31] Koerner, Stephanie, 'Revisiting the Dewey–Lippmann (1925–7) Debate, Faro and Expertise in the Humanities', in John Schofield (ed.), *Who Needs Experts? Counter-mapping Cultural Heritage* (Ashgate, 2014), 13–42, 25.

[32] Wolferstan, Sarah, 'Ethnography of a "Humble Expert": Experiencing Faro', in John Schofield (ed.), *Who Needs Experts? Counter-mapping Cultural Heritage* (Ashgate, 2014), 43–53, 48.

[33] de L'Estoile, Benoît, Neiburg, Federico, and Sigaud, Lygia, 'Introduction: Anthropology and the Government of "Natives," a Comparative Approach', in Benoît de L'Estoile, Federico Neiburg, and Lygia Sigaud (eds), *Empires, Nations, and Natives: Anthropology and State-Making* (Duke University Press, 2005), 1–29, 13–14; de L'Estoile, Benoît, 'Rationalizing Colonial Domination? Anthropology and Native Policy in French-Ruled Africa', in Benoît de L'Estoile, Federico Neiburg, and Lygia Sigaud (eds), *Empires, Nations, and Natives: Anthropology and State-Making* (Duke University Press, 2005), 30–57; and Lima, Antonio Carlos de Souza, 'Indigenism in Brazil: The International Migration of State Policies', in Benoît de L'Estoile, Federico Neiburg, and Lygia Sigaud (eds), *Empires, Nations, and Natives: Anthropology and State-Making* (Duke University Press, 2005), 197–222.

[34] Boswell, Christina, *The Political Uses of Expert Knowledge—Immigration Policy and Social Research* (Cambridge University Press, 2009), 7.

unless they serve either to justify turf claims by states or organizations, or simply to justify whatever states or organizations were going to do anyway.

The implications are twofold. First, it means that states will not give much credence to what experts say unless it aligns with and protects their own positions, and states will instrumentalize expert knowledge to serve their own purposes, simply reinforcing sovereignty paradigms in international law. Second, experts may become co-opted by this machinery, as it may be in their own interest, if they are to survive and feel they are being listened to, to favour state interests from the starting point, and to only introduce the interests of non-state actors when they also align with an authorized narrative. Subversive ideas about heritage, for instance, and its potential political uses, are likely to receive little attention and consequently to not be adequately safeguarded internationally.

For instance, the mandate of an expert on World Heritage Sites is to conserve the 'Outstanding Universal Value' (OUV) of those places on behalf of governments and UNESCO, and not necessarily to advance the (potentially contradictory) interests of the people who live around those areas.[35] Experts must serve the narrative authorized by governments and UNESCO first and foremost, and only incidentally other interests.

Other important features of expert knowledge to take into account are that knowledge will be considered 'expert' only as a function of the qualifications and institutional affiliations of those producing it, and, more importantly, that the assessment of expertise depends also on substantive and procedural requirements that are often contingent on the interests of those using said knowledge.[36] In the heritage context, the implication is that expertise will be considered in terms defined by UNESCO, an intergovernmental organization composed of and dependent on states.

Knowledge in this respect cannot be considered as simply a means to resolve problems (a Weberian account); it necessarily has features that operate as social control techniques (a Foucaultian account).[37] But knowledge in itself constitutes a set of interests—it is not only a means of legitimizing external interests. In this sense, not only do experts have an incentive to serve the structures of the organization within which they operate and on some level the interests of the states that compose that organization, but they also have interests of their own.[38]

But organizations like UNESCO, or at least the World Heritage Centre within UNESCO, tend to use knowledge not necessarily symbolically, but for the most part instrumentally. Technical or standard-setting organizations seem to be 'fundamentally concerned with improving the quality of their outputs'.[39] Even then, this instrumental use is only likely to take place when organizations are under pressure to adjust their outputs to society, and believe that the use of expert knowledge will lend legitimacy to their activities.[40] More importantly, that might result in a

[35] Walker, Dominic, 'Local World Heritage: Relocating Expertise in World Heritage Management', in John Schofield (ed.), *Who Needs Experts? Counter-mapping Cultural Heritage* (Ashgate, 2014), 181–201, 182.

[36] Boswell (n 34) 24–5.

[37] Boswell (n 34) 29.

[38] Boswell (n 34) 38–9.

[39] Boswell (n 34) 47.

[40] Boswell (n 34) 60.

naïve suggestion of uses of expert knowledge having no political implications, which would suggest that instrumental uses of knowledge can happen instead of symbolic uses. Symbolic uses, which are highly political, are always present, at the very least as a necessary (even if unintended) consequence of instrumental uses of expert knowledge.

Part of the problem seems to be with the definition of heritage itself (discussed in Chapter 2), which is in some ways a chicken-and-egg problem. A narrow definition of heritage is defended by experts, who then use that narrow definition to perpetuate their own professional positions. In the words of Graham Fairclough,

> as long as heritage is defined primarily as the things we wish to pass on, instead of defining 'the' heritage as everything we have inherited, only some of which will in the end form part of our generation's legacy, the practice of heritage will require gatekeepers who are exercised with selectivity on grounds of quality, significance, value (in the narrow, also most sterile sense) and practicality, and who will need to be, or require the help of, a particular set of experts; more to the point, other views of heritage will be forced to act as supplicant heritages.[41]

A possible response to that would be to follow Fairclough and significantly broaden the definition of heritage (a possibility also discussed in Chapter 2). But I would add to that in saying that more than a larger domain of heritage is desirable; rather, an entire rethinking of the relationship between the authorizing institutions of heritage and their purposes is needed. For instance, is UNESCO's culture mandate with respect to heritage about safeguarding cultural heritage supported and guided by (often developed) states, or is it about promoting aspirations of peoples that may or may not align with states? An answer to this question incidentally affects the place of experts, and what interests they actually serve.

Which is all to say, expert knowledge producers and holders must not assume that what they do is necessarily in the interests of humanity as a whole, nor that what they do is not contingent on the politics of the organization that invites them into their fold. To assume otherwise simply replicates the status quo. And part of that replication happens in the way experts portray communities in the heritage context.

A variety of instruments adopted by UNESCO for the safeguarding of heritage—most notably the WHC and the ICHC, but also others—have treaded the difficult line of trying to determine what heritage's worth is, why it should be protected, and for whom heritage should be safeguarded. These instruments have attempted to bridge the gap between the languages of law and of heritage, and in the process have created their specific expert language through which governance in the field is pursued. A professional vocabulary of international cultural heritage law exists, and the question is where it stands in relation to the two vocabularies from whose collision it originally derived (heritage and law).

Even within this seemingly small and cohesive universe of international cultural heritage law under UNESCO, there is a lot of room for disagreement, and much of

[41] Fairclough, Graham, 'What Was Wrong with Dufton? Reflections on Counter-Mapping: Self, Alterity and Community', in John Schofield (ed.), *Who Needs Experts? Counter-mapping Cultural Heritage* (Ashgate, 2014), 241–8, 246–7.

it can be traced back to what Laurajane Smith has called 'the Authorized Heritage Discourse' (AHD),[42] and the conservation paradigm discussed in Chapter 1. AHD is the notion of heritage as a professional (expert) vocabulary, which, by determining the rules of the game, determines what heritage is, what heritage worth protecting is, how it should be protected, and for whom it should be protected.

In addition to expertise in certain types of heritage, heritage experts also share a common label of 'heritage expert', which stands behind the larger dimensions of the AHD. Heritage expertise is subsequently translated into the expertise of the heritage lawyer, who appropriates (sometimes inaccurately) assumptions and debates of the heritage field in order to set up the legal frameworks for international cultural heritage law. International cultural heritage law then becomes a highly specialized field of law which caters to the AHD, instead of cultural owners.

A lot of work is done in heritage studies and management to promote democratic and inclusive heritage practices, challenging the AHD. However, the discussion in this book is about the mainstream which is still defined by the AHD. The majority of practices, processes, laws, and institutions about heritage internationally are still strongly embedded in the AHD.

The lesson of heritage experts and the AHD, even within the relatively well-defined normative environment of UNESCO, teaches international law more generally that the class of experts is corruptible and will naturally lean towards serving its own endogenous purposes, for the self-preservation of experts as needed participants in the legal process. The heritage case study then works as an experiment with Foucault's idea of discourses as forms of expertise, constituting and governing meanings and social relations.[43]

3.2.1 The Authorized Heritage Discourse and the role of expertise in heritage regime-making

Experts play a key role in determining what is relevant in a certain field of knowledge. Expertise is a discourse, and, according to Foucault, discourses do not simply reflect their objects of analysis, but in fact create them, and in the process position and license certain people to speak about it at the expense of others.[44] Additionally, the language, the professional grammar in which these things are expressed, contains within itself the tools for its proliferation.[45] In other words, cultural heritage experts do not only describe what cultural heritage is, they in fact create (or destroy) heritage by their affirmation that something does (or does not) qualify as 'heritage'. By creating the category of heritage, they offer cultural manifestations a second life

[42] Smith, Laurajane, *Uses of Heritage* (Routledge, 2006).

[43] See in particular Foucault, Michel, *Les mots et les choses: une archeologie des sciences humaines* (Gallimard, 1966); and Foucault, Michel, *The Archaeology of Knowledge* (trans. A. M. Sheridan Smith) (Routledge, 1972).

[44] Foucault, *The Archaeology of Knowledge* (n 43) 49. For a summary of Foucault's theories and their relationship to law, see Golder, Ben and Fitzpatrick, Peter, 'The Laws of Michel Foucault', in Ben Golder and Peter Fitzpatrick (eds), *Foucault's Law* (Routledge, 2010), xi–xxvi.

[45] Foucault, *Les mots et les choses* (n 43) 55.

as representations of themselves.[46] In a play between utopia and the territorialization of heritage appears the expert, the savant, specialized in humanities, asked to advise, direct.[47]

Heritage is defined and governed by philosophies that go back to a specific Euro-American way of imagining the relationship between the past and the present, and a late-modern obsession with vulnerability, uncertainty, and risk.[48] These philosophies, while originating historically for the most part from laypeople,[49] have since been captured by experts, who are the official spokespeople for what heritage is and what is should mean. The risk of losing our heritage, our memory, is calculated and defined by experts, who make that risk manageable.

In this connection, the AHD and the conservation paradigm are self-referential discourses, which engender a set of consequences. Mainly, they need to establish their own reality, and thus create their own boundaries. One of these is the disconnection of heritage from the present and present-day values. The other is that heritage passes on to the near-exclusive domain of experts in determining the meaning and nature of heritage.[50] Even in early efforts to institutionalize heritage, experts assumed a prominent role. For instance, in the US National Park Service, the figure of the 'park ranger' was from the beginning the sole interpreter of the material traces of human and natural history, and the only one capable of translating them to tourists. The past and nature thus became separate from the people visiting the parks, and needed to be translated in terms in which ordinary citizens could understand them.[51]

Importantly, expertise does not seem to be the driving motor at the beginning of international lawmaking in the heritage field. Shortly after the creation of UNESCO, archival documents show that it was local citizen associations and even consortia of city mayors who were pushing for the implementation of UNESCO's culture mandate in the heritage field.[52] It was only later on, when the Cold War gained momentum and UNESCO needed to be depoliticized, sanitized, and 'scientificized', that communities were pushed aside and 'neutral' experts, who could 'discipline' the political unevenness of heritage into a normalized field, became the central figures

[46] Hafstein, Valdimar Tr., 'Célébrer les differences, renforcer la conformité', in Chiara Bortolotto (ed.), *Le patrimoine culturel immatériel* (Éditions de la Maison des sciences de l'homme, 2011), 75–97, 90.

[47] 'C'est dans ce jeu entre l'utopie et sa déclinaison territorialisée, qu'apparaît la figure de l'expert, en l'occurrence le savant ou l'universitaire, specialist en sciences humaines, requis pour conseiller, voire orienter.' Grenet, Sylvie and Hottin, Christian, *Avant-propos: Un livre politique*, in Chiara Bortolotto (ed.), *Le patrimoine culturel immatériel* (Éditions de la Maison des sciences de l'homme, 2011), 9–19, 13.

[48] Harrison, Rodney, *Heritage: Critical Approaches* (Routledge, 2013), 8–9.

[49] Laypeople in this specific context are in fact socioeconomic elites, who could afford to devote time and energy to heritage conservation and preservation. In a way, heritage efforts have since then been riddled with a certain white, male, middle-class mentality, which has permeated discussions about the inclusion of communities in heritage governance. See Waterton, Emma and Smith, Laurajane, 'The Recognition and Misrecognition of Community Heritage', *International Journal of Heritage Studies* 16(1–2) (2010), 4–15, 5.

[50] Ibid., at 11–12.

[51] Harrison (n 48) 104.

[52] UNESCO Archives, Protection des bien culturels, Folder 069:7, Parts I-IV, *passim* (including letters from craftsmen organizations and civil society groups concerned with preservation of historical monuments and sites in countries like the Netherlands, France, Belgium, and the United States).

of the heritage process.[53] The scientificization of heritage work also meant that the need for preserving heritage could be conveyed to a broader, global, audience. The international heritage system is also set up in ways to route around political problems, to avoid international law being involved in disputes over ownership, territory, and property. Thus the values of the law in this moment work to distance the community actors because as non-experts they will want to articulate much broader claims about their rights as particular people, rather than one single claim about the abstracted heritage of humankind.

The inevitable consequence of a heritage governance system that privileges expert rule is that other stakeholders, particularly cultural owners themselves, are excluded. And cultural owners, while often connected to and proud of their own heritage, also have other interests in heritage conservation beyond conserving heritage for heritage's sake, or may also have other interests altogether that take precedence over heritage. One example is the well-known destruction of the Bamiyan Buddhas in Afghanistan by the Taliban regime in 2001. It has been stated that the destruction of these statues marked a turning point in the decision to invade Afghanistan and overthrow the Taliban regime. It has also been stated that '[t]he act of destroying the statues came to be viewed as an explicit defiance of international conventions and a form of symbolic violence that was directed at the world's heritage, and hence at the whole world'.[54]

And, while the predominant narrative about the destruction of the Buddhas states that they were destroyed out of religious intolerance (after all, the Buddhas stood defiantly as symbols of a religion of infidels),[55] an alternative account by Sayed Rahmatullah Hashimi suggests that the statues were destroyed instead because of the reluctance of international (heritage) bodies (more specifically the UNESCO delegation that was in Afghanistan to investigate the destruction of artefacts in the Kabul Museum) to perceive interests other than those of heritage conservation:

> The scholars told them that instead of spending money on statues, why didn't they help our children who are dying of malnutrition? They rejected that, saying, 'This money is only for statues'. The scholars were so angry. They said, 'If you are destroying our future with economic sanctions, you can't care about our heritage'. And so they decided that these statues must be destroyed.... If we had wanted to destroy those statues, we could have done it three years ago [when Mullah Mohammed Omar originally ordered the destruction of the statues]. So why didn't we? In our religion, if anything is harmless, we just leave it. If money is going to statues while children are dying of malnutrition next door, then that makes it harmful, and we destroy it.[56]

[53] See generally Maurel, Chloé, *La pensée et l'action de l'UNESCO dans le domaine de la culture. 1946–1974*, Mémoire (Université Paris I, 2001); and Wells, Clare, *The 'Politicisation' of United Nations Specialised Agencies? UNESCO, the UN and the Politics of Knowledge 1945–82*, PhD thesis (Trinity College Dublin, 1984).

[54] Harrison (n 48) 186.

[55] See e.g. O'Keefe, Roger, 'World Cultural Heritage Obligations to the International Community as a Whole?' *International and Comparative Law Quarterly* 53 (2004), 189–209; and Francioni, Francesco and Lenzerini, Federico, 'The Destruction of the Buddhas of Bamiyan and International Law', *European Journal of International Law* 14(4) (2003), 619–651.

[56] Quoted in Harrison (n 48) 186.

Granted, the mandate of the organs offering money for the conservation of the statues only allowed them to do that, but that is precisely the problem. By foregrounding only the preservation of heritage in the terms established by experts, without regard for the aspirations of the communities affected, the regime neglected background conditions that were necessary for creating an environment conducive to preserving relics of a past that had a lesser meaning in that community's everyday life, conditions necessary for the relics' physical survival. Instead, a situation was created in which the statues had an effect on that community's life, but a negative one, that needed to be eliminated. Further, the reality of this localized conflict and its history also created the institutional need for culture experts to 'decode' the context, and the context was decoded in the experts' vocabulary, backfiring in the worst possible way from the experts' standpoint.

3.2.2 Expert rule in international heritage regimes

Cultural heritage instruments under UNESCO all offer some degree of deference to expert rule. The 1954 Hague Convention, for instance, determines that personnel engaged in the protection of cultural heritage are to be respected and allowed to continue their work even if they fall into enemy hands.[57] This broad protective measure for cultural heritage experts already points out to the importance of expert rule in the regime. Expertise becomes central to this system forty-five years later, when the Second Protocol to the Hague Convention was approved.[58] When describing the requirements for granting enhanced protection for certain cultural heritage, the Second Protocol highlights the role of experts in proposing properties for inclusion in the enhanced protection list.

Enhanced protection is granted only to 'cultural heritage of the greatest importance for humanity',[59] and it is up to experts or states (the latter being validated by the Committee for the Protection of Cultural Property in the Event of Armed Conflict that is established by the Second Protocol, which is also composed of experts 'qualified in the fields of cultural heritage, defence or international law')[60] to determine what that is.[61]

Experts thus operate at least on the same level as states (and arguably a level above, seen as experts also form the Committee, which is the single decider of what heritage qualifies for enhanced protection) in delineating the scope of application of the provisions of the Second Protocol, and ultimately determine what cultural heritage is for the purposes of the law. Even if those experts are nominated by states, and

[57] Hague Convention, Article 15.

[58] Second Protocol to the Hague Convention of 1954 for the Protection of Cultural Property in the Event of Armed Conflict (adopted 26 March 1999, entered into force 9 March 2004) 2253 UNTS 172 (Hague Protocol II).

[59] Ibid., Article 10. [60] Ibid., Article 24.

[61] Ibid., Article 11. See also Guidelines for the Implementation of the 1999 Second Protocol to the Hague Convention of 1954 for the Protection of Cultural Property in the Event of an Armed Conflict (adopted March 2012), Guidelines 47 and 51.

act in as state representatives, they are still experts, as opposed to delegates.[62] This choice represents a compromise in the negotiations of the Second Protocol, which oscillated between a pure expert body and a pure intergovernmental committee.[63]

The 1970 Convention also relies on expertise. But expert rules appear indirectly, in the litigation and other dispute settlement processes around the return of cultural property. Cases have been dismissed for the lack of sufficient expert opinion to corroborate claims of historical title, for instance, or the lack of expert corroboration as to the origins of an object. Similarly, expertise is required to interpret the domestic laws of other countries as to such matters as ownership.[64] This reliance on expert rule places experts above community members, with the former deemed neutral in disputes over ownership of movable heritage items.

The WHC is also very deferential to expert rule. The preamble mentions that protection cannot be complete without the use of experts, and that it is essential that protection mechanisms be 'organized on a permanent basis and in accordance with modern scientific methods'. The WHC was drafted with the advice of the International Council on Monuments and Sites (ICOMOS),[65] a leading NGO of cultural heritage experts. The instrument having been drafted by experts, it is only natural that the role of experts is central to its operation. Even though the WHC attributes to the state the primary duty of identifying cultural heritage properties situated in its territory,[66] and of protecting heritage, the protective duties are expected to be discharged through scientific and technical assistance.[67] Little to no mention is made of communities' involvement in protecting heritage, and, more specifically, in determining what their heritage actually is. While Article 5, on the measures for the protection of heritage, does mention in its first paragraph the need to adopt policies aiming 'to give the cultural and natural heritage a function in the life of the community', the remaining four paragraphs refer to the importance of expertise and expert training,[68] which shows an imbalance in how experts and cultural owners are perceived in the international legal process of heritage protection.

Also significantly, the World Heritage Committee, the main administering body responsible for the implementation of the WHC, is composed of representatives of States Parties assisted by NGOs composed of experts in cultural heritage issues, with grass-roots organizations largely excluded from the process.[69] The same can be said of the Secretariat, the bureaucratic arm of the WHC, which can be assisted by expert NGOs, but seemingly not by grass-roots organizations.[70] States Parties are

[62] See Toman, Jiří, *Cultural Property in War: Improvement in Protection—Commentary on the 1999 Second Protocol to the Hague Convention of 1954 for the Protection of Cultural Property in the Event of Armed Conflict* (UNESCO Publishing, 2009), 528.

[63] Ibid., 519–26.

[64] For a reflection on these matters, see Kaye, Lawrence M., 'The Recovery of Stolen Cultural Property: A Practitioner's View—War Stories and Morality Tales', *Villanova Sports & Entertainment Law Journal* 5(1) (1998), 5–17, 13–15.

[65] See Smith (n 42) 95. [66] WHC, Article 3. [67] WHC, Article 4.

[68] WHC, Article 5. [69] WHC, Article 8.3.

[70] WHC, Article 14. In fact, the Operational Guidelines to the Convention, when specifying the meaning of 'other organizations', only refers to 'other international and nongovernmental organizations with appropriate competence and expertise'. Operational Guidelines for the Implementation of the World Heritage Convention (2015 version). Guideline 38.

even encouraged, in their activities to implement the treaty, to bring together their own experts and expert representatives from other bodies.[71] The Committee relies on these expert NGOs for decisions going from inscription on the World Heritage List (which, according to the Operational Guidelines to the Convention, must be based on 'objective and scientific considerations')[72] to the discharge of funds for heritage protection assistance.[73] These funds, incidentally, may be used only for activities aimed at generating or consolidating cultural heritage expertise.[74] One of the few mentions of community involvement in the World Heritage system is the idea of local communities acting as 'partners' in the protection and conservation of World Heritage.[75] It is telling that communities are not mentioned as having anything to do with the process of indicating what the World Heritage actually is. In this way, the WHC ends up creating a cultural and discursive climate in which expert values and ideologies become dominant in determining cultural development and change.[76] Local communities are only marginally involved in the process, in an almost tokenistic fashion.

The UCHC, by its turn, does not consider community involvement at all, and is purely an expert-driven instrument. The main governing body of the UCHC is the Meeting of the State Parties, which has created a Scientific and Technical Advisory Body, composed solely of experts, whose function is to implement the rules annexed to the UCHC.[77] These rules further reinforce the exclusivity claim of experts over the realm of underwater heritage, by containing rules dedicated to archaeological exploitation of this heritage, and imposing high thresholds of technical knowledge for access to heritage. Even the cultural connections to heritage are to be documented through strict regulations overseeing scientific activities.[78] A recent recommendation by the Advisory Body on the inclusion of NGOs in the implementation of the UCHC recommends that only NGOs with proven 'competence, expertise and experience' in underwater cultural heritage be allowed to participate, thus excluding NGOs who might have experience with underwater heritage, but lack expert backing to direct the meanings that can be attributed to underwater heritage.[79]

The preamble of the UCHC mentions 'the public at large' as a party whose cooperation is essential in the protection of this type of heritage, but the actual text of the treaty does not mention the participation of communities or 'the public', restricting

[71] Operational Guidelines for the Implementation of the World Heritage Convention (2015 version). Guideline 15.

[72] Ibid., Guidelines 23 and 143–51. See also Annex 6 to the Operational Guidelines—Evaluation procedures of the Advisory Bodies for nominations.

[73] WHC, Articles 13 and 21. Article 21 in fact states that 'Such requests [for international assistance] *must* be supported by experts' reports whenever possible' (emphasis added).

[74] WHC, Articles 22–23.

[75] Operational Guidelines for the Implementation of the World Heritage Convention (2008 version). Guideline 40.

[76] Smith (n 42) 99–100.

[77] UCHC, Article 23.

[78] Rules concerning activities directed at underwater cultural heritage, Annex to the Convention on the Protection of the Underwater Cultural Heritage. Rule 6.

[79] Convention on the Protection of the Underwater Cultural Heritage—Scientific and Advisory Body. Recommendation 4/MAB 1, adopted at the first meeting in Cartagena, Spain, on 13–15 June 2010. Doc. UCH/10/1.MAB/220/6 REV.

itself to the setting up of means for expert action to protect underwater heritage by conserving it preferably *in situ*, and access by non-expert actors is deemed acceptable only to the extent it is non-intrusive.[80] In this way, underwater heritage is actually frozen and stripped of any possible meaningful cultural connection to local communities. Heritage is to be appreciated from a distance, not to be interacted with, not to be really experienced, but just gazed at. States can claim a stake on underwater cultural heritage by proving cultural, historical, or archaeological ties,[81] but it is still the state's prerogative to make the actual claim, and nowhere in the instrument or the recommendations of the advisory body is it indicated that communities are to be involved in this process.

Finally, the ICHC is the most recent key instrument under UNESCO relating to cultural heritage.[82] Even though community involvement is an important part of the system created by the ICHC,[83] in practice it has not lived up to its promise in the early years of the implementation of the instrument.[84]

According to the Operational Directives to the ICHC, States Parties should consult not only communities, groups, and individuals who are bearers of ICH, but also experts and research institutes. States are encouraged to create consultative bodies to bring together communities and experts to help in the identification of ICH, the drawing of inventories, and the preparation of nomination files, among other activities.[85]

This is an important shift from the original text of the ICHC, which did not really speak about expert participation in its implementation. However, expert participation *is* seen as an important element, since one of the great shortcomings of the ICHC is precisely the lack of expert knowledge on intangible heritage. The Subsidiary Body on modalities of participation has studied the matter, and concluded that communities must be returned the research results of work on ICH.[86]

Article 15 of the ICHC determines that, at the national level, communities, groups, and individuals concerned with intangible heritage shall participate in

[80] UCHC, Article 2. [81] UCHC, Article 11.4.

[82] My argument regarding the Intangible Heritage Convention was first rehearsed elsewhere. See Lixinski, 'Selecting Heritage' (n 30).

[83] See Blake, Janet, 'UNESCO's 2003 Convention on Intangible Cultural Heritage: The Implications of Community Involvement in "Safeguarding"', in Laurajane Smith and Natsuko Akagawa (eds), *Intangible Heritage: Key Issues in Cultural Heritage* (Routledge, 2009), 45–74, 62; and Aikawa-Faure, Noriko, 'From the Proclamation of Masterpieces to the *Convention for the Safeguarding of Intangible Cultural Heritage*', in Laurajane Smith and Natsuko Agakawa (eds), *Intangible Heritage* (Routledge, 2009), 1–44, 37.

[84] For a fuller analysis, see Lixinski, 'Selecting Heritage' (n 30); and Lixinski, Lucas, *Intangible Cultural Heritage in International Law* (Oxford University Press, 2013).

[85] General Assembly of States Parties to the Convention for the Safeguarding of the Intangible Cultural Heritage, Operational Directives for the Implementation of the Convention for the Safeguarding of the Intangible Cultural Heritage (June 2008), *available at* <http://www.unesco.org/culture/ich> (last accessed 9 April 2009). Rule 77.

[86] See Intergovernmental Committee for the Safeguarding of the Intangible Cultural Heritage, *Report of the Rapporteur of the subsidiary body on the modalities for the participation of communities or their representatives, practitioners, experts, centers of expertise and research institutes in the implementation of the Convention*, presented at the Second Extraordinary Session (Sofia, Bulgaria, 18–22 February 2008). Doc. ITH/08/2.EXT.COM/CONF.201/INF.4, of 12 February 2008, para. 12.

policymaking regarding and management of their own intangible heritage. While a valuable development, this inclusion is limited to the national level (where there is much less international control, and less uniformity of practice), and it does not necessarily compensate for the overall exclusion of community input during the drafting of the treaty and its safeguarding system.

Janet Blake, in her study that served as the basis for the drafting of the ICHC, highlighted the importance of involvement of communities in the implementation of the treaty.[87] According to the ICHC and the early practice under it, however, community participation is restricted to the national level, and communities seem not to have a space at the international level of implementation of the ICHC. Instead, it seems that communities are replaced by experts at the international level. Bulgaria has warned against this shift, and the need to preserve communities as the essential non-state actor in terms of ICH safeguarding.[88]

Experts thus have a much more decisive role, in 'evaluating' requests for funding and inscription, whereas communities play a supporting role at best. Experts in a way become the implementers of the ICHC, and act as 'culture brokers', or mediators rendering the culture of a group accessible to the population at large.[89] Cultural owners themselves are props or bit players in the spectacle of heritage, rather than its stars. The stars are the experts, where their eagerness to create the category of heritage leads to a global project consisting in privileging aspects of artistic creation connected to an almost 'show business' understanding of heritage worth protecting: heritage appealing to a broad public will be that which offers the glitz and blitz of a cabaret show, instead of more subtle forms of heritage.[90] The 'traditional' structures of the local communities are far from having their authority reinforced;[91] rather, 'traditional' in the heritage context is associated with primitive, and needs to be disregarded, or at least it becomes part of the heritage product itself (a notion I will come back to presently). In a sense, then, background rules become merged with their own object of protection, only reinforcing the notion that international workers will end up missing 'opportunities for weaving their efforts into the existing local context'.[92]

[87] See Blake, Janet, *Developing a New Standard-Setting Instrument for the Safeguarding of Intangible Cultural Heritage: Elements for Consideration* (UNESCO Publishing, 2001), 70.

[88] See Intergovernmental Committee for the Safeguarding of the Intangible Cultural Heritage (n 86) Annex 1.

[89] Bortolotto, Chiara, 'Introduction: Le trouble du patrimoine culturel immatériel', in Chiara Bortolotto (ed.), *Le patrimoine culturel immatériel* (Éditions de la Maison des sciences de l'homme, 2011), 21–43, 37.

[90] 'Ici, les volontés de sauvegarde et de patrimonialisation manifestées par les experts épusent un projet global consistant à valoriser les multiples aspects de la creation artistique ou sont liées au monde du spectacle.' Fournier, Laurent-Sébastien, 'La Tarasque métamorphosée', in Chiara Bortolotto (ed.), *Le patrimoine culturel immatériel* (Éditions de la Maison des sciences de l'homme, 2011), 149–66, 160.

[91] A suggestion made by David Kennedy with regard to the work of humanitarians: 'Identifying local conditions as "traditional" may well reinforce the authority of precisely the institutions humanitarians seek to change.' Kennedy, David, *The Dark Sides of Virtue: Reassessing International Humanitarianism* (Princeton University Press, 2005), 140.

[92] Ibid., at 141.

Not all is gloomy in the domain of community participation, however. A new set of operational directives for the ICHC aimed at raising awareness about intangible heritage was approved in June 2010 (and left intact in the 2016 revision), which advances much stronger forms of community involvement, and uses much stronger language in referring to states' obligation to involve communities. Even though these rules refer to a rather harmless aspect of the ICHC, they can be read as a back door through which stronger views about the legal bite of the treaty and more effective means of community involvement are sneaked into the system. These revised directives include principles on awareness-raising, which require not only that free, prior, and informed consent be sought, but also that control over the uses of heritage be ultimately given to the communities, rather than the state seeking an eventual nomination.[93] Additionally, the UNESCO Recommendation on the Historic Urban Landscape of 2011[94] attempts to include more community participation and bottom-up approaches to governance in the World Heritage Convention system. As a recommendation, though, it is a soft law instrument, and as such it is not binding upon UNESCO Member States, or on the body in charge of implementing the WHC.[95]

Therefore, it seems that for the most part communities are once again placed in the back seat of international standard-setting and safeguarding of cultural heritage. There are positive steps forward, but they still fall short of fully empowering communities to control their own heritage and influence decision-making regarding it internationally.[96] Communities should be able to control the meaning of their heritage, and the different uses of it. In a way, communities are defined and justified because of their heritage, and that heritage is fostered and sustained by the creation of community.[97]

What is gained from including communities is, for one, to displace traditional constructions of culture away from its normal understanding as something to be gazed upon, towards something that is effectively lived and renewed, thus upending the conservation paradigm.[98] Of course, there is always a risk that community involvement in heritage processes will result in tokenistic and unsustainable

[93] Operational Directives for the Implementation of Convention for the Safeguarding of the Intangible Cultural Heritage (2016), paras 100–102.

[94] Recommendation on the Historic Urban Landscape, including a glossary of definitions, of 10 November 2011.

[95] For a more positive outlook, suggesting this Recommendation does in fact have the potential to represent a major overhaul of the World Heritage System, see Gardner, Maggie, 'UNESCO to Recommend a New Approach for Protecting Historic Cities: Bringing Technocracy to the People?', *Cultural Heritage & Arts Review* (Summer 2011), 17–21.

[96] For a more positive outlook on the matter, see Kurin, Richard, 'Safeguarding Intangible Cultural Heritage: Key Factors in Implementing the 2003 Convention', *International Journal of Intangible Heritage* 2 (2007), 10–15, 15.

[97] Crooke, Elizabeth, 'The Politics of Community Heritage: Motivations, Authority and Control', *International Journal of Heritage Studies* 16(1–2) (2010), 16–29, 17.

[98] See Hemming, Steve and Rigney, Daryle, 'Decentring the New Protectors: Transforming Aboriginal Heritage in South Australia', *International Journal of Heritage Studies* 16(1–2) (2010), 90–106, 93.

projects,[99] and that the promise of community participation will remain unfulfilled.[100] It is always necessary to negotiate with a range of actors, and understand their motivations and needs, as part of the management process.[101] There are diverse forms of community engagement with heritage across the globe, and they are contingent upon local conditions.[102] At the global level, there is a sense in which this diversity has been filtered internationally and become expert participation. But that is not enough internationally, and I would suggest means need to be developed through which communities can also be in charge of their heritage's management internationally.

The analysis of the provisions from these treaties suggests that community involvement in the international governance of heritage is barred by the required expert participation, which is by its turn made a requirement by experts themselves (jointly with states who fear the consequences of ceding authority to communities). The politics of expertise in heritage processes prevents the actual custodians of heritage from being meaningfully involved in lawmaking affecting their own heritage. Naturally, such a process makes it more difficult to fully safeguard heritage. More importantly, it creates dissonances about what heritage means, with experts and states more often than not sticking together, sometimes in opposition to community-grown sentiments and aspirations.

The reliance on expert knowledge for the making of international law seems to problematize international legal governance in the field of heritage, by creating a dichotomy between heritage holders and heritage experts. The function of heritage experts as 'translators' of the aspirations of cultural owners does not seem to function well enough to warrant their monopoly over the background. Experts, however, provide fundamental tools for understanding what heritage is, and what is at stake when one thinks about heritage safeguarding. But other actors' views need to be considered. Among these actors, museums are also key in interpreting heritage and its meanings, and a discussion of their role with respect to heritage is the object of the next section.

3.3 Museums

Museums are key stakeholders not only with respect to movable heritage, but also intangible heritage[103] and underwater heritage. Specialized museums cover a wide

[99] See Perkin, Corinne, 'Beyond the Rhetoric: Negotiating the Politics and Realizing the Potential of Community-Driven Heritage Engagement', *International Journal of Heritage Studies* 16(1–2) (2010), 107–22, 107.

[100] See generally Chirikure, Shadreck, Manyanga, Munyaradzi, Ndoro, Webber, and Pwiti, Gilbert, 'Unfulfilled Promises? Heritage Management and Community Participation at some of Africa's Cultural Heritage Sites', *International Journal of Heritage Studies* 16(1–2) (2010), 30–44.

[101] See Perkin (n 99) at 108. For a general critique, see Greer, Shelley, 'Heritage and Empowerment: Community-Based Indigenous Cultural Heritage in Northern Australia', *International Journal of Heritage Studies* 16(1–2) (2010), 45–55; and Mansuri, Ghazala, and Rao, Vijayendra, 'Community-Based and -Driven Development: A Critical Review', *The World Bank Research Observer* 19(1) (2004), 1–39.

[102] See e.g. Watson, Steve and Waterton, Emma, 'Editorial: Heritage and Community Engagement', *International Journal of Heritage Studies* 16(1–2) (2010), 1–3, 2.

[103] For an examination focused on intangible heritage's role in museums, see Brown, Michael F., 'Exhibiting Indigenous Heritage in the Age of Cultural Property', in James Cuno (ed.), *Whose*

range of heritage domains, and they are therefore deserving of particular consideration. And, even though museums themselves employ a range of experts, as discussed in Section 3.2, there are also specific dimensions to their presence in the heritage field that are worth highlighting.

Traditionally, museums have played an important role in educational activities, and also in the make-up of national identity. National museums, for instance, not only play the role of educating the public, but in doing so they also help foster national identity, and even, in the case of former imperial powers, help showcase the empire and its achievements, often as a means to strengthen national pride in the metropolis. The role of the national museum has even withstood globalization.[104]

The museum is a product of the late eighteenth and early nineteenth centuries, where museums precisely following the patterns and flows of colonialism; creating 'museums of conquest'.[105] It takes 'the forms of collections of locally made art and industry, and of imperially gathered trophies'.[106] That happened in spite of original intentions to create museums of and for the world, as was the case with the British Museum,[107] at least to the extent that the 'world citizens' meant European citizens. In these museums, archaeological context would be replaced by the context that 'allow[s] truths to emerge that could not emerge if the objects were studied only in the context of objects like them'.[108] By putting objects from several different cultures all under one roof, universal truths can be arrived at, beyond nationalist politics.[109] Also, anthropology's input into certain imperial museums helped make a case for the presence of certain characteristics in peoples under colonial domination 'that justified bringing their colonial subordination to an end'.[110] But, predominantly, imperial museums showcased the glory of the empire first and foremost.[111]

The experience of museums has become internationalized, thanks to the tourism industry and its global rise.[112] While tourism will be discussed in detail in Chapter 5, it suffices now to point out how globalizing forces flow towards colonial patterns, in true path-dependence mode. New national museums control and reinforce taxonomies of difference, by creating spectacles of said difference.[113] As a result, the same colonial imprint that is carried by communities (discussed below) is reinforced by institutions like museums, in spite of their attempts at defending their own role, and the importance of 'universal museums'. There is thus a 'negative cloud surrounding museums institutions', which has been argued to be detrimental to the achievement of their mission.[114]

Culture? The Promise of Museums and the Debate over Antiquities (Princeton University Press, 2009), 145–64.

104 Young, Linda, 'Globalisation, Culture and Museums: A Review of Theory', *International Journal of Heritage Studies* 5(1) (1999), 6–15, 6.

105 Jenkins, Tiffany, *Keeping their Marbles: How the Treasures of the Past Ended Up in Museums . . . and Why They Should Stay There* (Oxford University Press, 2016), 80.

106 Ibid., at 11.

107 For this history, see MacGregor, Neil, 'To Shape the Citizens of "That Great City, the World"', in James Cuno (ed.), *Whose Culture? The Promise of Museums and the Debate over Antiquities* (Princeton University Press, 2009), 39–54, 40.

108 Ibid., at 42.

109 Ibid., at 50. See also Jenkins (n 105).

110 Brown (n 103) at 148.

111 Ibid.

112 Young (n 104) at 12.

113 Ibid., at 13.

114 Jenkins (n 105) 181.

In addition to the colonial imprint and its implications for how we understand community, it is also important to reassess the notion that museums are visited and exist primarily for educational purposes, which is a position still taken by many major museums and their directors.[115] Recent literature has suggested that the reasons people visit museums go beyond education, and are indeed primarily outside of education; people visit museums for the 'enacting of a performance that provides institutional and structured reinforcement of a visitor's sense of self, their ideological positions, and the cultural values that underpin both of these'.[116] Museum visiting is thus itself a form of heritage-making,[117] and therefore community engagement with these stakeholders is key to understanding their function.

There are issues with how a museum's 'community' is defined, though. The liberal defence of the universal museum tends to stress the role of museums in serving the community at large, as opposed to archaeologists. But that community is usually the one that is geographically closer to the community primarily, and then visitors from outside that space. Historically, this 'public' was mostly composed of experts.[118] For a museum to claim that it serves the whole of humanity because it receives large numbers of international tourists is also misleading, at least to the extent that the absolute majority of international tourists in museums are relatively affluent (or at least middle-class),[119] as opposed to, for instance, the communities from where many of the museum's artefacts may have come, through subsistence digging (discussed in more detail in Chapter 5).

Museums, it has been argued, 'have value as repositories of objects dedicated to the dissemination of knowledge and the dissolution of ignorance, where the artifacts of one culture and one time are preserved and displayed next to others without prejudice'.[120] This idea lines up with the liberal defence of the value of museums, and a liberal stance on international cultural heritage law more generally. Perhaps more perniciously, this type of argument is seen as flowing from a cosmopolitan take on heritage and its value, and in going against cultural nationalism and its divisive and retentionist tendencies. As the argument goes, because there is no cultural continuity between, for instance, ancient Egypt and modern-day Egypt, ancient Egyptian artefacts should not be seen as belonging to Egypt, which uses them in favour of nationalist identity politics.[121] Further, an argument is made that if resources were used to ensure artefacts from a number of cultures entered a

[115] de Montebello, Philippe, 'And What do You Propose Should be Done with Those Objects?', in James Cuno (ed), *Whose Culture? The Promise of Museums and the Debate over Antiquities* (Princeton University Press, 2009), 55–70, 61. See also Boyd, Willard L., 'Museums as Centers of Cultural Understanding', in John Henry Merryman (ed.), *Imperialism, Art and Restitution* (Cambridge University Press, 2006), 47–64.

[116] Smith, Laurajane, 'Theorizing Museum and Heritage Visiting', in *The International Handbooks of Museum Studies*, vol. 3 (Wiley, 2015), 459–84, 465.

[117] Ibid., 459.

[118] Jenkins (n 105) 54.

[119] Smith, 'Theorizing' (n 116) 466.

[120] Cuno, James, 'Acknowledgements', in James Cuno (ed.), *Whose Culture? The Promise of Museums and the Debate over Antiquities* (Princeton University Press, 2009), ix.

[121] See generally Cuno, James, *Who Owns Antiquity? Museums and the Battle over Our Ancient Heritage* (Princeton University Press, 2008); and Cuno, James, 'View from the Universal Museum', in John Henry Merryman (ed.), *Imperialism, Art and Restitution* (Cambridge University Press, 2006), 15–36.

country's territory, as opposed to preventing artefacts leaving a territory, a 'cosmopolitan aesthetic experience', would be best achieved,[122] one that is more in line with UNESCO's objectives. Here, as elsewhere in this book, cosmopolitanism becomes a proxy for a specific view of the world that privileges developed nations, at the expense of developing countries and communities therein.

But this argument can also be seen as favouring communities. As discussed in Chapter 5, often national heritage strategies, by privileging a certain version of identity that is tied to an ancient empire on that territory (notably in countries like Greece,[123] Egypt, and Turkey, but also Italy, Nigeria,[124] and many others), end up alienating communities from the heritage where they lie, to the extent their own current identity is not integrated into a specific narrative produced for tourism purposes. So, the disassociation between a nation state and the territory's ancient history can in fact liberate community identity that does not fit the reified version prepared for outside consumption, and allow other understandings of heritage and other identities to be better integrated into contemporary economic and political structures. But that is not to say that the artefacts representing the ancient civilization should then be free to go anywhere. Rather, its commodification should be used to promote the development of the communities within the territorial state.

An important part of the liberal defence of museums is to place museums against archaeologists, and highlight the frictions between the two fields.[125] Archaeologists have embraced context over artefacts as the primary object of study of their discipline, and have supported excavations only under their direction. That is all part of the AHD. A consequence of this attitude is that several archaeological journals, in support of the profession's stance against illicit looting, now refuse to publish studies based on unprovenanced artefacts.[126] The publication of studies based on unprovenanced artefacts has long been a practice of museums (sometimes in cooperation with collectors) to launder artefacts, and give them legitimacy.[127] Now archaeologists refuse to engage in this activity, and museums wish to return to the *status quo ante*. In their defence, museums again appeal to the educational value of heritage and notions of freedom of (academic) expression, arguing that the publication of these artefacts is the only way to preserve whatever is left of the information that cannot be recovered from the destroyed context.[128]

[122] Appiah, Kwame Anthony, 'Whose Culture is It?', in James Cuno (ed.), *Whose Culture? The Promise of Museums and the Debate over Antiquities* (Princeton University Press, 2009), 71–86, 78.

[123] Merryman, John Henry, 'Whither the Elgin Marbles?', in John Henry Merryman (ed.), *Imperialism, Art and Restitution* (Cambridge University Press, 2006), 98–113, 100.

[124] On Nigeria specifically, see Appiah (n 122) 74.

[125] Boardman, Sir John, 'Archaeologists, Collectors, and Museums', in James Cuno (ed.), *Whose Culture? The Promise of Museums and the Debate over Antiquities* (Princeton University Press, 2009), 107–24, 107.

[126] Owen, David I., 'Censoring Knowledge: The Case for the Publication of Unprovenanced Cuneiform Tablets', in James Cuno (ed.), *Whose Culture? The Promise of Museums and the Debate over Antiquities* (Princeton University Press, 2009), 125–42.

[127] See generally Felch, Jason and Frammolino, Ralph, *Chasing Aphrodite: The Hunt for Looted Antiquities at the World's Richest Museum* (Houghton Mifflin Harcourt, 2011).

[128] Owen (n 126) at 127.

Underlying this anecdote is the creation of a dichotomy between museums and the archaeological profession, in which one form of expertise is replaced with another, which includes accusations of archaeologists co-opting the practice of collection away from the public in general.[129] Museums act as defenders of public access, going against archaeologists and depicting them as an elitist class of experts who would rather not have the world know its own history than let the market function on its own terms (that is, allowing unprovenanced objects to be studied and those studies published, thus creating more incentives for illicit digging). The problem once again lies in the different definition of the communities that each side serves: museums serve their own community of (middle-class and developed-world-bound) visitors, whereas archaeologists claim to act responsibly by protecting context and indirectly the economic interests of the communities of origin (but at least ostensibly primarily serve the goals of the discipline and consequently the AHD). Notably, the liberal argument in favour of publication of unprovenanced artefacts points at the hypocrisy of the archaeological profession in refusing to publish those studies, but doing nothing 'to condemn or even openly discuss human rights abuses, [and] widespread corruption' (and implying that museums do some of that work when they put together exhibitions about those countries).[130]

John Merryman has argued that the majority of international law affecting museums is objectoriented, whereas some law (in particular the 1970 Convention) is nation-oriented.[131] Object-oriented instruments are more in tune with museums, and better protect the cosmopolitan mandate of international heritage law and of UNESCO, according to Merryman.[132] But, by being object-oriented, museums and international law reinforce the conservation paradigm and their own version of the AHD, and exclude communities from these processes just as much as a nation-oriented instrument would.

As a response to these criticisms, community-controlled museology has emerged as a field of study.[133] But community engagement is not always an optimal tool of governance, according to Michael Brown, as it 'may be indispensable in some cases and little more than a distraction in others, especially when the goal of the exhibition is comparative and analytical rather than celebratory'.[134] Nevertheless, the incipient possibilities of community-oriented approaches with respect to museums as well is a means to engage stakeholders in a way in which they are not just consumers of culture, but, in fact, produce heritage as well, and can control its meanings in a way that would otherwise not be possible.[135]

[129] Watt, James C. Y., 'Antiquities and the Importance—and Limitations—of Archaeological Context', in James Cuno (ed.), *Whose Culture? The Promise of Museums and the Debate over Antiquities* (Princeton University Press, 2009), 89–106, 97.

[130] Owen (n 126) at 128.

[131] Merryman, John Henry, 'The Nation and the Object', in James Cuno (ed.), *Whose Culture? The Promise of Museums and the Debate over Antiquities* (Princeton University Press, 2009), 183–208, 183.

[132] Ibid., at 195. [133] Brown (n 103) at 159. [134] Ibid.

[135] On the importance of controlling museum exhibitions in the Indigenous context, see Thomas, David Hurst, 'Finders Keepers and Deep American History: Some Lessons in Dispute Resolution', in

3.4 Collectors and Corporate Actors

These two categories of private actors have specific interests in cultural heritage. They are grouped together here because their entry point into the world of heritage is usually through economic engagement, either by the act of purchasing objects (collectors) or by investing in and around heritage (corporations). Much of this discussion will therefore be revisited in Chapter 5, but it is important to frame these stakeholders in the context of other actors in the field of heritage.

Collectors have long had a history of involvement with cultural heritage. Erin Thompson has collated and systematized much of the history of collecting in the West.[136] She argues that the motivations and beliefs of collectors need to be engaged with so they can be channelled in more productive ways that simultaneously satisfy their expectations and do not endanger heritage.[137] Some of these motivations are religious (like English collectors in the twelfth century claiming to buy ancient Roman statues in Rome in order to prevent locals from starting to worship them again,[138] or contemporary iconoclasm).[139] Relatedly, a classic argument made by some collectors contemporarily and historically,[140] and discussed further in Chapter 5, is that they rescue antiquities by purchasing them out of the black or grey market. The argument goes on to say that collectors, art dealers, and countries of origin all share fundamentally the same goals for the preservation of cultural heritage, diverging only in the detail of implementation of said interests.[141]

But this argument neglects a long history of collectors using artefacts to gain social status, and in doing so manipulating the artefacts, sometimes by destroying them (as fragments can be more useful than whole objects).[142] Restoration practices have changed dramatically, to be sure, but they have in the past led collectors (as well as museums) to deface or join together parts of different works (sometimes from vastly different periods) as a means to pursue a certain narrative about the objects.[143] In this way, any claim by collectors that they preserve the past in spite of other actors ignores a long history in which collectors, much like states and experts, also pursue their own agendas with respect to heritage.

Collectors often rely on fairly complex networks of other collectors and dealers, which present sophisticated engagement with a number of stakeholders. But this engagement with other collectors and dealers is in stark contrast with

John Henry Merryman (ed.), *Imperialism, Art and Restitution* (Cambridge University Press, 2006), 218–53, 244.

136 Thompson, Erin L., *Possession: The Curious History of Private Collectors from Antiquity to the Present* (Yale University Press, 2016).

137 Ibid., 2 and 173. 138 Ibid., 16. 139 Ibid., 163. 140 Ibid., 160.

141 Coggins, Clemency Chase, 'A Licit International Traffic in Ancient Art: Let There Be Light!', *International Journal of Cultural Property* 4(1) (1995), 61–80, 61.

142 Thompson (n 136) at 26. 143 Ibid., 39.

collectors' general attitudes towards governments.[144] Part of it can be explained, as Thompson argues, through a certain culture of entitlement that collectors in upper socioeconomic strata enjoy vis-à-vis the government, for instance in their engagement with tax systems, and the payment of duties that are used to control the movement of heritage objects.[145] The manipulation of customs regulations led sometimes to the disassembly of objects (since parts are less valuable than wholes for taxation purposes), or to lies about whether antiquities had been heavily restored or otherwise contemporarily manipulated.[146] This same sense of entitlement is used to justify behaviour that leads collectors to believe current possessors 'are unworthy owners who are neglecting or damaging artifacts'.[147] Custom laws that, as discussed in Chapter 2, are influential and excluded communities with the promise of law enforcement, still fall short, being exploited by other actors instead.

The unworthiness argument, or the 'underserving local',[148] has the effect of alienating communities from their own heritage, putting the interests of collectors (often wealthy citizens of wealthy countries) above the interests of local communities (often less wealthy people in developing countries).[149] Relatedly, collectors often believe they are better positioned because they can better appreciate the works (and the past more broadly),[150] a line of argument also often advanced by museums.

The connection between dealers and museums is an important element to be explored, as the social networks developed by collectors under the umbrella of museums, and the philanthropy of collectors that benefits museums, are important elements in the movable heritage realm.[151] Further, the behaviours of museums and collectors tend to frustrate the objectives of the law on movable heritage in fairly similar ways.

In this context, too, collectors and dealers are pitted against archaeologists, with the idea that archaeologists assume collectors and dealers to be guilty of engaging illicitly in the market unless they can prove the legality of their actions.[152] The reverse seems to be true from the perspective of collectors, too, who often assume that archeologists' interest in the mundane, and the reconstruction of all aspects of life in the past, gets in the way of the true appreciation of the aesthetic (or contemporary social) attributes of antiquities.[153] Further, non-archaeologists find it difficult to engage satisfactorily with archaeological processes, given their distance justified on

[144] Ibid., 144–5. [145] Ibid., 147. [146] Ibid., 150. [147] Ibid., 161.

[148] For a discussion of these portrayals in popular culture, see Lixinski, Lucas, 'Moral, Legal and Archaeological Relics of the Past: Portrayals of International Cultural Heritage Law in Cinema', *London Review of International Law* 4(3) (2016) 421–37.

[149] Thompson (n 136) 165. [150] Ibid., 166.

[151] Ibid., 180–1. For connecting stakeholders in the somewhat comparable universe of contemporary art, including museums, auction houses, and artists, see Thornton, Sarah, *Seven Days in the Art World* (W. W. Norton & Company, 2008).

[152] Coggins (n 141) 62. See also Matsuda, David, 'The Ethics of Archaeology, Subsistence Digging, and Artifact Looting in Latin America: Point, Muted Counterpoint', *International Journal of Cultural Property* 7(1) (1998), 87–97, 90.

[153] Thompson (n 136) 108–9.

grounds of scientificism.[154] But, as Thompson argues, such engagement is central for shifting the incentives that lead collectors to adopt predatory attitudes towards heritage.[155]

Corporate actors in particular are often seen as negatively impacting cultural heritage, and more broadly not engaging sufficiently with communities and other local stakeholders.[156] Corporate actors often treat heritage as a development resource (a position discussed in more detail in Chapter 5).[157] There are, however, situations in which corporate actors see themselves as contributing positively to cultural heritage safeguarding, though, and even leading efforts in the field.[158] J. Paul Getty, for instance, as an individual collector, used his collection to project and pursue his corporate plans. He saw art and business as inextricably linked, at least to the extent that this contributed to his imagination to advance his commercial interests.[159] While there certainly are other, legitimate, means in which corporate actors engage with heritage, in the remainder of this section I will instead focus on forms of engagement that often displace communities in the process. This discussion will focus on peacetime actions and therefore exclude the Hague Convention regime. It will therefore not focus on situations like the conflicts in Mali and Syria, still ongoing at the time of writing,[160] since they trigger questions that go beyond the involvement of non-state actors beyond the state, at least to the extent these non-state actors aim to become the state.[161]

That cultural heritage can be negatively affected by non-state actors is a fairly commonplace idea.[162] There are three general ways in which heritage has been threatened by corporate actors: direct exploitation for commercial gain; direct destruction of heritage as collateral damage in resource exploitation projects; and indirect damage to heritage resulting from, for instance, water pollution caused by nearby industrial plants, or damage from tourism.[163]

Among the ways in which corporations can impinge upon cultural heritage is, for instance, the development of hydroelectric dams that lead to the submergence of archaeological sites, or mining operations that can impact on tangible sites and

154 Ibid., 181. 155 Ibid., 182.

156 See e.g. Perrone, Nicolás M, 'The International Investment Regime and Local Populations: Are the Weakest Voices Unheard?', *Transnational Legal Theory* 7(3) (2016), 1–23.

157 Coombe, Rosemary J. and Baird, Melissa F., 'The Limits of Heritage: Corporate Interests and Cultural Rights on Resource Frontiers', in William Logan, Máiréad Nic Craith, and Ullrich Kockel (eds), *A Companion to Heritage Studies* (John Wiley and Sons, 2015), 337–54.

158 Paterson and Telesetsky (n 1) 550. 159 Thompson (n 136) 115.

160 But on Mali, the ICC issued a judgment on 27 September 2016 in the *Al Mahdi* case, about the destruction of the World Heritage Site in Timbuktu. *Prosecutor v Al Mahdi* (Judgment and Sentence) ICC-01/12-01/15-171 (27 September 2016); and *Prosecutor v Ahmad Al Faqi Al Mahdi* (Reparations Order) ICC-01/12-01/15 (17 August 2017). This case is further discussed in Chapter 7.

161 See generally Lostal, Marina, *International Cultural Heritage Law in Armed Conflict: Case-Studies of Syria, Libya, Mali, the Invasion of Iraq, and the Buddhas of Bamiyan* (Cambridge University Press, 2017); and Vrdoljak, Ana Filipa, 'Cultural Heritage, Human Rights and the Privatisation of War', in Andrea Durbach and Lucas Lixinski (eds), *Heritage, Culture and Rights—Challenging Legal Discourses* (Hart, 2017), 61–90.

162 See for instance Francioni, Francesco, 'Public and Private in the International Protection of Global Cultural Goods', *The European Journal of International Law* 23(3) (2012), 719–30.

163 Paterson and Telesetsky (n 1) 551.

the intangible heritage of communities where mining takes place.[164] Not to say anything of the activities of looters, private collectors, and museums, which can be seen as forming transnational crime networks,[165] and has been discussed above.

When it comes to looters, collectors, and museums, it seems to be fairly clear that their activities are condemned by international heritage instruments, particularly the 1970 Convention, as discussed. In economic development scenarios, though, rules are not as clear-cut. In fact, it has been argued that there is an emerging international norm that would see economic development as a permissible justification for destroying cultural heritage, even if said norm puts increasing demands on host states to make good faith efforts to preserve artefacts and to mitigate the harm caused by development projects to sites.[166] Thus, the destruction of cultural heritage as an international wrong could be justified on grounds of performance of due diligence. But here there is another layer to be added; that of competing norms and priorities. The primary norm against the destruction of cultural heritage needs to be balanced with the state's right to development, it seems. Or the wrong can be justified on grounds of economic necessity, as was the case with the construction of the Aswan Dam in Egypt.[167]

It seems that, in cases of economic development activities impacting on heritage, one of the mitigating factors (which may speak to due diligence) is the involvement of local communities in the management of the resources (cultural and economic), and their involvement in the choices about the fate of the cultural sites to be affected by the development project.[168] This type of participation, it seems, dilutes the responsibility of the territorial state. In that respect, arguably the involvement of communities influences the standing of states even above the involvement of experts (even though experts are the ones who ultimately make the cultural impact assessment studies) or corporate actors (but, again, it is in the furtherance of corporate actors' interests). Mining is acknowledged as placing greater pressure on the cultural heritage of local communities, and also as raising democratic legitimacy concerns with respect to UNESCO heritage treaties.[169] But mining can also be an opportunity to realize a certain cultural future that is beyond the reach of many communities, due to the injection of resources and mitigating actions around cultural awareness and heritage safeguarding.[170]

Further, the pressures from corporate actors are a stark reminder that, yes, cultural heritage is important, and its safeguarding is important, but that is one competing

164 For a case study, see Bainton, Nicholas A., Ballard, Chris, Gillespie, Kirsty, and Hall, Nicholas, 'Stepping Stones Across the Lihir Islands: Developing Cultural Heritage Management in the Context of a Gold-Mining Operation', *International Journal of Cultural Property* 18 (2011), 81–110.

165 For an exposé, see Felch and Frammolino (n 127).

166 Wangkeo, Kanchana, 'Monumental Challenges: The Lawfulness of Destroying Cultural Heritage During Peacetime', 28 *Yale Journal of International Law* (2003) 183–274, 187.

167 Wangkeo (n 166) 209. See also Fagan, Brian M., *The Rape of the Nile: Tomb Robbers, Tourists, and Archaeologists in Egypt* (Westview, 2004).

168 Bainton et al. (n 164) 90–1; Wangkeo (n 166) 269.

169 Affolder, Natasha, 'Mining and the World Heritage Convention: Democratic Legitimacy and Treaty Compliance', *Pace Environmental Law Review* 24(1) (2007), 35–66, 39–43.

170 Bainton et al. (n 164) 82.

need among many for several communities. Economic imperatives usually mean that heritage is addressed later in the relevant processes, and social change is initiated by economic activities long before people realize the need, or galvanize the resources, to safeguard cultural heritage.[171]

Corporations can also be positively involved in safeguarding the heritage their activities put pressure on, as case studies have shown.[172] Corporate interest is driven by entrepreneurial opportunities, concerns about reputation of corporate actors, best corporate practices, and internal leadership priorities.[173] In the WHC context, there are seven positive roles non-state actors can play: world heritage partnerships for conservation; direct implementation of the treaty via no-go pledges;[174] contributions to rapid-response facilities or the World Heritage Fund; participation in national initiatives to prepare nominations for the World Heritage List; corporate planning; industry cooperation; and lobbying within and outside the WHC framework.[175] Not all of those forms of engagement apply to corporate actors, but most of them do. Private restoration banking is a tool that falls within this framework, and has been successfully deployed with respect to natural heritage sites.[176]

Corporate tools can also lead to the development of participatory techniques to prepare cultural heritage plans in a manner that is consistent with and appropriate for the involved community.[177] A risk with this positive involvement, of course, is the dependency on the corporate actor's resources for the continuation of safeguarding activities. The emergence of formalized community structures can work as an important counterweight to the dependence on corporate resources, and also increase the pressure on the corporate actor for compliance, transparency, and accountability.[178]

Other situations involving economic uses of heritage seem to find less support. For instance, salvage of underwater cultural heritage is prohibited under the terms of the UCHC, and therefore the actions of a private company registered in a state party to the UCHC in salvaging underwater heritage in the waters of another party could trigger the first state party's responsibility, if it can be proven that said state breached their due diligence obligations. What said due diligence duties would mean is unclear, as it would imply the extraterritorial application of the UCHC, which may be incompatible with the treaty's text and find limited support in the law of the sea regime.

Competing situations thus arise. On one hand, when it comes to World Heritage Sites and ICH cultural spaces, corporate actors can be seen as putting pressure on communities, but using this pressure to potentially engage them directly in the management process. There are associated risks of community aspirations being co-opted by and translated into what serves corporate profit-maximization tools, and that is one reason why the state plays a vital role in balancing otherwise asymmetrical relationships. On the other hand, the posture of the UCHC with respect

171 Ibid., 83. 172 Ibid. 173 Paterson and Telesetsky (n 1) 550.
174 For details, see Affolder (n 169) 59–60. 175 Paterson and Telesetsky (n 1) 552.
176 Ibid., 560–1. 177 Bainton et al. (n 164) 94. 178 Ibid., 101.

to salvage, discussed above and in more detail in Chapter 5, places corporate actors in the same position as communities, as violating the principle of *in situ* preservation and endangering the archaeological integrity interests that are paramount in the UCHC.

In these scenarios, the 'community' can be seen as either part of the heritage management process, or as anathema to it. They can be the underserving locals from whom collectors rescue heritage, or the obstacles to development who try to defend the heritage they live around (and on which they often depend for their livelihoods). But who are 'communities', and what are the terms under which they are defined? What baggage does the process of defining communities carry, and how does it affect the prospects of community-based forms of heritage management? The next section explores these questions, and attempts to weave together the other subsections of this chapter that have defined the roles of multiple stakeholders vis-à-vis the elusive 'local community'.

3.5 Communities

Historically, heritage has always had a particular relationship with community, as a social gathering place, for instance, and in a way that helps distinguish cultural heritage from environmental conservation.[179] In fact, early engagements with the idea of community have been used to dislocate national politics in favour of some other stakeholder. In England, said stakeholder was the Church of England, which used its community as a proxy for humanity as a means to make claims for control over heritage uses (in that case, churches) going beyond what the English private law of property allowed.[180]

One of the big challenges with communities, of course, is how to define what a 'community' is, in a manner that is neither hegemonic nor allows for the perpetuation of inequalities within the group. Many of the same charges levelled at states apply here as well, as states are often criticized for speaking on behalf of specific elites, as opposed to representing dissonant voices. Likewise, a community's representative speaks on behalf of their own interests, or the interests of the community's governing forces, perpetuating the *status quo*. The alternative, to impose norms that would make communities more inclusive, begs the question: 'more inclusive in whose eyes?', and ends up with accusations of imposition of external hegemonic norms of conduct.

Because of the difficulties of understanding who the community is, and how its agency is operationalized, references to community involvement in international lawmaking and governance seem to be few and far between. And experts appear again almost by default, as a means to engage meaningfully with non-state actors,

[179] Miele, Chris, 'Heritage and its Communities: Reflections on the English Experience in the Nineteenth and Twentieth Centuries', in Melanie Hall (ed.), *Towards World Heritage: International Origins of the Preservation Movement 1870–1930* (Ashgate, 2011), 155–179, 155.

[180] Ibid., 177–8.

but still filtered in a way in which communities' views are represented 'objectively'. The problem, of course, as demonstrated by David Kennedy[181] among others, is that experts can abuse their own positions of authority, and perpetuate their own positions at the expense of the communities they should be representing.

Communities are given some nominal of voice or representation in international heritage law. Recent instruments like the ICHC explicitly mention the need for community involvement, and the WHC's Operational Guidelines have been amended to precisely promote more engagement from communities.

This type engagement is important, as it gives communities the chance to discuss heritage in their own terms, parallel to the state (even if it is still ultimately the state that has the prerogative to nominate heritage for safeguarding under these instruments). However, all of this engagement is still filtered by experts. And, as a result, heritage holders are treated first as objects, rather than subjects, with respect to their own heritage. They are informants about what heritage is and why it should be protected, but do not get to make the final decisions about those themes. In the process, they themselves become part of the heritage on whose behalf they speak. And, in the midst of this, the notion of community needs to be problematized further, if one is to take the possibilities for the exercising of community agency seriously, beyond treating communities as objects of protection.

Thinking of heritage beyond the expert, and driven by communities, is important in articulating the potentials of heritage in serving counter-hegemonic social movements. In a sense, heritage 'from without and from below' has a latent power that is seldom recognized or used.[182] This section examines some of those promises, framing them in the broader context of colonialism and relations that informs how we talk about heritage holders and communities in many instances as 'natives'.

One of the bigger challenges with involving communities in the management of their own heritage is to define who the community is. In the context of formerly colonized countries, 'community was a fundamental political institution within the European, and especially British, political systems'.[183] The colonial effects of defining communities are still felt today, as communities are still defined within this script of 'metropolitan normalcy', in which they are never fully autonomous subjects with agency, and their passivity cannot be broken unless a different script is presented.[184]

An alternative to defining the community within colonial contexts is to define it based on territoriality—connection to places.[185] This connection applies with

[181] Kennedy, David, 'Challenging Expert Rule: The Politics of Global Governance', *Sydney Law Review* 27 (2005), 5–28; and Kennedy, David, *A World of Struggle: How Power, Law and Expertise Shape Global Political Economy* (Princeton University Press, 2016).

[182] Robertson, Iain J. M., 'Introduction: Heritage from Below', in Iain J. M. Robertson (ed.), *Heritage from Below* (Ashgate, 2012), 1–27, 23.

[183] Kelly, John D. and Kaplan, Martha, *Represented Communities: Fiji and World Decolonization* (University of Chicago Press, 2001), 5.

[184] Ibid., 24.

[185] Droit, Roger-Pol, 'Lieux communs', in François Barret-Ducrocq (ed.), *Communauté* (Éditions UNESCO, 2006), 230–5, 231.

respect to Indigenous[186] and non-Indigenous[187] communities alike, but here I will explore the Indigenous connections in more detail.

In the Indigenous context, Irene Watson has argued that the 'colonial project now archives an historical narrative where Europe is the subject of sovereignty and non-Europe the object of sovereignty.'[188] Place and territory emerge as ways of contesting that framework, resisting the idea of Indigenous identity as 'contained within the representations of the exotic, the "primitive" '.[189] But a connection to place, if articulated outside Western paradigms of property, can promote agency by renewing relationships to land and identity.[190] Essentially, though, what seems to be most relevant is not necessarily place, but the potentials of place as a catalyst for rethinking the entire place of community agency in the legal system.

But even this connection to place can have the risk of replicating structures of domination, at least to the extent territory is often thought of as an attribute of statehood. If it can be separated from the state, however, and treated simply as a reference point, that can allow communities to congregate organically. But, even then, it is the territory that is the focal point, and arguably the community becomes an accessory to the territory. Also, as Waterton and Smith have suggested, the assumption that identity is embedded within sites makes non-experts passive. Consequently, '[t]his lack of a serious examination of precisely *how* identity is tied up with heritage likewise works to flatten out any involvement by non-expert individuals or groups in contemporary society'.[191] The dependence on territory can have negative impacts on the possibilities of community participation in heritage management.[192]

The promise of community involvement in heritage is to 'realign' the very concept of heritage, and to suggest that everyone is a heritage expert.[193] The presence of expertise in heritage is not at the origins of the field, if one considers the origins of archaeology in the nineteenth century in countries like England as the activity of amateurs, county societies who wanted to increase local interaction with their own heritage.[194]

In France, this move is connected to the Second World War occupation by collaboration with Nazi Germany (Vichy France). According to Florence Weber, reactions

[186] Watson, Irene, *Aboriginal Peoples, Colonialism and International Law: Raw Law* (Routledge, 2015).

[187] Waterton, Emma, 'Whose Sense of Place? Reconciling Archaeological Perspectives with Community Values: Cultural Landscapes in England', *International Journal of Heritage Studies* 11(4) (2005), 309–25.

[188] Watson (n 186) 7. [189] Ibid., 57. [190] Ibid., 14–15.

[191] Waterton, Emma and Smith, Laurajane, *Heritage, Communities and Archaeology* (Bristol Classical Press, 2009), 30.

[192] See generally Ubertazzi, Benedetta, 'The Territorial Condition for the Inscription of Elements on the UNESCO Lists of Intangible Cultural Heritage', in Nicolas Adell, Regina F. Bendix, Chiara Bortolotto, and Markus Tauschek (eds), *Between Imagined Communities and Communities of Practice: Participation, Territory and the Making of Heritage* (Universitätsverlag Göttingen, 2015), 111–22.

[193] Schofield, John, 'Heritage Expertise and the Everyday: Citizens and Authority in the Twenty-First Century', in John Schofield (ed.), *Who Needs Experts? Counter-mapping Cultural Heritage* (Ashgate, 2014), 1–11, 1–2.

[194] Henson, Don, 'The Academy and the Public', in Stephanie Koerner and Ian Russell (eds), *Unquiet Pasts: Risk Society, Lived Cultural Heritage, Re-designing Reflexivity* (Ashgate, 2010), 209–22, 210.

against the past of collaboration with Nazi Germany helped solidify 'folklore' as a scientific endeavour. The position adopted by Vichy France was one of close connection between folklore and political movements closely aligned to collaboration. As a means to push against that, a depoliticization of heritage was favoured.[195] The motives are somewhat different, but the rationale is the same: stripping heritage of its political value, and consequently shifting agency in the creation and protection of heritage away from political agents.

In the process of depoliticizing anthropology (which is an important field in thinking about heritage), 'postwar ethnology became resolutely antihistorical'. It also became sharply divided between anthropology and sociology, the latter looking at European modernity, and the former entrenching the 'exotic', the 'primitive', the 'native' as necessarily separate from the rest of society,[196] a division which still finds echoes today.[197] This division further allowed for the separation of heritage holders from their heritage, depriving them of their agency. The 'native' is separate from the 'civilized' world, and is thus an object of study, not a subject.

Similarly, Waterton and Smith have argued that there are three different phases to the discussion of community in the context of heritage, all of which map ostensibly sociological debates, but lack critical engagement with the notion of 'community'. This lack of critical engagement has resulted in the embedding and dissemination of a specific definition of community in heritage policy, one that assumes that the dominant 'we' (white and middle- or upper-class) are individuals, while 'they' have community (a notion that 'we' dropped on the way to modernity).[198]

Another consequence of that shift from politics to science domestically is that heritage became a site for class struggle, with experts representing educated middle-class elites, in contrast to, for instance, metal detectorists in the 1970s and 1980s representing uneducated, poorer segments of society.[199] A consequence of this translation of expert knowledge into class is to highlight the neglect of economics in heritage processes, and how expert rule in the heritage and other contexts is by and large a product of the aspirations of the 'haves', with little to no consideration for the interests of the 'have-nots'.

But expert interest can also be a driver of economic uses of heritage. For instance, in Salvador (capital of Bahia, a state in north-eastern Brazil, and also the first capital of Brazil during Portuguese colonization), tourism agencies were quick to use anthropological interest in Salvador as a means to develop new 'cultural tourism attractions' in the city.[200] But even those still cater to middle-class consumers, as

[195] Weber, Florence, 'Vichy France and the End of Scientific Folklore (1937–1954)', in Benoit de L'Estoile, Federico Neiburg, and Lygia Sigaud (eds), *Empires, Nations, and Natives: Anthropology and State-Making* (Duke University Press, 2005), 88–107.

[196] Ibid., 102.

[197] Fumaroli, Marc, 'Le Lien Culturel?', in François Barret-Ducrocq (ed.), *Communauté* (Éditions UNESCO, 2006), 33–9, 36–7.

[198] Waterton and Smith (n 191) 23–4.

[199] Henson (n 194) 212–13.

[200] de Magalhães, Marta, 'Exotic Objects, Uncanny Encounters: Anthropological Knowledge, Tourism and Challenges of Representing a World Heritage Site', in Stephanie Koerner and Ian Russell (eds), *Unquiet Pasts: Risk Society, Lived Cultural Heritage, Re-designing Reflexivity* (Ashgate, 2010), 223–37, 226.

opposed to the heritage holders themselves, and end up portraying authorized versions of the culture for tourism consumption.[201] Tourism will be explored in more detail in Chapter 5.

If the role of the heritage expert is to represent at a fundamental level the interests of heritage, as opposed to those of heritage holders or public opinion,[202] it is of course only natural that those mandate lenses will tint the work of the expert, who will then only engage with a community in a way that makes the heritage holder part of the heritage itself, and subordinates the heritage holder's identity and claims to those of heritage on whose behalf the expert still seems themselves as speaking.

> The phrase 'the public' compresses into one illusory entity a multiplicity of voices and silences, opinions, counter-opinions and non-opinions. It is evidently a function of the vagueness of the concept of 'public opinion' that it can be mobilised or ignored depending on what is required of it and by whom.[203]

Heritage's function of producing narratives and myths describing origins is a construct of Western scientific positivism.[204] As such, Western readings of heritage and why it is worth protecting limit the possible uses of heritage and squeeze heritage into a mould that requires a distance between observer and observed. In that sense, a specific function of thinking of heritage as contributing to a positivist world view is precisely to enshrine the heritage holder as object of heritage, as opposed to its narrator and agent. The expert is the narrator, the native is at best an informant incapable of connecting their own heritage to broader narratives of nationalism and cultural diversity that justify domestic and international legal protection of heritage.[205] This role of the expert as narrator suits particularly well the notion of heritage and tradition in many instances being invented precisely to pursue a broader national political agenda,[206] one that counter-hegemonic narratives around heritage coming from heritage holders themselves would not suit.

The English example considered earlier reminds us that the community to whom heritage belongs is not exclusive to Indigenous peoples, but a lot of the discussion in

[201] Collins, John, 'The Sounds of Tradition: Arbitrariness and Agency in a Brazilian Cultural Heritage Center', *Ethnos: Journal of Anthropology* 72(3) (2007), 383–407, 386.

[202] Burström, Mats, 'More than a Sensitive Ear: What to Expect of a Professional Expert', in John Schofield (ed), *Who Needs Experts? Counter-mapping Cultural Heritage* (Ashgate, 2014), 101–112, 103.

[203] O'Keeffe, Tadhg, 'Who Would Believe Experts? Interrogating the Discourses of Archaeologists and Interest Groups in Two Recent Heritage Disputes in Ireland', in John Schofield (ed.), *Who Needs Experts? Counter-mapping Cultural Heritage* (Ashgate, 2014), 113–32, 122.

[204] Ickerodt, Ulf, 'The Social and Political Significance of Prehistoric Archaeology in Modern and Post-modern Societies', in Stephanie Koerner and Ian Russell (eds), *Unquiet Pasts: Risk Society, Lived Cultural Heritage, Re-designing Reflexivity* (Ashgate, 2010), 81–98, 83.

[205] For a contrary view, see Geirmar, Haidy and Tilley, Christopher, 'Negotiating Materiality: International and Local Museum Practices at the Vanuatu Cultural Centre and National Museum', *Oceania* 73(3) (2003), 170–88, 184, who in particular suggests that

> museum processes of objectification may be seen to work in both ways: whilst people may be compared to the other museum material we have been examining in that they are given heightened meaning by being collected together as objectification of [customary practices], as personified 'resources' they are a vital part of the reproduction of social practice.

[206] See generally Hobsbawm, Eric, 'Introduction: Inventing Traditions', in Eric Hobsbawm and Terence Ranger (eds), *The Invention of Tradition* (Cambridge University Press, 1982), 1–14, 10.

this section focuses on Indigenous rights, as there are more debates around the native as object in the Indigenous context. But I would suggest that in non-Indigenous contexts, too, communities are often seen as objects. In the English case, local historical societies who initially made the push for heritage protection soon found themselves in the position of only being relevant if they were part of the professional, expert archaeologists' narrative of that place. Failing that, communities were more likely to be an obstacle to heritage protection than an agent in those processes.

Certain accounts of culture that use the heritage of vulnerable communities often frame the need for those accounts in terms of need for preserving a dying culture for the benefit of future generations. This rhetoric of benevolence, however well-intentioned, has the effect of perpetuating paternalistic attitudes of the majoritarian society. It also has the effect of deflecting debate away from harm that can be caused in other contexts (particularly with respect to the appropriation of and control over the meanings of the vulnerable community's culture).[207] In a sense thus experts, in pursuing their goal of documenting and cataloguing culture, can still engage in significant harm to culture when they objectify heritage holders and turn them into the heritage themselves. Experts also get to control that identity, by proclaiming the existence of 'authentic' manifestations of that identity, that cultural heritage.[208] Said risk exists even in a seemingly scientific and neutral way as listing heritage for protection and safeguarding.

Listing, in fact, seems to for the most part reinforce the objectification of heritage holders, as discussed in more detail in Chapter 7. To the extent heritage holders do not participate actively in the processes through which their heritage is recognized and safeguarded at the international level, they immediately become the 'object-seen', while the expert remains in the position of 'seeing-subject'. The heritage holder is constituted only within the limits of what the expert allows, which is also an act of judgement. And the subject–object relation is synonymous with the relation of dominant to subordinate. It is not a relationship distorted by power, but, '[r]ather, recognition is contiguous with the deployment of power'.[209] Similarly, invented tradition can also be a place where the colonial encounter is articulated, and particularly where modes of command by the colonizer are normalized, offering the colonized models of behaviour.[210]

Engagement between communities and experts can be beneficial, at least in theory, as long as it is based on long-term relationships in which, for instance, the community can influence the expert's research questions while at the same time the expert is helped in conducting their research. Further, experts need to be mindful

[207] Examining these tensions in the context of literature based on folk tales, see Wright, Nancy E. and Collins-Gearing, Brooke, 'The Rhetoric of Benevolence as an Impediment to the Protection of Indigenous Cultural Rights: A Study of Australian Literature and Law', *Journal of Australian Studies* 29(85) (2005), 57–68.

[208] Watson (n 186) 69. See also Lixinski, 'A Tale of Two Heritages' (n 29).

[209] Looking at these issues in the context of recognition politics, see Schaap, Andrew, 'Political Reconciliation Through a Struggle for Recognition', *Social & Legal Studies* 13(4) (2004), 523–40, 531.

[210] Ranger, Terence, 'The Invention of Tradition in Colonial Africa', in Eric Hobsbawm and Terence Ranger (eds), *The Invention of Tradition* (Cambridge University Press, 1982), 211–62, 212.

of the collateral phenomena in the environment in which they operate, influenced by and influencing the exercise of expertise.[211] In post-national international law-making more generally these collateral phenomena can usually be mapped by identifying the effects of specific legal initiatives on the background norms that are meant to support pluralism—do they, for instance, by promoting recognition also promote subordination of the community? Or do experts reinforce structural discrimination when treating communities as separate and exotic, or as Claude Lévi-Strauss's 'fragile flowers of difference'?

In some respects, making heritage governance's problems hinge on a dichotomy of 'expert v community' seems to background thinking of heritage as 'global v local', which is arguably where arguably concrete, practical, and context-dependent solutions to distributed global problems may lie.[212] And there is a sense in which the idea of a 'global society' is but the end goal of narratives of progress that are closely tied to the distinction between 'civilized' and 'uncivilized'.[213] But in large measure the expert is the authorized bridge between the global and the local, so it plays an important role in articulating solutions, unless we are to do away with the current system.

Surely, agency for cultural heritage can exist, as some jurisprudence in countries like India indicates. There, deities themselves have legal personality and standing to sue in cultural heritage cases.[214] And domestic law of India in this respect has been upheld in Canadian courts in a case involving a resource development project, on the basis of comity.[215] In that respect, heritage (intangible cultural heritage in particular) can potentially have intrinsic value,[216] and itself be considered a subject.[217] But, failing that, it is people (and 'peoples') with agency who must be the actors to whom we turn. Articulations of the role of peoples in international law, however, are limited, as John Morss shows.[218]

In the terms of colonial relations which permeate much of international law,[219] the 'native' resides in an unknowable past form, whereas the subject of legal relations,

[211] Walker (n 35) 196.

[212] Koerner, Stephanie, 'Contextualizing Contradictory Trends of Globalisation Risk Society', in Stephanie Koerner and Ian Russell (eds), *Unquiet Pasts: Risk Society, Lived Cultural Heritage, Re-designing Reflexivity* (Ashgate, 2010), 11–31, 13.

[213] Bowden, Brett, *The Empire of Civilization: The Evolution of an Imperial Idea* (The University of Chicago Press, 2014), 61.

[214] Paterson, Robert K., 'The "Curse of the London Nataraja"', *International Journal of Cultural Property* 5(2) (1996), 330–8.

[215] Ibid., 331.

[216] Godden, Lee, 'Preserving Natural Heritage: Nature as Other', *Melbourne University Law Review* 22 (1998), 719–42, 725.

[217] Hall, C. Michael, Mitchell, Ian, and Keelan, Ngawini, 'Maori Culture and Heritage Tourism in New Zealand', *Journal of Cultural Geography* 12(2) (1992), 115–28, 115–16.

[218] See generally Morss, John R., *International Law as the Law of Collectives: Toward a Law of People* (Ashgate, 2013).

[219] Anghie, Antony, *Imperialism, Sovereignty and the Making of International Law* (Cambridge University Press, 2007); Becker Lorca, Arnulf, *Mestizo International Law: A Global Intellectual History 1842–1933* (Cambridge University Press, 2014); Pahuja, Sundhya, *Decolonising International Law: Development, Economic Growth and the Politics of Universality* (Cambridge University Press, 2011).

with agency, seems to exist in 'an unknowable future formal ideal'.[220] And one must take heed of accounts suggesting that the idea of 'civilization' has not quite been abandoned, that 'the postcolonial moment . . . represent[s] more of a blip on history's radar screen (granted, a significant blip), than an altogether about-face or sea change in the nature of European/Western and Nonwestern relations'.[221]

Therefore, it would seem that colonialism and its persistent legacy is destined to make the 'native' an object. If the potentials of substate actors as agents of post-national lawmaking are really to be tapped into, then greater strides need to be made in the way we think of those actors, beyond subjecting them to the translating efforts of experts.

If the promise of communities governing their own heritage at the international level is to be fulfilled, communities need to be rethought beyond their currently limited potential role as informants in a limited context, and reconsidered as being polyvalent and multi-interested. Acknowledging the multiple interests that those actors have would require not filtering them at all. Expert filtering, after all, tends to pigeonhole interests and identity. And filtering through the state, which could potentially account for the multiplicity of interests, is at the root of why we are having this discussion to begin with.

The rethinking needed here is more fundamental than simply rejigging roles and allowing communities to the table as an add-on to current structures. Those current structures are prepared to subordinate communities, and will do so whenever they appear in lawmaking contexts. Perhaps a possibility is to downgrade experts to just another interested community, as opposed to stage managers. That parity could potentially open the field more widely to engagement by other non-state actors, whose interests would not need to be filtered by the expert in its stage manager role.

A possible avenue would be what Michel Callon and others have called 'dialogical democracy' through 'hybrid forums'.[222] These fora bring together experts, non-experts, laypersons (in the case of heritage, community cultural owners), and politicians in order to breach the bureaucratic divide between the expert and layperson poles, and to correct asymmetries between them. The non-expert groups can then rebalance the interests at stake and generate their own forms of knowledge that have a bearing in governance. Further, general principles are relativized and made case-sensitive, acknowledging and taking into account the needs of local communities. Cultural owners thus move from context to the background themselves, and have an active role in informing the decisions of the prince.

In that sense, one can see the abandonment of the idea of 'documentary' expertise in favour of one of 'participative' expertise. More specifically, expertise stops being a profession, and becomes a position that gives free course to the confrontation of

[220] Schaap (n 209) 536 (quoting Povinelli, Elizabeth A., 'The Cunning of Recognition: Real Being and Aboriginal Recognition in Settler Australia', *Australian Feminist Law Journal* 11 (1998), 3–27, 26).

[221] Bowden (n 213) 7.

[222] Callon, Michel, Lascounes, Pierre, Barthe, Yannick, and Burchell, Graham, *Acting in an Uncertain World: An Essay of Technical Democracy* (MIT Press, 2011). Discussed in Rodney Harrison, *Heritage: Critical Approaches* (Routledge, 2013), 223–5.

expertises, of expert vocabularies; in other words, the plural capabilities of speaking of something, thus engaging with dialogical democracy more fully.[223] Communities that participate in and live heritage become experts over those who document heritage.

This idea of 'dialogical democracy' is connected to that of 'participatory development', defined as involving local community actors in decisions about their development (including, in our case, decisions about heritage management, inasmuch as heritage can be seen as a vehicle for promoting development). But a critique of participatory development inspired by the work of Slavoj Žižek and articulated by Ilan Kapoor suggests that this model, to a large extent, still relies on expertise as a means to outline the 'rules of the game'. More specifically, experts are still responsible for determining the rules of participation; who gets to be a community, when communities get to speak, and in what contexts. It reflects to a large extent the experience of the ICHC, which nominally includes communities, but the actual rules drafted by experts on community participation in effect exclude local actors. Nonetheless, because the rules on their face call for community participation, they create a ' "feel good" community experience, but elide[] the behind-the-scenes stage management. [They] promote[] the sharing of power, but manage[] to centralize power by personalizing and mythologizing the role of the facilitator'.[224] In other words, even mediators are still in far too powerful a position, and affect governance in invisible yet very palpable ways. One set of experts needs to be checked by another set of experts. If communities are indeed elevated to the status of experts, as treaties like the Faro Convention[225] promise, there is a possibility to untangle and ameliorate some of these tensions.

This promise is complicated in the actual implementation of international heritage treaties, in part because of the reliance on states to make determinations at the international level about who the community is, and whether they have been sufficiently engaged in heritage management processes.[226] This point has been addressed elsewhere,[227] and will also be taken up in following chapters. For now, it is important to remark that, even disregarding the colonial baggage of 'community', or perhaps precisely because of it (seen as the colonizer having got to define community in order to serve the colonial enterprise, and within the bounds of statehood), communities are constrained in how their agency is exercised in international legal processes.

Nowhere is this colonial imprint more tangibly felt than with respect to Indigenous communities. While the objective of this book is to think about 'the community'

[223] Tornatore, Jean-Louis, 'Du patrimoine ethnologique au patrimoine culturel immatériel: suivre la voie politique de l'immatérialité culturelle', in Chiara Bortolotto (ed.), *Le patrimoine culturel immatériel* (Éditions de la Maison des sciences de l'homme 2011), 213–27, 226–7.

[224] Kapoor, Ilan, *The Postcolonial Politics of Development* (Routledge, 2008), 64.

[225] Framework Convention on the Value of Cultural Heritage for Society, Signed in Faro on 27 October 2005. Council of Europe, ETS No. 199. Entry into force: 1 June 2011.

[226] For a case study, see generally Aykan, Bahar, 'How Participatory is Participatory Heritage Management? The Politics of Safeguarding the Alevi *Semah* Ritual as Intangible Heritage', *International Journal of Cultural Property* 20 (2013), 381–405.

[227] Lixinski, *Intangible Cultural Heritage* (n 84).

more generally, some specific experiences regarding Indigenous communities merit being flagged. For instance, one of the few attempts to institutionalize community involvement in international heritage management has been through the World Heritage Indigenous Peoples Council of Experts (WHIPCOE),[228] an initiative taken in response to concerns about the lack of involvement of Indigenous peoples in the management of World Heritage sites internationally.[229] Here, like with other community-based initiatives, failure stemmed from colonial legacies and state sovereignty.[230]

One of the bureaucratic objections to WHIPCOE was that it would involve engaging a large number of 'unwieldy bureaucratic procedures, for an issue which only concerns a limited number of States Parties and which can be treated by other means'.[231] Even if this objection is deemed valid with respect to Indigenous peoples, it does not hold true with respect to communities in general, as every country would have local communities affected by a number of heritage management practices and laws. Therefore, in this instance, the focus on Indigenous peoples' special rights was used as an argument against community aspirations. This argument against translating 'community' as 'Indigenous community' is one of the reasons why this book does not focus solely on Indigenous communities. The ghettoization of communities is one of the strategic problems with promoting more community-based forms of governance over heritage, and needs to be combatted.[232]

But the Indigenous rights movement offers a number of lessons that can be useful for community-based heritage management. For instance, an important lesson from the Indigenous movement is that, historically, international standard-setting concerns about Indigenous peoples have often moved forwards without acknowledging the need for Indigenous participation in establishing rights pertaining to them (with the 2007 UN Declaration on the Rights of Indigenous Peoples a notable exception,[233] alongside the 2016 American Declaration on the Rights of Indigenous Peoples).[234] Another lesson draws from recent action around involving Indigenous peoples in participatory processes, which has been on the agenda of the UN Human Rights Council, which revived in some way the proposal for WHIPCOE, but even more broadly, by saying that UNESCO needed to create procedures to involved Indigenous communities directly in international decision-making.[235]

[228] On Indigenous involvement more generally, see Ahmed, Mohsen Al Attar, Aylwin, Nicole S., and Coombe, Rosemary J., 'Indigenous Cultural Heritage Rights in International Human Rights Law', in Catherine Bell and Robert Patterson (eds), *Protection of First Nations' Cultural Heritage: Laws, Policy and Reform* (University of British Columbia Press, 2009), 311–42.

[229] Meskell, Lynn, 'UNESCO and the Fate of the World Heritage Indigenous Peoples Council of Experts (WHIPCOE)', *International Journal of Cultural Property* 20 (2013), 155–74, 155.

[230] Ibid., 156. [231] Cited in ibid., 164.

[232] On strategic choices of the Indigenous rights movement in general, see Karen Engle, *The Elusive Promise of Indigenous Development: Rights, Culture, Strategy* (Duke University Press, 2010).

[233] Ahmed et al. (n 228) 315.

[234] American Declaration on the Rights of Indigenous Peoples (ADRIP), AG/RES. 2888 (XLVI-O/16) (Adopted at the third plenary session, held on 15 June 2016).

[235] See generally United Nations Human Rights Council, *Final report of the study on indigenous peoples and the right to participate in decision-making—Report of the Expert Mechanism on the Rights of Indigenous Peoples*, UN Doc. A/HRC/18/42, of 17 August 2011, para. 38.

Other opportunities for community engagement involve the requirement of prior and informed consent before a community's heritage is used internationally, a mechanism that is already being used in the broader context of access and benefit-sharing in the area of traditional knowledge and genetic resources,[236] and which also has specific potential for ICH.[237] In the area of traditional knowledge, access and benefit-sharing protocols have been successful in promoting community development (in spite of it not being a clear objective of the international treaty that serves as the foundation of these protocols), as well as overall conservation of natural resources (often with cultural significance for affected communities), bringing together corporate actors, states, experts, and communities.[238]

Appealing to the access and benefit-sharing mechanism shifts the legal form to safeguard heritage away from 'heritage' and 'property, towards 'contracts'. This shift, while contravening many of the foundations of the field, and somewhat unfamiliar in international legal spaces, presents novel possibilities of community control over heritage, which have been engaged in more detail in Chapter 2.

But is community-based governance over heritage the panacea it seems to be? As the discussion here has highlighted, the first major obstacle is defining the malleable and unfathomable 'community'. Further, a local community is not necessarily the only stakeholder in the safeguarding of heritage, particularly if we buy into a notion of heritage as a tool with multiple possible uses.

My point in this chapter (and in this book) is not to advocate for community-based governance as the answer to all of international heritage safeguarding's shortcomings. While I do argue that it is an important element in improving the international system, there are inevitable shortcomings. The chapters that follow will engage with the potentials and shortcomings of community participation in different contexts related to international heritage governance.

There is a multitude of stakeholders involved in the field of international heritage law. States, as the primary addressees of international treaties under UNESCO, constitute a central stakeholder, but one that is committed to relatively little in a system that is highly deferential to state sovereignty and allows the state to be the primary determinant in the potential uses of heritage.

The system is not a complete monopoly of states, though, and non-state actors are invited to the table. Those, however, are mostly expert organizations, and not communities directly. As a type of community in their own right, experts have specific interests and uses when it comes to heritage, and those do not necessarily align with the interests of the local communities for whom experts are meant to act as translators. As a result, experts alienate many heritage users from their rule, which is increasingly challenged.

Even museums challenge the rule of experts, and place themselves in the position of stewards of communities and of cosmopolitanism. Communities, however, are defined in fairly narrow terms, in a way that reinforces colonial imprints of

[236] For a recent overview and review of literature, see Robinson, Daniel F., *Biodiversity, Access and Benefit-Sharing: Global Case Studies* (Routledge, 2015), 29–44.

[237] See Lixinski, *Intangible Cultural Heritage* (n 84).

[238] Robinson (n 236) 176–7.

international heritage law. Domination also often happens when corporate actors get involved in heritage management and safeguarding.

The idea of 'community' is thus burdened with colonial legacies, and with asymmetrical conditions vis-à-vis other stakeholders, in spite of it being their heritage that is being used by everyone else, under the banners of cosmopolitanism, education, or economic development. The international system turns a blind eye to this exclusion (and, by doing so, in effect reinforces it). The chapters that follow will attempt to locate better ways in which communities can be directly involved in the international management of their own heritage. Property, discussed in Chapter 2, is one of these means, but other possibilities remain to be explored.

4

Temporalities of International Heritage Law

Heritage is a means to relay a society's relationship with its own past, be it a past that the people embrace, ignore, accept as is, or wish to change. Heritage helps us convey not a historical 'truth', but what a society wishes to tell themselves (and others) 'about what they forget, remember, memorialise and/or fake'.[1] But the way heritage tells the past is necessarily affected by certain contingencies of the moment when the past is told, as well as the contingencies of when heritage was created in that past and the present. As such, heritage simultaneously oscillates between negotiating the past in the present and also negotiating the present through the past. This understanding qualifies us to understand the historically contingent and embedded nature of heritage, and its role in the production of power, identity, and authority in any given society.[2] In other words, 'what counts as heritage changes all the time; it is no finished product pickled in amber but an ever-changing palimpsest'.[3]

This fluid relationship with time is incompatible with law and the conservation paradigm. As will be discussed here, sometimes the law freezes heritage in time, while at others culture is written out of the law and this exclusion creates a time freeze to other contexts, like in genocide. The relationship between genocide and culture is vital to the very definition of genocide. After all, culture necessarily binds together a group; more so than biology. Even if culture ultimately was excluded from the legal definition of genocide in the 1948 Convention,[4] it was always an important part of the debate. In fact, Raphael Lemkin came up with the notion of genocide having in mind the destruction of a group's cultural identity. Its biological destruction was the ultimate crime, to be sure, but the destruction of those elements that bind the group together, such as their religion, their language, their cultural achievements, were all part of the original definition of genocide that was ultimately negotiated out of the 1948 Convention.[5]

[1] Harvey, David C., 'Heritage Pasts and Heritage Presents: Temporality, Meaning and the Scope of Heritage Studies', *International Journal of Heritage Studies* 7(4) (2001), 319–38, 320.

[2] Ibid., 321.

[3] Lowenthal, David, 'Why Sanctions Seldom Work: Reflections on Cultural Property Internationalism', *International Journal of Cultural Property* 12 (2005), 393–423, 395.

[4] Convention on the Prevention and Punishment of the Crime of Genocide (adopted 9 December 1948, entry into force 12 January 1951), 78 UNTS 277.

[5] For an account, see Novic, Elisa, *The Concept of Cultural Genocide: An International Law Perspective* (Oxford University Press, 2016); Bevan, Robert, *The Destruction of Memory: Architecture at War* (Reaktion Books, 2nd edn, 2016); Vrdoljak, Ana Filipa, *International Law, Museums, and the Return of Cultural Objects* (Cambridge University Press, 2006); and Vrdoljak, Ana Filipa, 'Genocide and Restitution: Ensuring Each Group's Contribution to Humanity', *European Journal of International*

The law of genocide's relationship with cultural heritage is a good way to think through international heritage law's relationship with time because, first, it helps move us beyond time as being primarily about definitional issues (as discussed in Chapter 2). Second, it shows how culture can contribute to thinking about international norms as needing to operate across temporal boundaries, and that culture can hold the key to that engagement. Third, it helps revisit a time at which culture and biology were connected at least as an idea, even if the law ultimately created a split. Finally, it assists in thinking about heritage practices under the conservation paradigm and their potential for dramatic effect, especially if the law turns a blind eye to these potentials by excluding certain relationships as belonging to a different temporal framework. Fixed temporalities harm communities by privileging claims staked by states and the rise of expert rule in the twentieth century, ignoring ongoing past relationships with heritage. They also freeze relations in time, whereas communities' engagement changes over time. Conversely, fixed temporalities create blind spots that prevent the law from playing a role in genocide prevention, thus also having exclusionary effects with negative consequences.

Recent developments in international criminal law, particularly in the jurisprudence of the International Criminal Tribunal for the former Yugoslavia (ICTY) and the International Criminal Court (the latter discussed in Chapter 7), have brought back to the fore the importance of thinking about cultural heritage in the context of ethnic conflicts. The shelling of Dubrovnik, among other acts against cultural heritage, was seen as informing the intent for international crimes,[6] and its destruction was intentional because of the town's recognizability to the outside world.[7] The ICTY in general engaged with destruction of heritage as evidence of criminal intent, but not a method of these crimes,[8] which is different from Lemkin's intentions in defining the cultural elements of genocide.[9] So, while culture did not all of a sudden trump the biological contours of the legal definition of genocide, it at least added some nuance to understanding what drives crimes like genocide, and the role that culture plays in making a group identifiable.

Despite this omission from the law, and only small incremental regaining of the connection between culture and the criminal act, in fact there is much that can be said about this connection's relevance in the field of genocide studies. The literature on genocide studies, particularly anthropological interventions in the field, has successfully established time and again that culture is an important factor to be taken into account when trying to predict, mitigate, understand, or even overcome the atrocity of genocide if it ultimately happens. Acts of genocide, unfortunately, can

Law 22(1) (2011) 17–47, 29–30. Also for an account, and advocating the inclusion of cultural genocide in the international legal definition, see Starrenburg, Sophie H., 'Effectively Protecting Cultural Heritage: Incorporating Cultural Genocide into the International Legal Definition of Genocide', BA thesis (Leiden University, 2014).

6 As discussed by Vrdoljak, 'Genocide and Restitution' (n 5) 36–9; and Vrdoljak, Ana Filipa (January 2009), 'Cultural Heritage in Human Rights and Humanitarian Law', working paper available at <http://works.bepress.com/ana_filipa_vrdoljak/15> (accessed 29 October 2017), 47–9.

7 Bevan (n 5) 116. 8 Ibid., 12. 9 Novic (n 5) 4.

contribute to the formation of national identity, determining the boundaries of who is and is not part of a people within the boundaries of a country.[10]

The relationship between genocide and national identity, and thereby heritage, helps highlight the need to better understand how (international) heritage law operates in shaping identities over time, and, specifically with respect to mass atrocity and international criminal law (a matter revisited in Chapter 7), the role that heritage law has had in creating the conditions leading to atrocity, but also its potential for post-atrocity transformation. The latter is particularly relevant in that it opens international heritage law up to a more aware engagement with the politics it has helped create, even if only by its silence. To highlight the responsibility of international heritage law in this context thus underscores the fact that, whereas heritage can have a more fluid relationship with time, the law cannot. International heritage law being caught in between, it ultimately defers to certain fixed understandings of time that are incompatible with heritage's nature, and end up affecting a certain set of practices surrounding heritage that align with the scientific and apolitical conservation paradigm, to the detriment of heritage's status as living culture.

Even if my intervention in this book is on the system of international heritage law and its relationship to communities' control over their heritage, this chapter may also be seen as contributing to the growing field of genocide studies with respect to culture—but with a twist. While taking on board the literature on the connection between genocide and culture, I wish to take it a step further, and frame those ideas in the context of culture that is institutionalized, normalized, and in many ways authorized. More specifically, I wish to look at the ways in which heritage law, policy, and practices can influence our understanding of the causes of genocide. I show that heritage law, policy, and practice can comprise an important element in understanding the temporalities of atrocities with an ethnic component, of which genocide is the most gruesome. And I argue that human rights approaches to heritage safeguarding, inasmuch as they represent community involvement in heritage management, can help navigate these temporalities in a way that can mitigate tensions before genocide happens, or allow for more constructive engagements with heritage in the aftermath of tragedy (even if there are downsides).

In order to support the claim, what follows looks the relationship between international heritage law and time, as a means to set up the broader problems with temporalities in this area. Next, I look at the interaction among cultural heritage law, policy, and practice at three different moments of genocide: before, during, and after. I use different case studies to highlight each of those moments, all the while mapping out events that, when framed at an abstract level, can help our understanding of the connection between genocide and cultural heritage. Some of these case studies spill across different moments, underscoring the fluidity of heritage's relationship with time. After the discussion of these three moments, I examine the potentials of a human rights approach to heritage law and management as a means to defuse a lot of the negative potential uses of heritage law, since a human rights

[10] O'Neill, Kevin Lewis, 'Anthropology and Genocide', in Donald Bloxham and A. Dirk Moses (eds), *The Oxford Handbook of Genocide Studies* (Oxford University Press, 2010), 182–96, 185.

approach to heritage can be used to engage different substate groups as a vital part of how heritage is understood, appreciated, used, and safeguarded, in spite of enforceability problems, the discussion of which falls outside the scope of this book.

4.1 International Heritage Law and Time

As indicated above, heritage and time are connected, as heritage is a story we tell in the present about the past, and project it onto the future. However, such a fluid relationship between heritage and time is not allowed by international heritage law. UNESCO was created only after the Second World War, and it has since engaged in prolific standard-setting activity in the field of culture in general, and cultural heritage in particular. One result of this activity is wider international protection of cultural heritage, which is for the most part positive. But every bright side casts a shadow, as discussed in Chapter 8, which in this case is that heritage seems to be portrayed today as the product of events that only happened from the middle of the twentieth century onwards.[11] For our present purposes, it means that heritage's role in shaping identity and power in events prior to the creation of UNESCO is largely ignored, and those statements about power and authority are taken for granted, as unaltered historical narratives.[12]

Another consequence of the creation of UNESCO and its standard-setting activity has to do with the nature of international law, and particularly international treaties. It is a rule of international law that treaties do not retroact, unless they explicitly indicate so.[13] As such, the new order of heritage only applies to heritage's existence after the treaty enters into force. The law cannot be a tool to renegotiate the meanings and uses of heritage in the past; it can only really impact on the status quo at the moment the law enters into force. That is not to say that the law cannot change that meaning at all, but it must do so using legal categories that are only forward-looking, and that engage with the past in at best rudimentary and secondary ways. Consequently, the past becomes a sacred, pure truth against which heritage is tested, as opposed to being itself a contingent phenomenon. The power relationships of the past become established truths that can certify or deny the value of heritage, instead of being themselves fluid concepts that have often created, recreated, and eliminated heritage. This relationship with time is also consistent with the conservation paradigm discussed in Chapter 1, and reinforces the disconnect between law and non-law also discussed in Chapter 1.

[11] Harvey (n 1) 325. [12] Ibid., 325.

[13] See for instance the Vienna Convention on the Law of Treaties (adopted 23 May 1969, entry into force 27 January 1980) 1155 UNTS 331 (VCLT):

> Article 28. Non-retroactivity of treaties. Unless a different intention appears from the treaty or is otherwise established, its provisions do not bind a party in relation to any act or fact which took place or any situation which ceased to exist before the date of the entry into force of the treaty with respect to that party.

While this provision does not apply directly to a number of UNESCO treaties (concluded before the entry into force of the Vienna Convention), it applies as a matter of customary international law.

A 1997 UNESCO 'Declaration on the Responsibilities of the Present Generations Towards Future Generations'[14] engages with the way the present relates to the future in important ways for our purposes, given its source. In this Declaration, UNESCO reaffirms the importance of international human rights instruments to understanding the rights of future generations,[15] as well as the key role of environmental instruments.[16] The World Heritage Convention (WHC) is one of these environmental instruments and is the only heritage treaty explicitly mentioned in the Declaration (which was adopted before the Intangible Cultural Heritage Convention—ICHC), which may speak to the connections between heritage and environment being stronger than usually admitted, as discussed in Chapter 6.

The Declaration focuses on the relationship between the present and the future, not mentioning the role of the past. While that choice is understandable, it also sits uneasily with heritage, as discussed earlier. For instance, the one provision in the Declaration that makes explicit reference to the role of heritage is restricted to urging recognition of the responsibility for the identification and safeguarding of heritage, taking for granted that heritage will play a positive role for future generations, and not engaging with its role in shaping the present through its past.[17] Therefore, in an instrument that tackles temporalities head on, UNESCO steers away from engagement with the past, and focuses instead on the present and future. But, in doing so,

[14] Declaration on the Responsibilities of the Present Generations Towards Future Generations (12 November 1997).

[15] Preamble:

> Considering the provisions of the International Covenant on Economic, Social and Cultural Rights and the International Covenant on Civil and Political Rights, both adopted on 16 December 1966, and the Convention on the Rights of the Child, adopted on 20 November 1989, ... [and] Stressing that full respect for human rights and ideals of democracy constitute an essential basis for the protection of the needs and interests of future generations.

See also:

> Article 2—Freedom of choice. It is important to make every effort to ensure, with due regard to human rights and fundamental freedoms, that future as well as present generations enjoy full freedom of choice as to their political, economic and social systems and are able to preserve their cultural and religious diversity.

[16] Preamble:

> Recalling that the responsibilities of the present generations towards future generations have already been referred to in various instruments such as the Convention for the Protection of the World Cultural and Natural Heritage, adopted by the General Conference of UNESCO on 16 November 1972, the United Nations Framework Convention on Climate Change and the Convention on Biological Diversity, adopted in Rio de Janeiro on 5 June 1992, the Rio Declaration on Environment and Development, adopted by the United Nations Conference on Environment and Development on 14 June 1992, the Vienna Declaration and Programme of Action, adopted by the World Conference on Human Rights on 25 June 1993, and the United Nations General Assembly resolutions relating to the protection of the global climate for present and future generations adopted since 1990.

[17] See:

> Article 7—Cultural diversity and cultural heritage. With due respect for human rights and fundamental freedoms, the present generations should take care to preserve the cultural diversity of humankind. The present generations have the responsibility to identify, protect and safeguard the tangible and intangible cultural heritage and to transmit this common heritage to future generations.

it also ignores the contingencies that determine the present, and consequently the future.

With respect to specific UNESCO standard-setting in the area of heritage, the drafters of the 1970 UNESCO Convention on Cultural Objects[18] initially wanted an instrument that could promote the return of cultural objects to their countries of origin. More specifically, the newly decolonized countries that pushed for and produced the initial draft of this instrument wanted their heritage, their cultural artefacts, returned. They wanted to use heritage as a means to contest the power relationships that were created and made possible by colonialism. But this proposal was defeated by the former colonial powers at the negotiating table. Thus, the treaty that was ultimately approved is very explicit in that it does not apply to situations that happened before the treaty's entry into force.[19] Thus, colonialism and its history are on some level legitimized by the law, which does not allow heritage to be used as a means to contest said history, and its power relationships. The law protects and enshrines colonialism through heritage, alongside its identities and power relations.[20] The main effect on communities is to undermine the practice, discussed in Chapter 2, which uses the terms of the 1970 Convention to try and promote the repatriation of cultural objects in favour of Indigenous communities.

Finally, heritage is often defined by the law as necessarily being of a certain age. That can be an actual age requirement, such as 100 years for furniture or certain antiquities under the 1970 Convention,[21] or 100 years underwater for the Underwater Cultural Heritage Convention,[22] as further discussed in Chapter 2. Or it can simply mean that many legal definitions of heritage require it to be intergenerational, or that it is of importance for future generations of a given group, such as the ICHC's definition of intangible heritage as being 'transmitted from generation to generation'.[23] But the processes through which heritage is recognized and authorized by these instruments seem to create this one-way relationship with time, in which heritage is (re)created by the act of international safeguarding. For instance, the WHC, which is the flagship instrument of UNESCO in this realm, only speaks of heritage's importance for future generations.[24] The contingencies of heritage at the moment the tradition was created seem to be ignored, if they have happened before the relevant international instrument became applicable (which happens nearly

[18] Convention on the Means of Prohibiting and Preventing the Illicit Import, Export and Transfer of Ownership of Cultural Property 1970 (adopted 14 November 1970, entered into force 24 April 1972) 823 UNTS 231 (1970 Convention).

[19] See for instance Article 7, which repeatedly refers to the application of the Convention only to situations that happen 'after the entry into force of this Convention'.

[20] For additional discussion of this matter, see particularly Vrdoljak, *International Law, Museums, and the Return of Cultural Objects* (n 5).

[21] Article 1(k) for furniture, and Article 1(e) for other collections.

[22] Convention on the Protection of the Underwater Cultural Heritage 2001 (adopted 2 November 2001, entered into force 2 January 2009) 2562 UNTS 3 (UCHC). Article 1.1.a.

[23] Convention for Safeguarding of the Intangible Cultural Heritage 2003 (adopted 17 October 2003, entered into force 20 April 2006) 2368 UNTS 3 (ICHC). Article 2.1.

[24] Convention concerning the Protection of the World Cultural and Natural Heritage 1972 (adopted 23 November 1972, entered into force 15 December 1975) 1037 UNTS 151 (WHC). Article 4.

always, given the relative newness of these instruments, which have not been around for more than one or two generations).

International heritage treaties end up reinforcing a certain view of heritage that freezes it in time, in a way akin to some of the effects of property law that the move to heritage was meant to avoid, as discussed in Chapter 2. But, in freezing heritage, and particularly doing so in the name of state sovereignty (as argued in Chapter 2), international heritage law can get in the way of one of its main objectives. As Lowenthal has argued:

> Self-regarding chauvinism is perhaps now more than ever a potent and stubborn impediment to global sharing. National and local self-esteem are sacred writ in UNEESCO and other cultural [heritage] protocols. Equating heritage with identity justifies every group's claim to the bones, the belongings, the riddles, and the refuse of every forebear back into the mists of time. All that stands in the way of everyone's reunion with all their ancestors and ancestral things is its utter impossibility. [. . .] It is impossible because the essentialist credo that fosters these claims flies in the face of historical reality. There are no well-attested, or long-enduring, or pure, or unchanged social or cultural entities.[25]

Therefore, the relationships between heritage law and time do not seem to help resolve broader tensions between heritage and time. If anything, they reinforce the strains, and make the words of Tunbridge and Ashworth ring true when they refer to heritage practices as 'the present select[ing] an inheritance from an imagined past for current use and decid[ing] what should be passed on to an imagined future'.[26] That the law is not attuned to this malleable connection with time has the effect of not only limiting its reach, but also alienating stakeholders closest to heritage, namely, communities.

Bearing in mind this fraught relationship between heritage (practices and law) and time, the following sections discuss the possible relationships between heritage at the different moments of genocide, and whether, even within the limited temporalities of the law, international heritage law can have any impact on genocide in its prevention, perpetration, and overcoming its effects.

4.2 Before: Heritage Practices as an Instigator of Ethnic Schisms

Cultural heritage shapes identity, and as such it can not only create the identity of a community in its own terms, but it can also create a community in opposition to a real or imagined 'other'. Cultural heritage and national identity have long been linked as a matter of practice (through archaeology), and even in the law. The 1970 Convention, for instance, focuses on the heritage of nation-states, and recognizes cultural heritage as 'one of the basic elements of civilization and national culture'.[27]

[25] Lowenthal (n 3) 405.
[26] J. E. Tunbridge and G. J. Ashworth, *Dissonant Heritage*, p. 6. Cited in Harvey (n 1) 324.
[27] Preamble.

The connection between heritage practices and nationalisms has existed for a long time. Heritage has been manipulated politically to promote certain founding myths of different nations or peoples, particularly along ethnic lines.[28] While this connection has often been used to promote independence from colonialism, it has also often been used in ways that create or nurture ideas about racial superiority, as a means to justify domination or even genocide. Memories and historical representation become a form of hate speech, one that creates divisive memories around a ruling elite, and at the expense of another group.[29]

But this connection to nationalism is not necessarily meant, in the law, to be divisive. After all, UNESCO was created with the idea of promoting lasting peace, and one of the ways in which this can be accomplished is by promoting cultural exchange and understanding the cultures of other peoples.[30] Further, the same 1970 Convention says that states have obligations with respect to not only their own heritage, but that of all nations.[31] One of the problems, of course, is that the text of the 1970 Convention, because it was pushed by decolonizing nations, is unclear in that respect. But, for the most part, it would be difficult today to make a claim for international heritage law allowing the creation of this type of divisiveness. Nevertheless, there have been past instances of just such use.

The quintessential example is interwar Germany. In that Germany, two categories of action can be observed: one is the manipulation of the discipline of archaeology to create the myth of the Aryan super-human, of noble, Nordic origin; the second type of action is the direct destruction of the heritage of the other. That first myth helped create German nationalism, but it did not by itself entirely justify the annihilation of the Jewish race. More was done to reinforce the impure and undesirable 'other', particularly the Jewish other, and that was the official labelling of Jewish art under the Reich as 'degenerate'.

On the first instance, Bettina Arnold and Henning Hassmann have characterized archaeology in a post-Second World War Germany trying to come to terms with that past as the result of a Faustian bargain. Their analysis in particular points to the state of archaeology, and the uses of heritage practice, in Nazi Germany. As universities were purged, the Nazi leadership not only removed from departments figures who were not sympathetic to their cause, but also boosted the field of archaeology. Also, as the war ended, many young thinkers had been lost to war, or to post-war economic conditions, and German universities had been occupied by the Allies. As a result, theoretical developments in the US and UK were largely

[28] For a collection of essays, see Kohl, Philip L. and Fawcett, Clare (eds), *Nationalism, Politics, and the Practice of Archaeology* (Cambridge University Press, 1995).

[29] Musi, Maja, 'The International Heritage Doctrine and the Management of heRitage in Sarajevo, Bosnia and Herzegovina: The Case of the Commission to Preserve National Monuments', *International Journal of Heritage Studies* 20(1) (2014), 54–71, 58. See also Lowenthal, David, *The Heritage Crusade and the Spoils of History* (Cambridge University Press, 1998).

[30] Constitution of the United Nations Educational, Scientific and Cultural Organization (UNESCO) (adopted 16 November 1945, entered into force 4 November 1946) 4 UNTS 275 (UNESCO Constitution), Preamble.

[31] Preamble.

resisted as occupation acts themselves, particularly the notion that archaeology should seek to establish universal laws of human behaviour; rather, the impulse for classification of classic German archaeology prevailed, one that privileged difference rather than commonality.[32] The work of Gustav Kossinna was particularly influential in establishing the idea of 'cultural provinces', and weaving a narrative of Germany as a nation descended from a superior, Nordic race.[33] This type of research was tapped into by the Nazi propaganda machine, particularly with respect to the use of runes, of which the swastika is perhaps the most enduring example.[34] Historic preservation more generally in Nazi Germany adopted aesthetic principles that were tied to cleanliness, health, and a moral and racial purity of the national community. Historic preservation was therefore inherently political, and helped produce and maintain Nazi ideology.[35]

Similarly, during the Second World War Germany engaged in a process of cleansing of art and culture. In many respects, *Kristallnacht*—the concerted destruction of Jewish-owned businesses—was a precursor to these events, and a proto-genocidal act.[36] The ensuing purge of art and culture included Germany 'stealing back' artefacts that had been taken from Germany during previous wars (most notably the Napoleonic wars), either as loot or war compensation.[37] It also included the policies on 'degenerate art', in which all art and cultural objects that did not fit the criteria of 'German-ness' or enhance the new foundational myth of the Reich was to be disposed of (but not always destroyed; many of these items were sold at auction around Europe and the US and financed the Nazi State's war efforts).[38]

All of those acts were legitimized by German law at the time, and there was in fact a systematic legal effort, documented by Lemkin, to discriminate, segregate, and eventually eliminate a people and its culture.[39] These acts could have been read as an omen of things to come, at least to the extent that the laws on degenerate art in particular created an inferior cultural 'other' that needed to be expunged. Thus one of the first genocides in history officially labelled as such was perpetrated.

The United Nations in 2014 published a 'Framework of Analysis for Atrocity Crimes'.[40] This tool outlines a number of risk factors that must be taken into

[32] Arnold, Bettina and Hassmann, Henning, 'Archaeology in Nazi Germany: The Legacy of the Faustian Bargain', in Philip L. Kohl and Clare Fawcett (eds), *Nationalism, Politics, and the Practice of Archaeology* (Cambridge University Press, 1995), 70–81, at 70–1. See also Arnold, Bettina, 'Justifying Genocide: Archaeology and the Construction of Difference', in Alex Laban Hinton (ed.), *Annihilating Difference: The Anthropology of Genocide* (University of California Press, 2002), 95–116.

[33] Arnold and Hassmann (n 32) 71–2.

[34] Ibid., 77.

[35] Hagen, Joshua, 'Historic Preservation in Nazi Germany: Practices, Patterns, and Politics', in Glenn Hooper (ed.), *Heritage at the Interface: Interpretation and Identity* (University Press of Florida, 2018) 56–71, at 69–70.

[36] Bevan (n 5) 18.

[37] Nicholas, Lynn H., *The Rape of Europa: The Fate of Europe's Treasures in the Third Reich and the Second World War* (Vintage Books, 1995), 121. Also, on how the restitution of taken artefacts can be seen as a form of restoration of a people's dignity, and specifically reparations for genocide, see Vrdoljak, 'Genocide and Restitution' (n 5).

[38] Nicholas (n 37) 7–25.

[39] Novic (n 5) 18.

[40] United Nations, *Framework of Analysis for Atrocity Crimes: A Tool for Prevention* (2014).

account when mass atrocities (understood as genocide, crimes against humanity, and war crimes) are about to happen. Among those risk factors, growing nationalist movements is often highlighted as a common risk factor for mass atrocities,[41] as are ideologies based on the supremacy of a specific identity, or extremist versions of identity.[42] Heritage law and practice that fosters nationalism falls under this category, particularly as it connects to violation of cultural rights (such as the right of access to, and enjoyment of, cultural heritage).[43] Specifically, another risk factor is the enactment of legislation that discriminates against specific groups (such as the legislation on degenerate art), as well as the destruction or plundering of property connected to a group's cultural or religious identity.[44] The commemoration of events that glorify past atrocity is also a risk factor,[45] and is connected to intangible heritage in the aftermath of atrocity (to be discussed later). The destruction of heritage, like in the drafting of the Genocide Convention, is seen as a precursor to the physical elimination of a group.[46]

So, even though international heritage law itself seems no longer to support the idea of heritage being used to create division, that may still be possible, if one takes the connection between heritage and identity to mean a connection between heritage and *national* identity. As it stands, because international law still largely depends on the nation-state for much of its functioning, and considers it to largely be its basic unit of operation (as discussed in Chapters 1 and 3), there is a lingering risk that nationalism could be pursued again due to the lack of clarity in international law. So domestic practices and law can still create divisiveness, and not be subject to the necessary scrutiny, as they will be on the surface still complying with international heritage law. A stronger set of rules is needed to scrutinize domestic practice in a way that is more broadly consistent with thinking of heritage as creating harmony, rather than division. The risk factors prepared by the United Nations can be useful guidelines in this context.

In relation to communities, the analysis in this section reminds us that the state can use heritage law to create a nation that excludes and dehumanizes certain communities, while imagining others altogether. That communities themselves have no say in how heritage is authorized by the law renders them easy prey to these malicious uses of the law. Were their roles recognized, heritage would not be so easily manipulated.

4.3 During: Heritage Practices as a Means to Propel Genocidal Acts

Part of the justification for genocide during conflict is the idea of bringing a certain people into modernity, turning genocide into largely a project of social

[41] Ibid., 10. [42] Ibid., 13.

[43] Ibid., 11. On the connection between cultural rights and cultural heritage, see Committee on Economic, Social and Cultural Rights, *General comment No. 21—Right of everyone to take part in cultural life (Art. 15, para. 1(a), of the International Covenant on Economic, Social and Cultural Rights).* UN Doc. E/C.12/GC/21, of 21 December 2009.

[44] UN Framework of Analysis (n 40) 16. [45] Ibid., 17. [46] Novic (n 5) 26.

engineering.[47] This kind of justification already existed before and during the Holocaust in the Second World War, and it remained present in other instances of genocide through history. That is the kind of narrative articulated in the context of Indigenous peoples, and it also applies largely to what happened in Cambodia.

In Cambodia, it was not so much the law, but practices around heritage that were used during the genocide. More specifically, music, song, and dance were used to invent a tradition of progress of a renewed Khmer identity, among other practices.[48] Built heritage, particularly Angkor Wat, was ostensibly preserved, as it stood as a symbol of a glorified past civilization that was aspirational for the future of Cambodia, but also temporally distinctive from the present civilization that needed rebuilding (or, failing that, erasure).[49] At work sites, Cambodians were inundated with revolutionary arts, and they were used as a means of indoctrination.[50] These practices aimed, among other things, at demonizing foreigners and non-Khmer ethnic groups in order to revive the ancient glory of the Khmer Empire and race.[51]

This type of behaviour conforms to Cambodian heritage law at the time, too. By virtue of a 1956 agreement between Cambodia and France, the management of archaeological heritage was largely delegated to French institutions, who employed a specific scientific approach to heritage, and in many ways used it to preserve a Khmer identity they had created during French colonization of the country. Specifically, this agreement gave France the prerogative to administer Cambodian heritage, with the exception of religious buildings in use, and certain tombs.[52] This agreement was to be interpreted in a way that made it consistent with Buddhist customs. As the Khmer Rouge advanced, and (Buddhist) religion was pushed aside as impure,[53] the framework crumbled, but even if it had stood France was not to be involved, as the practices Khmer Rouge engaged in were living heritage and as such were excluded from the relevant agreements. Cultural heritage, particularly archaeological artefacts, also played an important role in the transition *from* the Khmer regime. For instance, the 1992 transitional law specifically discusses criminal penalties applicable to looting of cultural artefacts in a general piece of criminal legislation that contains only a handful of crimes.[54] The Extraordinary Chambers in the Courts of Cambodia, charged with international criminal accountability as a transitional

[47] Hinton, Alexander Laban, 'The Dark Side of Modernity: Toward and Anthropology of Genocide', in Alexander Laban Hinton (ed.), *Annihilating Difference: The Anthropology of Genocide* (University of California Press, 2002), 1–40, 10–13.

[48] Ibid., 19. [49] Bevan (n 5) 160.

[50] Shapiro-Phim, Toni, 'Dance, Music, and the Nature of Terror in Democratic Kampuchea', in Alexander Laban Hinton (ed.), *Annihilating Difference: The Anthropology of Genocide* (University of California Press, 2002), 179–93.

[51] Arnold, 'Justifying Genocide' (n 32) 109.

[52] Bilateral Agreement between Cambodia and France concerning the regime applicable to archaeological finds in the former state (1956), Art. 4, among others.

[53] Hinton (n 47) 19.

[54] Provisions Relating to the Judiciary and Criminal Law and Procedure Applicable in Cambodia During the Transitional Period (1992), Art. 44.

justice mechanism in Cambodia, also has heritage under its jurisdiction, even if this competence has not been used.[55]

Particularly with respect to the applicable international law, the 1954 Hague Convention applies to what happens during the conduct of conflict.[56] As genocide often happens as part of a broader situation of war, this treaty can be applicable, even if it only refers to monuments and sites.[57] During the drafting of this instrument, it was highlighted that the prosecution of war crimes and genocide is important for the protection of cultural heritage.[58] Legal categories are often created with a specific past event in mind,[59] and, in this case, the actions of Nazi Germany were the main engine behind this instrument.

That the Hague Convention refers only to physical heritage would seem to be inconsistent with the history around it, and also with current understandings of cultural heritage. As Ana Vrdoljak has documented, the United Nations War Crimes Commission, even prior to the 1954 Hague Convention, had already discussed the applicable international humanitarian law rules as referring not only to the objects and sites themselves, but also the intangible heritage associated with their use.[60] Therefore, the intangible values of heritage sites are every bit as important in thinking about their uses in situations of atrocity.

One of the important distinctions when thinking about the applicability of this regime to ethnic conflicts comes in the determination of the importance of the heritage. Some commentators read the language on 'importance' of the cultural heritage as meaning importance to a group, regardless of whether it is represented by the state. Others, however, take a more conservative approach, and read the regime as being applicable only to heritage that the state deems of importance.[61] Therefore, in ethnic conflict and genocide within ethnic conflict, the heritage of the minority group can be pushed aside and not be subject to legal protection, as it is unlikely to be deemed of importance by the state perpetrating the genocide. Communities are again at a disadvantage if they challenge the territorial state, and the law at the very least turns a blind eye to this type of situation (at worst, the law effectively condones the situation).

The example of Cambodia also highlights a limitation of international heritage law's relationship with time. Because heritage is defined as either of a specific age, or intergenerational (as discussed above), international law has no effect on invented

[55] I am thankful to Sarah Williams for this insight.

[56] Convention for the Protection of Cultural Property in the Event of Armed Conflict with Regulations for the Execution of the Convention 1954 (adopted 14 May 1954, entered into force 7 August 1956) 249 UNTS 240 (1954 Hague Convention).

[57] But on intangible cultural heritage and armed conflict, see Chainoglou, Kalliopi, 'The Protection of Intangible Cultural Heritage in Armed Conflict: Dissolving the Boundaries Between the Existing Legal Regimes?', *Santander Art and Culture Law Review* 2/2017(3) (2017), 109–34.

[58] Cited by Vrdoljak, 'Genocide and Restitution' (n 5) 32.

[59] Bowen, John R., 'Culture, Genocide, and a Public Anthropology', in Alex Laban Hinton (ed.), *Annihilating Difference: The Anthropology of Genocide* (University of California Press, 2002), 382–96, 389.

[60] Vrdoljak, 'Cultural Heritage in Human Rights and Humanitarian Law' (n 6) 18–19.

[61] For this discussion, see ibid., 32–3.

tradition that propels genocide.[62] Two other related assumptions affect the application of general international heritage law (outside the 1954 Hague Convention) as genocide is being perpetrated: (1) a situation of genocide is a state of emergency that entails a suspension of the law; and (2) it is also a fairly sudden and uncontrollable state of exception, where themes like culture and heritage rank second. In fact, even though it has been argued that heritage treaties not specific to wartime do apply in times of war as well,[63] cultural rights are often seen as subject to suspension in times of emergency.[64] Further, the regime of the 1954 Convention does not necessarily apply, unless genocide happens as part of a traditional (and often international) armed conflict, and, as a consequence, ethnic conflict is not easily accommodated.[65] There seems therefore to be a gap in applying those values that make us look at heritage in a way that promotes harmony, as opposed to division (discussed above). Therefore, once again, one is left with the mandates of domestic laws and practices, and international law's values are of limited influence. Communities, without a seat at the international table, are left at the mercy of states that may be actively persecuting them.

But practices of heritage domestically can also work to help move beyond the legacy of genocide. Projects in Cambodia have allowed for the preservation of archival material and other records of the events there.[66] The next section explores this relationship between the law and practices of heritage and post-genocide in more detail.

4.4 After: Heritage Practices as a Means to Overcome Genocide

One of the most widely studied examples of using cultural heritage law and practice to tackle the legacies of genocide is Rwanda. But heritage (and anthropology) also played a role in Rwanda in creating the conditions for genocide, and understanding that context is important for the narrative of heritage in the aftermath of

62 For a collection of essays investigating the idea of contemporary cultural heritage, see Waelde, Charlotte, Cummings, Catherine, Pavis, Mathilde, and Enright, Helena (eds), *Research Handbook on Contemporary Intangible Cultural Heritage: Law and Heritage* (Edward Elgar, 2018).

63 Francesco Francioni, 'Au-delà des traités: l'émergence d'un nouveau droit coutumier pour la protection du patrimoine culturel', *Revue générale de droit international public* (2007). See also Marina Lostal, *International Cultural Heritage Law in Armed Conflict: Case-Studies of Syria, Libya, Mali, the Invasion of Iraq, and the Buddhas of Bamiyan* (Cambridge University Press, 2017).

64 For instance, the International Covenant on Civil and Political Rights allows for the provision on minority protection (Art. 27) to be suspended, as long as the suspension is not discriminatory (Art. 4). International Covenant on Civil and Political Rights (adopted 16 December 1966, entered into force 23 March 1976) 999 UNTS 171 (ICCPR).

65 Lixinski, Lucas, and Schreiber, Lara, 'The Limits of Framing in International Law: The Shortcomings of International Heritage Protection in the Isis Conflicts', *RUMLAE Research Paper No. 17-4* (2017).

66 UNESCO, 'UNESCO supports a project of preservation for the Tuol Sleng Genocide Museum premises and its archives to keep alive the memory of Cambodian history', available at <http://www.unesco.org/new/en/culture/themes/museums/museum-projects/archive/unesco-supports-a-project-of-preservation-for-the-tuol-sleng-genocide-museum-premises-and-its-archives-to-keep-alive-the-memory-of-cambodian-history/> (accessed 29 October, 2017).

the Rwandan genocide. Divisions between Hutus and Tutsis were reinforced over time by colonial powers with the assistance of archaeology and anthropology, where Eurocentric stereotypes helped manipulate and warp distinctions that did not necessarily exist. Violence was then structured by cultural assumptions, and also legitimated by them.[67]

After the events of 1994, the country reemerged and attempted to use heritage as a means to reshape its own national history. Its constitution, for instance, recognizes genocide memorials as part of the country's cultural heritage and cultural identity.[68] The main (legally prescribed)[69] narrative suggests that the divisions between Hutus and Tutsis were created by colonial powers in a misunderstanding of what the divisions actually entailed. These divisions were socioeconomic, having to do with the occupation of each one of the groups, rather than an actual ethnic division. But the colonizers saw that division as being based on ethnic grounds, and helped create fundamental differences between the two groups. By privileging one group over the other, colonizers also created resentment that, after Rwandan independence, continued to simmer until it violently exploded in 1994. Therefore, new archaeological evidence was needed to refute the colonial version of history, and remake the Rwandan nation.[70]

While it may seem like a sound strategy, this manipulation of heritage in the same way it was once manipulated may actually perpetuate the political paradigms it seeks to challenge.[71] The focus on archaeological evidence seems to revive and perpetuate a certain scientificism that, as we saw above with respect to both Germany and Cambodia, often has negative effects, partly because of its apolitical nature. While the intention in Rwanda may have been to use scientific methods to deconstruct colonial racist stereotypes that would otherwise hinder the development of the country's identity,[72] it can also have the effect of perpetuating a sense of separateness between the two groups.

This connection between science and transition is not unique to the Rwandan case. In South Africa, too, a more 'scientific' approach has been used with respect to heritage in the aftermath of apartheid, with the result that cultural heritage has been 'cleansed' in favour of natural heritage, which is seen as neutral and less politically charged.[73] Part of the impulse here may be to use allegedly value-neutral science to wipe the slate clean, which is similar to approaches to human rights in transitional contexts that focus on criminal law as the main response to transition.[74] If one erases

[67] Taylor, Christopher C., *Sacrifice as Terror: The Rwandan Genocide of 1994* (Berg, 1999). Cited in O'Neill (n 10) 191–2.

[68] Art. 51.

[69] Giblin, John Daniel, 'Decolonial Challenges and Post-Genocide Archaeological Politics in Rwanda', *Public Archaeology* 11(3) (2012), 123–43, 128.

[70] See generally Reid, Andrew, 'Cattle, Identity and Genocide in the African Great Lakes Region', *Archaeology International* 4 (2000), 35–8.

[71] Giblin, 'Decolonial Challenges' (n 69), 123–4.

[72] Ibid., 127.

[73] Lixinski, Lucas, 'Cultural Heritage Law and Transitional Justice: Lessons from South Africa', *International Journal of Transitional Justice* 9(2) (2015), 278–96.

[74] For a general critique, see Engle, Karen, 'Anti-Impunity and the Turn to Criminal Law in Human Rights', *Cornell Law Review* 100(5) (2015), 1070–127.

the politics, one can start again. However, pushing the politics aside also has the (unintended) consequence of perpetuating the same conditions that made atrocity possible to begin with.

Thus, this move to scientificism can also replicate ideas about the formation of identity that have been used as justifications for genocide in other instances, alongside slavery and exploitation.[75] But heritage can play an important role in dealing with trauma, as long as one understands that it is neither necessarily good nor intrinsically bad in post-atrocity situations. Rather, heritage should be understood as part of a healing complex, and one that has not been created anew in the aftermath of the latest atrocity.[76] Past uses of heritage matter just as much as the current ones, again highlighting the relationship between time and heritage law and practices.

There is another element in the relationship between time and heritage that needs to be considered in this context. More specifically, atrocity can often reset the clock for a certain community that becomes defined by the events it endured.[77] In Rwanda, as its own constitution makes it, genocide is the defining moment of the nation, and heritage law and practice has been built around genocide, and moving away from it. But memorializing genocide can have the effect of authenticating the roles that cultural difference played in making the atrocity possible.[78]

International heritage law, again, seems not to have much to say on the matter. As I have argued elsewhere in the context of transitional justice,[79] and in Chapters 1 and 3, international law seems to enable a scientific approach, and does not interfere much with the way states choose to use their own heritage in the aftermath of atrocity. The context of Bosnia and Herzegovina can also help shed some light on this relationship. During the Balkan wars in the 1990s, culture was often a target of destruction. For instance, a key Bosnian library in Sarajevo was targeted so that records claiming the land as Bosnian could be erased, in order to privilege a history of the region as Serb.[80] After the dissolution of Yugoslavia, and the genocide that happened there, Bosnia and Herzegovina became an independent country. Annex 8 of the Dayton Peace Agreement was dedicated to the protection of cultural heritage in the new country, and time and again it reinforced cultural value on ethnic grounds (as opposed to national) as a basis for protection of heritage.[81] But, like in Rwanda, a safer, more distant past is used as the common ground for a shared heritage.[82] In doing so, heritage manipulates time, in a way that the law is all too happy to authorize, if anything by simply ignoring it.

[75] Hinton (n 47) 13.

[76] Giblin, John Daniel, 'Post-Conflict Heritage: Symbolic Healing and Cultural Renewal', *International Journal of Heritage Studies* 20(5) (2014), 500–18.

[77] Yusin, Jennifer, 'The Itinerary of Commemoration in the Kigali Memorial Centre: On Trauma, Time and Difference', *Culture, Theory and Critique* 57(3) (2015), 338–56, 339.

[78] Ibid., 355.

[79] Lixinski, 'Cultural Heritage Law and Transitional Justice' (n 73).

[80] Bevan (n 5) 56.

[81] Dayton Peace Agreement, Annex 8: Agreement on Commission to Preserve National Monuments (December 14, 1995), Arts 4 and 6.

[82] Bevan (n 5) 230.

The implementation of these structures was supported by existing UNESCO regimes. The nation state was still relied on 'as the carrier and developer of collective cultural memory and identity, overlooking settings where the primary mode of group identification and legitimization occurs at different (lower) levels'.[83] In the lead-up to the dissolution of Yugoslavia, heritage was reinterpreted in essentialist, religion-based terms, as a means to construct difference and prompt the destruction of cultural resources that up until close to that time had been shared by different groups in the country.[84] The Dayton Agreement gave heritage a 'pivotal role in post-conflict reconstruction and intercommunity reconciliation'.[85]

But, relevant as heritage was, its governance was difficult on the ground, precisely because of some of the limitations of international heritage law that still focuses on the nation state and its territory for the management of heritage. Especially in a situation like the former Yugoslavia, it may be that some of the most important heritage to be safeguarded for a specific group is outside the borders of the state where that group ended up in the division of territory.[86] But the law ends up requiring that identity be re-grounded on the existing territory of the new state. Heritage ends up being ascribed to territory, rather than communities, in this context.[87]

This territorialization of heritage forces identity in a way that can be even more divisive. As Musi highlights,

> what until the 1980s used to be a pluralist and heterogeneous society must now cope with the legacy of extreme ethno-nationalist modes and practices of identity during conflict and with a hybrid system that maintains 'national' (ethnic) affiliation as crucial for its functioning. The task of configuring a memory to sustain the identity of the new state is thus particularly complicated by at least two factors: (1) the impossibility of shaping the country as one nation and (2) the appeal of nation-state models of identification at the level of the constituent peoples (i.e. Bosniacs, Croats, Serbs).[88]

Therefore, the process of dealing with atrocity, alongside the problematic relationship between heritage law and identities that do not correspond with territorial boundaries, may end up recreating and normalizing some of the divisions that existed prior to atrocity. The same risks associated with the relationship between heritage law and temporalities (as in Rwanda) exist with respect to territory in the aftermath of genocide.

What these two examples show is that, in dealing with the legacies of genocide, heritage law and practice are often called upon to play specific roles. These roles do not necessarily take into consideration the limitations of the application of heritage law. Time does not seem to be a specific obstacle to the application of heritage law (except with respect to formal retroactivity issues), but temporalities play a role in defining what role heritage is to play in the larger picture. If the atrocity is to become

[83] Musi (n 29) 54. [84] Ibid., 55. [85] Ibid., 55–6.

[86] Montenegro, another country to come out of the dissolution of Yugoslavia, made specific provision for the protection of heritage located extraterritorially. See Protection of Cultural Property Act (2010), Art. 6.1.

[87] Musi (n 29) 55. [88] Ibid., 58.

a defining moment only after which the new community emerges, there is a risk that heritage law and practices will, in an effort to start anew, ignore the role that structures of heritage law and practice have played in creating the atrocity to begin with, and may end up replicating some of those biases. Additionally, international heritage law and practice, in forgetting about those conditions, and being conceptually restricted to the state as the primary international actor and subject, can potentially also ignore internal power structures and attachments to heritage that do not match the official line of the state. Communities are thus excluded, and left at the mercy of state structures endorsed by international law.

Can the answer to some of these challenges be found in a different field of international law, though? What, if anything, can international human rights law, particularly with respect to cultural rights and heritage, do in order to mediate some of these tensions between heritage law and time? The next section explores some of these possibilities.

4.5 (How) Can a Human Rights Approach to Heritage Help Alleviate These Tensions?

One of the challenges with the applicable rules of international law, as indicated above, is that international law regulates the activities of states, and, as such, it embraces a state-centric articulation of culture and cultural heritage, to the detriment of entities that may be in disagreement with a national project of statehood.[89] This bias is particularly present in instruments on cultural objects, and less important on instruments on intangible cultural heritage.[90] In fact, the intangible cultural heritage regime's embrace of communities is important for a human rights approach to heritage management.[91]

While a full exploration of the relationships between human rights and heritage law is beyond the scope of this chapter (and this book, for that matter),[92] a few words are useful to frame the debate.[93] Cultural heritage, and international cultural heritage law with it, has been consistently used over time as a means to build identities, and human rights have become a cogent legal discourse to safeguard those identities. The example of the movement for promoting the human rights of Indigenous peoples is particularly telling: the international Indigenous movement since the 1970s has chosen to use culture as the main banner behind which to rally support for the Indigenous cause, and therefore as the catalyst for the very idea of human

[89] See also Vrdoljak, Ana Filipa, 'Human Rights and Cultural Heritage in International Law', in F. Lenzerini and A. F. Vrdoljak (eds), *International Law for Common Goods: Normative Perspectives on Human Rights, Culture and Nature* (Hart, 2014), 139–74, 142.

[90] Ibid., 146.

[91] But with limitations. See generally Lucas Lixinski, *Intangible Cultural Heritage in International Law* (Oxford University Press, 2013).

[92] But see for instance Durbach, Andrea and Lixinski, Lucas (eds), *Heritage, Culture and Rights Challenging Legal Discourses* (Hart, 2017).

[93] Drawn from Lixinski, Lucas, 'ESIL—International Human Rights Law Symposium: International Human Rights Law and International Cultural Heritage Law: Cooperation, Conflict or Cooption?'

rights of Indigenous peoples.[94] A human right to heritage is difficult to establish, and, when proclaimed, is difficult to enforce.

International human rights law and international heritage law are also seen as mutually reinforcing with respect to rights to access and participation in decision-making on heritage matters, necessary for the promotion of community participation in heritage governance that is central to this book's thesis. This idea of promoting community participation, even if it is also difficult to enforce and implement in light of the existing legal framework, gets one closer to the idea of a human rights approach to heritage management and governance.

At the same time, though, heritage is often in opposition to narratives of progress in human rights discourses. The definition of heritage contained in the ICHC says that 'consideration will be given solely to such intangible cultural heritage as is compatible with existing international human rights instruments'.[95]

All the while, and parallel to these tensions, there is a real risk of a 'human dimension of heritage' being expanded so as to co-opt all of heritage under the umbrella of a 'human rights approach'. While a human rights approach can be helpful, and it is certainly an important means for the international enforcement of legal claims surrounding culture, there is also much that can be obscured by a treatment of heritage as being a human rights concern.

The relationship between human rights and cultural heritage can be looked at in at least two principal disciplinary ways. One way of going about describing this relationship is to think of the extent human rights establish claims to historical narrative by assigning roles of victims and perpetrators. This relationship, alongside other relationships, describes human rights generally in terms broader than human rights 'law'. Another way is the idea of community participation in the management, conservation, and safeguarding of heritage (and human rights as an enabler of participation), which is in line with this book's broader call for community engagement. But one big obstacle from an international legal standpoint is the notion that state sovereignty is still paramount in the field of heritage, whereas (contemporary) international human rights law is largely premised on the erosion or cession of sovereign attributes by states.[96]

A direct connection between heritage and human rights in the realm of community participation makes problematic assumptions about the ways in which heritage obligations are met. The most common mechanism for heritage protection at the international level is that of listing, discussed in more detail in Chapter 7. The most famous such list is the World Heritage List, with over a thousand properties listed in over 160 countries around the globe. However, the listing of heritage is

EJIL: Talk! (12 February 2016), available at <http://www.ejiltalk.org/esil-international-human-rights-law-symposium-international-human-rights-law-and-international-cultural-heritage-law-cooperation-conflict-or-cooption/> (accessed 30 October 2017).

[94] The work of Karen Engle is particularly significant in this respect. See Engle, Karen, *The Elusive Promise of Indigenous Development: Culture, Rights, Strategy* (Duke University Press, 2010).

[95] ICHC, Article 2.1.

[96] Blake, Janet, 'Taking a Human Rights Approach to Cultural Heritage Protection', *Heritage & Society* 4(2) (2011), 199–238.

not necessarily conducive to the idea of a human rights approach to heritage, as it is largely dependent on state sovereignty, and does not include communities in the international selection and management of their heritage. Perhaps the most problematic aspect of heritage listing as the primary means of (international) heritage protection, which creates tension with human rights ideas, is the gap that exists between what is promised to communities when their heritage is being 'prepared' for ins cription in a UNESCO list, and what they actually get. For instance, heritage listing can foreground one specific aspect of a place's history, and in the process erase other histories people might be more connected to, or expect local skills in the management of a heritage area that are not present among the local population. Or it can impair the right of local inhabitants of a heritage site to privacy and to live their everyday lives without being surrounded by tourists on a quest for an 'authentic' insight into the place and its people (a notion criticized in Chapter 1).

Another important instance in which there is a tension between heritage and human rights in the listing process is when the heritage itself is seen as potentially conflicting with human rights. The 'human rights exception' in Article 2(1) of the ICHC speaks to that, and has been analysed in more detail elsewhere.[97] One example is that of the human towers,[98] a Spanish manifestation of heritage that stirred considerable debate when first proposed for inclusion in the Representative List of the Intangible Cultural Heritage of Humanity, because of its potential for violating human rights. What this particular type of tension seems to do is replay the debates between universalism and relativism in human rights law, now using cultural heritage as a proxy. Because cultural heritage is in some ways more 'institutionalized' than 'cultural practices' (at least listed heritage is), it seems to lend new breath to debates on universalism and relativism of international human rights law.[99] I would suggest this is a counterproductive move, as it tends to antagonize cultural heritage and downplay its contribution to community cohesion that allowed for the birth of notions of rights to begin with.

The possible relationships between human rights and international heritage law are often obscured by a focus on trying to understand how human rights and heritage relate to each other not as bodies of law, but simply as broader sets of ideas and practices, not necessarily connected to the legal field. While there is some liberating appeal in not necessarily focusing on the narrow legality of these categories and the institutions around them, the legal dimension is nevertheless important, at least to the extent law is a language of power which can aid in advancing any common goals that may exist between human rights and heritage.

A human rights approach to heritage, thus, means rethinking the way heritage is articulated and managed. On the articulation side, heritage becomes central to identity, which aligns with our discussion so far. On the management side, it means

97 Lixinski (n 91).

98 Inscribed in 2010. UNESCO Intangible Cultural Heritage, Human towers, at https://ich.unesco.org/en/RL/human-towers-00364.

99 Also taken up recently by Lenzerini, Federico, *The Culturalization of Human Rights Law* (Oxford University Press, 2014).

including more actors in the management of heritage. Heritage management is no longer the monopoly of the state; instead, communities who claim that heritage as their own, who practice that heritage, and/or live around certain heritage, become an integral part of the decision-making process around whether heritage should be protected, how, for whose benefit, and for the pursuance of which values.[100]

This type of approach can potentially help address some of the limitations of heritage law and practice discussed here. Firstly, if heritage becomes the domain of communities, rather than experts, scientific approaches to heritage are more likely to give way to more politicized approaches. Everyone becomes a heritage expert, in a sense. Secondly, human rights law provides a clear framework to place substate entities at the forefront of the process of heritage management, as provisions on minority protection would suggest. Thirdly, international human rights law is potentially a vocabulary of power and emancipation that is much more present in the context of atrocities than is heritage, and this pervasive process can help relay the importance of heritage in this context.

But there are some potential downsides, too. First, even if communities are included, there are still lingering questions as to who gets to speak on behalf of the community. As it stands, international law (particularly in the field of heritage) is very deferential to states in this type of definition, allowing for the replication of a number of problematic structures. Secondly, provisions on minority protection and cultural rights, as indicated above, can be derogated in the context of emergencies, thus frustrating some of the possibilities on the ground. And thirdly, the pervasiveness of human rights can co-opt the potentials of heritage law on its own, and polarize discussions around heritage in a language of entitlements and rights that is not necessarily conducive to harmony and understanding, or even in a language of punishment and prosecutions of crime against heritage, which is consistent with the turn to criminal law in human rights,[101] and many of the efforts around linking cultural heritage and atrocity,[102] which will be revisited in Chapter 7.

A human rights approach can help include otherwise neglected communities, and shift power onto them in making decisions about how their heritage is used, which can be particularly useful with respect to oppressed minorities. Also importantly, human rights standards can help international heritage law come to terms with its own temporal contingencies. Human rights cannot always undo the past and redress historical grievances, but it has more of a vocation to do so than international heritage law. That is so in spite of the limits of enforceability of group rights in international human rights, even if there is some emerging level of recognition of legal personality of groups in international human rights law.[103]

[100] See also Francioni, Francesco and Lixinski, Lucas, 'Opening the Toolbox of International Human Rights Law in the Safeguarding of Cultural Heritage', in Andrea Durbach and Lucas Lixinski (eds), *Heritage, Culture and Rights Challenging Legal Discourses* (Hart, 2017), 11–34.

[101] Engle, 'Anti-Impunity' (n 74).

[102] For a collection of essays, see Francioni, Francesco and Gordley, James (eds), *Enforcing International Cultural Heritage Law* (Oxford University Press, 2013).

[103] See *Kaliña and Lokono Peoples v Suriname* (Merits, Reparations and Costs) Inter-American Court of Human Rights Series C No. 309 (25 November 2015).

That is particularly the case with respect to the intertemporal application of law. Whereas international heritage law is largely thought of as being under classic public international law mechanisms of non-retroactivity, international human rights law in several instances has worked around those limitations by introducing doctrines like 'continuing violation', which contend that a violation of the international norm is repeated anew each day for as long as it is not redressed,[104] as opposed to the classic international law mechanism of assuming the critical date for an international dispute as a one-off event.[105] Therefore, international human rights law's influence on international heritage law can influence not only community participation more generally, but also the system of international heritage law's fraught relationship with time and inability to satisfactorily tackle historical injustices.

Cultural heritage is an important means of channelling identity in specific practices and sites. The law and practices around cultural heritage help normalize and authorize these identities in ways that can be conducive to harmony or conflict. Scientific approaches to heritage do not take sides, but seem to have been used very often in negative ways. And international heritage law seems inadequately equipped to deal with the challenges of the different moments of genocide, because of a fraught relationship between heritage and time that is enshrined in the law in a way that glosses over tensions (again, in an attempt to promote scientificism and the conservation paradigm). The same happens with international law's relationship with states as the central actors, in a way that reinforces potentially dangerous nationalism associated with heritage. Therefore, a human rights approach to heritage, that helps challenge scientificism and state-centrism, can be an important tool in helping heritage become a better catalyst for preventing, mitigating, and addressing traumatic events like genocide. But there are important limitations to be taken into account if heritage is to live up to its full potential in mediating identity in a constructive and harmony-conducive way.

These limitations spill over not only in the way we conceptualize the possibilities and limits of international heritage law, but also in the ways in which this international law is implemented. The next three chapters focus on several issues of implementation of international heritage law across a range of topics. While a human rights approach can help heritage become a language of emancipation, other mechanisms can help heritage also become a toolbox for redistribution. We therefore start with international heritage law's relationship to economics, and the possibilities for economic uses of heritage to emancipate and promote the development of communities.

[104] See for instance *Chiragov v Armenia* ECHR 2011 App. No. 13216/05 [97]–[127]; cf. *Case of the Moiwana Community v Suriname* IACHR 2005 Ser. C No. 124 [37]–[43]; *De Becker v Belgium* ECHR 1962 App. No. 214/56; *Loizidou v Turkey* EHCR 1995 App. No. 15318/89 [100]–[105]; *Hutten-Czapska v Poland* EHCR 2006 App. No. 35014/97 [152]–[153].

[105] *Island of Palmas Case* (United States v Netherlands) (1928) II RIAA 829, 834.

5

International Heritage Law and the Market

There are four main areas of significance of heritage: economic, social, political, and scientific.[1] As discussed in previous chapters, the scientific value of heritage is the most important one from the expert's perspective, but it can have alienating effects. The social value of heritage is the one that matters most for communities, but it is difficult to define. Communities may also wish to make use of political values of heritage, but those are usually constrained (or even ruled out) by the Authorized Heritage Discourse (AHD) framework, and, when available, overwhelmingly favour the nation state. And the economic values of heritage are usually seen as somewhat taboo, even if those perceptions are slowly changing outside the law.

International heritage law's relationship to the market is fraught to say the least. It oscillates between potentially outlawing the market outright, such as the prohibition on the traffic of cultural objects in the 1970 Convention or the prohibition of salvage in the 2001 Underwater Heritage Convention (UCHC), to simply not mentioning the possibility of cultural heritage being in the market, such as the World Heritage Convention (WHC) and the Intangible Cultural Heritage Convention (ICHC).[2] The effect across heritage instruments is to push the market into the invisible and un(der)regulated private.[3] Much of this troubled relationship stems from a rejection of the possibility that heritage could belong in the market. Across many civil law jurisdictions, for instance, heritage is classically thought of as *res extra commercium*, or a thing outside the stream of commerce.[4] And that is because heritage is just too special; to add it to the market would be distasteful.[5] This

[1] Loulanski, Tolina, 'Revising the Concept for Cultural Heritage: The Argument for a Functional Approach', *International Journal of Cultural Property* 13 (2006), 207–33, 207.

[2] The system for the protection of heritage during wartime is excluded from this chapter. For an analysis of the Hague system and the trade in cultural objects, see Fitschen, Thomas, 'Licit International Art Trade in Times of Armed Conflict?', *International Journal of Cultural Property* 5(1) (1996), 127–32.

[3] For a critique, see Muir Watt, Horatia, 'Private International Law beyond the Schism', *Transnational Legal Theory* 2(3) (2011), 347–427.

[4] Siehr, Kurt, 'The Protection of Cultural Heritage and International Commerce', *International Journal of Cultural Property* 6(2) (1997), 304–25, 304 and 318. Common law countries seem to be more permissive, though. See Fincham, Derek, 'A Coordinated Legal and Policy Approach to Undiscovered Antiquities: Adapting the Cultural Heritage Policy of England and Wales to Other Nations of Origin', *International Journal of Cultural Property* 15 (2008), 347–70. For a discussion of other domestic categories, see John Henry Merryman's remarks in Shapiro, Daniel, 'Opinion: Legal Issues in the Trade of Antiquities', *International Journal of Cultural Property* 3(2) (1994), 365–95, at 367–8.

[5] Ashworth, Gregory J., 'Heritage and Economic Development: Selling the Unsellable', *Heritage & Society* 7(1) (2014), 3–17, 5.

idea aligns with the conservation paradigm that is typical of international heritage law, and it has been referred as having 'an air of fundamentalism'.[6] The market values of heritage are often seen as being in conflict with its cultural values, and an obstacle to them.[7] It is in communities' best interest, the story goes, to preserve cultural values above all, and those are a stand-in for the conservation paradigm.

This treatment of heritage as too special for trade stems from a well-intentioned desire to protect it.[8] If heritage is outside the stream of commerce, then it cannot be vulgarized, it will always be special, and it will always have a value that transcends numbers and figures, or so the argument goes. It is a terrific idea in theory. But in practice heritage has an economic dimension that is quite fundamental to its process.[9] Cultural objects are still traded (in fact, the 1970 Convention is often blamed for the creation or at least great expansion of the black market in antiquities), or at the very least heritage is impacted by economic activities around it (such as intense tourism in places like Angkor Wat, which ends up jeopardizing the World Heritage Site). So, when the law excludes the economic possibilities of heritage, the market does not go away; it simply moves elsewhere, often into the invisible private, or to other fora that are less sympathetic to the cultural needs of heritage, because their goals lie more in the promotion of economics (such as the World Tourism Organization—UNWTO).

Also importantly, the economics of heritage can highlight an important distinction between market and source nations. Market nations for the purposes of this chapter will be roughly characterized as wealthier nations who consume heritage in other countries, or import heritage from other countries for internal consumption. Source nations, on the other hand, are commonly poorer, postcolonial countries[10] with rich histories, which tend to be visited by hordes of tourists interested in certain aspects of their heritage, or to have their artefacts taken to museums in other countries, often as part of a colonial enterprise. This distinction originates in the debates around movable cultural heritage, but it will be used throughout this chapter in other contexts, too. It evokes tensions discussed in Chapter 2 about who the museum's 'community' is, and the difficulties of defining a community on a Westphalian political plane.

This chapter engages with the economics of heritage, and what the market means (and can mean) for communities who live around heritage. I will explore the economics of cultural heritage, and its potential impacts on how we read and apply

[6] Mason, Randall, 'Be Interested and Beware: Joining Economic Valuation and Heritage Conservation', *International Journal of Heritage Studies* 14(4) (2008), 303–18, 304. For a useful table comparing economic, heritage, and functional values of historical buildings, see Krus, Anna, 'Heritage—Function—Economy: Three Perspectives on Values in Estate Management', in Mikko Mälkki, Raine Mäntysalo, and Kaisa Schmidt-Thomé (eds), *Economics and Built Heritage—Towards New European Initiatives* (Helsinki University of Technology, 2008), 71–90, 80.

[7] Deuchar, Stephen, 'Sense and Sensitivity: Appraising the *Titanic*', *International Journal of Heritage Studies* 2(4) (1996), 212–21, 212.

[8] Chechi, Alessandro, *The Settlement of International Cultural Heritage Disputes* (Oxford University Press, 2014), 65.

[9] Ashworth (n 5) 3.

[10] Italy is a notable exception, even though it is a market nation as well in other contexts.

international heritage law, as well as its potential impacts on addressing issues of community engagement in the economics of heritage. One of the often-made promises to communities is that listing their heritage, making it available to the world, will translate into development and boost the local economy. In practice, though, it seems that most of the money spent on cultural heritage ends up benefitting other parties. So, once again, communities end up alienated from their heritage, as control over it tends to pass to those that have more tangible economic stakes. An international heritage law oriented towards communities therefore needs to be mindful of the impact economics has on heritage and the relationship between heritage and local communities. It must also promote means of translating the economics of heritage into benefits for those whose heritage it really is.

One of the big problems with engaging heritage in the market, of course, is that it contradicts international law's impulse to think of heritage as an absolute, a common good that belongs to all of humanity. To make heritage less than an absolute implies acknowledging it has no intrinsic value, and that its values are defined relationally. Here, bridging law and non-law, as discussed in Chapter 1, is crucial. That proposition seems to be acceptable to a number of heritage studies scholars, and the vast majority of economists engaged in cultural heritage matters, but finds less receptive minds among international lawyers in the field. One of the advantages of accepting that heritage has no intrinsic value in this case is that it allows engagement with the market. The dark side, of course, is that one may be taking the first step down a slippery slope that will vulgarize and ultimately destroy cultural heritage. But, as reiterated throughout this volume, heritage is only important if it means something to the people who will ultimately live with it and care for it. Allowing them to perceive and engage with heritage beyond its symbolic dimensions is a means to expand the range of cultural heritage that local communities will want to care for, all the while providing them with the means to safeguard their own cultures.

This chapter engages with the literature on the economics of heritage, which for present purposes can be divided in two generations. The first generation of economic studies of heritage engages with the econometrics of heritage, and the market impacts of cultural heritage, tackling matters such as the impact of heritage listing on the prices of buildings in historic cities. This is the type of literature that will be of more immediate interest to international lawyers, as it makes a case for the undeniable presence of the market in cultural heritage matters, in spite of the law's best attempts to shield heritage from it.

The second generation of literature on the economics of heritage engages economic insights and methods to understand the dynamics of the production of value with respect to heritage. This literature has as a starting point that economics is much larger than the market *sensu stricto*. Economics is a way of explaining the world, understanding behaviour and motivations. So, this second generation tends to answer questions about why and how we value cultural heritage, and whether tools to safeguard heritage are adequate to pursue those whys and hows. Here, the law is largely a competitor to economics. As these two social sciences come together, they compete in their task to assign value to heritage, and design the means to safeguard value. This generation of literature, therefore, is still valid for our present purposes in understanding and challenging some of the assumptions international heritage law makes about cultural heritage's engagement with the market.

Ultimately, this chapter will tackle the promises and pitfalls of a heritage market, from the law's perspective. Many voices in law have spoken in favour of a (regulated) market for heritage, and, while I agree with the broad lines of the outcome they propose (a regulated market), I am also wary of the potential downsides of said market, and the (neo)liberal politics that seems to underlie a lot of their justifications for it. I will therefore propose a different way of configuring an engagement of the law with a market in cultural heritage, beyond the elusive promise of 'liberating the economic potential of cultural heritage' (to borrow from Hernando de Soto's much-criticized idea with respect to land ownership). For example, I do not think the market should ultimately control what heritage is, and whether it is safeguarded, as there are other (non-economic) interests at stake.[11] But the market does not need to always be in opposition to heritage safeguarding, either, and the fact that there are non-economic interests does not mean economic interests ought to be expunged.

The chapter proceeds as follows: Section 5.1 will look at the current engagement of international cultural heritage treaties under UNESCO with the market. Section 5.2 will present the literature on heritage economics, and the promises and pitfalls of development through cultural heritage. Section 5.3 will examine how those promises play out in the international standard-setting bodies that do engage with heritage in an economic sense, such as the World Tourism Organization (UNWTO), the World Trade Organization (WTO), and, from an adjudicatory point of view, the International Centre for the Settlement of Investment Disputes (ICSID). Section 5.4 will examine the effects of the economics of heritage on issues of community engagement and governance over heritage. Section 5.5 will flesh out the idea of a market on cultural heritage.

5.1 Economic Matters in International Heritage Treaties

As I suggested above, the relationships between international treaties on the safeguarding of cultural heritage and the market is problematic. These relationships oscillate between prohibiting the market outright on one extreme, to turning a blind eye to the market's existence. UNESCO's posture vis-à-vis the market was originally friendlier, inasmuch as it conflated ideas in a liberalized market with the objectives of cultural exchange.[12] But somewhere along the way that spirit was lost, in favour of the conservation paradigm's aversion to economics.

The 1970 Convention on the Means of Prohibiting and Preventing the Illicit Import, Export and Transfer of Ownership of Cultural Property, for instance, seems to largely outlaw the trade in cultural objects that states have declared to be heritage

[11] Fechner, Frank C., 'The Fundamental Aims of Cultural Property Law', *International Journal of Cultural Property* 7(2) (1998), 376–94, 382.

[12] Vrdoljak, Ana Filipa, *International Law, Museums and the Return of Cultural Objects* (Cambridge University Press, 2006), 184.

of national importance.[13] Much of the literature on the market in cultural heritage, from a legal perspective, also relates to the movement of cultural objects,[14] so the 1970 Convention is central to understanding the relationship between heritage and the market. This instrument was drafted at the behest of decolonizing states (source nations), who saw their cultural artefacts being taken by their former colonizers, and wanted to have those items returned.[15] It came after failed attempts under the League of Nations, where its decolonization mandate was read in free trade terms that significantly impaired the ability of the League to successfully negotiate a treaty on the return of cultural objects, perpetuating colonial structures.[16] This move from decolonizing states is firmly grounded in an assertion of these new states' sovereignty, and, in effect, many of these countries (most notably the Congo) treated cultural objects as a resource as valuable as the mineral resources that had been exploited by colonial powers. Therefore, there is a strong political and economic content to cultural objects, which are seen as key to galvanizing the country's population around a single identity (on the political side), but also key to their future wealth (on the economic side).

But, as the 1970 Convention was negotiated, the former colonial powers, alongside the United States (which wanted freedom to expand the collections of its own museums) opposed full restitution (as market nations), and instead a compromise was struck in which cultural objects were to be returned if they were illegally taken after the entry into force of the treaty, but past events would not be addressed by this instrument.

Therefore, in actuality, the text of the negotiated 1970 Convention did not make all trade in cultural objects illegal, nor is it averse to the market in principle;[17] it simply restricted taking new objects out of source nations without that country's authorization, as long as those objects had been recognized as important by the state themselves. But what happened in effect was a hastening to protect whatever heritage was still left in source nations, thus reducing the supply of new artefacts down to a trickle, while market nations also decided to hold on to their collections, as they could no longer determine when they would be able to get new objects. This affirmation of sovereign rights by source nations therefore created the appearance of a total ban on the market, even if in actuality it is just a much reduced market, and one that seems to take into account the interests of the local populations (as presumably represented by the source nations).

One of the results of this greatly reduced market is the rise of the black or grey market in antiquities.[18] Figures vary significantly, as does the estimation of the

[13] Convention on the Means of Prohibiting and Preventing the Illicit Import, Export and Transfer of Ownership of Cultural Property 1970 (adopted 14 November 1970, entered into force 24 April 1972) 823 UNTS 231 (1970 Convention), Article 4.

[14] See e.g. Messender, Phyllis Mauch (ed.), *The Ethics of Collecting Cultural Property: Whose Culture? Whose Property?* (University of New Mexico Press, 1991).

[15] For a full history, see Vrdoljak (n 12) 206–11.

[16] Ibid., 104.

[17] Prott, Lyndel V., 'The International Movement of Cultural Objects', *International Journal of Cultural Property* 12 (2005), 225–48, 225.

[18] For a discussion, see Ulph, Janet and Smith, Ian, *The Illicit Trade in Art and Antiquities: International Recovery and Criminal and Civil Liability* (Hart, 2012), 1–26. See also Campbell, Peter B., 'The Illicit

market's worth relative to other similar markets.[19] But, regardless of what the precise figures are, for our present purposes what matters is that there is a sizeable market in antiquities, which largely exists as a response to a great reduction of the ability of international law (in its application by source nations) to allow engagement with the market.

There is, however, still a thriving licit market in movable cultural heritage. Much of this market, though, is framed as falling outside the scope of the 1970 Convention. As the 1970 Convention does not apply retroactively, all objects that left their countries of origin before the entry into force of the treaty for them are considered to be licitly exported, as far as international law goes (domestic law varies, but, for our present purposes, we will focus on the relevant international instruments). And they can therefore be freely traded. The black market in antiquities exploits this loophole through creating mechanisms to prove that the objects left the territories of the states in question before the Convention's entry into force, thus laundering the cultural artefacts. Provenance documents are thus key to create a legitimate market in antiquities.[20]

One of the problems with this licit market is that, because it is largely unregulated by international law (since the Convention's primary goal was to curb the trade of cultural heritage), it ends up regulated by the private sphere. It is the industry members themselves (dealers, museums, and collectors) who set the international standards for what counts as adequate proof that an object can be licitly traded, and set up the standard of due diligence required of the industry to ensure that the objects can be in the market.[21] They are even allowed to create a system where secrecy is permitted to an extent that is unheard of in other areas of international trade.[22] As mentioned, the 1970 Convention had a negative impact on market nations, who suddenly had the supply of new cultural artefacts greatly reduced. But it left open a loophole through which trade could continue. And currently whether an item of cultural heritage can be traded through this loophole is a determination to be made by precisely those actors who are interested in there being a free market in antiquities, and through regulations that are largely hidden in the private sphere and not subject to publicity and scrutiny in the way that the 1970 Convention is. There is hence a lot of room for abuse of the loophole, and examples abound of when said

Antiquities Trade as a Transnational Criminal Network: Characterizing and Anticipating Trafficking of Cultural Heritage', *International Journal of Cultural Property* 20 (2013), 113–53.

[19] For a discussion and critique, see Durney, Mark, 'Reevaluating Art Crime's Famous Figures', *International Journal of Cultural Property* 20 (2013), 221–32.

[20] For an analysis of the workings of the market through the perspective of a museum based in the United States, see Felch, Jason and Frammolino, Ralph, *Chasing Aphrodite: The Hunt for Looted Antiquities at the World's Richest Museum* (Houghton Mifflin Harcourt, 2011).

[21] This is of course a rough characterization of the market, and from the perspective of international law. In effect, the private aspects of the market are strictly regulated domestically through property law, and there is a tension between the private nature of property and the public nature of culture that is mediated in the political sphere. See generally Kuzmarov, Betina, 'The Coherence of the Concept of Cultural Property: A Critical Examination', *International Journal of Cultural Property* 20 (2013), 233–56, 235.

[22] Prott (n 17) 238–9.

abuse has in fact happened. The loophole is even more glaring if one considers that communities of origin are not part of the private ordering at stake here.

Therefore, as far as the 1970 Convention goes, it is not so much that it entirely excludes the market; it is rather that it pushes the market to a condition of semi-invisibility. This semi-invisibility happens in two main ways. First, the 1970 Convention claims the market can only exist if authorized by source nations (which is unlikely to happen, as those states are fearful of the slippery slope and political effects of allowing any cultural artefacts into the market officially). Second, there can be a market if the transactions exploit a loophole in the 1970 Convention negotiated by market nations, and the oversight of which is anchored by rules that further push the market into the private. The market is not so much outlawed as it is made invisible by the politics of a treaty that privileges assertions of sovereignty by nation states struggling to (re)shape their identities in the aftermath of colonialism.

Interests that make the market invisible, and are also hostile to the market, can be seen in the UCHC as well. The UCHC was actually drafted largely as a response from the underwater archaeology community to the rise in commercial salvage of underwater ships. The law of salvage itself was traditionally not meant to apply to shipwrecks, but rather to ships as they sank. However, it was extended to shipwrecks and underwater cultural heritage by analogy, due to the efforts of admiralty courts in common law countries.[23] As commercial salvage operations grew in number and scope, the field of underwater archaeology also expanded, and soon the two clashed. As a response to pressures coming from the archaeological community, a new instrument was drafted, initially under the auspices of the International Law Association, and then taken up by UNESCO.[24] The UCHC deals with salvage in its Article 4, which excludes the bodies of salvage law and law of finds from underwater heritage, unless it is authorized by competent authorities, deemed to be fully compatible with the UCHC, and that salvage ensures maximum protection of the instrument.[25] Because the UCHC privileges conservation *in situ* (that is, underwater) over all other forms, it is not surprising that it is somewhat hostile to any attempt at lifting heritage from the ocean floor. It is also deeply concerned with the dispersion of artefacts from a site, more so than their commercialization per se.[26] Thus, the case against commercialization is largely built on the interests of expert communities, rather than other stakeholders.[27] Communities that engage with underwater heritage are excluded, even if subsistence diving is central to their way of life.

The fraught relationship between the salvage market and the UCHC is one of the reasons, it seems, why it has not been as widely ratified as other UNESCO

[23] For this history, see generally Dromgoole, Sarah, *Underwater Cultural Heritage and International Law* (Cambridge University Press, 2013).

[24] For some of this history from the perspective of one of the participants in the International Law Association process, see Nafziger, James A. R., 'The UNESCO Convention on the Protection of the Underwater Cultural Heritage: Its Growing Influence', *Journal of Maritime Law & Commerce* 49(3) (2018) 371–400, 388–98.

[25] Convention on the Protection of the Underwater Cultural Heritage 2001 (adopted 2 November 2001, entered into force 2 January 2009) 2562 UNTS 3 (UCHC), Article 4.

[26] Dromgoole (n 23) 210. [27] Ibid., 219–20.

heritage treaties.[28] While Article 4 seems to open a means for commercial salvage, the UCHC's Rules (which are an Annex, and thus an integral part of the UCHC by virtue of the Law of Treaties)[29] make commercial salvage impermissible under the UCHC. Rule 2 says that 'commercial exploitation of underwater cultural heritage for trade or speculation or its irretrievable dispersal is fundamentally incompatible with the protection and proper management of underwater cultural heritage. Underwater cultural heritage shall not be traded, sold, bought or bartered as commercial goods'.[30] Therefore, the UCHC entirely excludes the market, and is hostile to it. Of course, non-ratifying countries can still apply salvage law, and therefore there are two parallel bodies of law, one based on domestic law of market nations that favours commercial exploitation (the law of salvage), and an international instrument that, because it is so hostile to the market, fails to find support and change the attitudes of market nations. Therefore, hostility towards economics here also translates into a market that, while regulated by a body of customary law, still fades into the private (the domestic laws of different countries, or even industry self-regulation),[31] and again a private that is overseen by those favouring commercial exploitation of heritage, without input from affected communities.

The two treaties discussed above push the market into the private, and that push seems to stem from a degree of hostility towards it. Other UNESCO treaties are less visibly hostile towards the market, but they still render it invisible by simply not dealing with it at all. It seems that these instruments see the market as vulgarizing heritage in some way, and therefore are also hostile to economics, but less visibly so.

The WHC, for instance, does not mention the economic aspects of heritage at all. It mentions economic conditions as a reason why heritage is threatened,[32] or that economic resources are needed for the protection of heritage.[33] It also mentions the need for economic studies before assistance is given to states.[34] But it does not engage with the idea that World Heritage can be the object of economic relations. In fact, economic motivations for seeking World Heritage List status is seen by many involved in the drafting and early implementation of the WHC as a failure of the system.[35]

The Operational Guidelines for the Implementation of the World Heritage Convention mention other relations between heritage and economic forces. For instance, in defining cultural landscapes (a category that was added to the World Heritage Convention by virtue of the Operational Guidelines), it states that they can be created by the influence of economic forces that influenced humans shaping

[28] For a full discussion of this relationship, see ibid., 226–39.

[29] Vienna Convention on the Law of Treaties (adopted 23 May 1969, entry into force 27 January 1980) 1155 UNTS 331 (VCLT), Article 2(1). See also UCHC, Article 33, stipulating that the Annex is an integral part of the UCHC.

[30] UCHC Annex, Article 2.

[31] For an example, see Dromgoole (n 23) 214–16.

[32] Convention concerning the Protection of the World Cultural and Natural Heritage 1972 (adopted 23 November 1972, entered into force 15 December 1975) 1037 UNTS 151 (WHC), Preamble.

[33] Ibid.

[34] Ibid., Article 24.

[35] Cameron, Christina and Rössler, Mechtild, *Many Voices, One Vision: The Early Years of the World Heritage Convention* (Ashgate, 2013), 235.

of the environment around them,[36] the same applying to heritage canals.[37] The Guidelines also acknowledge that economic process can be part of the broader setting within which World Heritage sites exist, and which needs to be included in the management of these sites.[38] But, even if economic forces can be a factor that creates or is part of heritage, it is still first and foremost a threat in this document. The Operational Guidelines follow the lead of the WHC in conceptualizing economic forces as a threat to heritage that needs to be contained.[39]

The WHC Operational Guidelines engage somewhat more with the commercialization of heritage when discussing the uses of the World Heritage emblem, which is admittedly a tool for the marketing of heritage sites.[40] But the Operational Guidelines specify that the emblem is off limits to tourism operators and other commercial enterprises, 'except under exceptional circumstances and when manifest benefit to the World Heritage generally or particular World Heritage properties can be demonstrated'.[41] If such use is authorized, then the World Heritage Fund should get a share of the revenues.[42] And, while tourism in World Heritage Sites is acknowledged by the Guidelines, it is only mentioned as part of the obligations of states in either preparing nominations or in reporting on the status of certain World Heritage Sites. Therefore, the relationship between the WHC (and the system under it) and economics is also one that pushes the economic dimensions of cultural heritage into the private, or something that is undesirable when it involves UNESCO directly (such as the use of the World Heritage emblem). Heritage is not to be vulgarized by its commercial exploitation; it is to be safeguarded in spite of it. Economic uses of heritage can form heritage, but, once heritage is recognized as such, these very uses become the enemy—pressures that can lead heritage astray, and challenge its integrity and authenticity. By implying this negative impact, the World Heritage system also seems to be implying that the engagement of communities around heritage sites is not helpful to the protection of heritage. Heritage is not to be lived or treated as a resource, it seems. It is to be gazed upon and kept intact for the benefit of present and future generations, reinforcing the conservation paradigm and its exclusionary effects vis-à-vis communities. However, the economic exploitation of heritage does not cease by fiat of the WHC. Indeed, the Operational Guidelines admit this possibility, but do not regulate it. By not regulating the economics of heritage, the WHC misses an opportunity, and allows the economics of heritage to move elsewhere, to fora such as the UNWTO, which is discussed in Section 5.3.1.

The last major UNESCO treaty that needs to be considered in its relationship to the market is the ICHC. This instrument is important, as discussed in earlier chapters, in that it promotes a novel way to think about heritage. Heritage moves from

[36] Operational Directives for the Implementation of the Convention for the Safeguarding of the Intangible Cultural Heritage (adopted 2016), para. 47. See also the 'Guidelines on the inscription of specific types of properties on the World Heritage List' that are an annex to the Operational Guidelines for the Implementation of the World Heritage Convention.

[37] Guidelines on the inscription of specific types of properties on the World Heritage List, para. 20(ii).

[38] Operational Guidelines, para. 112.

[39] Ibid., paras 98 and 111.c.

[40] Ibid., paras 264 and 275.

[41] Ibid., para. 275(g).

[42] Ibid., para. 275(h).

being static to living; living heritage is capable of changing without losing its attributes, and it is only heritage to the extent that people interact with it. So, it would seem that the ICHC would be a particularly welcoming instrument to the relationship between heritage and the market.

However, the notion of the ICHC has a less than warm relationship with the economics of heritage.[43] In fact, the very term 'intangible cultural heritage' was coined as a negative reaction to the market. It was perceived by experts in the field that the term 'folklore' had been captured by commercial interests and turned heritage into kitsch. Therefore, a new term needed to be coined, and the ICHC drafters opted for 'intangible cultural heritage'. Therefore, the ICHC is premised, like other UNESCO treaties, on the idea of the market as a threat to cultural heritage. The market can 'folklorize' heritage, turn it into kitsch, and commodify it in a way that makes it something to be performed purely for economic gain, as opposed to its performance for the pursuance of a given group's identity, which is seen as the pristine objective of the ICHC.[44] In fact, the ICHC does not mention economics or the market at all in its text.

However, the Operational Directives for the Implementation of the Convention for the Safeguarding of the Intangible Cultural Heritage (2016 version) engage with the possibility of commercialization of ICH.[45] The Operational Directives recognize that commercial activities can emerge from intangible heritage (in fact, traditional craftsmanship is nothing if not an economic activity),[46] and embraces these activities to the extent they can promote awareness about the importance of ICH and generate income to its practitioners. But they also warn that commercial activities should not threaten the viability of ICH, and that communities should be the beneficiaries of any economic benefits accruing from the exploitation of their heritage.[47] Particularly, the commercial misappropriation of ICH is considered a threat (and is the reason why so much literature on ICH explores the potentials of intellectual property law to protect ICH),[48] and the Operational Directives insist that the commercial use must 'not distort the meaning and purpose of the intangible cultural heritage for the community concerned'.[49]

[43] For a discussion in a different context focused only on intangible cultural heritage, see Lixinski, Lucas, 'Intangible Heritage Economics and the Law: Listing, Commodification and Market Alienation', in Natsuko Akagawa and Laurajane Smith (eds), *Safeguarding Intangible Heritage: Practices and Politics* (Routledge 2018), 54–67.

[44] For a more in-depth discussion of the commodification of intangible heritage, as well as the move away from 'folklore' as a term of art, see generally Lixinski, Lucas, *Intangible Cultural Heritage in International Law* (Oxford University Press, 2013), 14–18 and 30–32.

[45] Operational Directives (n 36) paras 116–117.

[46] Commenting on Italian national jurisprudence that recognizes traditional economic activities as heritage, and affords them legal protection, see Andrea Biondi, 'The Legal Protection of Traditional Commercial Activities: Two Decisions of the Italian Constitutional Court', 4(1) *International Journal of Cultural Property* (1995) 129–36. And on intangible heritage that arises out of economic activities, see Kato, Kumi, 'Prayers for the Whales: Spirituality and Ethics of a Former Whaling Community—Intangible Cultural Heritage for Sustainability', *International Journal of Cultural Property* 14 (2007), 283–313.

[47] Operational Directives (n 36) para. 116.

[48] For a summary, see Lixinski (n 44) 175–204.

[49] Operational Directives (n 36) para. 117.

Amendments proposed (and ultimately rejected) to these two paragraphs in 2013 sought to further clarify the relationship between ICH and the market. These amendments sought to expand the number of activities of intangible cultural heritage that have economic dimensions, and acknowledge that trade in ICH could improve not only living standards, but also the quality of life of ICH practitioners. The amendments also expressly said that commercial activities can in fact contribute to the safeguarding of ICH, as opposed to just being in tension with it (as long as many conditions were met, including assessment and mitigation of potential negative effects).[50] Another amendment to the section on commercialization also recognized not only that commercial misappropriation and tourism were threats to ICH, but that listing itself on one of the ICHC's lists (to be discussed in more detail in Chapter 7 below) could, as an unintended consequence, create an economic threat to ICH.[51] These proposed amendments seemed to be both too critical of UNESCO, while also allowing for a more open engagement between cultural heritage and the market. They seemed to go a step too far in relation to what UNESCO and the ICHC organs were comfortable with.

The two paragraphs in the Operational Directives discussed above (in their approved version) are among the very few attempts within UNESCO to directly tackle the economics of heritage. They represent an important step forward, as they attempt to regulate a market in heritage. While heritage is still seen as an unspoiled good to be protected, and commerce and the market still figure largely as enemies of this untainted culture, the Operational Guidelines at least acknowledge that commercialization is bound to happen, that the market does not disappear, and, importantly, that the market can *create* cultural heritage. The market needs to be regulated, and the Operational Directives push for regulation in the way that most protects ICH, as is their mandate. But this treaty, like its predecessors, is still unwilling to concede that the market is not necessarily the enemy of heritage, and can in fact be important to articulate and pursue objectives that are not necessarily economic, but also have to do with the quality of life of heritage practitioners, and even the values of heritage. Heritage is still seen as being separate from commerce, and the line that divides the market and heritage, while more porous now than it was a few decades ago, is still present in the law. And the body of international law, in seeing economics only as a threat to heritage that must be combatted, ignores the fact that heritage is often born out of the destruction of other heritage, and that much heritage needs to constantly evolve and change to stay relevant, even if it may sometimes mean that it becomes something else entirely.[52]

[50] Intergovernmental Committee for the Safeguarding of the Intangible Cultural Heritage, *Draft Amendments to the Operational Directives on safeguarding, commercialization and sustainable development*, Doc. ITH/13/8.COM/13.a, 11 October 2013. Annex, para. 116.

[51] Ibid., para. 117.

[52] Holtorf, Cornelius and Kristensen, Troels Myrup, 'Heritage Erasure: Rethinking "Protection" and "Preservation" ', *International Journal of Heritage Studies* 21(4) (2015), 313–17, 315.

One of the possible bright sides of a more porous engagement with international heritage law (even if only through Directives and Guidelines, and not in the treaty texts themselves) is the recognition that heritage may have values other than itself. Heritage may be valuable not as an end in itself, but to promote a better quality of life for the people who live with and practise heritage. Heritage can also lift living standards of often impoverished communities in source nations, if they are allowed to exploit their own heritage. Having said this, there is a dark side to this engagement, which is the possibility that all of cultural heritage will be reduced to a price tag, and the short-term benefits of commercialization will ultimately threaten the viability and existence of heritage. But this is not necessarily what the market implies, nor is it what economists think of when they discuss the economics of cultural heritage. The following section surveys this literature, and its potentials and pitfalls for rethinking international heritage law and promoting a more community-centric version of it.

5.2 Heritage Economics and Development through Heritage

As discussed in Chapter 1, the conceptual focus of cultural heritage has shifted towards development, alongside a shift from monuments to people, and from objects to functions.[53] From an economic perspective, heritage is a catalyst of economic development, and also one of its engines. There are three dimensions to this debate: (1) heritage as an economic sector in itself; (2) heritage as an economic sector capable of attracting other economic activities; and (3) heritage as a means to manage economies by allowing the creation of images for dominant economic purposes.[54] That said, communities are usually in the microeconomic considerations around heritage, whereas most of these concerns seem to focus on the macroeconomic implications of heritage.

The literature on the economics of cultural heritage can be roughly divided into two generations, which overlap quite significantly. Many of the authors write in both generations, sometimes conflating elements of both in the same text. This literature also relies quite significantly on insights from environmental economics.[55]

The first generation focuses on the econometrics of cultural heritage, and the financial returns (or losses) that could be expected from heritage protection or exploitation. The second generation focuses on economics not only as a way of measuring the economy, but also as a way of explaining human behaviour. I will address each of these generations, and their potential relationships to international heritage law, in turn, before moving to a discussion of development in the context of international heritage protection.

[53] Loulanski (n 1) 207. [54] Ibid., 225.

[55] See for instance Claesson, Stefan, 'The Value and Valuation of Maritime Cultural Heritage', *International Journal of Cultural Property* 18 (2011), 61–80.

5.2.1 First generation: measuring the economic impacts of heritage safeguarding and promotion

Much of the literature here has grappled with questions trying to measure and collect statistics on,[56] for instance, rises in employment,[57] return on public investment in heritage protection,[58] the impact of heritage listing on the value of real estate properties,[59] and even the appraisal of specific heritage sites or artefacts.[60] These studies have measured the impact of tourism on the overall employment and income of a certain region around a World Heritage Site, for instance.[61] Or considered the costs associated with heritage projects or 'investments'. A study produced by a World Bank economist, for example, highlighted some of the questions asked by the World Bank when deciding whether to lend money for investments in cultural heritage, and a lot of those questions had to do with the costs of a project.[62] These include assessing cultural heritage as assets, and asking how much worse off the community would be if the site vanished. Or it can mean considering the benefits or costs of actions that alter the heritage site, which then becomes a question about the costs of change.[63] They are thus closely connected to communities' economic engagement with heritage.

Other literature highlights the type of costs associated with heritage that go beyond the monetary costs. These are known as opportunity costs, which are the costs of a missed opportunity. For instance, if the state chooses to preserve a heritage area, what are the costs of the missed opportunity to have it developed?[64] This is a question that affects in particular community governance over heritage, as the decision about opportunity costs is one that should presumably be made by communities themselves, but, as it stands, it is relegated by international law to states and experts as proxies for communities.

[56] On the collection of statistics, see generally Deloumeaux, Lydia, 'Current Challenges in Cultural Statistics: A Focus on Heritage', in Ilde Rizzo and Anna Mignosa (eds), *Handbook on the Economics of Cultural Heritage* (Edward Elgar, 2013), 187–206.

[57] Vaughan, D. R., 'The Cultural Heritage: An Approach to Analyzing Income and Employment Effects', *Journal of Cultural Economics* 8(2) (1984), 1–36; Greffe, Xavier, 'Is Heritage an Asset or a Liability?', *Journal of Cultural Heritage* 5 (2004), 301–9.

[58] Ruijgrok, E. C. M., 'The Three Economic Values of Cultural Heritage: A Case Study in the Netherlands', *Journal of Cultural Heritage* 7 (2006), 206–13, 211 (finding that 'cultural heritage protection is an economically sound investment').

[59] See for instance Elsorady, Dalia A., 'The Economic Value of Heritage Properties in Alexandria, Egypt', *International Journal of Heritage Studies* 20(2) (2014), 107–22 (finding there is a negative impact); Shipley, Robert, 'Heritage Designation and Property Values: Is There an Effect?', *International Journal of Heritage Studies* 6(1) (2000), 83–100 (finding there is no negative impact); and ECM Ruijgrok (n 58, finding there is actually a positive value).

[60] See for instance Deuchar (n 5).

[61] Bowitz, Einar and Ibenholt, Karin, 'Economic Impacts of Cultural Heritage—Research and Perspectives', *Journal of Cultural Heritage* 10 (2009), 1–8.

[62] Pagiola, Stefano, 'Economic Analysis of Investments in Cultural Heritage: Insights from Environmental Economics', *World Bank Staff Paper* (World Bank, 1996).

[63] Ibid., 1.

[64] Frey, Bruno S., 'Evaluating Cultural Property: The Economic Approach', *International Journal of Cultural Property* 6(2) (1997), 231–46.

One of the underlying assumptions of these studies is to treat heritage as a public good. However, a public good in the economic sense means something quite different from what it means in the heritage sense. For conservationists, cultural heritage is a public good because it is a practice or social process that benefits a large segment of society. Economically, a public good is simply something that belongs in the public domain. Economists seem to assume there is something intrinsic in the structure of a public good, whereas heritage is generated contingently and contextually.[65]

Many of these studies helped map the direct and indirect effects of cultural heritage projects on the economy.[66] Among the indirect effects, studies have measured input–output effects (rise in production in the local economy to service the heritage project), multiplier effects (the rise in local income spreads over to other sectors of the economy), acceleration effects (a merger of input–output and multiplier effects, but only applicable in the short term, while the heritage site is being prepared for outside consumption), ancillary spending (spending that tourists make on non-heritage services, like accommodation and food), derived effects (other heritage activities that are established around the initial heritage investment), gravitation (heritage areas are more attractive for people to live in, and attract investment in other areas as a result), and non-economic (such as reinforced local identity) and counteracting effects (wear and tear caused by tourists, pressures on infrastructure, and displacement effects). Displacement effects are particularly important, as they shed light on the idea that the economic success of a heritage site can displace other economic interests.[67]

Importantly, too, a project will only benefit the local economy if it can attract tourists from the outside, injecting new capital into the region. But that means a dependence on outside capital that will only be effective in the short term.[68] It also means that tourists coming to one place will likely not go elsewhere. There is a single finite pool of potential tourists that heritage tourism seems to share.[69]

Also with regard to tourism, this literature helps elucidate that the benefits accrued from tourism do not always end up in the local economy. Many of the benefits are enjoyed in effect by non-members of the local community, and only a fraction of the benefits can actually be counted as local benefits. Therefore, figures describing the economic impact of the tourism industry are necessarily distorted, if one considers the perspective of the community where tourism takes place (as they do not receive all the money that is nominally spent there).[70] Local communities pay for

[65] Mason, Randall, 'Conference Reports: Economics and Heritage Conservation: Concepts, Values and Agendas for Research, Getty Conservation Institute, Los Angeles (December 8–11, 1998)', *International Journal of Cultural Property* 8(2) (1999), 550–62, 554–5.

[66] See for instance Noonan, Douglas S., 'Market Effects of Historic Preservation', in Ilde Rizzo and Anna Mignosa (eds), *Handbook on the Economics of Cultural Heritage* (Edward Elgar, 2013), 344–63.

[67] Bowitz and Ibenholt (n 61) 3–5.

[68] Ibid., 6.

[69] Pagiola (n 62) 10. See also Bedate, Ana, Herrero, Luis César, and Sanz, José Ángel, 'Economic Valuation of the Cultural Heritage: Application to Four Case Studies in Spain', *Journal of Cultural Heritage* 5 (2004), 101–111.

[70] Pagiola (n 62) 11.

much of the costs of heritage development (particularly the opportunity costs), and do not necessarily accrue the benefits.[71]

One of the key limitations of these economic methods is that they cannot quite measure values that cannot be monetized, such as identity values, which also drive expenditure in heritage.[72] By focusing on outcomes over processes, economics finds it difficult to understand the processes that create and assign value to heritage.[73] Therefore, econometrics is not equipped to grasp the whole gamut of what heritage means beyond the objects themselves. International law, to a certain extent, can serve as a barometer of those meanings, even if it is also biased towards certain objectives, as previous chapters in this book have shown.

Another issue approached by some of the literature, that tries to grapple with socioeconomic differences between source nations and market nations, is that for many source nations profitability is a distinctive possibility when exploiting heritage, whereas most market nations can at most hope to break even in their costs. Therefore, the question of allocation of the economic surpluses arising from the exploitation of heritage is not often a question for market nations, but it is vital in the context of source nations, where (1) profitability can easily become overexploitation; and (2) the local needs to be contextualized so as to enable capitals to flow in that direction, as opposed to staying within the market nations (through tourism operators located there), or with the central government of the source nation.[74]

A potential downside of first-generation cultural economics in thinking about heritage is that economic values often do not match cultural values associated with heritage, at least in a classic understanding of economics.[75] The reduction of cultural heritage to monetary values is a fairly extreme form of commodification, and fundamentally opposed to conservation views.[76] Also, the logic of the market requires a definition of the 'heritage product' that is often difficult to pin down for monetizing purposes. It is difficult to know whether the product is tickets sold for admittance into a heritage site, the number of exhibitions, the cultural experiences, or something else.[77] The heritage product is an essential part of the heritage market, too, as it is the basis for the business model.[78]

What this first generation of heritage economics means for international law is, first, proof that a market in heritage exists and is unavoidable. It also shows that the econometrics of heritage are weighted against those who live with heritage.

71 Ashworth (n 5) 13. 72 Bedate, Herrero, and Sanz (n 69) 110.

73 Mason, Randall, 'Economics and Heritage Conservation: Concepts, Values, and Agendas for Research', in *Economics and Heritage Conservation—A Meeting Organized by the Getty Conservation Institute, December 1998* (J. Paul Getty Trust, 1998), 2–18, 2.

74 Zan, Luca, 'Economic Discourse and Heritage Conservation: Towards and Ethnography of Administrations', *Heritage & Society* 6(2) (2013), 167–84, 173–4.

75 Mason (n 65) 552–3. 76 Ibid., 554.

77 Klamer, Arjo and Zuidhof, Peter-Wim, 'The Values of Cultural Heritage: Merging Economic and Cultural Appraisals', in *Economics and Heritage Conservation—A Meeting Organized by the Getty Conservation Institute, December 1998* (The J. Paul Getty Trust, 1998), 23–58, 28.

78 Colbert, François, 'The Marketing of Heritage Venues or Destinations', in Ilde Rizzo and Anna Mignosa (eds), *Handbook on the Economics of Cultural Heritage* (Edward Elgar, 2013), 231–48, 240.

Therefore, international law can play an important role of carving a space for communities' involvement in the governance of their heritage, as long as it is willing to also consider the economic dimensions of heritage (which, as the previous section indicates, is not quite the case).

5.2.2 Second generation: the production of value in heritage and policy guidance

The second generation of literature on the economics of heritage attempts to explain the creation of values associated with heritage, and how they influence policymaking about heritage,[79] thus being capable of accounting for both tangible and intangible benefits people derive from heritage.[80] This literature moves away from conflating the economics of heritage with the business of heritage, and applies economic thinking more broadly.[81] This literature also expands the idea of multiple values, both monetary and non-monetary, that can be attributed to heritage. One of the monetary values, that is not exactly a figure but translates into one quickly, is the value of authenticity, which is very important to the conservation discourse,[82] as it indelibly establishes the intrinsic value of heritage.[83] Authenticity helps assert and shift control over heritage, as discussed in Chapter 1.[84] So, in some way, there is additional political value closely associated with the first monetary economics of heritage, inasmuch as it translates into control.

Non-monetary values include the option value (people would like to have the option to enjoy heritage in the future, even if they do not right now), the existence value (people benefit just from seeing a historic building on their way to work, for instance, even if they do not actually visit it), the bequest value (the importance of being able to leave heritage to future generations), the prestige value (heritage creates a sense of pride and cultural identity),[85] and the educational value (heritage helps teach about history, and it also helps train artists and designers, whose creativity ultimately benefits all of society).[86] These values derive from economic thinking, and do not necessarily align with other values attributed to heritage by other disciplines,

[79] See e.g. Throsby, David, 'Regional Aspects of Heritage Economics: Analytical and Policy Issues', *Australasian Journal of Regional Studies* 13(1) (2007), 21–30.

[80] Claesson (n 55) 63.

[81] Mason (n 6) 304.

[82] Krus (n 6) 74–5. See also Cruz, Jasmine T., 'The Economics of Heritage', *Business World* (27 December 2012).

[83] Mason, Randall, 'Assessing Values in Conservation Planning: Methodological Issues and Choices', in Marta de la Torre (ed.), *Assessing the Values of Cultural Heritage: Research Report* (The J. Paul Getty Trust, 2002), 5–30, 13.

[84] For a discussion of authenticity, see Lixinski, Lucas, 'A Tale of Two Heritages: Claims of Ownership over Intangible Cultural Heritage and the Myth of "Authenticity" ', *Transnational Dispute Management* 11(2) (2014).

[85] Amestoy, Victoria Ateca, 'Demand for Cultural Heritage', in Ilde Rizzo and Anna Mignosa (eds), *Handbook on the Economics of Cultural Heritage* (Edward Elgar, 2013), 89–110, 96.

[86] For a summary, see Mourato, Susana and Mazzanti, Massimiliano, 'Economic Valuation of Cultural Heritage: Evidence and Prospects', in Marta de la Torre (ed.), *Assessing the Values of Cultural Heritage: Research Report* (The J. Paul Getty Trust, 2002), 51–76. See also Frey (n 64) 233.

which is part of the reason why economics has had very limited impact on heritage,[87] particularly from regulatory and conservationist perspectives.

Given the limitations of classical economics, concepts such as 'cultural capital' can be used to make a bridge between the fields of heritage and economics, and the monetary and non-monetary values of heritage.[88] Cultural capital is a term that conveys the idea of heritage as yielding different values in the goods and services it produces, and assumes a separation (but still a relationship) between the economic and cultural values of heritage.[89] This relationship fits into a more holistic take on heritage. Cultural capital could perhaps operate as a gateway for international heritage law into economics, as it already performs a bridging function, and is associated with a holistic take on heritage that is consistent with regimes such as the ICHC.

These monetary and non-monetary values are often assessed through impact studies. Other forms of engagement of economic methods with heritage include willingness-to-pay studies (which measure how much people are willing to spend on the preservation of heritage), and contingent valuation studies, which can help in prioritizing management strategies, among other things.[90] These methods can be useful in that they identify the 'consumers' of heritage (which often align with the local community) to help determine priorities, for instance, in the identification and listing of heritage sites.[91] Choice modelling approaches can also be helpful, particularly as they can help measure the extent to which the measures safeguarding heritage manage the expectations of the local community, and help understand the value the local community places on the way its heritage is marketed.[92] They can therefore also be a tool to articulate the social relevance of heritage.[93]

As a result of the application of these methods, heritage is perceived by economists in this second generation as a 'merit good', which is a good that is made possible from the surplus of economic development,[94] meaning it is typically to be found in market, rather than source, nations, as in the latter the scarcity of resources usually means that public investment in heritage is sacrificed.[95] Even if this assumption is somewhat problematic (as discussed below), it is the notion of merit good that allows for economists to engage with other dimensions of cultural heritage within

[87] Mason (n 83) 10.

[88] Throsby, David, 'Cultural Capital and Sustainability Concepts in the Economics of Cultural Heritage', in Marta de la Torre (ed.), *Assessing the Values of Cultural Heritage: Research Report* (The J. Paul Getty Trust, 2002), 101–17, 101.

[89] Ibid., 103.

[90] For a review of methods, see Mason, Randall, 'Economics and Historic Preservation: A Guide and Review of the Literature', *The Brookings Institution Metropolitan Policy Program Discussion Paper* (2005), 11–18. See also Stefan Claesson (n 55) 62.

[91] Mazzanti, Massimiliano, 'Valuing Cultural Heritage in a Multi-Attribute Framework: Microeconomic Perspectives and Policy Implications', *Journal of Socio-Economics* 32 (2003), 549–69, 554.

[92] Choi, Andy S. et al., 'Economic Valuation of Cultural Heritage Sites: A Choice Modeling Approach', *Tourism Management* 31 (2010), 213–20, 213.

[93] Mason (n 6) 310.

[94] Mazzanti, Massimiliano, 'Cultural Heritage as Multi-Dimensional, Multi-Value and Multi-Attribute Economic Good: Toward a New Framework for Economic Analysis and Valuation', *Journal of Socio-Economics* 31 (2002), 529–58.

[95] Klamer and Zuidhof (n 77) 27.

their discipline.[96] These goods usually show a high degree of deference by economists to heritage experts, as it falls upon the expert to define what 'merit' is.[97] Merit goods have also been perceived as political, though, and have been criticized for inducing inefficiency and rent-seeking behaviours.[98] But it seems that economists would still rather defer to experts in their assessment of the worth of heritage, and, here, international heritage law can also play a part if it carves a role for communities to be able to present their views on heritage's merits alongside experts and states.

This type of thinking around heritage can also work to unravel the public/private distinction that, as discussed, can account for much of the lack of consideration of the economic dimensions of heritage in international heritage law. Valuation of heritage using multi-value frameworks can help compare what Mazzanti calls the political and economic 'jurisdictions' over heritage, where the political jurisdiction is the level of government providing for heritage (and thus mapping onto the law), and the economic jurisdiction 'includes all individuals receiving the cultural heritage benefits'.[99]

The public and private are essential to understanding the economics of heritage, too, seeing as much of heritage is privately owned, but it still regulated by public systems.[100] These mechanics have been discussed in more detail in Chapter 2. For present purposes, an economic history of heritage protection is also to some extent a private history of heritage (partly discussed in Chapter 3): it starts from heritage being acquired by private collectors as 'positional goods' (i.e. status symbols), moving to a philanthropic interest in the protection of heritage for the purposes of educating the poor, and finally becomes a publicly managed system for the protection of heritage important to galvanize national identity and consequently nationalist movements.[101]

Thus, economic thinking can assist in understanding how the public and private are both involved in the economics of heritage. And better integration between the public and the private, in legal forms such as public–private partnerships, can assist in articulating and mediating a number of these tensions.[102]

One of the downsides of this second generation, much like the first one, is that it seems to pervasively use neoclassical economics, which is a-contextual and a-historical, and thus fails to measure the meaning of heritage before ascribing value to it.[103] As a consequence, economic approaches to heritage largely fail to capture

[96] For a brief review of literature, see Mazzanti (n 94) 531–6.

[97] Peacock, Alan and Rizzo, Ilde, *The Heritage Game: Economics, Policy, and Practice* (Oxford University Press, 2008), 23.

[98] Mazzanti (n 94) 532.

[99] Mazzanti (n 91) 552.

[100] Seaman, Bruce A., 'The Role of the Private Sector in Cultural Heritage', in Ilde Rizzo and Anna Mignosa (eds), *Handbook on the Economics of Cultural Heritage* (Edward Elgar, 2013), 111–28, 113.

[101] Peacock and Rizzo (n 97) 8.

[102] For a case study, see Rypkema, Donovan D., 'Heritage and Development: The Role of Public–Private Partnerships', in Mikko Mälkki, Raine Mäntysalo, and Kaisa Schmidt-Thomé (eds), *Economics and Built Heritage—Towards New European Initiatives* (Helsinki University of Technology, 2008), 131–50.

[103] Stanziola, Javier, 'Modelling the Heritage World: Economic, Legal and Political Considerations', *International Journal of Heritage Studies* 4(3-4) (1998), 168–76, 170. See also Zan (n 74) 169.

the politics of heritage, and tend to excessively defer to experts for their determinations of the meaning of heritage,[104] thereby contributing to the alienation of local stakeholders from their own culture. Even if the notion of merit goods can be seen as having political value and can trigger uses of heritage in favour of minorities and other disadvantaged groups,[105] much of the thinking around heritage economics still makes these considerations secondary. It has been argued that identity values (which are closely aligned with the politics of heritage) can in fact be measured using economic methods, as they affect the perceived utility of heritage, but even then identity is subsumed under neoclassical economics.[106] But she same study concludes that 'identity is required for a very limited scope of cultural goods',[107] which can be seen as downplaying the political possibilities of heritage. The authors argue that only when heritage is sacred to a certain population, and still living heritage, can identity be a relevant consideration in establishing the parameters of protection.[108]

This second generation considers regulation as a way of getting information about the social value given to heritage, but one that is only partly effective, as incentives are seldom clearly laid out in the law (particularly international law).[109] But international law can also be a way of integrating politics into considerations about the values associated with heritage, and thus international heritage law, rather than compete with economics for assigning value to heritage, can in fact cooperate with it. As values are assigned in a more political manner, the development potentials of heritage can be fleshed out in a way that more clearly benefits communities and other local stakeholders.

5.2.3 Heritage and development

As indicated, many of the processes through which heritage is valued see it as a merit good. Heritage, then, is seen first and foremost as a cost, a burden on society, as indicated by much of the first-generation literature on heritage economics described above. But heritage can itself be a wealth generator that can be enlisted not for its own benefit, but also to further other objectives.[110] Hence the connection between cultural heritage and development. With respect to sustainable development, the linkages are discussed in Chapter 6. For now, I wish to focus on the discussion of economic development more broadly.

There seems to be an assumption underlying recent literature on the economics of heritage that heritage can be a 'universally applicable panacea for economic development at all spatial scales',[111] in spite of earlier studies that actually blamed poverty on culture.[112] That is a problematic assumption, at least inasmuch as the expectations

[104] Mazzanti (n 91) 565. [105] Mazzanti (n 94) 537.

[106] Bicskei, Marianna Bizer, Kilian, and Gubaydullina, Zulia, 'Protection of Cultural Goods—Economics of Identity', *International Journal of Cultural Property* 19 (2012), 97–118, 99.

[107] Ibid., 97. [108] Ibid., 110. [109] Peacock and Rizzo (n 97) 146.

[110] Ashworth (n 5) 11. [111] Ibid., 6.

[112] For a retelling, see Vives, Alberto Abello and Candela, Dina, 'La Cultura en la Superación de la Pobreza', in Alfons Martinell Sempere (ed.), *Impactos de la Dimensión Cultural en el Desarrollo* (Documenta Universitaria, 2013), 53–100, 66.

set upon the development potential of heritage are based on a resource (culture) that was not necessarily created for developmental purposes, is not managed by people sympathetic to the economic uses of heritage (experts), and can itself be an obstacle to development, as the earlier discussion on opportunity costs shows.[113]

Nevertheless, it is important to highlight that heritage has at least the potential to realize development.[114] The economic crisis of 2008 has moved along ideas about the potential of cultural heritage to promote development.[115] Regional organizations, and even UNESCO, have also engaged with the connection between heritage and development, but this connection has tended to centre on the potential of heritage as a cultural industry.[116] International law, alongside critiques coming from the field of international law and development, can help mediate the relationship between international heritage law and development in a way that treats heritage not simply as a resource to be exploited and ultimately exhausted, but as the foundation for much more diversified development possibilities.[117]

Aligning heritage with development implies challenging the conservation paradigm that riddles much of heritage (and particularly most of international heritage law). It means taking heritage under a paradigm that not only does not align with the goals of preservation, but in fact contradicts them. Heritage is in fact a development option, if we think of it as 'whatever the present selects from imagined pasts to satisfy contemporary needs'.[118] But this option implies thinking of heritage as a very dynamic, changing concept and set of practices, monuments, and sites (clashing with some of its relationship with time, discussed in Chapter 4), and it adds nuance to decisions around what heritage to choose for what purposes (including economic ones).

Heritage as a development driver cannot be relied upon too much, though. Studies indicate that heritage development is most effective in areas that, ironically, need it the least. Places most reliant on heritage will benefit the least from heritage development (as resources tend to flow externally), whereas places in which heritage is only a marginal addition will benefit the most.[119] Mono-functional uses of heritage as an instrument of development are therefore problematic.[120]

The private (once rendered visible, and regulated) can again play an important role in development through heritage, either through initiatives like public–private partnerships[121] or by the private actor soliciting and contributing money to heritage

[113] Ashworth (n 5) 367. And, decrying the lack of consideration of opportunity costs in the literature supporting heritage tourism as a driver of development, see Peacock and Rizzo (n 97)118–19.

[114] Ashworth (n 5) 7.

[115] Klamer, Arjo, Mignosa, Anna, and Petrova, Lyudmila, 'Cultural Heritage Policies: A Comparative Perspective', in Ilde Rizzo and Anna Mignosa (eds), *Handbook on the Economics of Cultural Heritage* (Edward Elgar, 2013), 37–86, 38.

[116] For a discussion, see generally Peacock and Rizzo (n 97).

[117] On a broader take on development and culture's role in it, based on cultural rights, see Martinell Sempere, Alfons and Funollet Obiols, Urgell, 'Derechos Culturales y Desarrollo: Una Propuesta de Análisis de Sus Impactos', in Alfons Martinell Sempere (ed.), *Impactos de la Dimensión Cultural en el Desarrollo* (Documenta Universitaria, 2013), 17–52.

[118] Ashworth (n 5) 8.

[119] Greffe (n 57) 307–9.

[120] Ashworth (n 5) 16.

[121] Rypkema (n 102).

activities. After all, from a built heritage perspective, most heritage-listed buildings are privately owned,[122] and that is not seen as incompatible with the requirements of international heritage listing. For example, in historic city centres like Florence or Venice, invariably large parts of the heritage sites are owned privately, and the successful safeguarding of this heritage depends on cooperation between public and private sectors. Once again, the community is integral to the process of safeguarding, and its role needs to be accounted for not only domestically, but also internationally, if international law is to engage with the economics of heritage effectively.

Tourism is also a private sector initiative that deeply influences development through heritage, even if it is seen by many as a 'vulgar' form of promoting development.[123] The role of tourism in the economics of heritage will be discussed in more detail below, but for now it is important to say that one of the problems associated with heritage tourism is the discrepancy between internalities and externalities. Heritage safeguarding costs money (internalities), but is usually enjoyed at zero cost by many tourists, who do not spend their money directly on heritage, but elsewhere like food and accommodation (externalities). Therefore, the economic returns of tourism are indirect and difficult to invoke in justifying the safeguarding of heritage.[124] Further, international law does not promote means to correct this discrepancy, as it is preoccupied with other interests related to tourism (to be discussed below). Tourism has both positive and negative effects on heritage,[125] and that is a reason why it should be more closely watched by heritage standard-setting bodies like UNESCO.

5.3 Alternative Fora for the Economic Dimensions of Cultural Heritage

An engagement with the economics of heritage may have largely escaped UNESCO, but international standard-setting fora concerned with economic matters have considered culture and heritage in their own activities. The engagement of economic bodies with heritage is in principle a positive thing, as it contributes to the defragmentation of international law. But the fact that these bodies are engaging with heritage not in cooperation with UNESCO, but instead occupying a gap left by UNESCO's reluctance to engage in economics, is not necessarily positive. These bodies, because of the 'institutional goggles' they wear, have mandates that are meant to privilege interests other than heritage, and, as UNESCO does not offer a counterbalance, a true engagement with the economics of heritage in a way that considers the blind spots of economics highlighted in the previous section seems

[122] Seaman (n 100) 112.
[123] In the context of the World Heritage Convention, see Cameron and Rössler (n 35) 236.
[124] Ashworth (n 5) 380.
[125] Bonet, Lluís, 'Heritage Tourism', in Ilde Rizzo and Anna Mignosa (eds), *Handbook on the Economics of Cultural Heritage* (Edward Elgar, 2013), 386–401, 400.

elusive. Further, and most importantly, communities may have even less access to these fora, and at the very least should not be expected to navigate an international bureaucratic maze.

This section will examine three examples of engagement with heritage in economic fora. These short case studies will focus on the institutions themselves, but in some instances will be expanded to cover the economic sector they focus on in general, to add more nuance and context to the discussion. The subsections that follow will examine the work of the two WTOs (the World Trade Organization and the older World Tourism Organization). The World Tourism Organization (UNWTO) is a standard-setting body par excellence, whereas the World Trade Organization (WTO) performs adjudicatory functions as well, thus adding another layer of nuance to the discussions. The third case study is of a body the exclusive purpose of which is dispute settlement—the International Centre for the Settlement of Investment Disputes (ICSID), part of the World Bank group.

5.3.1 World Tourism Organization: heritage tourism as development alternative or trap?

The UNWTO is a United Nations Specialized Agency responsible 'for the promotion of responsible, sustainable and universally accessible tourism'.[126] Its membership includes 157 countries, six Associate Members and 480 Affiliate Members (the latter largely being private sector entities, such as tourism operators, and educational institutions).[127] The UNWTO was created in 1970 to replace the International Union of Official Travel Organizations, which had been established in 1946 to replace the League of Nations' International Union of Official Tourist Propaganda Organizations.[128] The names of the predecessor organizations already point to the organization being primarily focused on the tourism industry, hence the importance of participation of Affiliate Members in its activities.

The UNWTO sees tourism as a key driver of development, and measures its economic impact at about USD 1.5 trillion a year (2014 figures).[129] And it has worked within the UN system to make sure tourism is seen as part of the development agenda across the board.[130]

With respect to cultural tourism, cooperation between the UNWTO and UNESCO goes back to at least 1994, where they held their first joint meeting and adopted the Samarkand Declaration on Silk Road Tourism.[131] Since then, these two organizations have held several joint meetings on other specific heritage sites, including a meeting in Tehran on the relationship between tourism and handicrafts (which are a form of ICH), in 2006.[132] A World Heritage and Sustainable Tourism

[126] UNWTO, *Who We Are*, at http://www2.unwto.org/content/who-we-are-0.

[127] Ibid. [128] UNWTO, *History*, at http://www2.unwto.org/content/history-0.

[129] UNWTO, *Why Tourism?*, at http://www2.unwto.org/content/why-tourism.

[130] UNWTO, *UNWTO & the UN System*, at http://icr.unwto.org/content/unwto-un-system.

[131] UNWTO, *History* (n 128). [132] Ibid.

programme was created in 2001, and a number of joint initiatives of the UNWTO and UNESCO fall under its umbrella.[133]

The definition of heritage tourism is very difficult, as statistics indicate that most cultural tourists do not travel primarily in order to access heritage, but for other purposes.[134] Heritage tourism can nevertheless be defined as 'the explicit and voluntary contact that tourists have, away from their normal places of residence, with cultural heritage through the visit or consumption of heritage goods and services'.[135] This definition includes visits to historical cities, monuments, places of worship, archaeological sites, museums, and, potentially, also performances of intangible cultural heritage. This definition is clearly oriented towards heritage as a product, rather than a process.[136]

Cultural heritage is also the object of Article 4 of the UNWTO's Global Code of Ethics of Tourism, which is its main standard-setting instrument.[137] Article 4 states that:

ARTICLE 4: **Tourism, a user of the cultural heritage of [hu]mankind and contributor to its enhancement**

1. Tourism resources belong to the common heritage of [hu]mankind; the communities in whose territories they are situated have particular rights and obligations to them;
2. Tourism policies and activities should be conducted with respect for the artistic, archaeological and cultural heritage, which they should protect and pass on to future generations; particular care should be devoted to preserving and upgrading monuments, shrines and museums as well as archaeological and historic sites which must be widely open to tourist visits; encouragement should be given to public access to privately-owned cultural property and monuments, with respect for the rights of their owners, as well as to religious buildings, without prejudice to normal needs of worship;
3. Financial resources derived from visits to cultural sites and monuments should, at least in part, be used for the upkeep, safeguard, development and embellishment of this heritage;
4. Tourism activity should be planned in such a way as to allow traditional cultural products, crafts and folklore to survive and flourish, rather than causing them to degenerate and become standardized.

This article, even if not legally binding, showcases a number of important principles on the relationship between tourism and heritage. It starts from the assumption that tourism works to enhance the cultural heritage. But the assumption here is that tourism simply provides the financial means to safeguard heritage, rather than tourism also being a means of selecting cultural heritage, which is a problem highlighted in the literature on the economics of heritage. Importantly, too, the article highlights the relationship between tourism and intangible heritage, indicating that tourism should be planned in a way that does not overtly commodify ICH, but rather allows it to 'survive and flourish'. Given the widespread presence of governments and private sector entities in the UNWTO membership, it would

[133] UNESCO World Heritage Centre, *Sustainable Tourism—UNESCO World Heritage and Sustainable Tourism Programme*, available at http://whc.unesco.org/en/tourism/.

[134] Bonet(n 125) 387. [135] Ibid., 387–8. [136] Ibid., 388.

[137] UNWTO, *Global Code of Ethics for Tourism*, at http://ethics.unwto.org/en/content/global-code-ethics-tourism.

seem the relationship between tourism and cultural heritage is balanced and takes into account cultural heritage values and priorities. The same attitude is pervasive in a UNWTO publication on tourism and intangible heritage, which highlights the possibilities of promoting tourism and development through the safeguarding of ICH.[138] Also importantly, this article does not mention communities.

The 2013 Siem Reap Declaration on Tourism Development in Cultural and Natural Heritage Sites expands on some of these principles. It highlights the need to establish partnerships between local and national authorities to promote more sustainable heritage tourism,[139] and the need to effectively communicate heritage meanings to tourists.[140] The role of local communities in communicating their heritage, and also the need to get them involved in the safeguarding of their own heritage, are also core recommendations of the Siem Reap Declaration.[141] The assumption here is that well-informed tourists, because of the attachments they develop to heritage and the place, are more likely to support tourism activities that benefit the local community.[142] This meeting took into account the specific needs of its host country, Cambodia, and particularly the tensions around the World Heritage Site of Angkor Wat.[143]

Also in 2013, a meeting on Silk Road tourism was held, and identified the safeguarding of heritage as one of five key thematic approaches to create 'opportunities for tourism growth'.[144] The document estimates that 40 per cent of global tourism is cultural tourism, and highlights the possible negative impacts of growth in visitor numbers.[145] What the document does not do is engage with the local populations, which is a particularly challenging task in a serial heritage site like the Silk Road, where there are not only multiple sites and landscapes, but also an array of manifestations of intangible cultural heritage.

From the perspective of UNESCO in an appearance at a UNWTO meeting on heritage tourism, it seems these are not major problems. As far as World Heritage Sites are concerned, at least, the position of UNESCO is that tourism contributes to enhancing the visibility of heritage sites, which is one of the objectives of the WHC (and most other UNESCO heritage treaties).[146] This speech paints a fairly positive

[138] Du Cros, Hillary, *Tourism and Intangible Cultural Heritage* (UNWTO, 2012).

[139] UNWTO, Siem Reap Declaration on Tourism Development in Cultural and Natural Heritage Sites (2013), A.3.

[140] Ibid.,B.2. [141] Ibid., C.6.

[142] Brooks, Graham, 'Communicating Heritage: A UNWTO Handbook for the Tourism Sector', paper presented at the *55th Meeting of the UNWTO Commission for Europe and Seminar on Tourism on World Heritage Sites: Challenges and Opportunities*, available at <http://europe.unwto.org/event/55th-meeting-unwto-commission-europe-and-seminar-tourism-world-heritage-sites-challenges-and-o> (accessed 30 October 2017).

[143] For a discussion of some of these tensions, in light of tourism promotion through media products like cinema, see Winter, Tim, 'Angkor Meets *Tomb Raider*: Setting the Scene', *International Journal of Heritage Studies* 8(4) (2002), 323–36.

[144] UNWTO, *Conclusions & Highlights of the 6th UNWTO International Meeting on Silk Road Tourism* (Dunhuang, Gansu, 1–3 August 2013), at http://silkroad.unwto.org/event/meeting-information-6th-unwto-international-meeting-silk-road-tourism.

[145] Ibid.

[146] Rao, Kishore, 'Remarks by Kishore Rao, Director of the UNESCO World Heritage Centre', at the *55th Meeting of the UNWTO Commission for Europe and Seminar on Tourism on World Heritage*

picture of the relationship between tourism and cultural heritage. While it does call attention to the possibility of over-exploitation of a site, and dangers to its integrity and authenticity (important elements as far as the WHC's system is concerned), overall it is supportive of tourism's interaction with heritage sites.

In practice, though, tourism's interactions with cultural heritage are often tense. On one hand, it is said that heritage can allow the community to take part in the positive aspects of globalization (by attracting tourists), while resisting the 'bad', homogenizing forces of globalization.[147] But on the other, in practice there seem to be deliberate strategies in many tourism sites to separate tourists from local communities and prevent their interaction, and that is usually the premise of high-end tourism.[148] One of the effects of this dissociation is that certain heritages are privileged over others, thus essentializing identity.[149] Another effect is that the separation in practice also means that the money flows that come with tourism do not reach the local communities directly. As they do not enjoy the benefits of the exploitation of the heritage around them, but bear burdens like traffic congestion, water scarcity, and price rises in restaurants and other local businesses and services, they are likely not only to be alienated from the heritage around which they live, but even to actively resent it.

Also importantly, in heritage sites that are currently used for non-tourist purposes, there may also be tensions between local communities and tourists. But it seems, at least in the case of religious sites, that conflicts can be mediated, and that heritage listing of religious sites can in fact enhance religious pilgrimage to those sites. It is unclear how the interaction between locals and tourists who also take part in the intangible heritage (the religious practice) of the site is perceived by the locals, but it seems locals enjoy the enhancement of the prestige and visibility of the place.[150] When it comes to living religious practices, though, there is a risk that lack of consultation with the practicing community will lead to further alienation, which, in the case of religious minorities, can also equate with state oppression.[151]

There are also different expectations about what the heritage tourism experience should look like, which are culturally sensitive. For instance, Chinese tourists expect tourist sites to be well-developed in terms of amenities, whereas Western tourists

Sites: Challenges and Opportunities, available at http://europe.unwto.org/event/55th-meeting-unwto-commission-europe-and-seminar-tourism-world-heritage-sites-challenges-and-o (accessed 30 October 2017).

147 Loulanski (n 1) 225.

148 Bell, Jonathan S., 'The Politics of Preservation: Privileging One Heritage over Another', *International Journal of Cultural Property* 20 (2013), 431–50, 444.

149 For a general critique of these effects, and how cultural heritage is largely made of signs and other identifiers made for tourists, see Waterton, Emma and Watson, Steve, *The Semiotics of Heritage Tourism* (Channel View Publications, 2014), 19.

150 For a discussion of these tensions, see Winter, Michael and Gasson, Ruth, 'Pilgrimage and Tourism: Cathedral Visiting in Contemporary England', *International Journal of Heritage Studies* 2(3) (1996), 172–82.

151 For an example, see Aykan, Bahar, 'How Participatory is Participatory Heritage Management? The Politics of Safeguarding the Alevi *Semah* Ritual as Intangible Heritage', *International Journal of Cultural Property* 20 (2013), 381–405.

tend to privilege more 'pristine' environments.[152] It would seem a site with more amenities would be more likely to be engaged with the local economy, even if it would mean changing the nature of the site (as far as the conservation paradigm is concerned). But the pressures from market nations, when they come to consume the heritage of source nations, might push for a model of engagement with heritage that is not particularly beneficial to local communities' economic development based on their heritage, nor to the creation of other economic avenues that make heritage less of a priority. In fact, a model that requires heritage to be kept pristine in fact reinforces the dependence of heritage sites on their own heritage for economic survival. This is another gap where international law can act, by reforming its expectations about integrity and authenticity of World Heritage sites, for instance, to allow for more development without compromising the World Heritage values of a site.

As indicated above, local communities (and even nation states) tend to reap more economic benefits from the exploitation of heritage if heritage is only a relatively small part of their economies. However, tourism models tend to favour tourism and stifle all other economic alternatives. Even World Bank financing for projects in developing countries tended to favour projects that would enhance tourism revenues. The result is the creation of economies that rely on a single service for most of their revenues, binding these countries to a very volatile 'product'.[153] This pattern is reminiscent of colonialism, in which colonies were made to grow monocultures, and then floundered when the market in commodities shifted.

From an international legal point of view, despite the UNWTO's best intentions, its standard-setting is still soft law, and does not create mandatory standards for states. Coupled with UNESCO's reluctance to set rules for the economic exploitation of heritage, the result is that the lofty objectives of 'cultural tourism' end up co-opted into political structures that favour short-term development for the central state at the expense of other developmental potentials that can provide long-term possibilities for local communities.[154]

5.3.2 World Trade Organization: culture as an exception to trade

Heritage does not seem to have a particularly prominent role in the WTO's activities. Likewise, communities are not factored in at all in the work of the WTO. Cultural heritage features in the organization's two main substantive agreements, but the provisions have seldom been invoked by Member States. Both the General Agreement on Tariffs and Trade (GATT) and the General Agreement on Trade in Services (GATS)[155] contain provisions that specify cultural heritage as a

[152] See generally Shepherd, Robert J. and Yu, Larry, *Heritage Management, Tourism, and Governance in China: Managing the Past to Serve the Present* (Springer, 2013). Reviewed by Tythacott, Louise, 'Book Review: "Heritage Management, Tourism, and Governance in China: Managing the Past to Serve the Present"', *International Journal of Heritage Studies* 21(8) (2015), 842–3.

[153] For this history and critique, see generally Goldstone, Patricia, *Making the World Safe for Tourism* (Yale University Press, 2001), 71.

[154] Winter (n 143) 332.

[155] General Agreement on Trade in Services, 1869 UNTS 183; 33 ILM 1167 (1994) (GATS).

possible exception to rules determining the free trade of goods and services. The WTO Ministerial Conference has also instructed the Council for TRIPS (the intellectual property agreement of the WTO)[156] to consider the implications of the protection of traditional knowledge (which is part of intangible cultural heritage),[157] but, for our present purposes, we will focus on cultural heritage more broadly defined.

Article XX.f of the GATT allows states to create barriers to free trade 'imposed for the protection of national treasures of artistic, historic or archaeological value'.[158] Differently from other exceptions to free trade contained in Article XX, this exception only requires that measures be 'imposed for', instead of them being 'necessary to'. Therefore, there would seem to be a lower threshold for countries seeking to protect their national cultures against free trade imperatives. One of the limitations of this provision, though, is that the 'treasure' in question needs to be of national importance. Further, the cultural value of the heritage is not considered, and the GATT instead refers to 'artistic, historical or archaeological value'.[159] This mismatch can perhaps be attributed to the differences in the vocabularies used in trade and in heritage protection, but it can have the consequence of essentializing heritage if this provision is interpreted too narrowly (in accordance with the interpretive practice of the WTO),[160] and reinforcing the conservation paradigm.

A WTO dispute under the GATT can help shed some light on how living cultures are read by the body of WTO law, too. In *EC-Seal Products*,[161] the WTO dispute settlement system considered an exception to trade which is largely based on culture (subsistence hunting of seals by Indigenous peoples, particularly the Inuit in Greenland). More specifically, it held that an Indigenous exception in the EC rules allowing for the hunting of seals on cultural grounds violated most-favoured-nation provisions in the GATT, by impacting on the ability of commercial seal hunters in Canada and Norway to market seal products in the European Union.[162] Therefore, the WTO was not particularly friendly to a proposed exception based on cultural identity, and deemed it to be incompatible with GATT principles. Culture (and the intangible cultural heritage of the Inuit

[156] Agreement on Trade-Related Aspects of Intellectual Property Rights, 1869 UNTS 299; 33 ILM 1197 (1994) (TRIPS Agreement).

[157] Voon, Tania, *Cultural Products and the World Trade Organization* (Cambridge University Press, 2007), 16. On the connection between Traditional Knowledge and ICH, see Lixinski (n 44).

[158] General Agreement on Tariffs and Trade 1994, 1867 UNTS 187; 33 ILM 1153 (1994) (GATT 1994), Article XX.f.

[159] Voon (n 157) 105.

[160] See generally Van Damme, Isabelle, 'Treaty Interpretation by the WTO Appellate Body', *European Journal of International Law* 21(3) (2010), 605–48. On a more hopeful note, see Voon (n 157) 143–9.

[161] Panel Reports, European Communities—Measures Prohibiting the Importation and Marketing of Seal Products, WT/DS400/R and Add.1/WT/DS401/R and Add.1, adopted 18 June 2014, as modified by Appellate Body Reports WT/DS400/AB/R/WT/DS401/AB/R, DSR 2014:II, p. 365.

[162] For a commentary, see Fakhri, Michael, 'The WTO, Self-Determination and Multi-Jurisdictional Sovereignty', *AJIL Unbound* (2015).

in this case) was seen as potentially discriminatory, and impossible to accommodate within the GATT framework. A more positive reading of the case suggests that free trade can overall be 'a mechanism of economic subsistence and cultural empowerment'.[163]

With the GATS, much of the debate around a cultural exception has focused on the audiovisual industries and the transmission of broadcasting signals, which a number of WTO Member States have said help develop and reflect a sense of national unity and identity.[164] Article XIV of the GATS provides for a public morals or public order exception to the free trade in services. This exception could in theory be invoked when cultural services are deemed as essential to national identity, as argued by a number of countries. However, the WTO has interpreted these provisions restrictively, and has imposed a fairly high threshold. So, the prohibition of trade in services could potentially be sanctioned with respect to religious mores of a country, but the case would be much weaker if it were simply a matter of preventing foreign ideologies from seeping into a country's culture.[165]

There is a potential tension between these cultural exceptions and the safeguarding of cultural heritage. While cultural heritage has often been aligned with national culture, it is also associated with cultural diversity more generally. Therefore, a provision that allows countries to bar the entry of cultural products from other places for the sake of protecting their national culture may in fact lead to a degree of stifling, as it prevents the cultural flows that are vital for the life of cultures.[166] But there is also something to be said about the overwhelming influence of one culture over another, which can also lead to the homogenization of a more fragile culture. Thus, one of the paradoxes of cultural heritage safeguarding (that it is supposed to enhance cultural exchange while preventing cultures from being too affected by said exchange) also plays out in this trade dimension of it, and it is one of the objectives of the 2005 UNESCO Convention on the Protection and Promotion of the Diversity of Cultural Expressions, which we turn to now.

5.3.2.1 The UNESCO Convention on the Diversity of Cultural Expressions (2005)

I have argued elsewhere that this treaty is not a heritage treaty,[167] and, while I maintain that position, this is the culture treaty under UNESCO that helps articulate the relationship between international trade law and culture, so it deserves some attention. 'Cultural diversity' in this treaty seems to revive the meaning of the term in the UNESCO Constitution, which had less of a cosmopolitan aspiration, and actually meant the protection of national cultures from foreign intrusion.[168]

[163] Vadi, Valentina, 'Cultural Heritage in International Economic Law', in Valentina Vadi and Bruno de Witte (eds), *Culture and International Economic Law* (Routledge, 2015), 53–71, 65.

[164] Voon (n 157) 39. [165] Ibid., 108–9. [166] Ibid., 60.

[167] Lixinski (n 44) 59–60.

[168] Carreiro Carril, Beatriz, *La Diversidad Cultural en el Derecho Internacional—La Convención de la UNESCO* (Iustel, 2011), 111.

This convention was drafted with the input of a number of experts and UNESCO Member States, as well as the WTO and other agencies.[169] This treaty defines cultural expressions in a much broader way than 'national treasures' under the GATT, and it allows for cultural values to be taken into account more fully when defining cultural products. It could hence be used as a means to broaden the interpretation of provisions like the GATT Article XX.f, but the conservative approach of the WTO adjudicatory bodies to taking into consideration non-WTO treaties may be an obstacle even at this level.[170] The UNESCO 2005 Convention has specific provisions on the relationship to other treaties, which were the hardest ones to negotiate. As a result of the negotiation process, though, they were significantly watered down, meaning in effect that the treaty can be disregarded if the GATT or GATS are interpreted more restrictively.[171] So, in spite of its premise, the 2005 treaty does very little to challenge WTO regimes and better address cultural sensitivities, and it does nothing to include communities into 'WTO regimes' processes of thinking about heritage as part of trade.

The relationship between international trade law and cultural heritage, therefore, is one of opposition. Cultural heritage is largely defined in nationalist terms, and as running counter to the cosmopolitan objectives of trade liberalization. Even if the protection of heritage is a permissible exception, it is interpreted in the narrow jargon of experts, which does not seem to be capable of accounting for cultural values determined by local communities. Even in instances such as the *EC-Seal Products* case where Indigenous culture is at stake, it is still determined largely from the outside, without much input from communities themselves.

5.3.3 ICSID: investment in heritage or heritage as an obstacle to investment?

The International Centre for the Settlement of Investment Disputes is part of the World Bank group, and it is dedicated to resolving disputes between states and foreign investors. The ICSID system has been praised for allowing non-state actors to exercise international legal personality in its proceedings, but, in the context of this book, the actors involved are more often than not the ones going against cultural heritage protection, while the state acts as the steward of heritage.

Investment treaty obligations are commitments to liberalize the economy, and to allow non-nationals to have stakes in the economy. The interference of non-nationals in the economy is protected against nationalist interests, and, if cultural heritage is seen here, as it is in the WTO, as being an instrument of nationalism, then investment treaty obligations can clash with cultural heritage law, including cultural heritage law created nationally to implement international heritage law treaties. Communities, if seen at all in this system, are considered part of the rationalist problem or as obstacles to investment.

[169] Voon (n 157) 184–5. For a fuller history of the drafting of this treaty, see Carreiro Carril (n 168) 211–19.

[170] As discussed in Lixinski (n 44) 59–60.

[171] Voon (n 157) 188.

One of the important questions that is often addressed by investment arbitration is in drawing a line between permissible (and non-compensable) regulation and impermissible (and compensable) violations of investment treaty commitments by a state.[172] Heritage safeguarding in principle falls in the former category, but is often alleged to be in the latter.

There are two main tests that can be applied in determining whether investment treaties have been violated. The first test, of sole effects, measures the impact of the regulation on the investment. The second one, based on police powers, disregards the actual impact that regulation has, and focuses instead on whether the state has the competence to pursue the regulation in the first place, and whether the regulation as implemented is suitably tailored for the pursuance of a valid objective. A third, more innovative proposition, creates a twofold test: the initial step is to determine whether the deprivation of rights suffered by the investor is the direct consequence of the regulation; the following step is assessing whether the deprivation of property was in fact the intention of the regulatory measure.[173] In the cultural heritage context, applying the sole effects test would mean disregarding the cultural value of heritage as a justification for a measure. It is a type of test that aligns well with neoclassical economics' failure to grasp non-monetary values (discussed above). The police powers test, in contrast, does allow for cultural heritage considerations to be taken into account, but it requires that they are listed as a permissible ground for regulation before investment takes place. This test might be suitable if the ratification of an international heritage treaty can in itself be sufficient to add cultural heritage to the list of permissible grounds for restriction. The alternative test, on the other hand, does not seem to require creating an exception a priori, and it may be more suitable in dealing with cultural heritage's relationship with investment. But it is also more demanding legally, and more expensive, which may impose a disproportionate burden on source nations, who usually are the ones who attempt to curb investment in the name of protecting their cultural heritage.

All of these tests focus on the state as a unitary set of interests, and make no room for communities to participate in international adjudicatory processes. Other international adjudication, discussed in Chapter 7, makes more room for community aspirations.

The sole effects doctrine was applied in *Compañía de Desarrollo de Santa Elena SA v. Republic of Costa Rica*.[174] In this case, land was expropriated from investors for the creation of a national park, which was subsequently added to the World Heritage List. The ICSID tribunal found that the expropriation was permissible in the pursuance of a public policy objective, but that compensation was due according to market value. So, the sole effects doctrine can accommodate public policy considerations, but it will still require compensation to be paid in full. In another case,

[172] Vadi, Valentina, *Cultural Heritage in International Investment Law and Arbitration* (Cambridge University Press, 2014), 4.

[173] Ibid., 66–9.

[174] *Compañía del Desarrollo de Santa Elena SA v. Republic of Costa Rica*, ICSID Case No ARB/96/1, Award of 17 February 2000. Discussed in Vadi (n 172) 120–1.

involving the cancellation of the construction of a hotel complex near the Giza Pyramids in Egypt, the WHC was directly invoked, and the arbitral tribunal said that the UNESCO treaty by itself could not justify the expropriatory measures.[175]

But other cases, looking at the discriminatory effects of investment-curbing measures, have been more sensitive to cultural heritage considerations. In particular, *Parkerings v. Republic of Lithuania* considered claim by a Norwegian investor of discrimination in their bid to build a parking lot under the Historic Town of Vilnius, a World Heritage Site. The ICSID tribunal held that compliance with WHC obligations in fact justified the rejection of the Norwegian project, and balanced obligations under international heritage law against obligations under international investment law. International heritage treaties were seen as giving the state considerable discretion in choosing adequate protective measures.[176] Thus, obligations under international heritage law can be used, in some circumstances, to impact investments, but not to stop them altogether. In *Parkerings*, a different bid was chosen, that was more suited to the imperatives of protecting the World Heritage Site. But cases in which the investment was stopped altogether have found a less sympathetic ear in ICSID arbitration.

A considerable shortcoming of this system when it comes to cultural heritage, and one that is also common to the other regimes discussed in this section, is that it is set up with a different objective in mind. Here, the objective of the system is to protect investors, so cultural heritage interests face a number of uphill battles. The main ones are that they can only be represented by states (meaning communities must rely on states to adequately measure and convey what the loss of their cultural heritage may mean), and that the system has a slight bias against the state (seen as it is built to protect investments). Another is that states in general opt for the promotion of development at the expense of cultural heritage, and are thus generally unwilling to impose the regulatory restrictions on investment in the first place.[177]

The lessons that can be drawn from looking at how cultural heritage is treated by other international legal bodies point at some recurring themes in this chapter and this book. The first lesson is that many of these bodies adopt fairly outdated understandings of what heritage is, and how and why it should be safeguarded. Another is that the economic thinking that guides these bodies is the first generation of cultural economics that has a hard time coming to terms with non-monetary values being attributed to heritage, particularly when those clash with the monetary values behind the objectives of these bodies. Further, the mandates of these bodies command them to think of heritage as a secondary consideration, and only inasmuch as heritage can serve the economic goals that are the objectives of the UNWTO, WTO, and ICSID. As a consequence, and most crucially for this book's purposes, community aspirations and sentiment are ignored, not only because heritage is secondary to

[175] *Southern Pacific Properties (Middle East) Limited v. Arab republic of Egypt*, ICSID Case No. ARB/84/3. Award on the Merits of 20 May 1992. Discussed in Vadi (n 172) 121–2.

[176] *Parkerings-Compagniet AS v. republic of Lithuania*, ICSID Case No ARB/05/08, Award of 11 September 2007. Discussed in Vadi (n 172) 128–9.

[177] Vadi (n 172) 132.

these bodies' mandates, but because neither these nor UNESCO's mandates can escape Westphalian, state-centric ways of analysing heritage obligations, particularly at intersections with other regimes. The layering of regimes, in the economic context, excludes communities, or, worse, sees them as part of the 'problem' and an obstacle to free global trade.

With these perspectives in mind, what can international heritage law do for communities in terms of allowing engagement with the economics of heritage? The next section explores some of the effects of the economics of heritage on community governance over heritage.

5.4 Effects on Community Participation

Even if cultural heritage is often seen as local and grounded on identity,[178] the attachment between locals and heritage can stem from reasons other than identity, including economic ones. Attachment to place can be borne by economic necessity to earn a living from tourism that surrounds a population,[179] particularly when other economic possibilities are made impossible by heritage preservation (for instance, certain agricultural practices can be made illegal in light of legislation protecting agricultural landscapes).

Economic necessity of a local community is also at odds with ostensible heritage goals in the case of subsistence digging. A case study in Central America helps elucidate some of the tensions in this regard. Mayan communities refer to cultural artefacts as *semillas*, which is the word in Spanish for seed. The reference is justified because these artefacts, like agricultural seeds, are seen as gifts from their ancestors. Therefore, artefacts have a highly revered status, and communities are reluctant to dig them out, let alone trade them.[180] However, subsistence digging still happens in many Central American nations, despite the efforts of many experts and agencies (including the Organization of American States). In a country like Belize, with an estimated population of 250,000, as many as 50,000 people are part-time artefact hunters and gatherers. The majority are subsistence diggers, who engage in the activity during the agricultural off-seasons.[181] But the discussion on the legality of excavation of archaeological artefacts by untrained persons is, arguably, secondary, in that it 'distracts from what should be the primary issue—the unequal power relationships that make subsistence digging a viable socioeconomic alternative for Latin America's indigenous populations'.[182] As international cultural heritage law in this

[178] See e.g. Olsson, Krister, 'The Value of Preservation: Analysis of the Decision-making Processes in Urban Heritage Management, in Mikko Mälkki, Raine Mäntysalo, and Kaisa Schmidt-Thomé (eds), *Economics and Built Heritage—Towards New European Initiatives* (Helsinki University of Technology, 2008), 113–29, 116.

[179] Bell (n 148) 445.

[180] Matsuda, David, 'The Ethics of Archaeology, Subsistence Digging, and Artifact Looting in Latin America: Point, Muted Counterpoint', *International Journal of Cultural Property* 7(1) (1998), 87–97, 88.

[181] Ibid., 91. [182] Ibid., 94.

context does not include Indigenous voices, or community voices in general, it is incapable of engaging with the economics of heritage in a way that creates alternative means of subsistence.[183]

The exclusion of Indigenous voices from heritage governance at the international level is a particular concern, even if I have argued (in Chapter 3) that communities more broadly should be included, not only Indigenous peoples. To think of only Indigenous peoples in this context assumes that the state can cater to other minorities successfully (which is not always true),[184] and also conveys the impression that heritage is only for 'the other', which is counterproductive in thinking about the role of heritage in society. But Indigenous peoples are the main category targeted in debates about the inclusion of communities in international heritage governance, and there have been attempts, ultimately failed, to include Indigenous groups in the World Heritage Committee.[185] The proposal was defeated for a number of reasons, including for our present purposes the notion that the bureaucratic obstacles would be too difficult for a problem that only affects a small number of states.[186] Here, the idea of targeting community participation measures only at Indigenous peoples backfired, as indeed relatively few states have Indigenous populations, whereas all states have communities. An alternative was proposed in the aftermath of the formal rejection of the proposal; that Indigenous peoples meet informally, and contribute to the work of the intangible cultural heritage bodies.[187] This is also a counterproductive move, in that it assumes that Indigenous peoples are only concerned with ICH, and that all other forms of heritage are out of their reach for governance purposes. Therefore, full governance proposals, in which communities can have a say about how their heritage is listed and managed, and also potentially claim the economic benefits of said exploitation, have so far been formally rejected. But they should still be on the agenda, expanding the scope of beneficiaries to include all communities, and not only Indigenous peoples. That is an important avenue to make sure communities can control their heritage,[188] and the economic aspects of it.

In non-Indigenous contexts, the devolution of management over heritage buildings, monuments, and sites to communities may engender better development results than centralized heritage management. This literature, focused on local government structures, suggests that adaptive reuse of heritage buildings, that maintains their use and relevance, is more likely to result in economic benefits for the community. Particularly, heritage restoration and its adaptive reuse can support the local economy by hiring local labour and expertise. Additionally, heritage status in these circumstances galvanizes communities around the cause of improving their

[183] Ibid., 94

[184] Miller, Barbara D., 'Heritage Management Inside Out and Upside Down: Questioning Outsider and Top-Down Approaches', *Heritage Management* 2(1) (2009), 5–10, 8.

[185] Meskell, Lynn, 'UNESCO and the Fate of the World Heritage Indigenous Peoples Council of Experts (WHIPCOE)', *International Journal of Cultural Property* 20 (2013), 155–74.

[186] Ibid., 164. [187] Ibid., 165–6.

[188] On how the current system with respect to ICH fails communities, see Lixinski (n 44), and Aykan (n 151).

own quality of life.[189] But this strategy assumes adaptive reuses of heritage places as a means to enhance other economic possibilities within the community, as opposed to international heritage law's stricter conservation paradigm (discussed in Chapter 1).

Tourism, one of the main avenues through which the economic dimensions of heritage are made visible, can have very negative impacts on communities' involvement in their heritage, too. More specifically, tourism demands crystallize certain narratives about heritage (usually those endorsed by international processes under UNESCO) that ignore and even denigrate alternative histories (regardless of whether they challenge or complement the authorized narrative). As a result, 'communities that value alternate meanings of a place are often disenfranchised and disempowered'.[190]

Heritage development thus creates a number of tensions between the local and the global, which is reflected in the way local heritage management is influenced by global practices.[191] The international (often the tourist from the market nation) requires brevity, selectivity, and immediacy, and can be very reductivist. The local, on the other hand, is much more nuanced and conflicted. The effect is that development can erase the subtlety and diversity of local heritage in favour of a homogeneous global, 'leaving local societies either to adopt the new heritages, abandoning the old, or to resent and resist the new heritage being imposed upon them'.[192] But the safeguarding of heritage can also have the unintended consequence of reinforcing boundaries within and among different communities.[193] That is the paradox of the protection of cultural diversity discussed above.

Tourism in a way replicates colonialism, as it is a form of imperialism. Tourism in places like Egypt, for instance, can have the effect of marginalizing modern local communities in favour of a focus on Ancient Egypt's heritage.[194] Tourists are not invited to engage with contemporary Egypt, and most of the revenue stays with foreign tour operators or the central government, very little of it actually trickling down to the locals who inevitably bear the burdens of tourism (overcrowding, pressure on scarce natural resources, etc.).[195] Moreover, the needs of tourists as perceived and interpreted by nation states can lead to the erasure of heritage that is far more meaningful to the locals (heritage which can assist the tourists in engaging more meaningfully with the culture as a whole) in favour of sanitizing an area for easy consumption.[196] In the World Heritage Site of Petra (Jordan), for instance, made

[189] Shipley, R. and Snyder, M., 'The Role of Heritage Conservation Districts in Achieving Community Economic Development Goals', *International Journal of Heritage Studies* 19(3) (2013), 304–21, 314.

[190] Bell (n 148) 432.

[191] Long, Darrin Lee, 'Cultural Heritage Management in Post-Colonial Polities: *Not* the Heritage of the Other', *International Journal of Heritage Studies* 6(4) (2000), 317–22, 317.

[192] Ashworth (n 5) 14.

[193] van Meijl, Toon, 'Pacific Discourses about Cultural Heritage and Its Protection: An Introduction', *International Journal of Cultural Property* 16 (2009), 221–32, 223.

[194] See in general Fagan, Brian M., *The Rape of the Nile: Tomb Robbers, Tourists, and Archaeologists in Egypt* (Westview, 2004).

[195] Bell (n 148) 443.

[196] Abu-Khafajah, Shatha and Rababeh, Shaher, 'The Silence of Meanings in Conventional Approaches to Cultural Heritage in Jordan: The Exclusion of Contexts and the Marginalisation of the

famous by *Indiana Jones and the Last Crusade*,[197] a recurring view articulated by locals is that the government and tourism agencies do not explain to tourists how the current population of the area relates to Petra. Large amounts of money are spent on Petra to attract more tourists and maintain the stone structures, with little regard for the opinion of the people who live in the area, and who are the successors of those who built Petra.[198]

While there is an important tension that needs mediation in defining the place of heritage safeguarding between the local and the global, communities should be favoured in determining whether and to what extent their heritage can be economically exploited.[199] After all, the 'truth' of heritage resides not in contextual information around an object, but, as Lyndel V. Prott stated, 'in the community's continued re-endorsement of value by use within that community'.[200] Thus, international heritage law that makes the use of heritage more difficult tends to diminish heritage's value. I suggest that international heritage law should allow communities to engage with their own heritage economically, even at the cost of eroding some of heritage's integrity in the short term. It will after all mean a much closer engagement with heritage, and reassertions of its value, leading to better long-term safeguarding.

First-generation econometrics, at least inasmuch as it means the gathering of statistical data, can help integrate communities more fully in the economic aspects of their heritage, and measure their contribution to the preservation of heritage.[201] It can thus be an important ally of international law in measuring the consequences of change in UNESCO governance.

This type of engagement will also help mediate the public/private divide when it comes to heritage, by making a lot of decisions about heritage more transparent (and public). It allows heritage to be safeguarded, not only by states in spite of (or sometimes even at the expense of) local communities, but by communities themselves. Societal consideration by a community is part of the challenge to be achieved by cultural heritage organizations that also administer the economic aspects of it.[202] On the private governance side, volunteerism is an important means of getting local communities involved,[203] and it is a feature that distinguishes cultural heritage organizations from other private sector entities.[204] Recognition of this type of governance structure internationally, and allowing them to be involved not only in fulfilling international mandates, but actually in establishing them, is likely to allow

Intangible', in Michelle L. Stefano, Peter Davis, and Gerard Corsane (eds), *Safeguarding Intangible Cultural Heritage* (The Boydell Press, 2012), 71–83, 79.

197 For a discussion of international heritage law's portrayals in cinema, see Lixinski, Lucas, 'Moral, Legal and Archaeological Relics of the Past: Portrayals of International Cultural Heritage Law in Cinema', *London Review of International Law* 4(3) (2016) 421–37.

198 Abu-Khafajah and Rababeh (n 196) 81.

199 Examining these possibilities in the context of museums, see Young, Linda, 'Globalisation, Culture and Museums: A Review of Theory', *International Journal of Heritage Studies* 5(1) (1999), 6–15.

200 Prott (n 17) 231.

201 Deloumeaux (n 56) 201.

202 Castañer, Xavier, 'Management Challenges of Cultural Heritage Organizations', in Ilde Rizzo and Anna Mignosa (eds), *Handbook on the Economics of Cultural Heritage* (Edward Elgar, 2013), 209–30, 220.

203 Seaman (n 100) 123–4.

204 Castañer (n 202) 226.

for better results in terms of heritage safeguarding. There are also possibilities with respect to cooperation with corporate actors which are worth exploring, but they require interaction with and accountability to the public (the community and the state) to work.[205] The state in particular has an important role to play in correcting for power imbalances in the relationship between community and corporate actor willing to exploit cultural heritage.[206]

The second generation of heritage economics, on the other hand, may be less helpful in enabling community governance of heritage. One of the limitations of the second generation of economic approaches is that the premise of heritage as a merit good implies deference to the judgement of experts over local communities, as indicated earlier. According to this idea, local communities are just part of the group of 'consumers' of heritage, who can have limited input on heritage management and choices by exercising their 'consumer sovereignty' through standard democratic processes.[207]

In general, one must also be mindful of the potential for over-promising in the context of community development. As is discussed in Chapter 6 on heritage and the environment, communities often hear promises about the development potentials of international heritage listing, and these promises often go unfulfilled. The consequence is resentment in the community towards the promises of international heritage mechanisms, which did not deliver the development and stripped away community agency. Therefore, any attempt at engaging international heritage law more closely with communities and the economic potentials of heritage must beware of what promises are made. But the law must intervene nevertheless, if anything to create a regulated international market in heritage. The next section discusses this possibility.

5.5 Is a Regulated International Market of Cultural Heritage Viable?

The argument for a licit international market in cultural heritage is not new, even if it has primarily focused on the market in cultural objects. It also depends on the notion of property over cultural heritage to a significant extent, a notion rejected by many,[208] but one that, as argued in Chapter 2, can have positive impacts in promoting more community-based heritage governance.

[205] For a case study, see Bainton, Nicholas A., Ballard, Chris, Gillespie, Kirsty, and Hall, Nicholas, 'Stepping Stones Across the Lihir Islands: Developing Cultural Heritage Management in the Context of a Gold-Mining Operation', *International Journal of Cultural Property* 18 (2011), 81–110.

[206] I have made this argument elsewhere. See Lixinski (n 44). See also dos Santos, Paula Assunção and Müller, Elaine, 'When ICH Takes Hold of the Local Reality in Brazil: Notes from the Brazilian State of Pernambuco', in Michelle L. Stefano, Peter Davis, and Gerard Corsane (eds), *Safeguarding Intangible Cultural Heritage* (Boydell Press, 2012), 213–22, 215 (referring to the experience of implementing the ICHC in Brazil).

[207] Peacock and Rizzo (n 97) 23–4.

[208] See for instance Carman, John, *Against Cultural Property: Archaeology, Heritage and Ownership* (Duckworth, 2005). For a critical review, see Funari, Pedro Paulo A., 'Book Review: John Carman, 'Against Cultural Property: Archaeology, Heritage and Ownership', *International Journal of Cultural Property* 15 (2008), 97–9.

The main proponent of the licit market in cultural heritage was John Henry Merryman, whose liberal views on the safeguarding of cultural objects have been deeply influential.[209] In his piece on the licit international trade in cultural objects, Merryman argued that an active international market in cultural heritage can (1) advance the international interest; (2) provide income to source nations; and (3) 'reduce the harm done by the black market'.[210] He starts from the assumption that international law in the area (mainly the 1970 Convention) is too restrictive, and that it fails to achieve its objectives. He argues that said objectives would be much better served if there were a regulated international market, as opposed to the near-complete ban of the 1970 Convention (discussed above).[211]

The justification for restrictions on the market, says Merryman, comes from either protectionism or retentionism (which he equates with cultural nationalism). Protectionism is related to keeping an object in its context (and thus near the community of origin), whereas retentionism has to do with the political value of the heritage (even if he also admits it may sometimes simply be a state's impulse to 'hoard' heritage that does not necessarily speak to national identity, but is nevertheless valuable).[212] He sees the merit in protectionism in some instances, but refuses to see retentionism as a valid justification for excluding heritage from the market.[213] The assumption that keeping a cultural object within national boundaries will accomplish the objectives that justify the action is largely undemonstrated.[214] Ultimately, he concludes that there are sufficient reasons for an international licit trade, based on either barter or a more conventional market approach,[215] all for the sake of internationalism.

Retentionism as a means to protect national politics is an argument that is in fact made, but an important point in favour of the circulation of cultural heritage is that it can actually be a trigger for the politics of heritage, and not a means to do away with the political potentials. As stated above, the main driver of the 1970 Convention is the decolonization process. However, and somewhat paradoxically,

[209] See for instance Merryman, John Henry, *Thinking About the Elgin Marbles: Critical Essays on Cultural Property, Art and Law* (2nd edn, Alphen aan den Rijn, 2009); Merryman, John Henry, 'Cultural Property Internationalism', *International Journal of Cultural Property* 12(1) (2005), 11–39; Merryman, John Henry, 'The Free International Movement of Cultural Property', *NYU Journal of International Law and Politics* 31 (1998), 1–14; Merryman, John Henry, 'Cultural Property, International Trade and Human Rights,' *Cardozo Arts & Entertainment Law Journal* 19 (2001), 51–68; Merryman, John Henry, 'Thinking about the Elgin Marbles', *Michigan Law Review* 83 (1984–1985), 1881–923; and Merryman, John Henry, 'Two Ways of Thinking about Cultural Property', *American Journal of International Law* 80(4) (1986), 831–53, among many others.

[210] Merryman, John Henry, 'A Licit International Trade in Cultural Objects', *International Journal of Cultural Property* 4(1) (1995), 13–60, 13.

[211] Merryman (n 210) 17.

[212] Ibid., 19. For a discussion of the interaction between the market and national identity and politics, see O'Hagan, John and McAndrew, Clare, 'Restricting International Trade in the Artistic Patrimony: Economic Rationale and Policy Instruments', *International Journal of Cultural Property* 10(1) (2001), 32–54, 40–2. And, for a case study in France, see Bivar, Venus, 'History for Sale: The International Art Market and the Nation State', *International Journal of Cultural Property* 13 (2006), 259–83.

[213] Merryman (n 210) 25.

[214] Peacock and Rizzo (n 97) 150.

[215] Merryman (n 210) 30.

that decolonization process was in part enabled precisely by the taking of cultural artefacts and their exhibition in Western museums.[216] In this context, the movement of cultural objects in fact benefitted a substate actor (a colony), and not the state itself. The ultimate result was the creation of a new state. Thus, heritage's political potential can actually be unleashed by entry into the market, as opposed to exclusion from it, as the retentionist view would suggest. But it could go two different ways. The first way is that it enhances national pride, which is a reason for touring exhibitions of the national treasures of a given country.[217] Or the circulation of heritage in the market could also benefit challenges to the politics of the nation state, as the heritage escapes that state's control.

Merryman's position embodies the liberal argument for a market in cultural heritage. Even if it is focused on cultural objects, it can also be largely applied to other types of heritage. The movement of heritage is not feasible for many heritage domains (particularly World Heritage), but the argument can be read as speaking about the engagement of heritage with the market in general, and not just specifically the commerce in objects. Protectionism is an important justification for excluding heritage from economics, as it means sheltering heritage from influences that can commodify it, inasmuch as commodification implies a process of decontextualization,[218] of translating heritage into a less nuanced, consumable idea. And retentionism can also be applied to other forms of heritage, as it has to do with the political uses of heritage in the name of state sovereignty (a possibility that, as discussed elsewhere in this book, is out of reach for substate actors as soon as heritage is presented by the state to the experts who 'sanitize' it). Therefore, Merryman's argument speaks not only to cultural objects, but to the relationship between heritage and economics in general.

The critique of this argument comes from a number of directions. First, a lot of the liberal argument for a licit market in cultural heritage invokes the interests of humanity, all the while equating 'humanity' and the 'universal' interests with 'civilized Europe', a position that lacks nuance, to say the least.[219] As discussed, the colonial imprints of heritage are still felt across the international safeguarding system, and this is another way in which one can find its echoes. But that is not to say that a market would not be possible at all; it would just have to be justified on grounds other than the purported protection of 'humanity's' interests. It can rather be justified in terms of community development, for instance.

[216] Ginsburgh, Victor and Mairesse, François, 'Issues in the International Market for Cultural Heritage', in Ilde Rizzo and Anna Mignosa (eds), *Handbook on the Economics of Cultural Heritage* (Edward Elgar, 2013), 151–70, 153.

[217] For instance, the exhibition of the artefacts of the National Museum of Kabul, Afghanistan, which were hidden away when the Taliban first gained control of the country, and were rediscovered after the regime was ousted from power. See Hiebert, Fredrik and Cambon, Pierre (eds), *Afghanistan: Hidden Treasures from the National Museum, Kabul* (National Geographic Society, 2008).

[218] Cf. Weihe, Hugo Keith, 'Licit International Traffic in Cultural Objects for Art's Sake', *International Journal of Cultural Property* 4(1) (1995), 81–90, 85 (suggesting that '[i]f "commodification" is an inevitable attribute, it is by no means *a priori* detrimental').

[219] Prott (n 17) 229.

Merryman, in his defence of a licit market, has argued that a licit market in cultural objects can in effect displace the black market.[220] However, there have been attempts at regulated markets domestically in important source countries like Syria and Egypt, and the situation soon became untenable, with enormous burdens on policing that made the system far too expensive for poor source nations.[221] Public–private partnerships could also be part of the answer for a licit market in this context.[222] However, both possibilities risk replicating the unequal and potentially exploitative models of the large archaeological campaigns of the 1950s and 1960s.[223] Proponents have even suggested that a mode akin to commercial salvage be implemented (a suggestion made before the UCHC).[224] Despite the risks, it seems that the involvement of private (commercial) actors can also have the potential to enhance entryways for communities to reclaim and interpret their own heritage.[225] But one must be wary of the possibility of abuse of private actor power in the commercial sphere, too, especially when private actors get to replace the state and exercise monopoly over cultural heritage, which is a distinctive possibility, for instance, in the use of intellectual property mechanisms for the commercial exploitation of intangible heritage.[226] The invisibility of the private, too, especially when communities are not a part of this private, is also a key cause for concern.

Another argument for a licit market relies on the deaccessioning of museum collections, especially considering that a very large proportion of collections of major museums is in storage units, and is not seen by the public.[227] An implication of this model is the establishment of a barter system among museums and cultural institutions.[228] This is a possibility also partly advocated by Merryman,[229] who recognizes that the 1970 Convention has favoured this approach, as it allows for heritage artefacts to circulate without turning them into marketable goods, as they stay within the realm of cultural institutions. He believes this system is insufficient, though, as it excludes private actors, and therefore cannot curb the black market.[230]

A market can also be a substitute for other heritage protection initiatives such as World Heritage Listing, according to some economists.[231] Economically, it might

[220] Cited in ibid., 234. [221] Ibid., 234.

[222] Ginsburgh and Mairesse (n 216) 159.

[223] Discussed in Harrison, Rodney, *Heritage: Critical Approaches* (Routledge, 2013), 42–68.

[224] Weihe (n 218) 86–7.

[225] Paterson, Robert K. and Telesetsky, Anastasia, 'Heritage Inc.: A Mini-Symposium on Heritage Protection and Private Actors. Held at the Faculty of Law, University of British Columbia, Vancouver, Canada, 16 March 2012', *International Journal of Cultural Property* 19 (2012), 549–71, 550.

[226] For a case study, see Fish, Allison, 'The Commodification and Exchange of Knowledge in the Case of Transnational Yoga', *International Journal of Cultural Property* 13 (2006), 189–206. For a discussion of the different languages of intellectual property and cultural heritage in the safeguarding of ICH, see also Lixinski, Lucas and Buckingham, Louise, 'Propertization, Safeguarding and the Cultural Commons: The Turf Wars of Intangible Cultural Heritage and Traditional Cultural Expressions', in Valentina Vadi and Bruno de Witte (eds), *Culture and International Economic Law* (Routledge, 2015), 160–74.

[227] Ginsburgh and Mairesse (n 216) 152. See also the discussion in Shapiro (n 4).

[228] Peacock and Rizzo (n 97) 98. [229] Merryman (n 210) 30–1. [230] Ibid., 31.

[231] Frey, Bruno S. and Steiner, Lasse, 'World Heritage List', in Ilde Rizzo and Anna Mignosa (eds), *Handbook on the Economics of Cultural Heritage* (Edward Elgar, 2013), 171–86, 180.

be more beneficial to simply let the market govern heritage, particularly when it comes to popular heritage sites.[232] That way, there are less regulatory constraints, and the community can be more directly involved. The problem in this liberalized market is that there is still relatively little control over where the economic benefits of heritage are reaped, and, as mentioned above, those tend to be outside the communities. Regulation could thus play an important role in guaranteeing that those economic surpluses benefit the communities.

Another argument in favour of a regulated market is that it will allow for greater exchange of information among the different stakeholders, in a way that can actually help reconcile tensions among private parties, governments, museums, and also communities.[233] As the market implies commodification, and commodification promotes a displacement and settlement of power with respect to heritage, it necessarily brings the affected parties to the table. And, assuming all parties (including communities) are invited to the table, the market in heritage is not only a means to promote development and bring revenue, but also an opportunity to flesh out broader issues about governance in the process.

One of the tensions around the governance of heritage by local communities is that those groups are often characterized as unwilling or unable to preserve heritage, lacking the expertise to identify it, or even willingly destroying heritage.[234] But, as David Lowenthal has pointed out in response to one of Merryman's articles, maybe it is not a bad thing that some heritage is let go: 'Packrats by nature, we preserve too well. Not only do we not need all we have, we need desperately to be rid of it. Moth and rust no longer suffice; culling and disposal must be integral to making and collecting.'[235] That is a fairly controversial position, and one that challenges one of the premises of the entire field of international heritage law. But, as discussed in Chapters 1 and 4, if heritage is to be allowed to evolve, it must also be allowed to disappear, in some instances, at a minimum so that new heritage can be created to occupy its place.

Even if heritage is to be preserved at all costs, though, in line with the conservation paradigm, a licit market can still promote useful tools in that respect. The economics of heritage can create incentives for the safeguarding of heritage for governments, and, particularly, for communities. The creation of a licit market is also an opportunity to create conditions to renegotiate the terms in which heritage is seen and exploited, and can therefore challenge some of the existing practices with respect to the dichotomies between source and market nations, the public and the private, the nation state and communities, and the local and the international.

[232] Ibid., 183.

[233] Coggins, Clemency Chase, 'A Licit International Traffic in Ancient Art: Let There Be Light!', *International Journal of Cultural Property* 4(1) (1995), 61–80, 61. For a case study in China, see Murphy, J. David, 'The People's Republic of China and the Illicit Trade in Cultural Property: Is the Embargo Approach the Answer?', *International Journal of Cultural Property* 3(2) (1994), 227–42.

[234] Shapiro (n 4) 381–2.

[235] Lowenthal, David, 'Why Sanctions Seldom Work: Reflections on Cultural Property Internationalism', *International Journal of Cultural Property* 12 (2005) 393–423, 396.

Heritage economics and the market in heritage can thus be a tool not only for commodification, but also for development. This development, however, is constrained not only by economic possibilities, but also by other principles closely aligned with heritage, and that cut through a number of heritage instruments, particularly the idea of sustainable development. This concept, its application to international heritage law, and its effects on community governance are the objects of the next chapter.

6

Heritage and the Environment

This chapter focuses on the role of the interaction between environmental governance and heritage governance. It shows how environmental requirements can further alienate communities from their heritage, and therefore thinking about heritage in its relationships to the environment is important to understanding the place of communities in the mandates heritage gives to and is given by international legal ordering. International heritage law is often seen as a sub-branch of international environmental law. As such, it should be implemented and enforced having the needs of the environment in mind. Communities' presence, or any human action, is more often than not seen as an interference with the environment, which in some ways aligns with the conservation paradigm's idea of protecting a pristine 'thing'. And yet, in spite of prioritizing the environment as an idea, there are very different ways in which the environment is perceived by international heritage treaties. The 1970 Convention, for instance, includes nature in its definition of cultural objects, when it speaks of 'objects of fauna and flora'.[1] It thus subordinates nature to culture, and reads nature as an artefact of culture. In doing so, the 1970 Convention overcomes the history of Western museums in treating nature as universal, as opposed to provincial, culture.[2] Culture, even though it was treated by the 1970 Convention as belonging to states (discussed in Chapter 2), was in this way elevated to an international concern, justifying international action.

The World Heritage Convention (WHC) creates a very close relationship by having categories of 'natural' and 'cultural' heritage, a connection that goes back to the original drafting of the treaty, and helps elucidate a lot of the relationship between nature and culture in international heritage law. When the WHC was being drafted, it was originally the proposal of two separate arms of UNESCO: the science branch, which was interested in the conservation of nature for scientific purposes; and the culture branch, which focused on the protection of cultural sites. The two projects were ultimately merged, with the aid of the budding international environmental movement (at the time preoccupied first and foremost with the conservation of natural sites, a goal which aligned with the objectives of the cultural treaty being

[1] Convention on the Means of Prohibiting and Preventing the Illicit Import, Export and Transfer of Ownership of Cultural Property 1970 (adopted 14 November 1970, entered into force 24 April 1972) 823 UNTS 231 (1970 Convention), Article 1.

[2] Jenkins, Tiffany, *Keeping their Marbles: How the Treasures of the Past Ended Up in Museums . . . and Why They Should Stay There* (Oxford University Press, 2016), 164–5.

drafted). But the merger of culture and nature (as discussed in Chapter 2) was never complete, and, at any rate, it reinforced a conservation paradigm or imperative according to which heritage is preserved according to scientific criteria, and for scientific purposes.[3]

The Underwater Cultural Heritage Convention (UCHC), which is closely connected to the Law of the Sea Convention, takes a different direction with respect to the status of nature, and instead looks at the possibility of culture being found around nature, and sometimes culture becoming nature. More specifically, the preservation *in situ* requirements of the UCHC have the effect of promoting a symbiotic relationship between nature and culture, which is further enhanced by the possibility of underwater heritage becoming reefs over time. But this relationship is only made possible through a scientific gaze, required by preservation *in situ*. Additionally, the UCHC contains provisions requiring the protection of the natural environment where underwater heritage is found.[4]

Lastly, the Intangible Cultural Heritage Convention (ICHC) makes environmental sustainability one of the key aspects of the definition of intangible heritage, and in fact a requirement for a cultural practice to be considered ICH,[5] as discussed below. Therefore, culture becomes contingent on a certain understanding of nature.

Across these instruments, one can see a number of different ways of reading the relationship between nature and culture, which may sometimes clash with each other, and promote objectives that, in their implementation, are often opposite. One of the key effects that the environment seems to have on heritage is to raise the stakes for the safeguarding of heritage. While the loss of culture is a moral and intellectual loss for all humanity, the loss of environment can potentially impair the survival of the human species. The merging of environmental and cultural considerations falls on the side of caution, and therefore enshrines the conservation paradigm discussed in more detail Chapter 1. The implementation of international heritage law, therefore, in aligning with environmental goals and mechanisms, sometimes does so at the expense of communities' aspirations in relation to their own heritage. Nowhere is this more palpable than in the area of sustainable development.

Heritage protection and sustainable development seem to walk hand in hand in the international arena.[6] Sustainable development and cultural heritage resource management can be linked in two principal ways: (1) sustainable growth leading to the preservation of the tangible cultural heritage resource; and (2) sustainable growth as a means of conservation of intangible heritage values and meanings.[7] The

[3] For this history, see Cameron, Christina and Rössler, Mechtild, *Many Voices, One Vision: The Early Years of the World Heritage Convention* (Ashgate, 2013), 3–26.

[4] Convention on the Protection of the Underwater Cultural Heritage 2001 (adopted 2 November 2001, entered into force 2 January 2009) 2562 UNTS 3 (UCHC), Article 1(a).

[5] Convention for Safeguarding of the Intangible Cultural Heritage 2003 (adopted 17 October 2003, entered into force 20 April 2006) 2368 UNTS 3 (ICHC), Article 2(1).

[6] Robinson, J., 'Squaring the Circle? Some Thoughts on the Idea of Sustainable Development', *Ecological Economics* 48 (2004), 369–84; Lélé, S. M., 'Sustainable Development: A Critical Review', *World Development* 19(6) (1991), 607–21, 610.

[7] Keitumetse, S. O., 'Sustainable Development and Cultural Heritage Management in Botswana: Towards Sustainable Communities', *Sustainable Development* 19(1) (2011), 49–59, 51.

problem with this idealistic vision is that it takes for granted certain problematic political and philosophical assumptions underlying both heritage management and sustainable development, which have a tendency to freeze and mummify the environment and culture without taking economic viability and livelihood into account.

Heritage is often associated with the notion of protecting a romanticized past, a way of life, and the conservation paradigm does precisely that: freeze heritage at a point in time where it corresponds with an idealized past, and preserve it that way in the interest of future generations. This is a critique often associated with World Heritage, but it also resonates with intangible heritage. Likewise, there is a narrative of environmentalism that tells environmental history as 'a modern fall from landscape grace'.[8]

The ideals behind environmental and heritage protection are very similar, both largely aspiring (in an admittedly essentialized reading of the liberal take on these two issues) to preserve a romanticized, untainted version of the past, when man lived in harmony with nature and culture flourished, creating the heritage that is so important for defining today's humankind. As a consequence of this convergence of ideals, heritage protection and environmental protection seem to want to freeze society (or certain segments of it) in this past, as a constant reminder of how good we once had it. But, because the implementation of these ideals is uneven, affecting some communities more than others, it creates problems for those affected, ultimately compromising the ability of environmental and heritage instruments to accomplish their goals.

Further, because the goals of heritage protection and sustainable development are implemented through a top-down imposition of reified notions of sustainable development and its requirements, and without full integration of considerations on the ground, they cannot always be maintained in the long term. Sustainable development and heritage protection are sometimes required from communities in ways that have the effect of hampering their development, ultimately causing communities to be obliterated by segments of society upon whom the same stringent requirements of sustainable development and heritage protection are not imposed.

This chapter addresses tensions that arise from the relationship between heritage and the environment, in particular through the lenses of sustainable development as a principle of heritage management that more and more influences heritage practice and communities' relationship with heritage. More specifically, the chapter looks at how sustainable development and heritage protection converge, and how this convergence can sometimes be self-defeating. I argue that, despite the many merits of sustainable development and heritage protection as ideals to be pursued, their indiscriminate application, particularly from the top down, can hinder their own success. I will use two case studies to justify some of my broader claims.

[8] Olwig, Kenneth Robert, '"Time out of Mind"–"Mind out of Time": Custom versus Tradition in Environmental Heritage Research and Interpretation', *International Journal of Heritage Studies* 7(4) (2001), 339–54, 340.

The first case study is the Marimba music and traditional chants from Afro-Colombian and Afro-Ecuadorian communities,[9] which is an expansion of the original listing done by Colombia alone.[10] In Colombia in particular, these populations are domestically protected by a wide-ranging piece of legislation called *Ley 70*, which states, among other things, that the development of Afro-Colombian communities, and the protection of their autonomy, is conditioned upon sustainable development requirements.[11]

The second case study is the inscription of East Rennell on the World Heritage List in 1998. East Rennell consists of the southern third of Rennell Island, which is one of the southernmost islands in the Solomon Island group. The site includes circa 37,000 ha of the island, and one of its main features is Lake Tagano, the largest lake in the insular Pacific (15,500 ha). Rennell was the first property from a Pacific island nation added to the World Heritage List, and the very first anywhere that is subject primarily to customary law for its management by local communities. The fact that local communities and customary law are so vital for the site would indicate a success of the promises of community involvement in heritage management. However, East Rennell was added to the List of World Heritage in Danger in 2013. Part of the purpose of this chapter is to investigate the failures of heritage listing as a means to promote sustainable development in East Rennell.

I have chosen these two cases for three main reasons. First, they represent the two most successful instruments under UNESCO in the field of heritage (the ICHC and the WHC). Second, they show how sustainable development can work in living cultures that are closely connected to their natural surroundings, but perhaps not in the same way that is often imagined within heritage circles. Third, the mismatch between what heritage instruments expect of communities and what communities expect of heritage listing highlights an important lesson about the viability of trying to entrench romanticized visions of the past despite developmental expectations.

The chapter proceeds as follows:[12] I will first examine how sustainable development became ingrained in the international legal discourse around cultural heritage. I will then critically assess the dark sides of sustainable development. Next, I will discuss the Marimba music and East Rennell inscriptions with an eye specifically on the role of communities portrayed or argued in the listing processes. I will subsequently re-examine some of the connections between heritage and sustainable development in light of the promises of increased forms of community governance in the field of heritage. I will suggest that community governance, if integrated in

[9] Marimba music, traditional chants and dances from the Colombia South Pacific region and Esmeraldas Province of Ecuador, UNESCO Intergovernmental Committee for the Safeguarding of the Intangible Cultural Heritage, *Decisions*, 10th sess., Decision 10.COM 10.b.13, ITH/15/10.COM/Decisions (30 November–4 December 2015).

[10] UNESCO Intergovernmental Committee for the Safeguarding of the Intangible Cultural Heritage, *Decisions*, 5th sess., Decision 5.COM 6.8, ITH/10/5.COM/CONF.202/Decisions (15–19 November 2010) 16 [38].

[11] *Ley 70 de 1993 (Ley de Negritudes)* (Colombia) ('*Ley 70*').

[12] Significant sections of this chapter have appeared elsewhere. See Lixinski, Lucas, 'Sustainable Development in International Heritage Law: Embracing a Backwards Look for the Sake of Forwardness?', *Australian Yearbook of International Law* 32 (2015), 65–86.

all levels of heritage governance (local, national, international), is potentially more capable of fulfilling the promise of sustainable development than current top-down approaches.

6.1 The Requirement of Sustainable Development in International Heritage Law

The WHC came into existence drawing on the momentum of the incipient environmental movement, and, because of the history detailed above, is often seen as an environmental treaty itself, with great potential to achieve environmental goals like biodiversity conservation.[13] According to at least one account, the WHC regime drew much inspiration from the United States' model of national parks, which was designed with a natural heritage site in mind (Yellowstone, to be more specific).[14] In this sense, environmentalism goes hand in hand with the birth of international cultural heritage law.

Because it was approved in the early 1970s, before 'sustainable development' had emerged as a concept in international fora, the WHC does not really mention the concept in its main text. That said, the 2015 Operational Guidelines for the Implementation of the World Heritage Convention[15] are filled with references to the concept and its relationship to heritage.[16] They clearly state that:

> Since the adoption of the *Convention* in 1972, the international community has embraced the concept of 'sustainable development'. The protection and conservation of the natural and cultural heritage are a significant contribution to sustainable development.[17]

The WHC protects two types of properties, cultural and natural,[18] and will only protect them inasmuch as they have 'outstanding universal value' (OUV).[19] Perhaps the relationship between sustainable development and heritage in the WHC is best

[13] Kunich, John Charles, 'World Heritage in Danger in the Hotspots', *Indiana Law Journal* 78(2) (2003), 619–58.

[14] Meller, H., 'Taking it to the Next Level: The Internationalization of Domestic Norms and Intangible Cultural Heritage', *Gnovis: A Journal of Communication, Culture, and Technology* 10(3) (2010) available at <http://www.gnovisjournal.org/2010/08/26/taking-it-next-level-internationalization-domestic-norms-and-intangible-cultural-heritage/> (accessed 30 October 2017).

[15] Operational Guidelines for the Implementation of the World Heritage Convention (2015).

[16] See in general Dailoo, Shabnam Inanloo and Pannekoek, Frits, 'Nature and Culture: A New World Heritage Context', *International Journal of Cultural Property* 15 (2008), 25–47.

[17] World Heritage Operational Guidelines, para. 6.

[18] But a third category of 'cultural landscapes', representing the mixture of cultural and natural heritage, has been put into place by para. 47 of the World Heritage Operational Guidelines. On this evolution, see Whitby-Last, K., 'Article 1: Cultural Landscapes', in Francesco Francioni and Federico Lenzerini (eds), *The 1972 World Heritage Convention: A Commentary* (Oxford University Press, 2008), 51–63.

[19] Convention concerning the Protection of the World Cultural and Natural Heritage 1972 (adopted 23 November 1972, entered into force 15 December 1975) 1037 UNTS 151 (WHC), Articles 1–2. On this concept, see Boer, Ben, 'Article 3: Identification and Delineation of World Heritage Properties', in Francesco Francioni and Federico Lenzerini (eds), *The 1972 World Heritage Convention: A Commentary* (Oxford University Press, 2008), 85–103.

explained by the fact that, unlike most other heritage instruments, the WHC has a special category of natural properties protected in Article 2 of the instrument, as discussed in Chapter 2.[20] And, on assessing the outstanding universal value of natural heritage properties, the Operational Guidelines state the following.

> For all properties nominated under criteria (vii)–(x) [concerning natural heritage], bio-physical processes and landform features should be relatively intact. However, it is recognized that no area is totally pristine and that all natural areas are in a dynamic state, and to some extent involve contact with people. Human activities, including those of traditional societies and local communities, often occur in natural areas. These activities may be consistent with the Outstanding Universal Value of the area where they are ecologically sustainable.[21]

This rule of the World Heritage Operational Guidelines is telling, as it assumes sustainable development is a necessary element for (natural) heritage to be protected in the first place. Further, it seems to temper the absolute of conservation of pristine heritage, and admit to the possibility that heritage is in fact engaged with, and that said engagement does not necessarily deal a fatal blow to the value of an area. However, the preservation of this OUV depends on sustainable uses. On a specific rule about 'sustainable use', the Guidelines say that:

> World Heritage properties may support a variety of ongoing and proposed uses that are ecologically and culturally sustainable and which may contribute to the quality of life of communities concerned. The State Party and its partners must ensure that such sustainable use or any other change does not impact adversely on the Outstanding Universal Value of the property. For some properties, human use would not be appropriate. Legislations [sic], policies and strategies affecting World Heritage properties should ensure the protection of the Outstanding Universal Value, support the wider conservation of natural and cultural heritage, and promote and encourage the active participation of the communities and stakeholders concerned with the property as necessary conditions to its sustainable protection, conservation, management and presentation.[22]

One way to read the above paragraph is to say that the preservation of OUV trumps any form of use of the property, however sustainable it might be. In this sense, the critique of the WHC as being too focused on the protection of a certain type of sterile monumentality, even at the cost of alienating heritage users, local communities, and other stakeholders, gains credence.[23] But this restriction refers specifically

[20] WHC, Art. 2:

> For the purposes of this Convention, the following shall be considered as 'natural heritage': natural features consisting of physical and biological formations or groups of such formations, which are of outstanding universal value from the aesthetic or scientific point of view; geological and physiographical formations and precisely delineated areas which constitute the habitat of threatened species of animals and plants of outstanding universal value from the point of view of science or conservation; natural sites or precisely delineated natural areas of outstanding universal value from the point of view of science, conservation or natural beauty.

[21] World Heritage Operational Guidelines, para. 90. [22] Ibid., para. 119.

[23] See e.g. de Nordenflycht, J., 'El Culto Postmoderno a los Monumentos: Patrimonio Local en Contexto Global', Paper presented at the International Council on Monuments and Sites 13th General Assembly and Scientific Symposium, Madrid, 1–5 December 2002, available at <http://

to the *use* of the heritage site, not necessarily to the broader idea of sustainable development as a core principle for the management of heritage.

Further, the Guidelines acknowledge that community involvement is key for sustainable use. The question remains as to how (and, most importantly, by whom) sustainable use is defined and enforced. As understanding the cultural and natural elements of sites, particularly landscapes, is critical to the safeguarding of the heritage,[24] communities can be key in bridging those concepts.

In fact, according to the Operational Guidelines, sustainable development principles must always be integrated into the management system that needs to be presented alongside any nomination.[25] This interpretation of the Guidelines is consistent with the conservation paradigm that is integral to much of heritage thinking. According to this paradigm, as discussed in Chapter 1, heritage needs to be protected for the enjoyment of future generations (in a tone that is strikingly similar to much of the discourse about sustainable development, which says nature must be preserved for the use of future generations). A key gap in this discourse is that the notion of the *intra*generational seems neglected, which means that stakeholders in the present are not in the same position, and must all abide to one specific view of what the future needs from the past, without much regard to what the present may have to say about, or its ultimate influence on, the feasibility of that future. The result of the lack of observance of intragenerational equity concerns is the further alienation of communities, since experts are privileged to speak on behalf of future generations. Heritage thus must be protected even if at the cost of not allowing present generations to enjoy it. This lack of connection between heritage and the human element that made it significant to begin with is very problematic, as it alienates stakeholders and freezes heritage at a certain point in time in which it can still be (falsely) considered pristine and unspoiled.[26]

Besides the WHC, the other core international legal instrument in the cultural heritage realm is the ICHC. The instrument is in many ways a response to criticisms against the World Heritage Convention for its focus on OUV, and its role in alienating local communities and other stakeholders.[27] As is discussed in more detail in Chapter 7, the ICHC has moved away from the WHC model towards a model of 'representativeness' and fostering of cultural diversity, rather than exceptional aesthetic (or other) value.[28]

The ICHC protects living cultures, including ways of life. To the extent sustainable development is also about a way of life, there are commonalities between the

www.international.icomos.org/madrid2002/actas/177.pdf> (accessed 30 October 2017); and Smith, Laurajane, *Uses of Heritage* (Routledge, 2006), 100.

[24] Dailoo and Pannekoek (n 16) 26.

[25] World Heritage Operational Guidelines, para. 132.5.

[26] To unpack this assumption see Lowenthal, David, 'Natural and Cultural Heritage', *International Journal of Heritage Studies* 11(1) (2005), 81–92, 89–90.

[27] For these criticisms, as well as a drafting history of the instrument, see Lixinski, Lucas, *Intangible Cultural Heritage in International Law* (Oxford University Press, 2013).

[28] Blake, Janet, *Commentary on the UNESCO 2003 Convention on the Safeguarding of the Intangible Cultural Heritage* (Institute for Art and Law, 2006), 119.

mandate of heritage protection in the intangible heritage context, and that of sustainable development.

With respect to sustainable development in the text of the ICH Convention, the instrument's preamble already acknowledges the relationship between intangible heritage and sustainable development by '[c]onsidering the importance of the intangible cultural heritage as a mainspring of cultural diversity and a guarantee of sustainable development'.[29] Article 2(1) of the ICHC, on the definition of intangible heritage, is further-reaching, in stating that '[f]or the purposes of this *Convention*, consideration will be given solely to such intangible cultural heritage as is compatible [. . .] with the requirements [. . .] of sustainable development'.

By making compatibility with sustainable development a requirement of the very concept of intangible heritage, the ICHC turns sustainable development into one of the core conceptual pillars of the instrument.[30] However, the Operational Directives for the Implementation of the Convention for the Safeguarding of the Intangible Cultural Heritage,[31] in contrast to the WHC Operational Guidelines, until recently scarcely mentioned sustainable development. Earlier versions of the Directives did not elaborate further on the requirement of sustainable development for the nomination to the intangible heritage lists. Sustainable development was instead mentioned as a bar to accepting certain contributions to the Intangible Heritage Fund (in the sense that potential contributors who are not committed to sustainable development will not be allowed to contribute to the fund),[32] or in the connection between the commercial exploitation and awareness-raising of intangible heritage and the effect of these activities on sustainable tourism.[33] Therefore, despite being nominally a core pillar of the ICHC, sustainable development's role in the intangible heritage realm was still somewhat undefined.

The 2016 version of the Operational Directives, by contrast, includes an entire chapter titled 'Safeguarding intangible cultural heritage and sustainable development at the national level',[34] covering matters like social development (including food security and gender equality), economic development (considering tourism and labour standards), environmental sustainability *sensu stricto*, and the connection between ICH and peace. The 2016 version of the Directives reiterates the rules on the fund in previous Directives, and advances them tremendously with the new chapter. The Directives envisage three pillars of sustainable development (social, economic, and environmental) which need coordination at the local level.[35] These

[29] Convention for Safeguarding of the Intangible Cultural Heritage 2003 (adopted 17 October 2003, entered into force 20 April 2006) 2368 UNTS 3 (ICHC), Preamble.

[30] On the connection between intangible heritage and sustainable development see Kono, Toshiyuki, 'UNESCO and Intangible Cultural Heritage from the Viewpoint of Sustainable Development' in A Yusuf (ed.), *Standard-Setting in UNESCO Volume 1: Normative Action in Education, Science and Culture* (UNESCO Publishing and Martinus Nijhoff, 2007), 237–65.

[31] Operational Directives for the Implementation of the Convention for the Safeguarding of the Intangible Cultural Heritage (2016).

[32] Operational Directives for the Implementation of the Convention for the Safeguarding of the Intangible Cultural Heritage (2010), para. 73.

[33] Ibid., paras 102, 111, and 117.

[34] ICH Operational Directives (2016), Chapter VI (paras 170–197).

[35] Ibid., para. 170.

new Directives stress the importance of community involvement and governance for the sustainability of heritage,[36] but, as discussed in Chapter 3, still problematically relegate community involvement to the domestic level.

Particularly with respect to environmental sustainability, the Directives state that:

> States Parties are encouraged to acknowledge the contribution of the safeguarding of intangible cultural heritage to environmental sustainability and to recognize that environmental sustainability requires sustainably managed natural resources and the conservation and sustainable use of biodiversity, which in turn could gain from improved scientific understanding and knowledge-sharing about climate change, natural hazards, the environmental and natural resource limits and that strengthening resilience among vulnerable populations in the face of climate change and natural disasters is essential.[37]

Therefore, the Directives acknowledge that communities are actors alongside experts, in many respects challenging assumptions in the conservation paradigm. However, its weak language, that only 'encourages' states to acknowledge the expertise of communities, is indicative of ingrained resistance to accepting the contribution of communities, if not by experts, then by states, who may fear the possibilities of ICH as a form of political emancipation.[38] Other language in the Directives reinforces this concern with climate change and disaster mitigation,[39] but also stresses the connection between communities and their Traditional Knowledge (TK) for the conservation of biodiversity.[40] Much like in the Convention on Biological Diversity (CBD),[41] then, TK is a key instrument for the achievement of environmental goals. But, unlike the CBD's focus on Indigenous and local communities, the ICHC Directives include all communities who practise ICH, 'as essential actors in sustaining the environment'.[42]

Some of the running themes in this connection between sustainable development and ICH, particularly with respect to the environment, highlight a connection that makes ICH largely a conduit for broader goals that exist outside the domain of cultural heritage. I suggest this view largely means a broad rejection of the idea of ICH (or heritage more broadly) as having intrinsic value,[43] and sees ICH as being a means for a different goal (in this case, sustainable development). Further, ICH in these Directives serves sustainability, as is required by the letter of the ICHC, while seeing sustainable development in a broader way that takes into account more than just the environment.

This connection between intangible cultural heritage and sustainable development is also representative of the more general relationship between intangible

[36] Ibid., para. 171. [37] Ibid., para. 188.

[38] For a discussion of the potentials and pitfalls of these strategies, see Lixinski, Lucas, 'Heritage Listing as a Tool for Advocacy: The Possibilities for Dissent, Contestation and Emancipation in International Law through International Cultural Heritage Law', *Asian Journal of International Law* 5(2) (2015), 387–409.

[39] ICH Operational Directives (2016), para. 191. [40] Ibid., para.189.

[41] Convention on Biological Diversity, 1760 UNTS 79; 31 ILM 818 (1992) (CBD).

[42] ICH Operational Directives (2016), para. 189.a.

[43] As I have argued elsewhere. See Lixinski (n 27).

heritage and development, to the extent that the survival of ICHC depends on the survival of the way of life of a certain community or group, and therefore on its economic viability.[44] There is thus a much closer connection between ICHC and development than the normal connection between 'general' cultural heritage and development: while the 'general' cultural heritage connection is based on external elements, and the development brought about by the exploitation of that heritage is not necessarily directed at the preservation of said heritage, the connection between the ICHC and development is a necessary element for the ICHC's very survival.[45]

Can this requirement of sustainable development in fact guarantee the economic viability and survival of a community, which is so important for the continuity of the very heritage one seeks to protect? For the answer, one needs to look at the extent to which the paradigms of sustainable development and of heritage protection are up to the task, and whether their 'backwards-looking' tendencies can actually address present and future needs. But, before that, one needs to better grasp the idea of sustainable development, and its critics.

6.2 The Dark Sides of Sustainable Development

Sustainable development came about as a concept in the 1980s, pushed forward largely by the efforts of the International Union for the Conservation of Nature and Natural Resources (IUCN),[46] with a marked focus on conservation.[47] It fits in the evolution of an environmental movement which, tellingly, has a history steeped in colonial structures, much like the concept of community (discussed in Chapter 3) and much of the economics of heritage (Chapter 5). More specifically, environmentalists saw in colonial rules on forestry a ready-made model capable of setting aside large reserves of natural resources. In many respects, '[e]mpire forestry resolved the tension between romantic preservationist notions and *laissez-faire* policies'.[48] By, for instance, expropriating lands of local communities who opposed imperial domination, and turning them into forest reserves for the greater good, governance projects beyond those of immediate natural conservation were also articulated under the guise of protection of public goods.[49]

The environmental movement's colonial legacy seems to have been largely forgotten, partly because of its own success.[50] However, its effect of alienating

[44] Blake (n 28) 119.

[45] See Blake, Janet, 'UNESCO's 2003 Convention on Intangible Cultural Heritage: The Implications of Community Involvement in "Safeguarding"', in Laurajane Smith and Natsuko Akagawa (eds), *Intangible Heritage: Key Issues in Cultural Heritage* (Routledge, 2009), 45–74, 48–9.

[46] The IUCN, incidentally, is also one of the key non-governmental organizations behind the regime of the World Heritage Convention, which again highlights the relationship between the environmentalist movement and the heritage movement.

[47] See Lélé (n 6) 610.

[48] Barton, Gregory A., *Empire Forestry and the Origins of Environmentalism* (Cambridge University Press 2002), 1.

[49] Ibid., 50. [50] Ibid., 144.

communities is still felt, even if this is not a clearly desired outcome of environmental action. In the evolution of the environmental movement, development, as opposed to just conservation, was gradually brought back into the fold as a means to reengage economics. Sustainable development became a key term.

The concept of sustainable development evolved through three distinct phases. The first phase, *pre-Stockholm*, includes the development of the concept and its parallels in pre-1972 religious and other customary traditions; Malthus's 'theory of limits' (the recognition that there are limits to growth caused by resource scarcity); and the idea of 'bigness' as a primary problem in certain libertarian/anarchistic branches of political economy.

During the second phase, comprising the road from the 1972 Stockholm conference to the World Commission on Environment and Development (WCED), concerns about the consequences of unmanaged growth emerged at the 1972 UN Conference on the Human Environment in Stockholm, which roughly coincided with the recognition by the Club of Rome of an impending global environmental crisis. The IUCN, working closely with the World Wildlife Fund and the United Nations Environment Programme (UNEP), formally integrated environmental and developmental concerns for the first time under the umbrella concept of 'conservation' in its World Conservation Strategy, which was launched in 1980. The concept of sustainable development was then picked up by the WCED and included in its 1987 report, *Our Common Future*.[51]

Thirdly, after the WCED, there has been a proliferation of 'sustainable development' definitions sharing the core values established at the WCED, due to the vagueness with which it was defined in the original report. The WCED victory was a political one: rather than pinning down a precise definition at the cost of consensus, the participants settled for a vaguer definition for which there was widespread agreement.[52]

Sustainable development has long defied a precise definition. But, it has been argued, it is precisely because the concept is so vague that it is so effective in gathering support behind its aims, whatever they are.[53] Many of the policy prescriptions being suggested under the guise of sustainable development, however, 'stem from subjective (rather than consensual) ideas about goals and means, and worse, are often inadequate and even counterproductive'.[54]

Since the 1980s, sustainable development has been linked with the idea of cultural diversity and self-determination, alongside the integration of conservation and development.[55] The main success of the movement has been in highlighting that environmental conservation does not necessarily constrain development, and nor does development necessarily mean pollution or environmental degradation.[56]

[51] World Commission on Environment and Development, *Our Common Future: Report of the World Commission on Environment and Development*, UN GAOR, 42nd sess., UN Doc. A/42/427 (4 August 1987).

[52] Mebratu, D., 'Sustainability and Sustainable Development: Historical and Conceptual Review', *Environmental Impact Assessment Review* 18 (1998), 493–510, 496–503.

[53] Lélé (n 6) 607. [54] Ibid., 608. [55] Ibid., 611. [56] Ibid., 613.

But that is just one reading of what sustainable development means. According to John Robinson, early environmental literature was split into two main fields. On one hand were those who favoured the preservation of natural areas in what was perceived to be a pristine (i.e. undeveloped) form. This 'preservationist' position was often expressed in explicitly romantic or spiritual terms and had its intellectual roots in American (United States) Transcendentalism and European Romanticism. The alternative 'conservationist' position also favoured the protection of natural areas, but this protection was essentially a form of enlightened self-interest, conserving land and resources for later human use, including resource extraction and what today we would call eco-tourism. This position was often, though not always, explicitly rooted in a utilitarian and social philosophy that had as its goal the greatest good for the greatest number, and promoted access to the wonders of nature for all.[57]

Debates on sustainable development also largely replicated these concerns. According to Robinson,

> In each case one side focuses more on questions related to values and fundamental changes in individual attitudes towards nature (the sustainability argument) while the other side takes what they believe to be a more pragmatic and collective approach, oriented towards efficiency gains and improvements in technology (i.e. sustainable development). Both sides of these divides often band together in marriages of convenience against what are seen as explicitly anti-environmental arguments, but the well-springs of their concern, and their ultimate goal, are rather different.[58]

Because it oscillates between techno-pragmatism and a romantic aspiration to bring about value change, it is easy to agree with Escobar's suggestion that 'much of the sustainable development discourse is a tale that a disenchanted (modern) world tells itself about its sad condition'.[59] It is, by and large, subsumed under an economic paradigm, one in which dominant forms of political power still get to assert and determine the meaning and priorities of development for all stakeholders, thereby enabling continued forms of colonialism.[60] Sustainable development, thus, 'can colonize areas of Third World social life that are not yet ruled by the logic of the market or the consumer, areas such as forests, water rights, and *sacred sites*'.[61]

One such area of the Third World is the Pacific coasts of Colombia and Ecuador, where (intangible) cultural heritage, identity, and sustainable development are intrinsically connected, with mixed results. The next section explores some aspects of the safeguarding of Afro-Descendant cultural heritage and the requirement of sustainable development that comes with it.

[57] Robinson (n 6) 371. [58] Ibid.

[59] Escobar, Arturo, 'Construction Nature: Elements for a Poststructural Political Ecology' in R. Peet and M. Watts (eds), *Liberation Ecologies: Environment, Development, Social Movements* (Routledge, 1996), 46–68, 53–4.

[60] Banerjee, S. B., 'Who Sustains Whose Development? Sustainable Development and the Reinvention of Nature', *Organization Studies* 24(1) (2003) 143–80, 144.

[61] Ibid., 159 (emphasis added, citations omitted).

6.3 Sustainable Development as a Component of Identity: The Marimba Music of Afro-Descendants in Latin America

I have written elsewhere about the Marimba music as Afro-Colombian ICH, based on a 2010 listing.[62] Since that inscription, in 2015, the inscription of Marimba music has been entirely redone, and is now a multinational nomination including both Colombia and Ecuador, both countries that share a history and present of Afro-Descendant struggles.

Populations of African descent (descendants from African slaves in Colombia and Ecuador) have existed for a long time in both countries, and their struggles with respect to land tenure and other human rights have been widely discussed.[63] In this chapter, I will engage with the binational nomination of the Marimba music on the Representative List, but, for the purposes of discussing the dark sides of sustainability, I will particularly focus on the Afro-Colombian communities affected, while mindful that many of the problems the Afro-Ecuadorian communities face are the same, particularly with respect to shrimp farming and other resource-extraction practices around their territories.

Afro-Colombians in particular have been protected by the Colombian legal order since at least 1991, when a new Constitution recognized their rights to the lands they have traditionally occupied.[64] Subsequent legislation (*Ley 70*) has sought to operationalize the rights protected in the Constitution, and a titling process has begun to grant collective title to Afro-Colombian communities.[65] However, as a condition for the protection of these communities as such, and the granting of collective rights, they are required to subsist through the use of sustainable techniques only.[66]

But what does Marimba music and chanting have to do with sustainable development? As I have argued elsewhere, the safeguarding of a part of a group's intangible heritage is a means to attempt to safeguard the culture as a whole, because there is an assumption that living cultures operate holistically, and to protect only part of a culture would be self-defeating.[67] Therefore, listing a part of a group's ICH works as a means to highlight and safeguard not only that part of the culture, but the entirety

[62] Lixinski, 'Sustainable Development in International Heritage Law' (n 12).

[63] For excellent reports on these matters, see the Bernard and Audre Rapoport Center for Human Rights and Justice, *Afro-Descendant Land Rights Project*, at https://law.utexas.edu/humanrights/project-type/afro-descendants/.

[64] *Constitución de 1991* (Colombia) transitory art 55.

[65] Ley 70 de 1993 (Ley de Negritudes) (Colombia) ('Ley 70').

[66] Ibid., Art. 49, which reads:

> The design, execution and coordination of the plans, programmes, and projects of economic and social development that the government and the Technical International Cooperation may put forward for the benefit of the Black Communities to which this Law refers should be carried out with the participation of the representatives of said communities, in order to respond to their particular needs, the preservation of the environment, the conservation and qualification of their traditional practices of production, the eradication of poverty, and the respect and recognition of their social and cultural life. These plans, programmes, and projects should reflect the aspirations of the Black Communities in areas of development.

[67] Lixinski (n 27).

of identity for the benefit of present and future generations. That holistic approach works to protect not only the cultural manifestation being listed, but also the economic activities that enable the community to continue practising those cultural forms (even if simply by allowing them to continue living together in the same area).[68]

And that is the point of *Ley 70*, cited in the 2010 nomination process as an important legislative tool for safeguarding Afro-Colombian identity.[69] *Ley 70* protects Afro-Colombian communities as a whole, including their cultures, livelihoods, and land rights.[70]

The Marimba music and traditional chants of Afro-Colombian communities were initially added to the Representative List of the Intangible Cultural Heritage of Humanity in 2010. According to the Nomination File, '[t]he expression being nominated is recognized as cultural heritage by Afro-Colombians from the south-western part of the country who share the historical condition of descending from slave contingents that were brutally imported to [what is now Colombia]'.[71] Marimba music, even though nominated as being a Pacific coast manifestation of heritage, is actually spread widely across the country, by virtue of internal migration. Women often leave communities with their children to seek educational opportunities, whereas the men stay to work the land and provide for their families. This aspect of migration makes the vitality of Marimba music all the more important as a means to safeguard identity.[72]

The 2015 Nomination File presents the communities affected as 'Afro-descendant communities from the beaches, forests and rivers along the coast of the south of Colombia and the north-west of Ecuador who share the same cultural heritage and have been settled in the same land since the 16th century'.[73] The areas indicated in the 2015 Nomination File cover a large part of the Afro-Descendant population in each country: 39% in Colombia, and 25% in Ecuador.[74]

Marimba music gains a new dimension for Afro-Colombians, according to the 2010 Nomination File, because community leaders and political organizations have emphasized 'the recognition of culture as the foundation of identity and a departure point to access autonomy and territorial rights and to build their own worldvision (*cosmovisión*)'.[75] In the 2015 Nomination File, 'Marimba music and traditional chants and dances are underpinned by Afro-descendants' social claims, including

[68] With specific regard to Colombia, see Rodríguez-Uribe, N. and Rodríguez-Uribe, D., 'Emerging Indigenous Voices: Safeguarding Intangible Heritage in Colombia and the Reaffirmation of Cultural Rights' in R. Amoêda, S. Lira, and C. Pinheiro (eds), *Heritage 2012: Proceedings of the 3rd International Conference on Heritage and Sustainable Development* (Green Lines Institute, 2012), 1469–79.

[69] UNESCO Intergovernmental Committee for the Safeguarding of the Intangible Cultural Heritage, *Nomination File for Inscription on the Representative List of the Intangible Cultural Heritage in 2010*, 5th sess., Document No. 00436 (November 2010) 3 ('*Marimba Nomination File (2010)*').

[70] *Ley 70* (n 65).

[71] *Marimba Nomination File (2010)*, Document No 00436, 2.

[72] Ibid.

[73] UNESCO Intergovernmental Committee for the Safeguarding of the Intangible Cultural Heritage, *Nomination File for Inscription on the Representative List of the Intangible Cultural Heritage in 2015*, 10th sess., Document No. 01099 (November 2015) 3 ('*Marimba Nomination File (2015)*'), 2.

[74] Ibid.

[75] Ibid., 3.

spiritual and religious aspects, which make it possible for them to express their identity following centuries of persecution through slavery and evangelization and being forced to survive in obscurity', and '[t]he communities recognize that each of these expressions of the element facilitates family and collective integration through ancestral practices that heighten the sense of belonging to a particular ethnic group connected to shared territory and history'.[76] Importantly, here the assertion of connection to a *cosmovisión* seems to have been dropped, and the focus is instead on less of a direct comparison with Indigenous peoples, and greater recognition of the autonomous cultural status of Afro-Descendant communities in these countries.

The *cosmovisión* of Afro-Descendant communities was originally somewhat different from Indigenous *cosmovisión*: while Indigenous *cosmovisión* is normally understood in terms of a harmonious relationship with nature, Afro-Colombians were not originally bound by this notion, because they were not originally from the land.[77] However, 'their championing of traditional practices of production and connection to land has turned out to be problematic for many whose options in terms of development are limited'.[78] To be sure, *Ley 70* requires that Afro-Colombian communities '(re)learn sustainable traditions and practices'.[79]

With respect to sustainable development, the 2015 Nomination File states that 'the element is involved in all aspects of family and community life relating, amongst other things, to respect for nature and the sustainable management of resources needed to make instruments'.[80] In other words, the environmental dimension deserves little to no attention, and the nomination does not focus on the broader culture in this respect, focusing instead on the specificities of Marimba. In this way, the Nomination File, and the representation of Marimba music and Afro-Descendant culture to the world as a consequence, tries to do two things simultaneously: it sees itself as interacting with the culture as a whole when depicting the relevance of Marimba music to Afro-Descendant culture; but at the same time it focuses only on a narrow reading of Marimba music (instead of the culture) when discussing limitations. There is a contesting of the definition of ICH at play here, and one in which sustainable development ends up being pushed into the background. Nevertheless, in its decision, the Intergovernmental Committee under the ICHC praised both States for preparing a 'high quality multinational file that testifies to the dialogical, dynamic and evolving nature of intangible cultural heritage'.[81]

There is an assumption that Afro-Descendant culture (that is, their ICH) is only worth protecting inasmuch as it conforms to the idea of sustainable development. However, the obligation to meet this requirement comes with no assistance from the State, and must be complied with against strong competition from industrial shrimp farming businesses operating in the same area as these communities.

[76] Ibid., 5.

[77] Engle, Karen, *The Elusive Promise of Indigenous Development: Culture, Rights, Strategy* (Duke University Press, 2010), 234.

[78] Ibid., 253. [79] Ibid., 242. [80] *Marimba Nomination File (2015)* (n 73) 6.

[81] UNESCO Intergovernmental Committee for the Safeguarding of the Intangible Cultural Heritage, *Decisions*, 10th sess., Decision 10.COM 10.b.13, ITH/15/10.COM/Decisions (30 November–4 December 2015), para. 5.

The expansion of agricultural projects in areas surrounding these communities, particularly shrimp farming, has put communities' ability to use only sustainable means to the test. More specifically, these shrimp farming businesses are not bound by the same stringent requirements of sustainable development, and use state-of-the-art techniques. Because they are located a short distance from Afro-Colombian communities, they essentially exploit the same resources as Afro-Colombian communities, except that they are capable of extracting much larger quantities of shrimp. Their industrial activity leaves little to nothing to be fished by the communities, who are required to abide by sustainable development requirements if their land titles are to be recognized and protected. Additionally, shrimp farming—through the use of fertilizers, antibiotics, and chemicals to regulate the pH of the water, all of which have devastating effects on the ecosystem—destroys the mangrove forests upon which Afro-Colombians depend.[82]

In Tumaco, one of the places in Colombia indicated in the 2010 Marimba Nomination File as particularly important for Marimba music, a state-of-the-art fishing port facility was opened in 1993, the same year as *Ley 70*, with the capacity for large-scale shrimp farming.[83] It is somewhat paradoxical that, in the same year as the Colombian government required Afro-Colombian communities in the region to only use traditional methods for shrimp farming, a large complex for industrial shrimp farming opened, in direct competition with these Afro-Colombian communities.

In Ecuador, shrimp farming also poses challenges to the survival of Afro-Descendant communities in the Esmeraldas region. Industrial shrimp farming offers very limited employment for Afro-Descendant community members (since these businesses tend to bring their labour force from other parts of Ecuador), and the effluents from the shrimp ponds flow into lakes and mangroves, killing animal species that are vital for the food security and economic activity of Afro-Ecuadorians.[84]

The inscription of Marimba music and chants on the Representative List of the Intangible Cultural Heritage of Humanity thus serves as a means to entrench a certain version of Afro-Colombian identity defined by *Ley 70*. The same can be said to happen in Ecuador, which also has special legislation on Afro-Ecuadorian rights, in addition to constitutional provisions.[85] Those versions include sustainable development but, as it turns out, (non-traditional) groups and businesses surrounding Afro-Descendant communities, who do not enjoy the protection of the distinctiveness of their culture, are also free to exploit resources and develop, gradually preventing Afro-Descendants from being able to exploit those resources themselves and from reaping any benefits from that exploitation.

[82] Escobar, Arturo, *Territories of Difference: Place, Movements, Life, Redes* (Duke University Press, 2008), 88–9.

[83] Ibid., 94–5.

[84] Rapoport Delegation on Afro-Ecuadorian Land Rights, *Forgotten Territories, Unrealized Rights: Rural Afro-Ecuadorians and their Fight for Land, Equality, and Security* (2009), 34–5. Available at https://law.utexas.edu/wp-content/uploads/sites/31/2016/02/ecuador-eng.pdf.

[85] Ibid., 24–9. See also Defensoría del Pueblo del Ecuador, *Informe Temático: El Pueblo Afrodescendiente en Ecuador* (2012), 19–38.

Afro-Colombians have advocated for protection of their distinctive culture. This protection has come to fruition through the passage of *Ley 70*, and is being further entrenched in the Representative List, giving their distinctiveness international recognition. Specific legislation in Ecuador is also very protective of Afro-Descendant rights, particularly as channeled through culture, and in articulating these rights in connection to the environment.[86] The listing of Marimba music is also seen by Ecuador as an important means of guaranteeing the cultural survival of these communities, as discussed above.[87] However, at the same time that their culture has been recognized and safeguarded, it has been modified. As a (successful) advocacy strategy, Afro-Descendants have chosen to align their identity with certain tenets of Indigenous *cosmovisión*, given the successes of the Indigenous rights movement. But that came at the cost of creating and requiring a certain connection with nature and sustainable development that is not necessarily compatible with their historical practices, and not conducive to their own development, particularly when in competition with other sectors of society that are not subject to the same requirements.

The Afro-Descendant example highlights the connection between protecting a way of life (and ICH as an emblem of that way of life) and environmental sustainability for humanity at large. It shows the potential unfairness of making ICH holders the custodians of the environment, at least if they are the only ones required to be sustainable against non-sustainable economic competitors. This discussion also problematizes the assertion that culture must necessarily lead to sustainability, at least to the extent that sustainability is read as belonging in the past, and the ICHC, as discussed, in effect promotes the tenet that heritage is supposed to change, to be in the present, and not in the past.

In this section I have explored the effects of thinking of sustainable development as part of a holistic identity, and the effects of entrenching that identity through heritage listing. The following section considers the listing of nature as heritage, and the effects of identity-based connections to the land and the heritage.

6.4 Community Involvement and Sustainable Development: East Rennell

The eastern part of Rennell, as mentioned above, was inscribed on the World Heritage List in 1998.[88] The nomination process was sponsored by the New Zealand government and took about ten years, starting in 1989 with a recommendation by the Solomon Islands government to pursue listing of Lake Tegano on East Rennell even though formally the Solomon Islands only became a party to the World Heritage Convention in 1992.[89]

86 Rapoport Delegation (n 84) 24–9.

87 *Marimba Nomination File (2015)* (n 73).

88 *Report of the World Heritage Committee*, 22nd sess., WHC-98/CONF.203/18 (30 November–5 December 1998) 25.

89 Government of the Solomon Islands, *Nomination of East Rennell, Solomon Islands, for Inclusion in the World Heritage List—Natural Sites*, File Name 854 (June 1997) 1 ('*East Rennell Nomination File*').

Rennell is the largest raised coral atoll in the world. Lake Tagano, which was the former lagoon on the atoll, is the largest lake in the insular Pacific (15,500 ha). Lake Tagano is brackish and contains many rugged limestone islands and endemic species. A dense forest covers most of Rennell, with a canopy averaging 20 m in height. Because of its particular geological features, combined with the strong climatic effects of frequent cyclones, the site is a natural laboratory for scientific study.[90]

The listing of East Rennell is in many ways special. It is the only item on the World Heritage List protected and managed solely under customary law. The land in East Rennell is not owned by the State. It is, rather, collectively owned by the Rennellese. Custom ownership is patrilineal, and all major decisions regarding ownership are made by the chiefs. In the East Rennell Nomination File, the Solomon Islands government recognized the essential role played by traditional owners by saying that 'the customary/traditional practices have provided protection in the past and these practices will be recognised and strengthened'.[91]

Local communities were an integral part of the nomination process, and participated actively in the drafting of the management and conservation plan.[92] The participation of local people was mentioned in the Solomon Islands' arguments for the site's 'outstanding universal value'. More specifically, participation of local communities would help with preserving the integrity of the site.[93]

Additionally, local communities were considered to be an essential part of the sustainable development objectives of listing. Workshops for local community leaders and provincial government members have been undertaken periodically as a means to raise awareness of broader cultural, economic, and resource management issues in the area. The local East Rennell Environmental Drama Group has been in charge of putting together performances, followed by group discussions, raising awareness to and identifying strategies to deal with management issues on the property.[94]

It was local communities, too, who decided against listing the entire Rennell Island. Communities in West Rennell opposed the listing (perhaps anticipating the potentials of resource exploitation in West Rennell, where most of the island's forest area is), whereas East Rennell communities were supportive. As a result, only the eastern half of the island was inscribed on the World Heritage List.

East Rennell's protection under customary law means a double-tiered system of primary and secondary rights. Primary rights mean collective ownership and the right to use and dispose of land, as well as to sell its products. Secondary rights mean limited collective ownership, which includes the right to collect products of the land, or use it as a garden. Any other uses must be authorized by the primary

[90] UNESCO, *World Heritage List: East Rennell*, UNESCO World Heritage Centre, http://whc.unesco.org/en/list/854.

[91] *East Rennell Nomination File* (n 89). [92] Ibid., 32. [93] Ibid., 39.

[94] *East Rennell Nomination File* (n 89) attachment 1, 5, para. 4.1.1 ('*Resource Management Objectives and Guidelines for East Rennell, Solomon Islands*').

landowner. Exploitation of forest resources on customary land can only happen with the consent of the landowners, and that includes decisions about the use of land for purposes such as tourism.[95]

In a letter from the Minister of Commerce, Employment and Tourism of the Solomon Islands to the Director of the UNESCO World Heritage Centre, dated 1 September 1998, the Minister acknowledged a UNESCO suggestion that cultural criteria be applied to the site, and promised to investigate the possibility further.[96] This means that East Rennell could have been inscribed on the World Heritage List not only for its outstanding natural features, but also in recognition of the outstanding culture of the region that enabled these natural features to be preserved. Unfortunately, the inscription took place only with respect to the natural values of the property, putting the cultural contribution of the local communities in a secondary position. By not listing East Rennell as a 'cultural landscape' and inscribing it solely as a natural property, communities felt their culture was not given the recognition they expected.[97]

However, when the listing was being negotiated with local communities, there was an expectation on the part of these communities that listing would also work as a means to validate and give recognition to their way of life, their culture.[98] In effect, the East Rennellese land was listed 'without them'.[99]

Even at the time of East Rennell's nomination, it was highlighted that '[a]pproaches attempted in the Solomon Islands to foster the establishment of protected areas have, in the past, met with little success because they lacked a participatory approach and failed to consider customary land tenure, traditional practices and enforcement'.[100] As a consequence, there was a promise that East Rennell would be different, and that customary law and practices would be taken fully into account. Participatory approaches to the development of the conservation area, further recognition and strengthening of customary land tenure, involvement of customary landowners in the identification of areas of significance (ecological, wilderness, and cultural), promotion of ecotourism, and reinforcement of traditional knowledge and management systems were all possibilities mentioned when it came to including communities.[101]

However, reality fell short of expectations. Local communities did not see the benefits to their livelihoods they expected from the listing, causing dissatisfaction

[95] *East Rennell Nomination File* (n 89) 45. See also Smith, A. and Turk, C., 'Customary Systems of Management and World Heritage in the Pacific Islands' in S. Brockwell, S. O'Connor, and D. Byrne (eds), *Transcending the Nature–Culture Divide in Cultural Heritage: Views from the Asia-Pacific Region* (ANU E-Press, 2013), 23–34, 23.

[96] *East Rennell Nomination File* (n 89) annex ('*Letter from Moses K. Mose, Ministry of Commerce, Employment and Tourism, to Bernd von Droste, UNESCO World Heritage Centre*').

[97] Smith, A., 'East Rennell World Heritage Site: Misunderstandings, Inconsistencies and Opportunities in the Implementation of the World Heritage Convention in the Pacific Islands', *International Journal of Heritage Studies* 17 (2011), 592–607, 597–9.

[98] Ibid. , 595. [99] Ibid., 597.

[100] *Resource Management Objectives and Guidelines for East Rennell, Solomon Islands*, File Name 854 (June 1997), attachment 1 8 [4.4].

[101] Smith (n 98).

with the World Heritage process. The process then became a means through which to articulate many grievances within the community.[102] Because customary land tenure was treated only as an instrument for biodiversity protection, as opposed to an essential expression of Rennellese culture that shaped the island,[103] a disconnect between local and international actors may have compromised the sustainable development of the area.

Of course, other factors, such as the civil unrest in the Solomon Islands, have also contributed to this disconnect. However, as Anita Smith suggests, 'the frustration and confusion expressed by the East Rennell community in relation to World Heritage is the outcome not primarily of the civil strife, but of the implementation of the World Heritage Convention in the Solomon Islands'.[104]

As a result of the traditional customary ownership and management of the site, it seems it was always assumed that traditional economic practices would be maintained. For instance, when it came to fishing, there was some concern from the Solomon Islands and IUCN that switching to nets was compromising the viability of certain species, particularly *Tilapia mozambica*, which was artificially introduced into Lake Tegano by the government as an additional protein source for the villagers.[105]

One of the main animal resources available on Rennell is the coconut crab, which is the largest land crab in the world, weighing up to 4.1 kg (9 lb). It is an occasional source of food for locals, and a valuable trade commodity.[106] It has been harvested to extinction in most islands in the region by the Rennellese themselves, either for their own consumption or for sale to outsiders. It matures very slowly, and can take up to 30 years to reach the harvesting size of 2 kg. They could still be found on the entire island of Rennell at the time of nomination, but they have gradually disappeared from the western (not World Heritage listed) part of the island, and are now increasingly difficult to spot in East Rennell. In a report to the World Heritage Committee, the government of the Solomon Islands noted this decline and a mission sent to the island raised concerns that increased harvesting pressure might lead to localised extinction of the species. It noted that harvesting of marine resources is unregulated by state law and traditional conservation measures have been supplanted by a more commercial approach, and that the management plan for the property, which would include measures to regulate the harvesting of coconut crab, was never implemented.[107]

Commercial logging is also putting some pressure on the East Rennellese ecosystem. Even at the time of the nomination it was pointed out that some Rennellese resource owners would be interested in logging. However, by the same token, the majority of the population (which included resource users, in addition to landowners) expressed concern about the environmental problems that could come from widespread logging, even if it was recognized that sustainable small-scale logging would be possible for the production of furniture and structural timber.[108] Logging started

[102] Ibid., 592. [103] Ibid., 593. [104] Ibid., 596.

[105] *East Rennell Nomination File* (n 89) 27. [106] Ibid., 27–8.

[107] UNESCO, *State of Conservation (SOC) Report: East Rennell (Solomon Islands)* (2013) UNESCO World Heritage Centre http://whc.unesco.org/en/soc/1876 ('*State of Conservation Report*').

[108] *East Rennell Nomination File* (n 89) 28.

in West Rennell in the years after the nomination and, even though it was subject to a licensing process on paper, in practice things proceeded differently. More specifically, logging took place beyond the limits prescribed by the Environment Act 1998[109] because resource owners granted licences to logging companies without government supervision, resulting in over-exploitation. Resource owners claim, and the State admits, that the government does not have the power to ban logging on land under customary ownership.[110] Broad strips of forest in West Rennell have been cleared and a series of logging roads built. Because the forests of East Rennell are ecologically linked to West Rennell, logging in the Western part of the island has affected the entire ecosystem.[111]

The logical consequence of this analysis of logging pressures undermines the notion that traditional local ownership is the answer to the preservation of the unspoiled natural beauty of Rennell. On the contrary, it shows that the recognition of traditional ownership, unchecked, can very easily lead to over-exploitation of resources for the sake of pure (and not necessarily sustainable) economic development.[112] The WHC Operational Guidelines, examined above, warn of that risk, and say that human activity will only be allowed to the extent it does not impact on the OUV of the heritage. But this attitude reinforces a conservation paradigm that is closely connected to notions of (Western) monumentality and importance, and which is deeply entrenched in the meaning of the term 'outstanding universal value'.

The differences in expectations between local communities and the international community are reflective of an expectation during the listing process. Even then, New Zealand, which was sponsoring the nomination, saw the nomination as a project about nature conservation, while the Solomon Islands considered it as a means to bring about economic development for its local population (mainly through tourism). 'There is, then, a wide gulf between the primarily ("sustainable") environmental objectives of the donor and the primarily economic ("development") imperatives of the local participants.'[113]

This gulf, which is at least partly responsible for the over-exploitation of natural resources in East Rennell, caused East Rennell to be moved to the List of World Heritage in Danger in June 2013. In the relevant decision, the World Heritage Committee refers explicitly to commercial logging and the over-exploitation of coconut crab and other marine resources.[114] This in danger listing happened despite the passage of the Solomon Islands Protected Areas Act 2010, which aimed at

[109] Environment Act 1998 (Solomon Islands) No. 8 of 1998.

[110] UNESCO, *State of Conservation (SOC) Report* (n 107).

[111] Ibid.

[112] Here, the Solomon Islands, like Colombia, fall under the banner of 'Third World', where the exploitation of resources is often an economic imperative for populations that would otherwise be hard-pressed to find resources to enable their survival and growth. Sustainability is more often than not an afterthought where economic development is the primary concern.

[113] Overton, J. and Purdie, N., 'Think Local, Act Global? Reflections on Sustainable Development in the Pacific Islands', *Development Bulletin* 41 (1997), 37–39, 38.

[114] UNESCO World Heritage Committee, *Decision: East Rennell (Solomon Islands) (N 854)*, 37 COM 7B.14, 37th sess., WHC-13/37.COM/20 (1627 June 2013).

increasing protection for areas of biological diversity and natural importance,[115] and explicitly included World Heritage Sites as protected areas.[116]

Part of the environmental troubles of the island can be traced back to the fact that only half the island is World Heritage listed. This means resources can be over-exploited in the unlisted part of the island, which is not subject to same requirements of sustainable development. The consequence is similar to that of the Afro-Descendant case mentioned above: because the adjoining areas to the heritage-listed areas are not subject to the same sustainable development requirements, the effect is that the entire region is under very similar environmental pressure, with the difference that communities in the protected area are also economically worse off.

The example of East Rennell also teaches us that community involvement should not happen only at the local level, and should also be fully integrated nationally and internationally. If East Rennellese communities had been allowed to more fully participate in the management of their heritage before UNESCO, misguided expectations about the system would have been mitigated, at the very least.

Finally, to expect sustainable development from communities without fully acknowledging the value of their culture beyond the protection of biodiversity is counterproductive. In the Solomon Islands, this caused dissatisfaction with the World Heritage listing process, and was overall unhelpful to the preservation of the natural values of the property. In Colombia and Ecuador, the expectation meant, quite simply, jeopardizing the continuance of a cultural system that the sustainable development requirement was supposed to protect to begin with.

6.5 Heritage Protection and Sustainable Development: Potentials and Pitfalls

The relationship between sustainable development and heritage, explained above, works to preserve both tangible and intangible heritage. But it has the consequence of freezing heritage and the environment at a certain moment in time, reinforcing a romanticized ideal of existence, one that thinks of traditional culture as necessarily connected to nature.

The very notion of thinking of Indigenous or 'non-Western' knowledge as necessarily heritage, or 'traditional' knowledge, may have harmful consequences for these communities, in that it freezes knowledge in the past and impairs their ability to pursue their own development.[117] It would be more accurate to think of 'custom' instead of 'tradition', where the former is mutable, while the latter in a way belongs to

[115] Protected Areas Act 2010 (Solomon Islands) Act No. 4 of 2010, s. 3.

[116] Ibid., s. 10(1)(c). Generally on environmental law in the Solomon Islands, see Boer, Ben, 'Solomon Islands: Condensed Version of Legal Review', in Ben Boer (ed.), *Environmental Law in the South Pacific: Consolidated Report of the Reviews of Environmental Law in the Cook Islands, Federated States of Micronesia, Kingdom of Tonga, Republic of the Marshall Islands and Solomon Islands* (IUCN, 1996), 189–241, 191.

[117] See Anderson, Jane E., *Law, Knowledge, Culture: The Production of Indigenous Knowledge in Intellectual Property Law* (Edward Elgar, 2009), 9–11.

a fossilized past, at least if we adopt Eric Hobsbawn's logic.[118] Much of the evolution towards intangible heritage is associated with the idea of protecting living cultures, but the very notion of 'heritage' is in itself charged with a connection to the past that is difficult to overcome.[119]

Besides the above, another common thread connecting the two ideas is the use of 'culture' as a screen behind which struggles happen. The work of Karen Engle is particularly illuminating in this sense. Engle examines three possible meanings of culture when translated into legal discourse and practice: culture as heritage, culture as land, and culture as development. The idea of culture as heritage stands at the weaker end of the spectrum. Engle argues that internationalist claims over heritage protection displace the beneficiaries of heritage: instead of protecting Indigenous peoples, legal attempts at protecting heritage in fact protect states, giving them the say in what heritage is worth protecting. Conversely, the idea of culture as grounded in land has to do with how discourses around the connection between Indigenous peoples and their lands have been successful in guaranteeing legal title to lands, but with the unintended consequences of curtailing the rights of Indigenous peoples over their property and creating alienation. Finally, treating culture as development means that, over time, 'culture as development' fails to address larger structural economic inequalities. Engle concludes by lamenting the marginalization of development claims, and the attendant failure to account for critical structural issues.[120]

The idea of translating culture into development fits well with what Engle refers to as 'post-neoliberal market reforms aimed at development and environmental preservation'.[121] Drawing on the work of Arturo Escobar,[122] she reiterates Escobar's call for means of alternative development,[123] exploring instances in which the imposition of sustainable development has effectively compromised a community's ability to protect or sustain itself.

In other words, imposing sustainable development requirements without any consideration as to whether they existed to begin with has the result of not supporting sustainable initiatives and, on top of it all, allowing competition from other stakeholders not bound to the (often costly) implementation of sustainable development programmes. This actually affects the possibilities for the development of these communities and, in the long run, their own existence. Compromising their existence means that their culture will cease to exist, and with it the heritage that is so treasured.

[118] Hobsbawm, Eric, 'Introduction: Inventing Traditions', in Eric Hobsbawm and Terence Ranger (eds), *The Invention of Tradition* (Cambridge University Press, 1982), 1–14, 2–4. According to Hobsbawn:

> 'Custom' is what judges do; 'tradition' (in this instance invented tradition) is the wig, robe and other formal paraphernalia and ritualized practices surrounding their substantial action.... Inventing traditions, it is assumed here, is essentially a process of formalization and ritualization, characterized by reference to the past, if only by imposing repetition.

[119] For a fuller exploration of the connection between heritage and an idealized past, see Lowenthal, David, *The Heritage Crusade and the Spoils of History* (Cambridge University Press, 1998).

[120] Engle (n 77). [121] Ibid., 184. [122] Escobar (n 82). [123] Engle (n 77).

What seems to be needed is an approach that fully acknowledges the input of local actors at the international level of heritage management. That way, goals and expectations from both ends of the spectrum (the global and the local) can be constantly readjusted and negotiated, so as to find alternatives that will promote development while securing a (realizable) degree of environmental preservation. That balance depends, of course, on the full recognition of the role culture plays in any sort of sustainable development, and that the alienation of culture, or its commodification, will often defeat the possibilities of environmental preservation at the local level.

Most models of sustainable development nominally include stakeholder collaboration (under the name of 'community empowerment').[124] However, it seems that there is a disconnect when it comes to international processes, in that community participation is assumed, and only verified at the initial stage, without any sort of meaningful follow-up. The implementation of sustainable development is contingent on local circumstances, and continued stakeholder collaboration should be an integral part of sustainable development.

Another problem with international heritage management is its insular approach to what a 'community' is, as discussed in Chapter 3. Often relying on essentialized assumptions about communities and their aspirations, communities will be repackaged (or repackage themselves, as an advocacy strategy) as a means to guarantee protection for themselves and their heritage (like the Afro-Descendants in the first case study), often with serious unintended consequences.

Also importantly, heritage managers tend to overlook the problems of excluding relevant sectors of local populations (like the West Rennellese, in our second case study).[125] Ideas about community involvement and social inclusiveness have uncritically turned into box-ticking exercises that fail to examine the definition or content of the term 'community'.[126] Communities engage with other heritage stakeholders in diverse ways, according to each sector of a community's different priorities.[127] More importantly, heritage and community create each other in the context of heritage management. 'Both the community concept and the idea of heritage become intertwined with the lived experience and expression of community. The community group is defined and justified because of its heritage and that heritage is fostered and sustained by the creation of community.'[128] For instance, even though there have historically been differences between people from eastern and western Rennell, these were deepened by the process of delimitation of the property boundaries for inscription on the World Heritage List. If previously

[124] Landorf, C., 'Managing for Sustainable Tourism: A Review of Six Cultural World Heritage Sites', *Journal of Sustainable Tourism* 17(1) (2009), 53–70, 55.

[125] Waterton, Emma and Smith, Laurajane, 'The Recognition and Misrecognition of Community Heritage', *International Journal of Heritage Studies* 16(1–2) (2010), 4–15, 10.

[126] Watson, Steve and Waterton, Emma, 'Editorial: Heritage and Community Engagement', *International Journal of Heritage Studies* 16(1–2) (2010), 1–3, 1.

[127] Crooke, Elizabeth, 'The Politics of Community Heritage: Motivations, Authority and Control', *International Journal of Heritage Studies* 16(1–2) (2010), 16–29.

[128] Ibid., 17.

these two populations were simply 'Rennellese' to the world, the process of heritage listing defined the East Rennellese community for UNESCO (and arguably the international community) in a way that, it turned out, was not fully consistent with their own aspirations.

And, even if more nuanced approaches are undertaken, there are still many pitfalls to be negotiated.[129] Even though a large number of the success stories from integrating community participation into heritage management come from natural heritage,[130] the example of East Rennell shows there is still much work to be done. For instance, there seems to be a persistent failure in recognizing that 'although the community may not acknowledge the importance of an archaeological site, it may well be important to them as another resource, such as a grazing area'.[131] Extrapolating this idea, heritage areas are, for involved communities, more than just their heritage: they are their means of livelihood and existence. Failing to recognize that leads to an overlooking of the fact that Afro-Descendants are being squeezed out by industrial shrimp farmers and, if they had the choice, would probably engage in industrial practices as well, to have a fighting chance of staying in their communities and improving their health and education access locally; and that the Rennellese would allow logging if it meant they could afford the luxuries of development, however unsustainable. Alternative forms of development are called for.

Heritage and sustainable development are concepts that go hand in hand. What they share includes the connected articulations in international heritage instruments, but also goes beyond that lip service. Conceptually, both areas embrace a sort of romanticized version of a past that needs to be rescued, a past of harmony between man, nature, and culture that has not yet been tainted by modernity, industrialization, and technology. As idyllic as that version may seem, it is also a largely untenable future, at least if it is applied in the current piecemeal, tokenistic way. Certain communities, cultures, and areas are singled out to epitomize those ideals, whereas the majority of the world's population is free to exploit the majority of the world's resources. Heritage systems, because of their focus on listing, serve this tokenistic approach quite well, and heritage lists, both tangible and intangible, have been used to advance ideals of sustainable development as an achievable vision.

However, only these isolated pockets have been subject to this vision. Leaving aside for a moment the fact that these pockets were excluded from the possibilities of development they actually craved on the ground (such as access to health and education services), they were made to compete for the same resources with actors who were not subject to the stringent requirements of that idyllic vision of a past that can guarantee humankind's future.

[129] Mansuri, Ghazala and Rao, Vijayendra, 'Community-Based and -Driven Development: A Critical Review', *The World Bank Research Observer* 19(1) (2004), 1–39.

[130] Chirikure, Shadreck, Manyanga, Munyaradzi, Ndoro, Webber, and Pwiti, Gilbert, 'Unfulfilled Promises? Heritage Management and Community Participation at Some of Africa's Cultural Heritage Sites', *International Journal of Heritage Studies* 16(1–2) (2010), 30–44, 31.

[131] Ibid., 32.

Despite critiques of the uses of sustainable development, the concept still remains, to a large extent, the most tenable principle of collective action for mediating tensions between the environment and economic development.[132] How can it be used in a way that addresses these criticisms, while at the same time preserving its important function as a flag behind which most people can stand?

The answer, I suggest, lies in community-based forms of governance, for both heritage and sustainable development (as they are intrinsically connected). There are shortcomings to community involvement, which include the essentialization of community identity, and overlooking internal dissent within communities. The question of who gets to speak on behalf of the community (that is, the community's agency) is particularly important. Also, it may happen that the answer from communities, in the short and medium terms, lies precisely in the unsustainable over-exploitation of natural resources, privileging development over sustainable development.[133] This notion of promoting development contravenes the goals of heritage protection and sustainable development, but, to the extent these can be seen as tools to preserve a group's capacity to exist in the future, they need to accommodate the needs of present generations as much as those of future ones.

In the examples of Afro-Descendant communities and East Rennell above, if those communities are involved in the determination of the sustainable development requirements they will be subject to, governmental agencies involved in the process will necessarily be made aware of the necessities of the time (in the Afro-Descendant case, the pressure from industrial shrimp farming companies, and, for both, the need to improve their own livelihoods through exploiting natural resources). Other stakeholders, too, will be required to comply with sustainable development norms, thus levelling the playing field. That way, Afro-Descendant and East Rennell communities, as well as communities elsewhere, will in fact be able to preserve their way of life and their heritage, for the benefit of present and future generations of the communities, as opposed to hanging on to a way of life imposed from outside that has no chance of long-term survival because of external influences, and is thus nothing more than a relic for outsiders to gaze upon and celebrate as a memento of a past that is never coming back.

The involvement of communities is fraught with difficulties, but not only in the implementation of sustainability values in international heritage law. In fact, community exclusion also pervades the entirety of the implementation and enforcement of norms and mechanisms that are much more deeply entrenched in international heritage. The next chapter focuses on these aspects of the functionality of international heritage law.

[132] See Sneddon, C., Howarth, R. B., and Norgaard, R. B., 'Sustainable Development in a Post-Brundtland World', *Ecological Economics* 57 (2006), 253–68, 260.

[133] For this situation in China, see Wai-Yin, Chan and Shu-Yun, Ma, 'Heritage Preservation and Sustainability of China's Development', *Sustainable Development* 12 (2004), 15–31.

7

Implementation and Enforcement of International Heritage Law

International heritage law, if it is to be effective, needs implementation and enforcement. Both activities are related inasmuch as they both promote compliance with the treaty systems, even if enforcement usually happens only after the treaty obligation has already been violated, and heritage impacted negatively.

The role of communities in the enforcement of international heritage law is somewhat diminished, since courts and other court-like bodies play the more central role in that respect. Further, international enforcement usually involves reframing heritage and its goals within the constraints of another area of international law, as heritage treaties themselves lack (judicial) enforcement mechanisms. In fact, there is a mismatch between the normative development of the field and the possibilities of enforcement within it.[1] The displacement of the claim away from international heritage law and its conversion into a claim under, for instance, international criminal law, allows for international enforcement, but it also creates an additional filter through which community aspirations have to attempt to break, and they are often unsuccessful.

In spite of these difficulties, communities can still be involved in showing how the negative impact on heritage also has a negative impact on community life (if that is the case), thus heightening the stakes of any enforcement procedure, and also informing, for instance, reparations and other remedies for the violation. But their role is still somewhat limited, and they can easily become part of the context, as opposed to a key stakeholder in the foreground of the case.

Despite a somewhat diminished role in enforcement, though, community involvement is most central for implementation. As argued throughout this book, community involvement is essential for the secure establishment of heritage values, and to ensure that heritage remains vital and relevant locally, which then promotes the international safeguarding goals of the treaty regimes under UNESCO. But, as also shown in this book, international heritage law has a way to exclude communities from the equation. This implementation happens on two different but interconnected levels, the domestic and the international, as

[1] Francioni, Francesco and Gordley, James, 'Introduction', in Francesco Francioni and James Gordley (eds), *Enforcing International Cultural Heritage Law* (Oxford University Press, 2013), 1–5, 1–2.

discussed in Chapter 2. Domestic implementation often happens at the behest of, and modelled after, international mechanisms. But it can also often take a dynamic of its own, such as when domestic systems promote integrated approaches to different heritage domains that are not feasible in the current fragmented international system.

The focus of the chapter (as of the book) is on international law, though, so most of the discussion of implementation in this chapter will focus on international implementation mechanisms, of which three are particularly relevant across heritage treaties: listing, funding for international heritage initiatives, and international cooperation. These mechanisms have allowed for significant developments in the field of international heritage law, but along the way certain compromises have been made in favour of state-centrism, which should be revisited.

This chapter focuses specifically on the law and politics of the implementation and enforcement of international heritage treaties at the international level. It looks at the different mechanisms under international heritage law for ensuring that states fulfil their obligations and pursue objectives that conciliate the demands of culture, nature, sovereignty, and communities. I argue that these objectives can sometimes be fundamentally at odds with one another, and that, in many respects, they downplay the importance of communities in the management of their own heritage, in spite of a wide range of experiences that show that heritage goals are best served when communities are closely involved.

Therefore, by mapping out the means of implementation and enforcement of the system of international heritage law, this chapter identifies another means through which the lack of coordination among the multiple heritage regimes (and their connections to other fields of international law) renders communities invisible. In the same stroke, the chapter also identifies ways communities are or can be more closely involved in the implementation and enforcement of international heritage law.

The chapter proceeds as follows. Section 7.1 will examine international safeguarding mechanisms across the multiple heritage regimes, focused on listing, heritage funds, and international cooperation. Section 7.2 focuses instead on enforcement mechanisms, introducing the dynamics of international heritage law vis-à-vis other specialized areas of international law, most notably international criminal law (ICL), which is a more recent development in comparison to international humanitarian law (IHL),[2] and is also more significant with respect to community involvement in international heritage law. Section 7.3 returns to implementation, but briefly focusing on some of the domestic dynamics as a means to highlight the stakes of the international.

[2] Explored in full detail by O'Keefe, Roger, *The Protection of Cultural Property in Armed Conflict* (Cambridge University Press, 2006), 317–43. See also generally Lostal, Marina, *International Cultural Heritage Law in Armed Conflict: Case-Studies of Syria, Libya, Mali, the Invasion of Iraq, and the Buddhas of Bamiyan* (Cambridge University Press, 2017).

7.1 International Safeguarding Mechanisms

Among the many different mechanisms for safeguarding different types of heritage, three come to the fore: listing, heritage funds, and international cooperation. These mechanisms deserve special attention because they exist across a large number of international regimes, and seem to be most directly connected to some of the basic objectives of international heritage protection. Listing creates visibility for heritage internationally; heritage funds allow for action to safeguard heritage, and are an incentive for poorer countries to enter into international heritage arrangements and contribute to a specific type of cosmopolitan discourse around heritage; and cooperation mechanisms are a way to enhance the prominence and role of organizations like UNESCO, ICOMOS, IUCN, and ICCROM, to name a few, while also allowing for the spread of a specific vocabulary and articulation of why and how heritage is safeguarded around the world (the conservation paradigm).

All the while, the pull of cosmopolitanism seems to work against community involvement. This section will examine each one of these mechanisms in detail, and the means through which certain stakeholders (and consequently their priorities) are privileged over others.

7.1.1 Listing[3]

Lists are increasingly a part of international legal governance, often displacing other legal forms on the global scale.[4] The list, according to Fleur Johns, is a 'trigger to intervention'; it is definite (even if only temporarily) and thus actionable, yet also endlessly amendable. And it has the power to personalize and depersonalize at the same time.[5] In the heritage context, it makes heritage globally recognizable, and thus makes the heritage of humankind personalized to every individual and state. But it also makes heritage homogeneous, and thus distanced from its local context and depersonalized. Heritage on a list is subject to a standardized set of requirements, ticks a number of boxes, and must thus be packaged in a specific way that is amenable to efficient global governance, potentially at the expense of the local communities who live with and safeguard that heritage.

In international heritage law, lists are one of the most often-used mechanisms for the implementation of many treaties under UNESCO. Listing in the heritage context involves recognition of heritage, but also a regime of preservation, conservation,

[3] Parts of the discussion of listing have been rehearsed elsewhere. See Lixinski, Lucas, *Intangible Cultural Heritage in International Law* (Oxford University Press, 2013); Lixinski, Lucas, 'Environment and War: Lessons from Cultural Heritage Law', in Rosemary Rayfuse (ed.), *War and the Environment: New Approaches to Protecting the Environment in Relation to Armed Conflict* (Martinus Nijhoff, 2014), 157–77; and Lixinski, Lucas, 'Heritage Listing as Self-Determination', in Andrea Durbach and Lucas Lixinski (eds), *Heritage, Culture and Rights: Challenging Legal Discourses* (Hart, 2017), 227–50.

[4] Johns, Fleur, 'Global Governance through the Pairing of List and Algorithm', *Environment and Planning D: Society and Space* 34(1) (2015), 126–49, 126.

[5] Ibid., at 127.

and restoration.[6] It can also be a tool for advocacy.[7] Heritage listing has a series of economic impacts on heritage, by restricting its economic value (for instance, by making exports more difficult), or by increasing the value of buildings or reducing it (as discussed in Chapter 5, and also below). Economically, listing is seen as a regulatory and commodifying measure, and its effects are mixed.[8] In terms of commodification, listing can promote loss of cultural value: the act of cataloguing Indigenous heritage, for instance, can be read as suggesting that Indigenous heritage is for sale, according to a UN report on Indigenous rights by Irene Daes.[9] Heritage listing also necessarily creates hierarchies, with the listed heritage rendered relevant and the unlisted expendable.[10] Internationally, the World Heritage List is probably the most famous inventory of cultural heritage, but other instruments also have their own listing mechanisms.

There are five main UNESCO conventions relating to the protection of cultural heritage: the 1954 Hague Convention,[11] with its two Protocols;[12] the 1970 Convention;[13] the 1972 World Heritage Convention (WHC);[14] the 2001 Underwater Cultural Heritage Convention (UCHC);[15] and the 2003 Intangible Cultural Heritage Convention (ICHC).[16] Four of these create lists of some sort (the exception being the UCHC), and three of them create international lists (the exception being the 1970 Convention, that only has an inventorying system at the domestic level).[17] I will focus on the three international lists.

[6] Klamer, Arjo and Zuidhof, Peter-Wim, 'The Values of Cultural Heritage: Merging Economic and Cultural Appraisals', in *Economics and Heritage Conservation—A Meeting Organized by the Getty Conservation Institute, December 1998* (J. Paul Getty Trust, 1998), 23–58, 25.

[7] Lixinski, Lucas, 'Heritage Listing as a Tool for Advocacy: The Possibilities for Dissent, Contestation and Emancipation in International Law through International Cultural Heritage Law', *Asian Journal of International Law* 5(2) (2015), 387–409.

[8] Klamer and Zuidhof (n 6) 37.

[9] Quoted in Lowenthal, David, 'Why Sanctions Seldom Work: Reflections on Cultural Property Internationalism', *International Journal of Cultural Property* 12 (2005), 393–423, 411.

[10] For a similar argument in the context of animal species conservation, see Braverman, Irus, *Wild Life: The Institution of Nature* (Stanford University Press, 2015), 133.

[11] Convention for the Protection of Cultural Property in the Event of Armed Conflict with Regulations for the Execution of the Convention 1954 (adopted 14 May 1954, entered into force 7 August 1956) 249 UNTS 240 (1954 Hague Convention).

[12] Protocol to the Convention for the Protection of Cultural Property in the Event of Armed Conflict (adopted 14 May 1954, entered into force 7 August 1956) 249 UNTS 358 (Hague Protocol I); and Second Protocol to the Hague Convention of 1954 for the Protection of Cultural Property in the Event of Armed Conflict (adopted 26 March 1999, entered into force 9 March 2004) 2253 UNTS 172 (Hague Protocol II).

[13] Convention on the Means of Prohibiting and Preventing the Illicit Import, Export and Transfer of Ownership of Cultural Property 1970 (adopted 14 November 1970, entered into force 24 April 1972) 823 UNTS 231 (1970 Convention).

[14] Convention concerning the Protection of the World Cultural and Natural Heritage 1972 (adopted 23 November 1972, entered into force 15 December 1975) 1037 UNTS 151 (WHC).

[15] Convention on the Protection of the Underwater Cultural Heritage 2001 (adopted 2 November 2001, entered into force 2 January 2009) 2562 UNTS 3 (UCHC).

[16] Convention for Safeguarding of the Intangible Cultural Heritage 2003 (adopted 17 October 2003, entered into force 20 April 2006) 2368 UNTS 3 (ICHC).

[17] 1970 Convention. Article 5(b) only creates a national list, providing that the Parties commit to '(b) establishing and keeping up to date, on the basis of a national inventory of protected property, a list of important public and private cultural property whose export would constitute an appreciable impoverishment of the national cultural heritage'.

The lists created by the 1954 Hague Convention[18] and its Second Protocol,[19] the WHC,[20] and the ICHC[21] have the common feature of trying to offer additional protection to some heritage by including it in international inventories. Prior to inclusion on an international list, the heritage needs to be included in a domestic list.

With respect to the Hague Convention system, two levels of protection have been devised in respect of cultural heritage: the regime of special protection created by the 1954 Convention[22] and that of enhanced protection created by the 1999 Second Protocol.[23] The mechanism by which these properties are identified is that of listing. Pursuant to the 1954 Convention, a List of Cultural Property under Special Protection was created for cultural heritage refuges identified as being 'of very great importance'. A second criterion was that these properties had to be sufficiently far from important military objectives or large industrial centres, and not used for military purposes.[24] That the list was only open to this rarefied type of heritage 'of very great importance' reinforced the idea of listing as a means to create hierarchies and privilege some heritage over other (as discussed in Chapter 2). However, the system proved to be excessively complex.[25] In addition to the detailed requirements of Article 8, a complex series of implementing regulations[26] also needed to be followed

[18] 1954 Hague Convention, Article 8 (on special protection).

[19] Hague Protocol II, Article 10 (on the List of Cultural Property under Enhanced Protection).

[20] WHC, Articles 11(2) (on the World Heritage List) and 11(4) (on the List of World Heritage in Danger).

[21] ICHC, Articles 16 (on the Representative List of the Intangible Cultural Heritage of Humanity) and 17 (on the List of the Intangible Cultural Heritage in Need of Urgent Safeguarding).

[22] 1954 Hague Convention, Chapter II (Special Protection): Article 8 provides that

> There may be placed under special protection a limited number of refuges intended to shelter movable cultural property in the event of armed conflict, of centers containing monuments and other immovable cultural property of very great importance, provided that they: (a) are situated at an adequate distance from any large industrial center or from any important military objective constituting a vulnerable point, such as, for example, an aerodrome, broadcasting station, establishment engaged upon work of national defense, a port or railway station of relative importance or a main line of communication; (b) are not used for military purposes.

Military use is defined in the same article as 'use[] for the movement of military personnel or material, even in transit'.

[23] Hague Protocol II, Chapter 3 (Enhanced Protection): Article 10 determines that

> Cultural property may be placed under enhanced protection provided that it meets the following three conditions: a. it is cultural heritage of the greatest importance for humanity; b. it is protected by adequate domestic legal and administrative measures recognising its exceptional cultural and historic value and ensuring the highest level of protection; c. it is not used for military purposes or to shield military sites and a declaration has been made by the Party which has control over the cultural property, confirming that it will not be so used.

Enhanced protection is granted, according to Article 11, if a list is submitted by the state party to the Committee, or by the International Committee of the Blue Shield or other accredited organizations. All parties to the Second Protocol may submit observations as to whether the heritage proposed should be inscribed on the list or not. A decision is made ultimately by the Committee. Enhanced protection can be granted on an emergency basis, too, upon the outbreak of hostilities.

[24] 1954 Hague Convention, Article 8(1).

[25] Forrest, Craig, *International Law and the Protection of Cultural Heritage* (Routledge, 2010), 99–100.

[26] Regulations to the 1954 Hague Convention, Articles 11-16.

if heritage was to be inscribed on the list. Moreover, given that the rule of military necessity continued to apply as an exception to special protection,[27] there was little difference in the level of protection afforded to listed versus non-listed properties.[28] As a result, only five refuges were ever inscribed (Vatican City, three refuges in the Netherlands, and one in Germany).[29]

One objection against the Hague Convention listing system is the difficulty of complying with the condition of adequate distance from an industrial centre or military objective. Another more pertinent objection to the very concept of listing is that, in the specific context of wartime, an inventory would provide a potential adversary essentially with a 'hit list' of important sites, particularly valuable if the other party to the conflict is not bound by the relevant instruments.[30] Despite these objections, however, the Second Protocol also creates a list, although it extends enhanced protection to cultural heritage 'of the greatest importance for humanity', which is protected by domestic legislation 'recognizing its exceptional . . . value', and is 'not used for military purposes or to shield military sites'. An accompanying declaration by the state confirming that the property will not be used in these ways is also required.[31] The notion of 'greatest importance for humanity' again reinforces the idea of hierarchies in listing while the other two requirements are fairly straightforward: the obligation of a mirror list of heritage worth protecting, and that the state protecting it will not employ the heritage for military purposes.

As Toman notes, 'the objective of Article 10 and the following articles of the Second Protocol is to remove the obstacles created by the restrictive definition and unrealistic conditions preventing larger registration of property under special protection'.[32] To that end, the protocol creates a new List of Cultural Property under Enhanced Protection. The system is modelled, for the most part, on the WHC.[33] The drafters discussed coordination between the Second Protocol and the WHC in this respect,[34] but, as discussed in Chapter 2, the Second Protocol adopted the definition in the Hague Convention by reference, and the drafters believed the difference in the definition of 'heritage' between the two instruments affected their scope of application too much and made closer coordination difficult. This refusal to look

[27] 1954 Hague Convention, Article 9. This article determines that all property under special protection is immune from attacks, unless it is being used for military purposes.

[28] Forrest (n 25) 99–100. [29] Ibid., 102.

[30] Hladík, Jan, 'UNESCO's Activities for the Implementation and Promotion of the 1954 Hague Convention for the Protection of Cultural Property in the Event of Armed Conflict and its Two Protocols', in María Teresa Dutli (ed.), *Protection of Cultural Property in the Event of Armed Conflict* (International Committee of the Red Cross, 2002), 57–77, 66.

[31] Hague Protocol II, Article 10.

[32] Toman, Jiří, *Cultural Property in War: Improvement in Protection—Commentary on the 1999 Second Protocol to the Hague Convention of 1954 for the Protection of Cultural Property in the Event of Armed Conflict* (UNESCO Publishing, 2009), 187.

[33] Henckaerts, Jean-Marie, 'New Rules for the Protection of Cultural Property in Armed Conflict: The Significance of the Second Protocol to the 1954 Hague Convention for the Protection of Cultural Property in the Event of Armed Conflict', in María Teresa Dutli (ed.), *Protection of Cultural Property in the Event of Armed Conflict* (International Committee of the Red Cross, 2002), 27–55. 43. UNESCO in 1993 even invited states to submit items of the World Heritage List for consideration for inscription in the Special Protection List. No nominations resulted from this effort. Hladík (n 30) 66.

[34] O'Keefe (n 2) 265–6.

beyond the 1954 text was a missed opportunity to promote closer coordination among heritage treaties within UNESCO. Although the notion of simply incorporating cultural heritage on the World Heritage List into the Enhanced Protection List was rejected, the presence of cultural heritage on the World Heritage List serves as a powerful guide to the 'greatest importance for humanity' threshold.[35] In fact, according to the guidelines implementing the Second Protocol, there is a presumption that heritage on the World Heritage List meets the criteria for enhanced protection.[36]

The system created by the Second Protocol appears to function better, and is decidedly less burdensome than the Hague Convention system. The process for inscription is more streamlined and in line with listing processes for other instruments in the field of heritage. However, it is still tied to the original treaty. Even if the Second Protocol is fairly clear in that the enhanced protection regime replaces the special protection one for parties to the Second Protocol,[37] the drafting history of the Second Protocol makes it clear that the necessity of staying within the parameters of the Convention was still very much in the mind of the drafters.[38]

The WHC contains the most notorious list—the World Heritage List. Additionally, the WHC also makes provision for the List of World Heritage in Danger. Taken together, the two lists cover more than 1,000 heritage sites across over 160 countries.[39] The World Heritage List can work as a bridge between international and national interests in cultural heritage protection, through its mechanisms like the Tentative List.[40] Importantly, a specific view of the relationship between the domestic and the international almost compromised the very existence of the World Heritage List. In the early negotiations of what became the WHC, the UNESCO Executive Board said that a universal list would be unadvisable, as it would detract too much from state sovereignty, and it would create difficulties in reconciling domestic and international interest as to whether a certain site had universal value.[41] Even accepting the notion of an inventory, drafters were still concerned with the disparate influence

[35] Toman (n 32) 188.

[36] Guidelines for the Implementation of the 1999 Second Protocol to the Hague Convention of 1954 for the Protection of Cultural Property in the Event of an Armed Conflict (March 2012). Guideline 36.

[37] Hague Protocol II:

> Article 4. Relationship between Chapter 3 [on enhanced protection] and other provisions of the Convention and this Protocol.
>
> The application of the provisions of Chapter 3 of this Protocol is without prejudice to:
>
> a. the application of the provisions of Chapter I of the Convention and of Chapter 2 of this Protocol [both on general provisions regarding protection];
> b. the application of the provisions of Chapter II of the Convention [special protection regime] save that, as between Parties to this Protocol or as between a Party and a State which accepts and applies this Protocol in accordance with Article 3 paragraph 2, where cultural property has been granted both special protection and enhanced protection, only the provisions of enhanced protection shall apply.

[38] Toman (n 32) 190–4.

[39] UNESCO World Heritage Centre, *World Heritage Lists*, available at http://whc.unesco.org/en/list/.

[40] Anglin, Raechel, 'The World Heritage List: Bridging the Cultural Property Nationalism–Internationalism Divide', *Yale Journal of Law & the Humanities* 20(2) (2008), 241–75, 243.

[41] UNESCO Executive Board, Possible International Instrument for the Protection of Monuments and Sites of Universal Value (22 April 1970). 84 EX/14, para 45.

of developed countries in the process, and urged UNESCO to focus its efforts on developing countries.[42]

The criteria for inscription on the WHC lists are determined in the Operational Guidelines for the Implementation of the World Heritage Convention, which are revised periodically. Prior to inscription on one of the international lists, it is necessary for the site to be inscribed on the Tentative List, which is a provisional international list from which properties are drawn for the official lists.[43] The Operational Guidelines 'encourage' States Parties to consult widely with stakeholders including local communities in the preparation of nominations for the Tentative List, but there is no requirement to that effect.[44] Canada, for instance, has in the past opened national consultations when putting together its Tentative List.[45]

The Tentative List is not seen by the implementing bodies as perennial, and states are encouraged to resubmit the items on their tentative lists every ten years, as a means to keep their assessment of the values of those sites current.[46] A proposal was made when the WHC was drafted that inscriptions on the World Heritage List would also need to be periodically renewed, but that proposal was ultimately rejected.[47] Periodical reassessments of the value of heritage could breathe life into the system, and allow for assessment of the value of heritage that kept pace with changes in heritage management practice, unlike the current system, that reinforces and perpetuates a specific conservation paradigm that is not attuned to the needs of local communities. States Parties can (and several do) submit retrospective statements of Outstanding Universal Value (OUV, discussed below) as a means to re-evaluate the way their heritage is listed, but that is an optional exercise.

Tentative Lists are considered by the World Heritage Committee as a valuable planning tool, inasmuch as they indicate where future nominations will be coming from.[48] But their value seems to be restricted to how well they can serve the other list, and they are not seen as a means to, for instance, evaluate heritage management practices in those sites as well. Only those on the principal World Heritage Lists will be scrutinized. Assistance and international cooperation is also available for the preparation of nominations to the Tentative List (as it is for the other lists).[49] In that way, a mechanism (list) that was meant to be a means to a broader objective (raising awareness) becomes a goal of its own.

Once on the Tentative List, the next step is inscription on the World Heritage List. For that, it is necessary to assess the OUV of the site. There are ten criteria (six cultural, and four natural), of which the site needs to meet at least one.[50] In practice,

[42] Meeting of Experts to coordinate, with a view to their international adoption, principles and scientific, technical, and legal criteria applicable to the protection of cultural property, monuments, and sites—Final Report (31 December 1968). SHC/CS/27/8, para. 86.

[43] Operational Guidelines for the Implementation of the World Heritage Convention (2015), paras 62–76.

[44] Ibid., para. 64. For an example, see Anglin (n 40) 254 (discussing the Okefenokee nomination).

[45] Anglin (n 40) 257–8.

[46] Operational Guidelines (n 43) para. 65.

[47] For details, see Cameron, Christina and Rössler, Mechtild, *Many Voices, One Vision: The Early Years of the World Heritage Convention* (Ashgate, 2013), 57–8.

[48] Operational Guidelines (n 43) para 70.

[49] Ibid., paras 74–76.

[50] Ibid., para. 77.

however, most sites meet multiple criteria, and worries about the size of the World Heritage List have meant that only properties meeting several criteria (and therefore more meritorious) are inscribed. An additional condition to OUV is the site's authenticity (applied only to cultural sites) and/or integrity (applied to all sites).[51] These criteria reinforce the conservation paradigm under which the World Heritage List is built, particularly the criterion of authenticity, which serves as a means to exert control over the possible meanings of heritage, authorizing some, and potentially unauthorizing others, as discussed in Chapter 1.[52] It does so by creating a sense of belonging to an international community that protects and treasures cultural heritage—the 'World Heritage Community'.[53]

After identifying the site's OUV, the nomination process proceeds in a specified format, which includes a number of sections or criteria: (1) identification of the property; (2) description of the property; (3) justification for inscription (which is where the statement of OUV goes); (4) state of conservation and factors affecting the property; (5) protection and management measures; (6) monitoring; (7) documentation (including photographs and video, but also any other documents); (8) contact information; and (9) signature on behalf of the state(s).[54] The state of conservation statement is the baseline for monitoring of the site. The protection and management statement includes a list of all the 'legislative, regulatory, contractual, planning, institutional and/or traditional measures most relevant' to the protection of the site. That is one avenue in which community engagement can be noted, even though this engagement, as with other possible avenues, is voluntary, and would fall only under the 'traditional' mode of protection, which has happened in relatively few instances, such as East Rennel (Solomon Islands), discussed in more detail in Chapter 6.

The other list under the WHC is the List of World Heritage in Danger, which also has a specific set of requirements: (1) that the property under consideration is on the World Heritage List; (2) that there is a serious and specific danger; (3) that major operations are necessary to conserve the site; and (4) that international assistance has been requested within the WHC.[55] The danger can be either ascertained or potential, and is measured according to different sub-criteria depending on whether the site is cultural or natural.[56] In a potentially important connection to the Hague Convention and Second Protocol regimes, the outbreak or threat of armed conflict is a potential danger for both natural and cultural sites.

These two lists work around a specific conservation paradigm that has the effect of sidelining communities from their own heritage. Even though the World Heritage Committee suggests states consult with communities, that is an optional exercise, at the discretion of the nominating state. As a result, minority populations, politically powerless groups, and expat communities tend to have their heritage excluded

[51] Ibid., paras 78–95.

[52] For a critique, see Lixinski, Lucas, 'A Tale of Two Heritages: Claims of Ownership over Intangible Cultural Heritage and the Myth of "Authenticity"', *Transnational Dispute Management* 11(2) (2014).

[53] Anglin (n 40) 248.

[54] Operational Guidelines (n 43) paras 130 and 132.

[55] Ibid., para. 177.

[56] Ibid., paras 179–180.

from the WHC processes.[57] These lists, because of their prominence, also have the effect of becoming ends in themselves, and co-opting other resources (particularly financial and international cooperation resources, discussed in the following subsections) for their purposes. Therefore, the WHC lists play a multitude of roles in being a template for domestic practice (through the Tentative List process), and in being the most visible means through which people perceive heritage internationally. The criteria for Outstanding Universal Value also ensure that the heritage is packaged in a way that conforms to a set of pre-approved narratives about the importance of the site, and said importance, once stated and authorized, need not be rediscussed, even if the reasons why people value the heritage change over time. The international system validates the state narrative about World Heritage.

Economically speaking, there are also advantages and disadvantages to World Heritage List status. On the positive side, listing provides attention and protection.[58] On the negative side, the listing process is not transparent, and therefore the selection is questionable, inducing rent-seeking behaviour. It can even be argued that the population at large are often so alienated from the process and the sites that their willingness to pay for access to and protection of those sites is of little relevance.[59] Further, the list has been overextended, diluting the importance of World Heritage status, and it may also create incentives to the destruction of the site by other actors, such as tomb raiders.[60] Finally, there are important displacement effects when all the funds for heritage protection go to listed heritage, at the expense of other important heritage, deepening the hierarchization of heritage.[61] The market or national lists can be valid alternatives.[62]

When it comes to the ICHC, the primary mechanisms under it are lists as well. Some of the lists emulate the WHC, whereas another tries to bring other values and ways of thinking about heritage to the table. In the former category are the 'Representative List of the Intangible Cultural Heritage of Humanity' (Article 16) and the 'List of Intangible Cultural Heritage in Need of Urgent Safeguarding' (Article 17). While the Representative List embodies the ICHC's attempt to move away from the 'outstanding' standard set in the WHC (and would therefore be in the latter category above), it ends up replicating many of the World Heritage List's shortcomings.

The listing mechanism was opposed by some delegations, notably the one from Norway, during the negotiations of the ICHC. The Norwegian delegate was of the opinion that a list-based mechanism would create a hierarchy of manifestations of heritage (the 'listed', which would somehow be 'better', and the 'unlisted'). The delegation argued that a catalogue of best practices alone would suffice to accomplish the objectives of the ICHC. The Indian delegate, on the other hand, thought that the listing approach was an effective one, even though it should be approached carefully so as not to create any sort of hierarchy. This was generally the accepted argument,

[57] Anglin (n 40) 271.

[58] Frey, Bruno S. and Steiner, Lasse, 'World Heritage List', in Ilde Rizzo and Anna Mignosa (eds), *Handbook on the Economics of Cultural Heritage* (Edward Elgar, 2013), 171–86, 174.

[59] Ibid., 176. [60] Ibid., 177–9. [61] Ibid., 178. [62] Ibid., 174.

as the listing would help in the awareness-raising that was necessary for the achievement of the treaty's objectives. Further, as highlighted by the Brazilian delegation, the listing mechanism at the international level mirrored the national obligation of inventorying, thus being also a desirable means to implement the ICHC.[63]

The criteria for the inscription of manifestations of heritage in these lists have been the subject of discussion of the Intergovernmental Committee. A first set of criteria has already been approved into the Operational Directives for Implementation of the Convention and revised a few times.

There are several criteria imposed for a manifestation of heritage to be inscribed on the list of intangible heritage in need of urgent safeguarding, and all of them must be met: (1) heritage must be intangible heritage in accordance with Article 2 of the Convention; (2) it must be in need of urgent safeguarding 'because its viability is at risk' or 'because it is facing grave threats as a result of which it cannot be expected to survive without immediate safeguarding'; (3) there must be a plan of safeguarding measures elaborated to enable the element to be practised and transmitted; (4) free, prior, and informed consent must be obtained from the concerned community, group, or individuals; (5) the element must be in the national inventory of intangible heritage of the concerned State Party; and (6) the state must give the authorization for such inscription.[64]

These requirements are verified through standardized forms for inscription, annexed to the Operational Directives.[65] The explanatory notes to these forms indicate that the safeguarding measures that must be included in the request for inscription must be a detailed plan within a time frame of approximately four years. These measures must be described so as to indicate the objectives of the safeguarding measures and results expected; the key activities to be carried out; the mechanisms for participation of communities, groups, and individuals; and the timetable and budget.[66] Also, the forms require that states prove that the concerned communities, groups, or individuals are willing and committed to the preservation of the intangible heritage the safeguarding of which is sought,[67] which is an important element of variation with respect to the listing mechanisms under other UNESCO treaties.

And the free, prior, and informed consent of the community, group, or individuals must be proven, which would be a key avenue to bring communities to the foreground. According to the wording of the explanatory note, this consent 'may be demonstrated through written or recorded concurrence, or through other means, according to the legal regimens of the State Party and the infinite variety of communities and groups concerned'.[68] This is so because the Committee has chosen to leave the door open for demonstrations of consent in accordance with the cultural

[63] Blake, Janet, *Commentary on the UNESCO 2003 Convention on the Safeguarding of the Intangible Cultural Heritage* (Institute for Art and Law, 2006), 79.

[64] Operational Directives for the Implementation of the Convention for the Safeguarding of the Intangible Cultural Heritage (adopted 2016), Rule 1.

[65] See *Form ICH-01 (2016)—Urgent Safeguarding List.*

[66] See *Form ICH-01 (2016)—Urgent Safeguarding List*, Explanatory Note, para. 3.b.

[67] See *Form ICH-01 (2016)—Urgent Safeguarding List*, Explanatory Note, para. 3.c.

[68] See *Form ICH-01 (2016)—Urgent Safeguarding List*, Explanatory Note, para. 4.b.

traditions of the parties concerned rather than imposing a single format. Free, prior, and informed consent was highlighted by scholars as a necessary element for dealing with ICH from the very beginning of the process leading to the adoption of the ICHC, even though many states opposed the idea of involving communities. This opposition seems to have resulted in the manipulation of the rule in international listing processes, with countries selectively applying more or less stringent forms of measuring community involvement depending on the volatility of certain manifestations of heritage listed.[69]

The criteria for inscription on the representative list are slightly different,[70] and in many ways impose a lesser burden on states seeking inscription. The criteria for inscription on the list of representative intangible heritage, which must be all met, are: (1) that the manifestation of heritage falls within the concept of Article 2 of the ICHC; (2) that the inscription will contribute to the visibility and awareness of the significance of ICH and will encourage dialogue, thereby entangling cultural diversity and being a testimony to human creativity; (3) that safeguarding measures are elaborated to protect and promote the element; (4) free, prior, and informed consent of the affected communities, groups, and individuals; and (5) that the element is present in one of the inventories required from States Parties.[71] Also, communities must be involved in the (domestic) preparation of the nominations for this list.[72]

The manifestation of the heritage to be inscribed must be described in reference to the significant features of it at the present (this is because the Committee is aware that the element may, and probably will, change in the future),[73] also including the discussion of the social and cultural functions played by it. The history of the element is not a required item in the description.[74] The free, prior, and informed consent of the communities, groups, or individuals must also be secured and proven, in the same fashion as the consent for inscription in the urgent list.[75]

Article 18 provides for programmes, projects, and other activities for the safeguarding of intangible heritage, and determines that the Committee (upon approval by the Assembly) shall select the ones that best reflect the objectives of the ICHC. In this way, an inventory of best practices, so important for the implementation of the ICHC, can be created.[76] This inventory is the category of lists meant to challenge the logic of the WHC and the conservation paradigm, as indicated above. One of the issues raised regarding this repository of best practices was whether it should be

[69] For a discussion with examples, see Lixinski, Lucas, 'Selecting Heritage: The Interplay of Art, Politics and Identity', *European Journal of International Law* 22(1) (2011), 81–100.

[70] For a comparison, see Intergovernmental Committee for the Safeguarding of the Intangible Cultural Heritage, Second Extraordinary Session (Sofia, Bulgaria, 18–22 February 2008), Decision 2.EXT.COM 17 (Report of the Intergovernmental Committee for the Safeguarding of the Intangible Cultural Heritage on its activities between the first and second sessions of the General Assembly of the States Parties to the Convention, paras 11–19).

[71] Operational Directives (2016), Rule 2. [72] Ibid., Rule 24.

[73] UNESCO, *Report on the Expert Meeting on Criteria for Inscription on the Lists Established by the 2003 Convention for the Safeguarding of the Intangible Cultural Heritage* (Paris, 5–6 December 2005).

[74] *Form ICH-02 (2016)—Representative List*. Explanatory Note, para. 1.

[75] Ibid., para. 4.b. [76] Blake (n 63) 86–8.

a selective listing, or a more inclusive one.[77] It was decided early on, in the first draft of this part of the Operational Directives, that the listing should be selective.[78] The main advantage of a selective listing of best practices is that it can more easily inform practice elsewhere. But, as with any hierarchization in listing, the 'best' (and therefore listed) practice is judged so by states and expert groups, with little to no input from communities themselves. Therefore, there is a risk that safeguarding practices that challenge the power of certain stakeholders with regard to defining heritage and its uses will not be given any visibility, reinforcing the power imbalances of the listing system.

The Operational Directives determine the criteria that must be met for the selection of a best practice: (1) the programme involves safeguarding, as defined in Article 2(3) of the ICHC; (2) the programme coordinates efforts for safeguarding at the regional, subregional, and/or international levels; (3) the programme reflects the principles and objectives of the ICHC; (4) it has demonstrated effectiveness in contributing to the viability of the ICH concerned; (5) it counts on the participation of the community, group, or individuals with free, prior, and informed consent; (6) it can serve as a subregional, regional, or international model for other safeguarding initiatives (that is, it can be 'transplanted' or emulated in other contexts); (7) the involved state(s), communities, groups, or individuals are willing to cooperate with the dissemination of best practices; (8) it is possible to assess the results of the programme, project, or activity; and (9) the programme 'is primarily applicable to the particular needs of developing countries'.[79] These criteria are further developed in a standardized form attached to the Operational Directives, accompanied by explanatory notes.[80]

Lastly, the ICHC has one more list (which replicates the conservation paradigm), in the form of the transitional clause about the incorporation of the items listed in the Proclamation of Masterpieces of the Oral and Intangible Heritage of Mankind (a precursor programme to the ICHC)[81] into the international lists created by the treaty. Article 31 provides that this list be incorporated, and that the incorporation of these items does not interfere with the criteria for inscription of other manifestations of heritage in the list.

While this clause is an important statement of the idea that the Masterpieces programme was a useful precursor of the ICHC, it is also a reminder that the treaty has moved away from that model.[82] The ICHC has moved away from the 'masterpieces'

[77] Intergovernmental Committee for the Safeguarding of the Intangible Cultural Heritage, First Extraordinary Session (Chengdu, China, 23–27 May 2007), *Discussion on the Implementation of Article 18 of the Convention for the Safeguarding of the Intangible Cultural Heritage*, Doc.ITH/07/1.EXT.COM/CONF.207/11, of 20 April 2007.

[78] Intergovernmental Committee for the Safeguarding of the Intangible Cultural Heritage, Second Session (Tokyo, Japan, 3–7 September 2007), *Preliminary Draft Directives for Implementing Article 18 of the Convention for the Safeguarding of the Intangible Cultural Heritage*, Doc.ITH/07/2.COM/CONF.208/12, of 30 July 2007.

[79] Operational Directives (2016), Rule 3.

[80] Form ICH-03 (2016)—Programmes, Projects, and Activities.

[81] Discussed in detail in Lixinski, Lucas, *Intangible Cultural Heritage in International Law* (Oxford University Press, 2013).

[82] Blake (n 63) 118.

approach—which, as seen above, was closer to the WHC model of outstanding value—towards a model of 'representativeness' and fostering of cultural diversity, rather than exceptional aesthetic (or other) value.[83]

The Operational Directives for the implementation of the ICHC determine that the incorporation is automatic into the Representative List, immediately following the adoption of the Directives.[84] States with proclaimed Masterpieces that are not parties to the ICHC assume rights and obligations under the treaty only with regard to those items of the Representative List.[85] These states have been notified by the Director General of UNESCO about the inscription, and the ensuing change in the legal regime of the safeguarding programmes.[86] The UNESCO Office of International Standards and Legal Affairs states that the items incorporated in the list do not automatically generate any rights or obligations upon the states where the manifestations of heritage are located, and that additional steps are required to create this regime (in this case, the notification to the Director General to be bound to the ICHC's regime).[87]

Taken together, these four lists exemplify the difficulties of implementing international heritage law, at least inasmuch as there is growing dissatisfaction with the limitations of the listing model, and a search for alternatives within it. The Representative and Urgent Safeguarding lists for the most part replicate other existing mechanisms (with their advantages and disadvantages), and even the transitional clause incorporating the list of masterpieces into the Representative List can be seen as challenging the Representative List's attempt at moving away from a hierarchization of heritage. However, the inventory of best practices attempts to challenge the status quo, not simply by praising heritage, but by making something more of the list, and using it as a means to inform policy development elsewhere.

The list then serves as a means to create international visibility for the listed heritage, and visibility is meant to generate awareness for the protection and safeguarding of the affected heritage. One of the problems with this visibility-generating exercise is that it too can create hierarchies of heritage, between the 'listed' and the 'unlisted', with listed heritage being somehow superior to unlisted. This was a concern during the negotiations of the ICHC, but dismissed because it was felt that the awareness-raising effects of listing would surpass the risks of hierarchization.[88]

Listing can also work as a means to galvanize identity, to the extent the listing process makes people feel they have an international presence against their state, which

[83] Ibid., 119. [84] Operational Directives (2016) Rule 57. [85] Ibid., Rule 58.

[86] States were given the opportunity to express their consent (within one year) to be bound to the new regime in what regards the items on the Representative List. In case this consent was not demonstrated, the Committee had the right to withdraw these manifestations from the List. All manifestations were kept on the Representative List, which means that either all states have consented to the new regime, or, in the cases where that did not happen, the General Assembly decided to still keep the manifestations on the List. See Operational Directives (2016), Rules 37 and 39.

[87] Intergovernmental Committee for the Safeguarding of the Intangible Cultural Heritage, *Note by the Office of International Standards and Legal Affairs on the Incorporation of Masterpieces into the Representative List under Article 31 of the Convention for the Safeguarding of the Intangible Cultural Heritage*. Doc.ITH/07/2.COM/CONF.208/14, of 23 July 2007, para. 14.

[88] For details, see Lixinski (n 81) 43.

is a consequence of the connection between human rights and cultural heritage, or the 'human dimension' of international heritage law.[89] More specifically, listing in this context can be seen as a declaration of a community's presence before UNESCO separate from their territorial state. But that recognition has very sharp limits, as discussed above. The system could be reformed to that effect (even if some suggest that lists are 'not the appropriate instrument[s] for forcible intervention'),[90] but it is unlikely any such reform would ever meet the approval of States Parties.

Fleur Johns, in exploring the convergence of lists and algorithms, explored three non-exclusive and overlapping categories of this convergence, which I will explore here only in connection with lists.[91] The categories are: (1) 'delivery mechanism for lawful authority'; (2) a shortcut within a legal regime; and (3) 'an output of legal work in its own right'. Heritage lists can operate in all these categories, and her typology assists in unpacking the work that lists do in international heritage law.

The WHC lists and the ICHC lists operate as delivery mechanisms for legal authority, to the extent that they allow the duplication of the purposes and requirements of the treaties, alongside the conservation or safeguarding paradigms under which they operate, at a smaller, and therefore more pervasive, scale. To add heritage to one of these lists gives content to the obligations under the WHC and the ICHC. Further, countries often design the domestic protection of cultural heritage around the requirements of international instruments, as a means to facilitate compliance and reporting, and therefore the list becomes a means to monitor domestic implementation almost in a box-checking mode.[92] This type of list also helps move from ideal to action by making an easily understandable formula or formulae available.[93]

As a shortcut (second category), lists are a means to allow the direction of resources to areas where they are most needed from certain vantage points, or a means to undermine rights and circumvent accountability. And heritage lists mean that inevitably the resources available for heritage conservation will go to listed manifestations of heritage, or that, in the event of a conflict, the listed heritage will be better defended than others (or, conversely, more prone to being targeted during conflict). Therefore, in heritage the function of the list as a shortcut serves as a means to reinforce certain hierarchies, often at the expense of stakeholders (usually local communities) who are not involved in the prioritization processes. In the case of the Hague Convention and the Second Protocol, one must consider heritage during ethnic armed conflict. With respect to this heritage, the shortcut can also mean that minority heritage gets selected out, and the state is not accountable for not protecting the heritage of the minority group, and thereby manipulating the listing process to advance a specific political agenda.

Third, as a product in its own right, the list 'operates as a structuring or background-conditioning device for an array of regulatory initiatives and legal interventions'.[94]

[89] Francioni, Francesco, 'The Human Dimension of International Cultural Heritage Law: An Introduction', *European Journal of International Law,* 22(1) (2011), 9–16.

[90] Anglin (n 40) 273.

[91] Johns (n 4) 131–3.

[92] *Mutatis mutandis,* see Johns (n 4) 131 (using CITES as her example).

[93] Ibid., 132.

[94] Ibid., 133.

I have already discussed how domestic implementation of heritage treaties often follows the listing model. Additionally, a heritage list being in itself a product also means a way to map out the possibilities of safeguarding, and pursuing a specific paradigm. The inventory of best practices under the ICHC is one such example, in which specific practices are selected and the list in itself becomes the yardstick against which safeguarding of intangible heritage in every context will be measured.

This categorization helps illuminate the work the list does beyond the more obvious idea of raising the visibility of heritage. By this raising of visibility, and thereby making heritage plain, heritage lists also push to the background (and thus do not explain) the nuances and difficulties of treating heritage in this hierarchized, commodified way.[95]

Finally, in terms of participation, different roles are attributed to different stakeholders. In many processes, states are only 'encouraged' to consult communities and other stakeholders, but are not required to do that. In some others, communities need to be involved. But, in both alternatives, there is also a fundamental problem with the modality of participation. Yes, that communities are involved is necessary, but it is unclear whether the current system, in which communities are involved in the 'identification' of heritage but excluded from its actual 'designation' as such (and subsequent management), is sufficient.[96] States retain the monopoly of designation, and are the only ones who can in effect make up the list. So, whereas community involvement of any sort is important, listing at its best still falls short of treating communities as full participants. Other mechanisms available under international law suffer from the same shortcomings.

7.1.2 Heritage funds

A number of heritage treaties establish funds to directly channel resources into heritage safeguarding activities. These funds rely heavily on voluntary contributions, but sometimes they are also endowed with mandatory contributions from the States Parties. In channelling resources for heritage safeguarding, they can significantly influence safeguarding activities, and are an important part of the implementation of international heritage law. In spite (or because) of their importance, they are often the most difficult negotiation points of heritage treaties.

Part of the heritage in wartime regime, and an innovation of the Second Protocol, is the specific Fund for the Protection of Cultural Property in the Event of Armed Conflict.[97] Inspired by the World Heritage Fund,[98] this fund is meant to support preparatory measures during peacetime, as well as fund emergency assistance and post-conflict recovery. Among these measures is the preparation of inventories for inclusion in the enhanced protection list. Although the idea of a fund was already mentioned as desirable during the drafting of the Hague Convention,[99] it was only

[95] Ibid., 136.

[96] Gauthier, Antoine, *Confessions d'un Gestionnaire: Les Possibilités et les Choix Liés au Patrimoine Immatériel à L'Échelle Nationale* (2014), 8.

[97] Hague Protocol II, Article 29.

[98] O'Keefe (n 2) 292.

[99] Toman (n 32) 597.

established by the Second Protocol. The Fund's resources come from voluntary contributions, as a means to avoid the imposition of additional burdens on the parties. As mentioned by the Argentina delegate during the negotiation of the Second Protocol[100] the Fund was designed in this way to avoid the difficulties experienced with implementation of the World Heritage Fund.

The most important (and largest) of the international heritage funds is the World Heritage Fund, which is one of the main reasons behind the WHC's success.[101] During the negotiations of the WHC, the funding formula was perhaps the most controversial part of the entire treaty, with states split on whether funding should be mandatory. Favouring mandatory funding (at 1 per cent of each state's contributions to UNESCO) were developing states, whereas developed states in general pushed for voluntary contributions only. The United States argued for voluntary funds, and State Department correspondence shows that they believed that mandatory contributions would not raise sufficient funds, and voluntary contributions had a better chance of creating a large enough fund.[102]

The World Heritage Fund has also been central in expanding the World Heritage List, with vast amounts of money being given to the preparation of nominations, and to support the Advisory Bodies' mandates.[103] A mechanism that was meant to serve heritage safeguarding more generally thus becomes a servant of the system itself. Additionally, allegations of mismanagement of the fund from within the World Heritage Committee have put the credibility of the entire system at risk.[104]

Articles 15 and 16 of the WHC establish the Fund and its financial formula. The Operational Guidelines state that the Fund should be used as a means to provide seed funding for projects that can attract funding and international assistance from other sources,[105] thus reinforcing the connection between funding and assistance more broadly. States are encouraged to participate in fundraising, and, when making contributions of any sort to the protection of World Heritage Sites, to channel those monies through the Fund,[106] probably in an attempt to increase the Fund's balance, and also as a means to centralize the administration of World Heritage activities around the world.

Article 17 of the WHC encourages alliances between public and private entities for fundraising,[107] thus allowing for limited engagement with non-state and non-expert actors in the realm of the World Heritage system. That initiative is part of a broader UN system agenda to engage more successfully with the private sector.[108] Importantly, all requests above USD5,000 must be endorsed by the Advisory

[100] Toman (n 32) 600.

[101] Lenzerini, Federico, 'Articles 15–16: World Heritage Fund', in Francesco Francioni (ed.), *The 1972 World Heritage Convention: A Commentary* (Oxford University Press, 2008), 269–88, 271.

[102] Cameron and Rössler (n 47) 25.

[103] Cameron and Rössler (n 47) 96.

[104] Ibid., 213.

[105] Operational Guidelines (2015), para. 225.

[106] Ibid., paras 228–229.

[107] Ibid., para. 230.

[108] Patchett, Lynne, 'Articles 17–18: Activities to Support the World Heritage Fund', in Francesco Francioni (ed.), *The 1972 World Heritage Convention: A Commentary* (Oxford University Press, 2008), 289–304, 301.

Bodies, meaning therefore that expert bodies get to control how funds are used, and the priorities of heritage conservation.[109]

Within the WHC, regional funds have been created, such as the African World Heritage Fund, aimed at conservation activities in Africa, and at increasing the representation of African states and African heritage on the World Heritage List.[110] This regional initiative, which has received multiple contributions from outside Africa, is seen as an example of cultural internationalism in action.[111] Other funds include the Nordic World Heritage Foundation and the German World Heritage Foundation.[112]

Lastly, it must be said that the World Heritage Fund is but a relatively small part of the monies devoted to the WHC and its protection system. In fact, the lion's share of the income for the World Heritage Convention comes through personnel costs that are borne by extra-budgetary funds.[113] While those funds allow for the better functioning of the system and for the Fund to be used more directly to support heritage safeguarding activities worldwide (as opposed to personnel costs, for instance), they also highlight the relative lack of transparency of the organization.

Under the ICHC,[114] states may further request international assistance for the safeguarding of intangible heritage in their territories (Article 23). This international assistance may be financial in nature, with money drawn from the fund created by the treaty. And any funds allocated shall generally be met by the State Party as a means to prove interest also from the State Party in protecting its intangible heritage (Article 24.2).[115] One important feature of these requests is that only states can ask for such assistance, in the same way that only states can propose manifestations of heritage to the lists created by the ICHC. This is yet another feature of the strict sovereignty upon which the treaty system is built.[116]

The 'Fund for the Safeguarding of the Intangible Cultural Heritage' is created by Article 25 of the ICHC. The resources of the fund come from contributions made by States Parties to the ICHC, voluntary contributions from states (whether a party to it or not), organizations from the UN system, private organizations and individuals, any other income deriving from the fund itself (investments, for instance), and specific fundraising activities (Article 28). Article 26 offers a creative compromise to the difficult negotiation of the financial commitments of states, as it creates a duty of contribution to which states can submit opt-out declarations (Article 26.2). And, even when a state does deposit a declaration to such effect, it is still under an obligation to 'endeavour' to withdraw the declaration and contribute fully to the system (Article 26.3).

The mandatory contributions by States Parties are not permitted to be of more than 1 per cent of the contribution each state normally makes to the UNESCO budget (Article 26.1). While this seems to be a small amount of money, the fund's reserves

109 Operational Guidelines (2015), paras 247–50.
110 Anglin (n 40) 269–70.
111 Ibid., 270.
112 Patchett (n 108) 291–2.
113 Lenzerini (n 101) 280–1.
114 See generally Jakubowski, Andrzej, 'Articles 25–28: Intangible Cultural Heritage Fund', in Janet Blake and Lucas Lixinski (eds), *The 2003 Intangible Cultural Heritage Convention–A Commentary* (Oxford University Press, forthcoming) (manuscript on file, cited with permission).
115 Blake (n 63) 102.
116 Ibid., 99.

in roughly ten years since the entry into force of the ICHC are over USD12 million; a significant amount,[117] even if the reliance on voluntary contributions is pervasive, which can be counter-productive especially for safeguarding efforts.[118] This money comes from these mandatory and voluntary contributions (regulated by Article 27) or other sources. Similarly to the World Heritage Fund, this seems to be quickly evolving into a successful means of promoting the objectives of the ICHC.

When it comes to the possible uses of the ICH fund, there are important limitations for community involvement. According to the Operational Directives for the Implementation of the ICHC, funds can only be used to involve non-state actors who are experts in intangible cultural heritage. Resources can also be used to invite members of communities to meetings of the ICH Committee, 'to be consulted on specific matters'.[119] Activities that favour community engagement with, and participation in the management of, ICH are not supported by the funds. The ICH fund therefore reinforces the ICHC's objectives that are aligned with the authorized heritage discourse (AHD) and the conservation paradigm.

Funding is therefore an important means of implementation and enforcement of international heritage treaties, and it can be an important avenue for engaging all actors that use heritage. However, the fact that the uses of the funds are allocated to pursuing the treaties' projects, and that those do not necessarily include community engagement, is a notable shortcoming. Seemingly, money will only be used to reinforce the version of the AHD and the conservation paradigm advanced in each treaty. But nothing prevents the funds from being spent on means that also advance alternative ways of engaging with heritage.

7.1.3 Cooperation mechanisms

Listing is itself a form of establishing cooperation.[120] But it is by no means the only one, and, while it receives the most attention, it is in fact in less-visible mechanisms, particularly in setting budgets for heritage safeguarding, that most safeguarding activity actually happens.[121] Beyond listing and money, though, there are still other mechanisms that are worth considering. International cooperation, even if an important principle in international heritage law, has had mixed results.

Technical assistance and cooperation are envisaged in the 1954 Hague Convention, under the umbrella of UNESCO. While it was originally envisaged that UNESCO's role would be subsidiary, the organization's role grew tremendously in the implementation of the treaty, particularly in the provision of technical assistance.[122] Technical assistance for the purposes of the Hague Convention is meant to be any assistance that is not financial,[123] a position seemingly replicated in other

[117] Intergovernmental Committee for the Safeguarding of the Intangible Cultural Heritage, Tenth Session (Windhoek, Namibia, 30 November–4 December 2015), *Draft Plan for the Use of the Resources of the Intangible Cultural Heritage Fund in 2016–2017*, DOC. ITH/15/10.COM/8, of 2 November 2015.

[118] Jakubowski (n 114).

[119] Operational Directives (2016), para. 89.

[120] Anglin (n 40) 244.

[121] Gauthier (n 96) 24.

[122] O'Keefe (n 2) 172.

[123] Ibid.

UNESCO treaties. The Hague Convention allows technical assistance not only at the request of affected states, but also at UNESCO's own initiative, a position that was opposed by some delegates during the drafting of the Hague Convention, but was ultimately supported by the overwhelming majority of negotiating states.[124] The outbreak of the first Iran–Iraq war in 1980 greatly strengthened UNESCO's role with respect to heritage in conflict, and assistance in particular, being an important incentive for negotiating what became the Second Protocol.[125] In this sense, response to a situation of crisis once again helped elevate UNESCO's role in providing technical assistance, and even helped advance the overall legal frameworks of international heritage law by serving as a catalyst for renewed standard-setting.

The 1970 Convention creates cooperation mechanisms, which are discussed in some more detail below, under enforcement. These mechanisms are essentially diplomatic and cooperative, and, alongside awareness-raising of looted cultural objects, they are the most successful aspects of the 1970 Convention's system, since its direct enforcement has met with limited results.[126] Applied to museums, they can be seen as meaning the widespread use of loans and itinerant exhibitions.[127] Article 17 of the 1970 Convention in particular discusses possibilities of technical assistance, in particular with respect to information and education, consultation and expert advice, and coordination and good offices. UNESCO may also offer its good offices in the event of a dispute among parties on the domestic implementation of the 1970 Convention. This cooperation mechanism also includes non-state stakeholders like museums, which is an important step in more community-centric international heritage law, especially if one agrees with the view, discussed in Chapter 3, of museums as representatives of the community at large when it comes to movable heritage.

Technical assistance is an important part of the cooperation possibilities under the World Heritage Convention, even if it is seen as only subsidiary to national efforts.[128] In fact, technical assistance lies at the heart of historical efforts to fashion the international protective system that became the WHC.[129] The possibilities for technical assistance rely primarily on the World Heritage Fund,[130] and have developed fairly quickly in the early years of the WHC, highlighting the inadequacy of the Fund, and also the lack of experts deemed qualified to safeguard World Heritage.

124 Ibid., 175–6. 125 Ibid., 236.

126 Blake, Janet, *International Cultural Heritage Law* (Oxford University Press, 2015), 40.

127 Halman, Talat, 'From Global Pillage to Pillars of Collaboration', in John Henry Merryman, *Imperialism, Art and Restitution* (Cambridge University Press, 2006), 37–46.

128 Operational Guidelines (2015), para. 233.

129 See e.g. Brichet, Robert, 'Study on the Legal Provisions Required for Ensuring the Protection of the Monumental Heritage', presented at the Meeting of Experts to coordinate, with a view to their international adoption, principles and scientific, technical, and legal criteria which would make it possible to establish an effective system for the protection of monuments and sites, SHC/CS/27/5, of 26 January 1968.

130 For a commentary, see Vrdoljak, Ana Filipa, 'Article 13: World Heritage Committee and International Assistance', in Francesco Francioni (ed.), *The 1972 World Heritage Convention: A Commentary* (Oxford University Press, 2008), 219–41; and Lemaistre, Anne and Lenzerini, Federico, 'Articles 19–26: International Assistance', in Francesco Francioni (ed.), *The 1972 World Heritage Convention: A Commentary* (Oxford University Press, 2008), 305–24.

Thus, funds have been consistently used to train personnel.[131] The WHC became a learning platform that merged different approaches to heritage conservation from around the world, and came by and large to embody the conservation paradigm.[132]

The international assistance provisions in the WHC echo the spirit of international campaigns such as the Aswan Dam and the flooding of Venice and Florence,[133] which were landmark international campaigns that cemented UNESCO's standing as a bona fide international organization in the area of heritage.[134] There are three categories of international assistance: emergency assistance, conservation and management assistance, and preparatory assistance.[135] Preference is given to, in this order: (1) a Least Developed Country (as defined by the UN Economic and Social Council); (2) a Lower Middle Income Country (as defined by the World Bank); (3) a Small Island Developing State; or (4) a state in a post-conflict situation. The educational value for the training of experts and for the general public is also a consideration.[136]

There have been critics of the World Heritage programme's ability to pursue international cooperation. Some have accused the programme of being too large and crumbling under its own bureaucratic weight, or of representing little more than a large marketing tool for tourism. Importantly in the realm of international co-operation, critics have also accused the programme of having 'left its original aims in the dust in favor of materialism and pacification', instead of protecting World Heritage.[137]

The bureaucratic weight of the World Heritage programme has also meant much time and energy is devoted to advancing specific political agendas of states, inspired by cultural nationalism, and against the 'philanthropic goals' of the WHC.[138] The World Heritage Committee in particular seems to have gradually shifted away from its primary reliance on the opinions of the advisory bodies (composed of experts), and World Heritage is increasingly a political battleground for interstate politics. Cultural heritage is a pawn for advancing broader political agendas of states.[139]

That the World Heritage system has been politicized is not necessarily a bad thing. But when the politicization happens only at the interstate level, and no other actors can engage politically with the uses of heritage, that can be a problem. The politicization of heritage processes shows not that the state is receding, but that it is exercising its sovereignty in disaggregated ways.[140] This disaggregation can allow for

[131] Cameron and Rössler (n 47) 151–2. [132] Ibid., 153.

[133] Vrdoljak (n 130) 223.

[134] Harrison, Rodney, *Heritage: Critical Approaches* (Routledge, 2013), 57–9.

[135] Operational Guidelines (2015), para. 235. [136] Ibid., para. 239.

[137] For these criticisms and more, see Keough, Elizabeth Betsy, 'Heritage in Peril: A Critique of UNESCO's World Heritage Program', *Washington University Global Studies Law Review* 10(3) (2011), 593–615, 598–9.

[138] Ibid., 605.

[139] Meskell, Lynn, Liuzza, Claudia, Berrtacchini, Enrico, and Saccone, Donatella, 'Multilateralism and UNESCO World Heritage: Decision-Making, States Parties and Political Processes', *International Journal of Heritage Studies* 21(5) (2015), 423–40, 427. See also Meskell, Lynn, *A Future in Ruins: UNESCO, World Heritage, and the Dream of Peace* (Oxford University Press, 2018).

[140] Meskell et al. (n 139) 430.

the input of non-state actors such as local communities, which would be a laudable development, but, at the time of writing, that does not seem to be the case, or at least community involvement at the international level remains optional, with undefined rules and roles. The problem with the system is not its politicization; it is who gets to be heard in this (now openly) politicized arena.

One advantage of the politicization of World Heritage processes, it seems, is that developing countries seem to be dominating the arena and controlling negotiations.[141] In fact, BRICS countries seemed to dominate most of the debates in the World Heritage Committee over the eleven years between 2004 and 2015.[142] While this shift to developing countries does not address the need to include communities, at least it can (partially) address the geopolitics of international heritage law, and challenge the system's colonial imprint.

The UCHC's approach to international cooperation is closely related to its approach to the management of underwater heritage, which rests on three principles: (1) preference to preservation *in situ*; (2) if recovery from the water is allowed, conservation and management should ensure the underwater heritage's long-term preservation; and (3) public access is to be encouraged, as long as it is non-intrusive.[143] One of the key strategies for the implementation of the UCHC then rests on the tight control of the uses of underwater heritage. That control strategy requires a well-established authorization scheme for the uses of underwater heritage, that is administered nationally.[144] But the use of national administration does not constitute an obstacle to international cooperation, at least not if one considers that the procedures are undertaken in strict observance of international rules. Technical cooperation in the development of these rules by UNESCO experts is a means of international cooperation in this realm.[145] Therefore, the UCHC unifies international practice and imposes its approach to conservation on the States Parties, much in the way the WHC has done.

The challenge with these very protective rules is to guarantee access to underwater heritage, which is the primary means to raise awareness and the visibility of UCH, key objectives of the UCHC.[146] The UCHC's compromise is to promote access *in situ*, which of course restricts access greatly to a certain elite who can afford the equipment and other resources.[147] Further, the UCHC rules prohibit amateur archaeology, unless it is supervised by a 'trained' archaeologist.[148] The result is the exclusion of stakeholders from their own heritage, and the reinforcement of the AHD and the conservation paradigm. Similarly, underwater memorials must remain undisturbed, according to the UCHC, but that may be incompatible with ceremonial practices such as, for instance, laying flowers or small objects next to graves.[149] Especially as First World War shipwrecks now enter the protective scope of the UCHC, attempts to engage with those sites might become prohibited, further

[141] Ibid., 431. [142] Ibid., 432.

[143] Dromgoole, Sarah, *Underwater Cultural Heritage and International Law* (Cambridge University Press, 2013), 307.

[144] Ibid., 313. [145] Ibid., 314. [146] Ibid., 320–1. [147] Ibid., 321.

[148] Ibid., 324. [149] Ibid., 328.

distancing relevant community stakeholders (for instance, veterans' associations) from the heritage.

With respect to the ICHC, Article 19 determines international cooperation for the safeguarding of intangible heritage, including the exchange of information and joint initiatives by States Parties, as long as it is consistent with national laws. Article 20 determines the purposes of international assistance, two of which are closely connected to the listing processes, either the international lists or the domestic inventories. The ICHC also highlights domestic, subregional, and regional activities as one of the purposes of international cooperation, what could be seen as a way in for substate actor involvement (even if within the sovereignty constraints of the system). Article 21 outlines the forms of international assistance. Of these, 'standard-setting' is a particularly relevant one, and one that refers to the establishment of international standards to be subsequently translated into regional and national legislative initiatives.[150] In this sense, the ICHC is not a product of input from previous national initiatives, but it is created to be the catalyst of national measures for the safeguarding of intangible heritage. Other forms include technical assistance and assistance in the preparation of nominations, along the same lines as the WHC.

These cooperative regimes achieve an important goal; that of promoting a uniform language and practice around heritage. But that practice is framed around the conservation paradigm, in an exclusionary manner. Slowly, political concerns are making their way into the international cooperation activities of these treaties, but, because of the rules upon which they operate, it is only the political interests of states that get a hearing, with non-state actors beyond expert advisory bodies (which by and large still work against the politics of heritage) largely excluded from the debates.

It seems one of the few opportunities communities have of influencing international cooperation mechanisms is by influencing the domestic implementation of those treaties, even if, as we will see below, those possibilities are also limited. If the answer does not lie in the sovereignty-laden confines of international heritage law treaties, perhaps there is something to be said about the enforcement of heritage treaties via other international legal regimes? The next section explores those possibilities.

7.2 Enforcement and the Reliance on Other Systems

The enforcement of international heritage law has given teeth to the field, and added a dimension different to the cooperation mechanisms already discussed, in addition to enhancing the visibility of international heritage law. As mentioned above, much of this enforcement happens through other regimes of international law, particularly IHL and ICL,[151] through a plurality of legal mechanisms that matches the cultural

[150] Blake (n 63) 95.

[151] On this relationship, from the perspective of IHL with respect to cultural heritage, see O'Keefe (n 2) 343–56.

pluralism that heritage law aims to safeguard.[152] For that reason, it is beyond the scope of this book to exhaustively examine the matter of enforcement; rather, it suffices to make the point that enforcement helps develop the field. In fact, it has been pointed out that cultural heritage helps develop international law more generally in three respects: (1) international crimes against heritage as war crimes and crimes against humanity; (2) the development of individual criminal responsibility under international law; and (3) the development of the law of state responsibility for intentional acts against cultural heritage.[153]

However, in helping develop international law more generally, the enforcement of heritage law also deepens the problem of exclusion of communities from their own heritage at the international level. More specifically, resolving international heritage matters through the rules and mechanisms of other regimes of international law adds to the difficulty of access of communities to those regimes, for the most part. It also packages international heritage law in a way that excludes much of the politics of heritage in favour of the politics (or lack thereof) of the other regimes. In this translation process, communities tend to be the first ones lost.

This section briefly explores some of these tensions in more detail. Before getting to them, though, it is necessary to place international heritage law, and particularly the cooperative mechanisms discussed in the previous section, in a spectrum where the enforcement of heritage law ranges between law and diplomacy. The more legal the dispute is, as shown below, the more likely it is to be resolved outside the field of international heritage law. By relying on different fields, international heritage law becomes part of the discussion about the fragmentation of international law. And nowhere is this fragmentation more in evidence in recent times than in the efforts to bring heritage into ICL, which, based on recent developments analysed below, can work to effectively bring communities into enforcement, rather than exclude them, in contrast with the international investment regime discussed in Chapter 5.

7.2.1 Between law and diplomacy

One of the big tensions associated with the adjudication of international heritage law (or any global public good, for that matter) is that, in deciding a dispute between two states (or between a state and a non-state party), international adjudicatory mechanisms are making determinations that should apply only to an isolated situation, but that have ripple effects throughout the entire regime. In dealing with a field like international heritage law, adjudication is therefore somewhat limited, despite its attempts to advance substantive values through the application of procedural rules.[154]

[152] Francioni, Francesco, 'Plurality and Interaction of Legal Orders in the Enforcement of Cultural Heritage Law', in Francesco Francioni and James Gordley (eds), *Enforcing International Cultural Heritage Law* (Oxford University Press, 2013), 9–21, 10.

[153] Francioni, 'The Human Dimension' (n 89) 10.

[154] For a discussion more generally, see Nollkaemper, André, 'International Adjudication of Global Public Goods: The Intersection of Substance and Procedure', *European Journal of International Law* 23(3) (2012), 769–91.

There are also a number of difficulties with the enforcement of international heritage law specifically, which would discourage a narrower focus on legal methods of dispute settlement. For instance, most treaties under UNESCO do not create binding dispute settlement mechanisms (even though some mention good offices, like the 1970 Convention, or conciliation, like the Hague Convention), and, because the treaties do not retroact, they also do not cover a wide range of heritage disputes, or at least do not allow for the meanings of heritage prior to the entry into force of the treaties to be rediscussed, as argued in Chapter 4. A combination of lax (or non-existent) dispute settlement mechanisms and loopholes in the treaty regimes would suggest that diplomatic means are often more adequate.[155]

However, diplomacy is also fraught with difficulties for enforcing international cultural heritage law. For instance, the diplomatic meetings of different heritage bodies are first and foremost the domain of states, with communities having little to no participation, as discussed. Experts can play an important role in translating community aspirations, but their tendency to see heritage as an end in itself, because of their mandates, limits the possibilities for action beyond the AHD. Diplomatic alternative dispute resolution mechanisms are available, too, but negotiation and mediation are often resisted for their inability to render binding decisions.[156]

So, even though diplomatic means seem to favour more political engagement with heritage, they do not necessarily favour communities' political engagement with heritage. Certain legal enforcement mechanisms outside of heritage, on the other hand, can in spite of their state-centric nature also open important avenues for communities to engage, such as international human rights adjudication, but those often come with trade-offs.[157] Most importantly from the perspective of international law, the enforcement of international heritage law through other bodies needs to handle the risks and promises of fragmentation of the international legal system.

7.2.2 The push and pull of fragmentation

The creation of a specialized international cultural heritage law court has been proposed elsewhere.[158] Such a court would be able to render specialized decisions that took into account the cultural values of heritage, and in the process reinforce the body of international heritage law.[159] An unsuccessful attempt under the League of Nations has shown how difficult this idea actually is in practice, and the notion was not taken up by any of the UNESCO treaties.[160] The same obstacles that exist

[155] For an in-depth exploration of the potentials and pitfalls of legal dispute resolution methods, see generally Chechi, Alessandro, *The Settlement of International Cultural Heritage Disputes* (Oxford University Press, 2014).

[156] Ibid., 181.

[157] For a critical discussion, see Francioni, Francesco and Lixinski, Lucas, 'Opening the Toolbox of International Human Rights Law in the Safeguarding of Cultural Heritage', in Andrea Durbach and Lucas Lixinski (eds), *Heritage, Culture and Rights Challenging Legal Discourses* (Oxford, Hart 2017), 11–34.

[158] For a review of the literature, see Chechi (n 155) 200–18.

[159] Ibid., 205.

[160] Ibid., 206.

with respect to the effectiveness of international law in general (state sovereignty, the complexity of disputes, and the overall relative effectiveness of international adjudication) speak against such an endeavour.[161]

Additionally, a new specialized regime would only contribute further to the fragmentation of international law, and to the possibility of conflicting normative findings in different fora. It would also further entrench the conservation paradigm, at least to the extent an eventual specialized court would put heritage (in its current configuration, and instead of heritage holders) at the very centre of its normative universe, and look at the safeguarding of heritage as its primary goal, and an end in itself. So, while such a system would be advantageous from the perspective of the dominant heritage paradigm, and could open the door for more effective community participation, its institutional mandate would likely favour the AHD too greatly, at the expense of other goals.

The alternative is to allow for the enforcement of international heritage law in other fora, which are not specialists in international heritage law matters.[162] That strategy can lead to better integration of heritage in the international system, and its placing among other competing priorities. The disadvantages are obvious, though: by making heritage just another thing the body has to worry about almost inevitably means making it low priority, and the body might well not have sufficient expertise to properly grapple with the needs of heritage. But it has been argued that these bodies have increasingly become more sensitive to cultural matters.[163]

Also, a number of these systems are not equipped to hear claims from non-state actors, at least not with respect to how they value their heritage. Thus, the participation of non-state actors is fairly restricted. The enforcement of cultural heritage through international criminal law, often hailed as a promising new avenue, is a good case study of the possibilities and challenges of enforcement of international heritage law through other means.

7.2.3 International criminal law as a case study

Assuming international cultural heritage norms are *erga omnes* norms,[164] which is one way of thinking about public goods,[165] we can strengthen their enforcement, seen as the assignation of *erga omnes* status is 'a strategic choice to solve the problem of under-enforcement of norms that protect the public interest'.[166] One of the ways

161 Ibid., 208–17.

162 For a discussion, see Francioni, 'Plurality and Interaction' (n 152) 17–20.

163 Chechi, Alessandro, 'Plurality and Coordination of Dispute Settlement Methods in the Field of Cultural Heritage', in Francesco Francioni and James Gordley (eds), *Enforcing International Cultural Heritage Law* (Oxford University Press, 2013), 177–205, 178.

164 See e.g. Francioni, Francesco, 'Au-delà des traités: l'émergence d'un nouveau droit coutumier pour la protection du patrimoine culturel', *Revue Internationale de Droit International Public* 111 (2007), 19–41; Francioni, Francesco, 'Beyond State Sovereignty: The Protection of Cultural Heritage as a Shared Interest of Humanity', *Michigan Journal of International Law* 25 (2003–4), 1209–28; and Graham, Gael M., 'Protection and Reversion of Cultural Property: Issues of Definition and Justification', *The International Lawyer* 21(3) (1987), 755–93, 756.

165 Nollkaemper (n 154) 776.

166 Ibid., 777.

through which this enforcement has taken place is international criminal law. It is beyond the scope of this book to discuss the matter in detail,[167] but this case study helps highlight some of the possibilities and pitfalls of enforcement of international heritage law through other means.

More generally, much of past experience with the criminal enforcement of heritage law has had the effect of reinforcing the AHD, by excluding certain actors and criminalizing their conduct (such as amateur archaeologists and subsistence diggers), much in the way that human trafficking as a way of enforcing women's rights has alienated sex workers.[168] An excessive emphasis on this 'global neoliberal penality'[169] can also be read as meaning that that cosmopolitan aspirations such as the defence of global public goods have failed and been sidelined. Neoliberal penality implies a turn to the absolute, and it individualizes conduct by getting structural issues out of the equation. Additionally, framing people as victims defines them by their victimhood, leaving behind the reason why they were persecuted to begin with.[170] In the heritage context, heritage is perpetuated as the sanitized object to be gazed upon (and defended), as opposed to being political.

The criminalization of acts against cultural heritage is a mechanism relatively common across a number of UNESCO heritage treaties, whether in peacetime or during conflict.[171] The Hague Convention, 1970 Convention, and UCHC in particular all have provisions criminalizing acts against heritage, as a matter of domestic or international criminal law.[172] But these provisions in heritage treaties have not always been echoed in ICL mechanisms and instruments.

International cooperation in criminal affairs is one realm in which the enforcement of heritage law can take place, particularly with respect to movable cultural heritage and the 1970 Convention. The use of international cooperation mechanisms means treating the traffic of cultural artefacts as transnational crime, much in the way drugs and human trafficking are addressed.[173] Loosely connected and interchangeable participants create the illusion of complexity in transnational criminal

[167] For a more detailed overview, see e.g. Mainetti, Vittorio, 'De Nuremberg à La Haye: L'Émergence des Crimes Contre la Culture et la Pratique des Tribunaux Internationaux', in Vincent Négri (ed), *Le Patrimoine Culturel, Cible des Conflits Armés: De la Guerre Espagnole aux Guerres du 21e Siécle* (Bruylant, 2014), 151–82.

[168] See e.g. Chang, Grace and Kim, Kathleen, 'Reconceptualizing Approaches to Human Trafficking: New Directions and Perspectives from the Field(s)', *Stanford Journal of Civil Rights & Civil Liberties* 3 (2007), 317–44. Discussing the competing approaches between transnational criminal law and human rights law, see Lee, Kelsey, 'A House Divided: Divergent Approaches to Sex Trafficking in International Law', *Temp. Int'l & Comp. L. J.* 30 (2015), 383–414.

[169] Harcourt, Bernard E., 'Neoliberal Penality: A Brief Genealogy', *Theoretical Criminology* 14(1) (2010), 74–92.

[170] I am thankful to Frédéric Mégret for this insight. See Mégret, Frédéric, 'The Anxieties of International Criminal Justice', *Leiden Journal of International Law* 29(1) (2015), 197–221. See also generally Engle, Karen, 'Self-Critique, (Anti) Politics and Criminalization: Reflections on the History and Trajectory of the Human Rights Movement', in J. M. Beneyto and D. Kennedy (eds), *New Approaches to International Law: The European and the American Experiences* (TMC Asser Press, 2012), 41–73; and Engle, Karen, 'Anti-Impunity and the Turn to Criminal Law in Human Rights', *Cornell Law Review* 100(5) (2015), 1070–127.

[171] On criminal sanctions in the event of conflict in particular, see O'Keefe (n 2) 274–88.

[172] Mainetti (n 167) 153.

[173] For a detailed discussion, see Blake (n 126) 48–50.

networks in general, and particularly with respect to heritage; however, there are underlying structures that can be mapped and combated against.[174]

But the criminal enforcement of cultural heritage offences is also fraught with difficulties. Hard evidence is difficult to obtain in a fragmented, secretive, and self-regulated market, where 'optical due diligence' is the norm,[175] investigations are expensive, and facts are often very complex.[176] Further, the international legal basis for criminal cooperation is treaties that deal primarily with private law matters, and devote relatively little attention to the criminal aspects of enforcement.[177] And the deterrent effect of criminal law does not seem to have a meaningful impact on heritage crime.[178] There are also difficulties associated with the training and use of law-enforcement personnel, who are often unable to properly identify and prosecute crimes against cultural heritage, particularly with respect to movable heritage, where heritage is often confused with licit art or handicrafts, or loopholes are exploited (as discussed in Chapter 5). In this respect, listing's ability to raise awareness of heritage might work to the benefit of heritage safeguarding, at least in relation to criminal enforcement.

There are a few ways in which transnational crime in cultural heritage is different from other transnational criminal networks. One reason is that heritage is a finite resource, which cannot be cultivated or manufactured; also, artefacts can appear legitimate on the market, as long as they are laundered. Therefore, laundering is a large part of the illicit trade in heritage, and commands the involvement of a number of stakeholders to make the activity seem licit.[179] Further, while there is a limited number of suppliers with respect to drugs or weapons, when it comes to antiquities, the number of suppliers at the bottom of the pyramid is much larger (think of subsistence digging, for instance).[180] The treatment of heritage trafficking as a crime ignores the more structural issues at stake, such as economic inequalities that lead to subsistence digging, discussed in Chapter 5. The fact that licit and illicit activities occupy the same space demonstrates the difficulties with the black-and-whiteness that criminal law requires. It also highlights the number of stakeholders that need to be involved with crime, including customs authorities of multiple countries, the domestic police in multiple countries, international cooperation agencies, museums, dealers, communities, etc. While this complexity makes enforcement more difficult, it can also nuance the absolutes of criminal law by inviting a plurality of views on the

[174] Campbell, Peter B., 'The Illicit Antiquities Trade as a Transnational Criminal Network: Characterizing and Anticipating Trafficking of Cultural Heritage', *International Journal of Cultural Property* 20 (2013), 113–53, 114.

[175] Fincham, Derek, 'Social Norms and Illicit Cultural Heritage', in Francesco Francioni and James Gordley (eds), *Enforcing International Cultural Heritage Law* (Oxford University Press, 2013), 206–27, 220.

[176] Ulph, Janet, 'Criminal Offenses Affecting the Trade in Art and Antiquities', in Janet Ulph and Ian Smith (eds), *The Illicit Trade in Art and Antiquities: International Recovery and Criminal and Civil Liability* (Hart, 2012), 78–146, 78.

[177] Gerstenblith, Patty, 'Enforcement by Domestic Courts: Criminal Law and Forfeiture in the Recovery of Cultural Objects', in Francesco Francioni and James Gordley (eds), *Enforcing International Cultural Heritage Law* (Oxford University Press, 2013), 150–74, 157.

[178] Fincham (n 175) 226.

[179] Campbell (n 174) 117.

[180] Blake (n 126) 27.

uses and value of heritage. Because the transnational criminal cooperation approach acknowledges the complexity of cultural heritage actions, perhaps it is better suited to deal with heritage situations than, for instance, international criminal law.

Specifically with respect to ICL, the statutes of international criminal tribunals in general do not contain specific provisions on cultural heritage, but rather lump cultural heritage alongside other 'protected property' such as schools, churches, and hospitals. One notable exception is the Extraordinary Chambers in the Courts of Cambodia (ECCC), the statute of which makes explicit reference to the Hague Convention regime as part of the law that the ECCC will enforce.[181]

With respect to other international criminal tribunals, they have had different interactions with cultural heritage matters. In Nuremberg, Nazi looting of art and cultural objects was part of the prosecution case presented by both the United States and France, and also a part of the International Military Tribunal's judgment, even if the judgment simply mentioned works of art and cultural artefacts as part of the property that had been stolen by the Nazis, and not a separate crime.[182] The International Criminal Tribunal for the Former Yugoslavia (ICTY) adopted a similar route, as its statute did not contain a separate category for crimes against heritage. However, the ICTY jurisprudence also innovated in lending greater significance to attacks against heritage. More specifically, the cultural significance of attacked sites led the ICTY to find that the destruction of heritage was not only a crime against protected property,[183] but also part of the intent of criminals being prosecuted, or, as an element of persecution, a crime against humanity in the ICTY Statute.[184]

The International Criminal Court (ICC) has adopted a different approach. Its statute clearly includes the competence to hear crimes involving the destruction of heritage, at least as war crimes, but also arguably as crimes against humanity. In the *Al Mahdi* case,[185] the ICC Prosecutor put the destruction of heritage (the World Heritage-listed city of Timbuktu, in Mali) as the central crime in the case.[186]

During an internal armed conflict in 2012–13, rebel and insurgent groups targeted cultural heritage in Mali, as part of a broader policy based on fundamentalist

[181] Mainetti (n 167) 166. This reference also makes sense in the context of Cambodian heritage law post Khmer Rouge, discussed in Chapter 4.

[182] Sandholtz, Wayne, *Prohibiting Plunder: How Norms Change* (Oxford University Press, 2007), 174–7.

[183] Ibid., 205–9. See also O'Keefe (n 2) 280–8.

[184] See e.g. Lenzerini, Federico, 'The Role of International and Mixed International Criminal Courts in the Enforcement of International Norms Concerning the Protection of Cultural Heritage', in Francesco Francioni and James Gordley (eds), *Enforcing International Cultural Heritage Law* (Oxford University Press, 2013), 40–64; Vrdoljak, Ana Filipa, 'Human Rights and Cultural Heritage in International Law', in F. Lenzerini and A. F. Vrdoljak (eds), *International Law for Common Goods: Normative Perspectives on Human Rights, Culture and Nature* (Hart, 2014), 139–74; Vrdoljak, Ana Filipa, 'Cultural Heritage in Human Rights and Humanitarian Law' in Ben-Naftali Orna (ed.), *International Humanitarian Law and International Human Rights Law* (Oxford University Press, 2011), 250–302; and Trindade, Ivonei Souza, *Caso Pavle Strugar: Um Estudo sobre a Proteção de Bens Culturais em Caso de Conflito Armado* (Casa de Autores, 2016).

[185] *Prosecutor v Al Mahdi* (Judgment and Sentence) ICC-01/12-01/15-171 (27 September 2016).

[186] The discussion of the *Al Mahdi* case is largely drawn from Lixinski, Lucas, and Williams, Sarah, 'Rethinking the Enforcement of International Criminal Law Beyond the Biology/Culture Divide' (manuscript on file, cited with permission).

readings of Islamic teachings, which saw the destruction of mausoleums as necessary. In Timbuktu, Sufi libraries and ancient tombs were targeted for destruction by insurgents who argued that '[their] destruction is a divine order'.[187]

Al Mahdi was charged with intentionally directing attacks against ten buildings in Timbuktu.[188] All but one of the ten buildings were part of the World Heritage Site.[189] By June 2012 the World Heritage Committee, upon the request of authorities in Mali, placed the city on the List of World Heritage in Danger.

During the prosecution of the crime, a plea agreement was reached, the first plea agreement in the context of ICC proceedings. The Trial Chamber's judgment on conviction and sentence was issued on 27 September 2016, accepting the plea and finding that Al Mahdi was responsible for the destruction of the heritage site. The Trial Chamber sentenced Al Mahdi to nine years' imprisonment, less time already spent in custody, which is the lower end of the sentence range agreed, but consistent with previous sentences in ICTY cases.[190]

The *Al Mahdi* case has important implications for the field of international heritage law, to the extent it advances a more community-centric version of cultural heritage law and the values associated with cultural sites. This approach has been referred to as a cultural relativist means of defining protected objects,[191] and is one that is in marked contrast with the more universalist approach of previous (ICTY) jurisprudence.[192] The ICC Trial Chamber stressed the importance of the mausoleums and mosques in Timbuktu for the community;[193] that said, it ultimately seems to have decided the case based on Timbuktu's international importance,[194] reinforcing an internationalist view of heritage in the judgment.[195] In fact, specific references Al Mahdi made to the status of the buildings as part of a World Heritage Site were taken into account, to determine that Al Mahdi clearly directed the attacks not only at the buildings themselves, but also to the cosmopolitan values enshrined in the UNESCO Constitution, of promotion of peace and mutual understanding through culture.[196] The Trial Chamber's reliance on its international listing sends an important message to heritage managers in particular, and highlights the importance of listing.

Listed status, and its use in *Al Mahdi*, also represents an advancement with respect to integrating different instruments in international heritage law, since the ICTY had not relied on the World Heritage List status of other heritage sites in its cases (particularly *Strugar*, about the destruction of the World Heritage Site of Dubrovnik).[197] In other words, the ICC's judgment also helps advance more

[187] Tharoor, Ishaan, *Timbuktu's Destruction: Why Islamists Are Wrecking Mali's Cultural Heritage*, *Time, World*, 2 July 2012, available at <http://world.time.com/2012/07/02/timbuktus-destruction-why-islamists-are-wrecking-malis-cultural-heritage/> (accessed 30 October 2017).

[188] *Al Mahdi*, Judgment (n 185) para. 38.

[189] Ibid., para. 39.

[190] Seven years in *Jokić*; eight years (reduced to seven and a half on appeal) in *Strugar*.

[191] Casaly, Paige, 'Al Mahdi before the ICC: Cultural Property and World Heritage in International Criminal Law', *Journal of International Criminal Justice* 14(5) (2016), 1199–220, 1206.

[192] Ibid., 1214.

[193] *Al Mahdi*, Judgment (n 185) para. 34.

[194] Ibid., para. 46.

[195] Casaly (n 191) 15–16.

[196] *Al Mahdi*, Judgment (n 185) para. 46.

[197] Trindade (n 184) 50.

coordinated efforts to enforce international heritage law instead of focus on individual instruments.

The Trial Chamber considered that World Heritage status,[198] as well as the connection people felt to Timbuktu in their ordinary cultural practices in the city, spoke to the gravity of the crime,[199] as opposed to being an aggravating factor to be considered in sentencing (in fact, it found there were no aggravating factors).[200] The collective practices of conservation and symbolic maintenance events involving the entire community were taken into account.[201] These community connections and events are essentially ICH associated with the World Heritage Site. The connection between tangible and intangible heritage[202] played a role in this judgment.[203] That connection helps articulate the 'victimhood' of the residents of Timbuktu, since focusing only on the World Heritage status would rather suggest that the 'international community' and Mali as the territorial state were the victims. Therefore, in engaging the intangible elements of the site, the Trial Chamber advances a more holistic view of cultural heritage, one that, while embraced by many scholars and UNESCO officials, is difficult to implement within the constraints of treaty texts. Importantly, this holistic vision also prioritizes the community not only in being the owner of the heritage, but also as the key stakeholder in the reparations phase. The community's current use of the site is key to assessing its importance, and reconstruction is allowed, even if it is not fully in line with the conservation paradigm.

The Trial Chamber walks a tightrope in this case. On one hand, it wants to acknowledge the harm done to the local community in Timbuktu, and how 'destroying the mausoleums ... was a war activity aimed at breaking the soul of the people of Timbuktu'.[204] This type of engagement speaks to the intangible elements connected to the site, discussed above, as well as to the identification of victims as being the local population. However, on the other hand, Timbuktu is on the World Heritage List, 'and, as such, their attack appears to be of particular gravity as their destruction does not only affect the direct victims of crimes, namely the faithful and inhabitants of Timbuktu, but also people throughout Mali and the international community'.[205] The Trial Chamber therefore draws an important distinction between direct (people of Timbuktu) and indirect (Mali and the international community) victims, which is important in the reparations phase of the case.[206]

In the Reparations judgment, the indirect victims did not participate in the proceedings, and received only a symbolic reparation of one euro.[207] The primary focus

[198] *Al Mahdi*, Judgment (n 185) para. 80. [199] Ibid., para. 79.

[200] Ibid., paras 86–88. [201] Ibid., para. 78.

[202] Explored in detail in Lixinski (n 81).

[203] Exploring the connection between conflict and intangible cultural heritage, see Johannot-Gradis, Christiane, 'Protecting the Past for the Future: How Does Law Protect Tangible and Intangible Cultural Heritage in Armed Conflict?', *International Review of the Red Cross* 97(900) (2015), 1253–75.

[204] *Al Mahdi*, Judgment (n 185) para. 80. [205] Ibid.

[206] *Prosecutor v Ahmad Al Faqi Al Mahdi* (Reparations Order) ICC-01/12-01/15 (17 August 2017); and Judgment on the appeal of the victims against the Reparation Order in *Prosecutor v Al Mahdi* (International Criminal Court Appeals Chamber) ICC-01/12-01/15 A (8 March 2018). See also generally commentary by Vrdoljak, Ana Filipa, 'Introductory Note to *Prosecutor v Ahmad Al Faqi Al Mahdi* (Int'l Crim Ct)', *ILM* 17 (2018), 57.

[207] See Reparations Order (n 206) paras 106–107.

was on the harm suffered by the community itself, with the Chamber asserting that the destruction of the buildings 'affected the entire community of Timbuktu'.[208] The Court considered that the most appropriate form of reparations was collective reparations,[209] thereby partially closing the door on individual reparations for economic loss, which are allowed 'only to those whose livelihoods *exclusively* depended upon the Protected Buildings'.[210] This finding was (unsuccessfully) appealed by the victims, with the Appeals Chamber stating that the consideration of the importance of collective reparations over individual ones was within the Trial Chamber's discretion, and that, at any rate, the order did not entirely exclude individual members of the community from accessing the collective reparations, through initiatives like micro-credit systems and cash assistance programmes.[211]

From the perspective of international cultural heritage law, the judgment is hence a positive development in a few respects. First, and most obviously, it elevates international heritage law, since *Al Mahdi* is the first time an international criminal tribunal has made an act against heritage the central part of a case. In doing so, the ICC has given more credence and validity to efforts to protect cultural heritage, and has advanced the possibilities for enforcement of cultural heritage norms. Secondly, the judgment, in recognizing the existence of direct and indirect victims, recognizes the centrality of ICH and community participation for the appreciation and management of heritage, even if it is heritage that received international recognition via a different treaty. In some respects, the ICC, even if only by implication, advances a more integrated approach to heritage, one that would have seemed less likely within the formalistic constraints of UNESCO treaties. In other words, were the ICC directly enforcing a UNESCO treaty with respect to heritage, it may have missed certain aspects of the relationship between people and their heritage. By using heritage as an idea, and UNESCO treaties and mechanisms only as part of the case's 'factual matrix', the ICC was free (and, in fact, compelled) to advance a more community-centric view of heritage, rather than one burdened by the conservation paradigm enshrined in treaties like the Hague Convention and the WHC.

The same is likely to happen in a case in the ICC docket at the time of writing, with the significant difference that this time the ICC is not constrained by the war crimes category, and can prosecute heritage as part of the crime of persecution, a broader category that further connects heritage to the community. Further, in this new case the ICC is also prosecuting other crimes alongside the destruction of heritage, meaning that it will contextualize heritage further as one among many aspirations of the community.[212]

With respect to the ongoing reparations phase, presumably local communities will be at the centre of the ICC's efforts. The implication of the centrality of

[208] Ibid., para. 62. For a defence of collective reparations in the ICC, see Mégret, Frédéric, 'The Case for Collective Reparations before the International Criminal Court', in Jo-Anne M. Wemmers (ed.), *Reparation for Victims of Crimes against Humanity: The Healing Role of Reparation* (2014).

[209] Reparations Order (n 206) para. 67.

[210] Ibid., para. 81 (emphasis in original).

[211] Appeal to reparations order (n 206) para. 39.

[212] *The Prosecutor v Al Hassan Ag Abdoul Aziz Ag Mohamed Ag Mahmoud* (ICC-01/12-01/18). Case Information Sheet ICC-PIDS-CIS-MAL-02-002/18_Eng (4 April 2018).

communities, and their wishes vis-à-vis the World Heritage Site, is that the universal value of heritage that was instrumental for Al Mahdi's conviction will play a lesser role, and the relative value to the local community is what will drive the reparations process. That quite possibly would mean the reconstruction of the mausoleums, except that the mausoleums have already been reconstructed, and even re-consecrated.[213] But the interests of indirect victims (the international community) in some respects may clash with those of the direct victims. For one, the reconstruction of the buildings in Timbuktu can mean the site loses its authenticity, a problem as authenticity is a precondition for a site to be on the World Heritage List, as discussed in Chapter 1.[214] Therefore, in assessing specific measures of reparation, the ICC may have a difficult task of conciliating competing demands of the local community and the cosmopolitan aspirations of the international community represented by UNESCO, and the conservation paradigm under which it operates. The Buddhas of Bamiyan, for instance, destroyed in 2001 by the Taliban regime in Afghanistan, cannot enjoy World Heritage status as a cultural site because the Buddhas are no longer there, and, if reconstructed, the site would not be authentic. Instead, the Bamiyan Valley is listed as a cultural landscape, which only requires 'integrity' as a listing criterion.[215]

One notable example of a cultural site on the World Heritage List that has been reconstructed in the aftermath of war is the Mostar Bridge in Bosnia, but the Mostar Bridge was only added to the World Heritage List *after* its reconstruction, and the reconstruction was factored into the statement on authenticity.[216] Timbuktu's current statement of authenticity does not make room for reconstructed buildings. That said, the site could still be reassessed by the World Heritage Committee, and its listing modified, primarily through reassessing the criteria for OUV, so that, like with the Mostar Bridge, the conflict is an important part of the site's meaning, thus making cultural heritage law engage with transitional justice narratives more effectively.[217] So, it may be that Timbuktu needs, as a result of the reparations process, to be re-inscribed under a different category on the World Heritage List. The relisting

[213] For more information on the reconstruction process, see Segall, Anna, 'Protecting Culture in Practice: The Unique Role of UNESCO', *International Humanitarian Law Magazine* 2 (2016), 8.

[214] In *Al Mahdi*, Judgment (n 185) paras 78–80, there are listed some aspects of the mausoleums that fulfill conditions of authenticity.

[215] World Heritage Committee, Decisions Adopted by the 27th Session of the World Heritage Committee in 2003, Decision 27 COM 8C.43; UNESCO, *Cultural Landscape and Archaeological Remains of the Bamiyan Valley*, available at http://whc.unesco.org/en/list/208 (last visited 15 December 2016). See also O'Keefe, Roger, 'World Cultural Heritage Obligations to the International Community as a Whole?' *International and Comparative Law Quarterly* 53 (2004), 189–209; Francioni, Francesco and Lenzerini, Federico, 'The Destruction of the Buddhas of Bamiyan and International Law', *European Journal of International Law* 14(4) (2003), 619–51; Francioni, Francesco and Lenzerini, Federico, 'The Obligation to Prevent and Avoid Destruction of Cultural Heritage: From Bamiyan to Iraq', in Barbara T. Hoffman (ed.), *Art and Cultural Heritage: Law, Policy and Practice* (2006), 28–41.

[216] World Heritage Committee, *Old Bridge Area of the Old City of Mostar*, available at http://whc.unesco.org/en/list/946 (last visited 15 December 2016).

[217] For a discussion of the potentials and pitfalls of this engagement, see Lixinski, Lucas, 'Cultural Heritage Law and Transitional Justice: Lessons from South Africa', *International Journal of Transitional Justice* 9(2) (2015), 278–96.

is probably inevitable, as the destruction of the mausoleums fundamentally alters the 'outstanding universal value' of the site.[218]

From the perspective of international heritage law, one of the consequences of there being no special category of heritage crimes is that the cultural layer that lends significance to a building is lost. Heritage is treated therefore as just property, rather than as something containing value beyond the market. As argued in Chapter 5, the economization of heritage is important; but it is important to lend it economic value that accounts for its cultural and social value, which a broad category of 'protected property' does not seem able to do.

7.3 Domestic Implementation

The implementation of international heritage treaties is imperative for the international enforcement of situations that are very often transboundary, and is ultimately imperative for the safeguarding of heritage. Failure to implement treaties results in norms falling through implementation cracks, in a replay of the public/private distinction that permeates much of international heritage law, as discussed in Chapter 1.[219]

With respect to the UCHC, for instance, the role of competent national authorities is key to pursuing the preservationist approach of the treaty.[220] But the implementation of this treaty highlights a problem that is common to most heritage treaties; that of determining competence domestically, and the implications of that choice. Often, the WHC is implemented under environmental agencies, the ICHC under cultural agencies, and the Hague Convention under the Armed Forces of the same country. Similarly, the UCHC is often implemented by maritime agencies, instead of cultural ones.[221] In this respect, it is no surprise that a fragmented approach to heritage exists, and the same fragmentation problems with international enforcement are replicated. The consequence here, as with international enforcement through other bodies, is that communities are excluded from a large number of the processes, simply because of their inability to navigate the bureaucratic maze. Further, and most importantly, a cohesive approach to heritage that bears the interests of communities in mind is impossible, as many of these implementing national authorities are less sympathetic to communities because the interests of communities are not their ultimate goal, it being rather maritime interests, the environment, or peace and security.

Additionally, when large economic opportunities are involved (as discussed in Chapters 3 and 5), treaty implementation gaps and democratic deficits become apparent.[222] The lack of compatibility between international and domestic means of

[218] But see the World Heritage Committee's *Warsaw Recommendation on Recover and Reconstruction of Cultural Heritage* (2018), at https://whc.unesco.org/en/news/1826/.

[219] See also Fincham (n 175) 212.

[220] Dromgoole (n 143) 308.

[221] Ibid., 309.

[222] Affolder, Natasha, 'Mining and the World Heritage Convention: Democratic Legitimacy and Treaty Compliance', *Pace Environmental Law Review* 24(1) (2007), 35–66, 35.

implementation creates a series of blind spots that allow for heritage to be negatively impacted. The public/private distinction once again operates against effective cultural heritage safeguarding. For instance, mining companies repeatedly express surprise at their ignorance of the impacts of World Heritage List status on their proposed activities in an area, highlighting the lack of clarity in the rules, and the subsequent dissatisfaction with the entire heritage safeguarding system.[223] Criticisms of the WHC often are not about procedural defects internationally, but rather show frustration with the non-participatory processes at the domestic level.[224]

In dealing with the domestic implementation of international cultural heritage law, I have argued throughout this book that the inclusion of communities in international processes is central. But, as far as international cultural heritage law is concerned, its state-centric nature requires that at least some of the domestic implementation happens through state authorities, who are committed to the conservation paradigm.[225] Assuming implementation can happen through authorities that are in principle sympathetic to community aspirations because they have mandates to that effect, an additional obstacle arises. More specifically, if domestic bureaucracies do much of the (at least initial) implementation work, there is a clear disincentive to relinquish control over heritage processes in favour of communities, as it means the state official receives no credit for the implementation work, and for the eventual success of heritage safeguarding at the national level. Therefore, one of the big challenges in the domestic implementation of international heritage law, if communities are to be more involved, is to figure out incentives for the state and its officials to relinquish control over heritage once the basic safeguarding structures are set in place.[226]

Further, there is a risk that community participation will bring the state closer into the lives of communities, making it ever-present, but 'without necessarily displaying a greater capacity to remedy their problems'.[227] Residents' voices can end up subsumed into a bureaucratic process, and only heard when they serve government purposes. Capacity for political response is often weakened, at least in discussions about local and urban development (of which much of heritage necessarily is a part in its translation into domestic law). Further, local government authorities also may end up feeling their administration practices are increasingly burdened by formalization, and in a manner that only pays lip service to communities, without fulfilling community aspirations.[228] Therefore, instead of relinquishing control, it may well be the case that community participation requirements only create more

[223] Ibid., 46. [224] Ibid., 47.

[225] For a more optimistic view, arguing that domestic implementation of the ICHC may in fact be changing the conservation paradigm domestically, see Blake, Janet, 'The Impact of UNESCO's 2003 Convention on National Policy-Making: Developing a New Heritage Protection Paradigm?', in Michelle L. Stefano and Peter Davis (eds), *The Routledge Companion to Intangible Cultural Heritage* (Routledge, 2017).

[226] I am very thankful to Harriet Deacon for this insight. Personal communication.

[227] Eslava, Luis, *Local Space, Global Life: The Everyday Operation of International Law and Development* (Cambridge University Press, 2015), 269.

[228] Ibid., 269–70.

work for bureaucrats, and therefore cause bureaucracies to dig their heels in through this layering of processes, rather than relinquishing control. That is a danger we need to be mindful of in constructing a community-centric international heritage law with domestic echoes. In this respect the convergence of law and non-law is very important as a way to deconstruct bureaucracies and bring them down to their key elements, including the question of 'who is the process meant to serve?'. But, in doing so, Luis Eslava admonishes that lawyers should be companions, rather than mediators.[229]

Domestic listing of heritage, even if it follows by and large the requirements set by UNESCO treaties, will still inevitably have a national flavour, by virtue of different ideological filters created by states not only in presenting their items for international listing, but even in creating the conditions for domestic listing. Most of these filters are inscrutable based on a reading of domestic legislation alone, but they tend to lean towards valuing local culture in a way that serves nationalism and the local tourist industry.[230] Further, while international heritage law has been fairly successful in making heritage management practices uniform across the world, as shown in previous sections, there are still elements of the local that cannot be accounted for by international heritage treaties. More specifically, domestic managerial and bureaucratic practices beyond heritage inevitably influence the way heritage is handled as a bureaucratic and managerial matter. Certain documents like the Nara Document on Authenticity[231] (and its counterpart Nara +20)[232] have drawn attention to the diversity in domestic administrative practices, and their impact on heritage.[233]

Domestic takes on heritage priorities can lead to contradictory results. Luca Zan reports on how different local government entities provided opposite advice on the site of Lijiang (China) in the same year. One entity recommended the preservation of the social life of the site, which included among other things permission for certain old buildings to be destroyed (preserving therefore the site's intangible heritage), while another entity suggested preserving the buildings and turning them into restaurants catering for tourists, even if it meant pushing the local population out of the old village centre (thus prioritizing the tangible heritage of the place).[234] This example shows a significant mismatch in managerial practice, in which both instances are attempting to safeguard heritage. The conservation paradigm that filters from international instruments is therefore not as uniform as one might think, and is dependent on the different priorities of each international instrument. That variation creates problems in domestic implementation, too, where other domestic readings of heritage influence decision-making. One example, also in China, is the

229 Ibid., 292. 230 Gauthier (n 96) 11.

231 Nara Document on Authenticity, WHC-94/CONF.003/INF.008 (adopted 6 November 1994).

232 Nara + 20: On Heritage Practices, Cultural Values, and the Concept of Authenticity (adopted 24 October 2014). For a commentary, see Orbaşlı, Aylin, 'Nara+20: a Theory and Practice Perspective', *Heritage & Society* 8(2) (2015), 178–88.

233 Zan, Luca, 'Economic Discourse and Heritage Conservation: Towards and Ethnography of Administrations', *Heritage & Society* 6(2) (2013), 167–84, 171.

234 Ibid., 174.

replica of the old village of Shuhe (part of Lijiang),[235] which, even though contradicting notions of authenticity of built heritage, allows for a better safeguarding of the intangible heritage in the original site of the village.[236]

These filters are not necessarily compatible with the UNESCO vision of cosmopolitanism, but they in fact act as an important counterweight to them, allowing for local involvement and local politics to filter through the system. Therefore, domestic implementation is a key means to allow for the voices of local communities to be heard. The problem is when domestic law does not open those possibilities, and that is one of the reasons why involvement of local communities at the international level is so important.

In the implementation and enforcement of international heritage treaties, communities are still largely excluded. Internationally, mechanisms are still largely subjected to state sovereignty, and the available financial resources are used to perpetuate the systems themselves, and the conservation paradigm under them.

The enforcement of international heritage law in other fora, where communities could potentially make use of available mechanisms, is overall rather opaque. Avenues like international criminal law, which has gained prominence in recent years, depoliticize heritage in a way that is not conducive to community engagement challenging the AHD and conservation paradigm.

Even if the implementation of those treaties often relies on domestic implementation (which would be an ideal way to involve non-state stakeholders), domestic implementation also often falls short of considering the interests of communities. Obstacles include fragmented bureaucracies, and the lack of incentives for governmental authorities to relinquish their prerogatives.

Overall, there are significant problems with the implementation and enforcement of international heritage law with respect to communities. But how do they fit in the overall picture of other themes and areas discussed in this book? The next chapter reframes the issues discussed in this and previous chapters in a broader narrative of international heritage law's bright and dark sides.

235 This is an entire old village that was replicated in a nearby site, and each building in the replica turned to a tourist-oriented use (souvenir shops, restaurants, information centres, etc.). That way, the government reasoned, the social fabric of the old village could be preserved, and residents remain on the site, but tourists could also enjoy the architecture by visiting the replica.

236 Zan (n 233) 175.

8

The Bright and Dark Sides of International Heritage Law

Having examined the ways in which international heritage law operates to exclude communities and privilege other stakeholders like states and experts, it is necessary to engage in the redefinition of the field. This chapter starts that work, by refocusing on the field of international heritage law as a whole, rather than the individual aspects of it that previous chapters have addressed. My objective in this chapter is to draw together multiple threads woven throughout the book. This chapter is based on an earlier piece,[1] and the evolution of my thinking with respect to the issues raised therein in the intervening years, as a result of closer engagement with the system of international heritage law this book has mapped and critiqued.

The notion that the aftermath of the Second World War provided a particularly fertile moment for international legal structures and institutions is commonplace. A bit less circulated is the idea that international laws and institutions related to culture were part of this special moment. Caught between its natural place in the reserved domain of sovereignty and an acute awareness that neglecting international oversight could lead to genocide (a term then being coined, and to whose etymology culture contributed more than is normally acknowledged, as discussed in Chapter 4),[2] the international law of culture found its place in the United Nations Educational, Scientific and Cultural Organization (UNESCO). Created with a cosmopolitan impetus that cultural understanding was the key to 'save succeeding generations from the scourge of war',[3] UNESCO promised lasting peace based 'upon the intellectual and moral solidarity of [hu]mankind'.[4]

[1] Lixinski, Lucas, '*Luci e Ombre*: The Bright and Dark Sides of International Heritage Law', *Italian Yearbook of International Law* 22 (2012), 133–53.

[2] Vrdoljak, Ana Filipa, *International Law, Museums and the Return of Cultural Objects* (Cambridge University Press, 2006), 163–72; and generally Novic, Elisa, *The Concept of Cultural Genocide: An International Law Perspective* (Oxford University Press, 2016).

[3] Charter of the United Nations (adopted 24 October 1945), 1 UNTS XVI (UN Charter), Preamble.

[4] Constitution of the United Nations Educational, Scientific and Cultural Organization (UNESCO) (adopted 16 November 1945, entered into force 4 November 1946) 4 UNTS 275 (UNESCO Constitution), Preamble.

Ever since its Constitution entered into force in November 1946, UNESCO has gone about pursuing these ideals, and its action in the field of heritage (both cultural and natural) is a remarkable example of putting national identities on display for the enjoyment of the whole of humankind, in an attempt to find unity in diversity. But this success, while a cause for celebration, has not come without its costs, its dark sides, unintended consequences, and blind spots. Preceding chapters have highlighted many of these; this chapter aims at revisiting the themes of the book, and taking stock of some of the brightest achievements of the international heritage system, and the dark sides or unintended consequences of these successes. Every light on an object casts a shadow, and the shiny edifice of heritage, while something to behold and celebrate under a bright light, casts its own shadow, too.

I argue in this chapter that, for every major success of international heritage law, there is a somewhat troubling dark side, which, even if for the most part not enough to compromise the entire enterprise of international protection of heritage, certainly is to be taken seriously. Far from attempting to discredit the heritage movement, my intention here, as with the rest of the book, is to generate discussion leading to a more self-aware international heritage law, one that takes into account its own shortcomings and exploits its strengths to the maximum, including having communities as a central part of its endeavours. To the extent heritage is becoming increasingly more prominent in international debates, such self-aware and responsible reading of heritage becomes more and more urgent. International heritage law can no longer avoid its own responsibility for world-making by conveniently placing itself at the margins of the international legal project whenever convenient. This field of law is long overdue in asserting its own position at the core of international legal governance. This book, and this chapter in particular, contributes towards that goal.

Section 8.1 highlights what I perceive to be international heritage law's greatest successes or bright sides. Section 8.2 in turn examines the dark sides that are roughly equivalent to the bright sides. I will present the bright sides fairly uncritically, and mostly from an orthodox perspective (discussed in Chapter 1). The heterodox critique in which this book engages, as well as its overarching argument for community inclusion, are most relevant in presenting the dark sides. My objective with this point-and-counterpoint method is to engage a dialectical analysis of the system of international heritage law, and to remind the reader that, even though this book has focused on the shortcomings of the field, there is a solid foundation for redefinition, if only the field can stop working on itself through the conservation paradigm (and praising its successes) to focus on the problem at hand more broadly and the aspirations of heritage holders (being aware of how the dark sides should inform reshaping legal mechanisms). Most of these dark sides are drawn from non-legal perspectives, as a stark reminder of the need for international heritage law to be more mindful of how power it constructs is narrated and negotiated outside the law, where heritage's engagements, and the effects of the law on culture, are actually felt, primarily by communities.

8.1 Bright Sides

8.1.1 Heritage as global governance: a uniform language

Arguably international heritage law's greatest success lies in establishing a common professional language for cultural management around the world, in line with the conservation paradigm. Hardly anyone even minimally involved with heritage could claim to be unaware of UNESCO's work, and the way its mechanisms operate. Everyone is familiar with the idea of listing as a principal tool for heritage protection and safeguarding. Importantly, too, heritage has become a good worth safeguarding even in fairly extreme situations, where possibly other goods of similar importance are at stake. One example is the ongoing (at the time of writing) conflict in Syria. While the main focus is, and should be, on the tragic consequences of the conflict for human lives and the capacity of the Syrian State and people to survive the conflict and overcome its aftermath, a fair amount of attention has also been dedicated to the destruction of the *souk* in Aleppo. The fact that the *souk* is listed as a World Heritage Site has made it part of the international discourse around the conflict, alongside human rights issues and whether the UN should be intervening in the conflict. UNESCO's Director-General, while invoking the status of the markets as a World Heritage Site, also said that:

> The human suffering caused by this situation is already extreme. That the fighting is now destroying cultural heritage that bears witness to the country's millenary history—valued and admired the world over—makes it even more tragic. The Aleppo souks have been a thriving part of Syria's economic and social life since the city's beginnings. They stand as testimony to Aleppo's importance as a cultural crossroads since the second millennium B.C. Syria is a signatory to the 1954 Hague Convention for the Protection of Cultural Property in the Event of Armed Conflict. As such it is bound to do its utmost to safeguard this heritage from the ravages of war.[5]

The status of the *souk* as a World Heritage Site was remarked on by many news vehicles reporting on the destruction, including Reuters, the *New York Times*, the BBC and the *Guardian*. But one of the noteworthy features of the quote above is how it underlines the values of the *souk* for the whole of humankind. Notably, the Director-General also refers simultaneously to two bodies of applicable law within UNESCO, the World Heritage Convention (WHC) and the 1954 Hague Convention.

Heritage has also become an important part of discussions around the conflict in Iraq (the looting of the Baghdad museum) and in Afghanistan (a conflict which was allegedly partly triggered by the destruction of the Bamiyan Buddha statues).[6]

[5] UNESCO Director-General Deplores Destruction of Ancient Aleppo Markets, a World Heritage Site, available at: http://whc.unesco.org/en/news/940 (last accessed 9 November 2018).

[6] Francioni, Francesco and Lenzerini, Federico, 'The Destruction of the Buddhas of Bamiyan and International Law', *European Journal of International Law* 14(4) (2003), 619–51; Francioni, Francesco and Lenzerini, Federico, 'The Obligation to Prevent and Avoid Destruction of Cultural Heritage: From Bamiyan to Iraq', in Barbara T. Hoffman (ed.), *Art and Cultural Heritage: Law, Policy and Practice* (Cambridge University Press, 2006), 28–41.

Hence, at least in these first decades of the twenty-first century, it is possible to suggest that heritage has become an integral part of central discussions about the future of the international community.

But perhaps the most prominent effect of UNESCO having created a uniform language for cultural management is how it has enabled professionals in archaeology, anthropology, biology, environmental sciences, museology, history, and other similar disciplines to come together and have their professional aspirations and practices translated internationally and then back again domestically. That engagement has happened even if, as discussed particularly in Chapters 2 and 7, these translation efforts are not always successful. The Chinese example discussed in Chapter 7 on the mismatch between different local governments in the same country with respect to heritage practices is illustrative. This translation happened not only through the listing mechanisms, which exist in several UNESCO instruments and have been replicated by a large number of states, but even in ideas about conservation and protection of heritage beyond listing. The importance of non-governmental organizations such as the International Council on Museum and Sites (ICOMOS) and the International Union for Conservation of Nature (IUCN), which hold prominent status within UNESCO (to the point that properties cannot be added to the World Heritage List without the consent of one of these organizations),[7] testifies to this feature.

8.1.2 UNESCO's success as an international organization

Because of this capacity to make heritage a part of global governance projects, and its successful promotion of a uniform vocabulary and set of practices for professionals involved in heritage matters across the world, UNESCO has been a very successful international organization, at least in the heritage field. And that feat is also symbolized by the widespread ratification of heritage treaties under UNESCO. For instance, the Intangible Cultural Heritage Convention (ICHC), approved in 2003, already has over 170 parties 15 years after its adoption. The World Heritage Convention (WHC) is one of the most ratified international treaties in existence, with 193 parties at the time of writing. These ratifications do not just mean abstract international commitments; they also translate successfully into domestic law and practice. A case in Brazil, for instance, used the status of Brasilia (the country's capital) as a World Heritage Site in order to enforce domestic regulations being challenged.[8] In this case, residents of Brasilia wanted to build fences around apartment buildings for security reasons, but contrary to urban planning regulations. After judgments by the first instance and the appeals court of the Federal District, the

[7] Operational Guidelines for the Implementation of the World Heritage Convention (2015), paras 31.e and 143–151.

[8] The World Heritage Convention is implemented in Brazil via federal legislation, and has the full force of law. Special Appeal (Recurso Especial) 840.918-DF (2008/0086011-1), Judgment of 10 September 2010.

Superior Court of Justice[9] found against those wanting to install the fences, and used the status of the city as a World Heritage Site as a means to shed light on the meaning of contested provisions of the Brazilian legislation. It also went further and said that provisions of the World Heritage Convention are self-executing, and must therefore be followed by all authorities involved in heritage management.

Not only cases, but also a wide array of domestic legislation have been adopted around the world implementing UNESCO treaties, and creating fairly consistent rules about heritage preservation and safeguarding, even though there can be inconsistencies as discussed above and in Chapters 2 and 7. UNESCO's Database of National Cultural Heritage Laws,[10] for instance, was initially created to prevent and combat the looting, illicit trafficking, theft, and illegal import and export of heritage, and quickly expanded to include information on the protection and safeguarding of all forms of heritage, cultural and natural. It is a valuable resource containing nearly 3,000 legislative texts, import and export certificates, and other valuable legal documentation on heritage. Because many of these 3,000 texts were enacted in direct relation to UNESCO instruments, it bears witness to UNESCO's success in the heritage field, where it has virtually become the world legislator on these matters.

8.1.3 Listing: awareness-raising in heritage matters

But promoting the enactment of national legislation is by no means the only highly successful mechanism promoted by UNESCO. As a matter of fact, some of these conventions' greatest success lies in raising awareness, not only to governmental agencies and heritage professionals, but also to the population at large, of the existence of heritage in the Member States' territories. And that success can be attributed to listing mechanisms analysed in Chapter 7. Here, I will focus on lists under two treaties in particular: the WHC and the ICHC.

The World Heritage Convention creates two lists: the List of World Heritage in Danger (Article 11(4) of the WHC), containing 54 properties; and the World Heritage List (Article 11(2) of the WHC), containing 1,092 properties at the time of writing. The lists include three categories of properties—cultural, natural, and mixed—covering over 167 out of the 193 States Parties to the World Heritage Convention.

Drafted with the objective of being similar to the WHC in structure and safeguarding mechanisms (the listing mechanism being the main transplanted feature), the ICHC also establishes two lists: the Representative List of the Intangible Cultural Heritage of Humanity (Article 16 of the ICHC), containing 399 items at the time of writing;[11] and the List of Intangible Cultural Heritage in Need of

[9] The Superior Court of Justice is the Brazilian equivalent to the High Court, entitled to hear all cases about the uniform application of federal law, except for cases about the interpretation of the Constitution, reserved for the Supreme Federal Court.

[10] Available at: http://www.unesco.org/culture/natlaws/ (last accessed 9 February 2017).

[11] Of these, 90 were inherited from the List of Masterpieces of the Oral and Intangible Heritage of Mankind, an initiative under UNESCO which preceded the ICH Convention.

Urgent Safeguarding, with 52 items (Article 17 of the ICHC). It additionally creates a Register of Best Safeguarding Practices (Article 18 of the ICHC), containing 19 such practices. These manifestations include 117 of the 178 States Parties at the time of writing.

Listing is not only a mechanism of awareness-raising on a website somewhere. It is a complete branding operation. Sites listed on the World Heritage List, for instance, are entitled to (and do) add the World Heritage Convention's logo throughout their premises, sometimes very prominently, but most often interspersed in smaller details of the building or site such as signs, text panels explaining the site to visitors, pamphlets, and even worked into the design of the site's iron gates (such as in the World Heritage Site of Hué, Vietnam).[12]

UNESCO is very explicit about the branding potential of the World Heritage Emblem:

> The Emblem also has a fund-raising potential that can be used to enhance the marketing value of products with which it is associated. A balance is needed between the Emblem's use to further the aims of the Convention and optimize knowledge of the Convention worldwide and the need to prevent its abuse for inaccurate, inappropriate, and unauthorized commercial or other purposes.[13]

The use of emblems to designate heritage certainly increases the appeal of heritage sites and practices, adding to their commercial potential, and their use for development. It also performs a function internal to UNESCO; that of raising awareness to the existence of the organization and the instruments under it.

Listing therefore is a core mechanism for awareness-raising about heritage, and the emblem is a big part of it. But there is more, arguably, to heritage than raising awareness about itself. Heritage has also been successfully used as a vehicle to promote multiculturalism, diversity, and cross-cultural understanding, an achievement to which I turn next.

8.1.4 Promotion of multiculturalism and diversity

The preamble to UNESCO's Constitution states that 'ignorance of each other's ways and lives has been a common cause, throughout the history of mankind, of that suspicion and mistrust between the peoples of the world through which their differences have all too often broken into war'. With that problem in mind, UNESCO has consistently endeavoured to promote cross-cultural dialogue, and its action in the field of heritage has been a prime area of action towards this objective. Heritage has thus been defined as a 'wellspring of cultural diversity',[14] and action has been taken at the normative level to guarantee cross-cultural understanding.

[12] Photograph by Rodney Harrison, published in Harrison, Rodney, *Heritage: Critical Approaches* (Routledge, 2013), 92.

[13] See at: http://whc.unesco.org/en/emblem/ (last accessed 9 February 2017).

[14] Convention for Safeguarding of the Intangible Cultural Heritage 2003 (adopted 17 October 2003, entered into force 20 April 2006) 2368 UNTS 3 (ICHC), Preamble.

UNESCO has been very effective in promoting cultural diversity through instruments such as the Convention on the Diversity of Cultural Expressions of 2005, and the 2001 UNESCO Universal Declaration on Cultural Diversity. Article 1 of the Declaration defines cultural diversity in the following terms:

> Culture takes diverse forms across time and space. This diversity is embodied in the uniqueness and plurality of the identities of the groups and societies making up humankind. As a source of exchange, innovation and creativity, cultural diversity is as necessary for humankind as biodiversity is for nature. In this sense, it is the common heritage of humanity and should be recognized and affirmed for the benefit of present and future generations.[15]

Heritage is thus an integral part of and vehicle for diversity. However, heritage has also caused (or at least fuelled) some cross-cultural conflicts. One example is that of the Dragon Boat Festival. The Dragon Boat Festival is a tradition dating back over 2,000 years. Originally Chinese, it has also spread to Malaysia, Singapore, and Korea. Celebrated on the fifth day of the fifth month of the lunar calendar, it consists of a series of rituals in memory of the poet Qu Yuan, including Dragon Boat racing and eating *zongzi* (a traditional rice dumpling).[16] In 2005, prior to the entry into force of the Intangible Cultural Heritage Convention (ICHC), South Korea inscribed the Gangneung Danoje Festival on the List of Masterpieces of the Oral and Intangible Heritage of Humanity (a programme that was a predecessor of the ICHC, as discussed in Chapter 7). This festival is a version of the Dragon Boat festival, and its inscription on the list of masterpieces caused a certain upheaval in China. One important question was that of the 'authentic' practitioners/holders of the tradition. Of course, the issue of authenticity is one of control, as discussed in Chapter 1 and elsewhere:[17] whoever holds the power over the 'authentic' label ultimately controls the heritage itself. But at the end of the day, China inscribed the Dragon Boat Festival on the Representative List in 2009, being able to also claim the tradition as its own. A similar situation has happened between South and North Korea, with respect to the Kimchi tradition.[18] What the Dragon Boat example in particular shows is that cultures and traditions are shared across borders and, as long as peoples are not too precious about controlling the meanings of heritage, heritage can in fact be used as a means to finding commonalities in difference, thus promoting diversity.

[15] Ibid., Article 1.

[16] UNESCO, Intergovernmental Committee for the Safeguarding of the Intangible Cultural Heritage, Nomination for Inscription on the Representative List in 2009 (Reference No. 00225)—The Dragon Boat Festival.

[17] Lixinski, Lucas, 'A Tale of Two Heritages: Claims of Ownership over Intangible Cultural Heritage and the Myth of "Authenticity"', *Transnational Dispute Management* 11(2) (2014).

[18] The Republic of Korea (South Korea) inscribed in 2013 the 'Kimjang, making and sharing kimchi in the Republic of Korea'. In 2015, the Democratic People's Republic of Korea (North Korea) inscribed the 'Tradition of kimchi-making in the Democratic People's Republic of Korea'. Note that even the official titles of the inscriptions make assertions to a culture being restricted to a specific country. That description can be read as a mechanism to avoid having the two countries work on a joint nomination (which would have been impossible considering the state of their bilateral relations), but it has the effect of also framing Kimchi as belonging to one specific country.

8.1.5 Promoting the right to culture

The notion of cultural diversity is closely connected to that of human rights (discussed in Chapter 4 and elsewhere),[19] and even what Francesco Francioni calls 'the human dimension' of international heritage law.[20] The connection between human rights and heritage happens primarily through the right to culture, but, at least in the area of Indigenous peoples' rights, it is also connected to the rights to equality,[21] property,[22] and physical integrity.[23] Human rights are also considered as guarantors of cultural diversity. In the language of the UNESCO Universal Declaration on Cultural Diversity:[24]

> The defence of cultural diversity is an ethical imperative, inseparable from respect for human dignity. It implies a commitment to human rights and fundamental freedoms, in particular the rights of persons belonging to minorities and those of indigenous peoples. No one may invoke cultural diversity to infringe upon human rights guaranteed by international law, nor to limit their scope.[25]

More specifically, cultural rights are seen by the 2001 Universal Declaration as a catalyst for cultural diversity:

> Cultural rights are an integral part of human rights, which are universal, indivisible and interdependent. The flourishing of creative diversity requires the full implementation of cultural rights as defined in Article 27 of the Universal Declaration of Human Rights and in Articles 13 and 15 of the International Covenant on Economic, Social and Cultural Rights. All persons have therefore the right to express themselves and to create and disseminate their work in the language of their choice, and particularly in their mother tongue; all persons are entitled to quality education and training that fully respect their cultural identity; and all persons have the right to participate in the cultural life of their choice and conduct their own cultural practices, subject to respect for human rights and fundamental freedoms.[26]

This provision focuses on language as a vehicle of cultural diversity, a notion reinforced by the preamble of the 2005 Cultural Expressions Convention, when it says 'that linguistic diversity is a fundamental element of cultural diversity, and reaffirming the fundamental role that education plays in the protection and promotion of cultural expressions'. It is important to note that language is an element of intangible cultural heritage, inasmuch as it is a vehicle for said heritage, according to the ICHC.[27] When it comes to languages as a vehicle for ICH, the drafting committee

[19] For a collection of essays, see generally Durbach, Andrea and Lixinski, Lucas (eds), *Heritage, Culture and Rights Challenging Legal Discourses* (Hart, 2017).

[20] Francioni, Francesco, 'The Human Dimension of International Cultural Heritage Law: An Introduction', *European Journal of International Law*, 22(1) (2011), 9–16.

[21] *Indigenous Community Yakye Axa v. Paraguay* (Merits, Reparations, and Costs) Inter-American Court of Human Rights Series C No. 125 (17 June 2005).

[22] *Community Mayagna (Sumo) Awas Tingni v. Nicaragua* (Merits, Reparations, and Costs) Inter-American Court of Human Rights Series C No. 79 (31 August 2001).

[23] *Community Moiwana v. Suriname* (Preliminary Objections, Merits, Reparations, and Costs) Inter-American Court of Human Rights Series C No. 124 (15 June 2005).

[24] Universal Declaration on Cultural Diversity (adopted 2 November 2001).

[25] Ibid., Article 4. [26] Ibid., Article 5. [27] Ibid., Article 2(a).

of the ICHC made a clear effort to say that only languages specifically important for ICH are protected under the convention, thus narrowing down the significance of language to intangible heritage.[28] But UNESCO has focused on the notion of language as a part of oral traditions in order to normatively protect languages and cultural diversity.[29]

8.1.6 Heritage as a tool for development

Besides the connection to human rights, UNESCO has also been successful in promoting the notion of heritage as a vehicle for development beyond the treaties, discussed in Chapter 5. It has been highlighted that development programmes must recognize the specific role of culture in their design, reflecting that direction through the inclusion of programmes for development of intangible and tangible heritage. The preservation of heritage is thus an important goal of development.

But the connection between heritage and development can be thought of in two different ways. On one hand, culture can be treated as a commodity only, and that is very problematic. On the other hand, culture can be thought of as integral to development politics, both a commodity and a tool for development more broadly. Economics is thus not necessarily the enemy of heritage; it just depends on how one conceptualizes economics. Development can be culture-sensitive and with great economic potential.[30] In this sense, culture and development can be connected from three different perspectives: culture as a generator of economic growth, employment, and development; culture as the cause of challenges to cultural and creative industries; and culture as an instrument of social inclusion and cohesion and to combat poverty. The safeguarding of cultural heritage in all of its forms is important for the promotion of cultural diversity, and places, objects, and living traditions are a permanent legacy that needs to be acknowledged and preserved.

Some aspects of this relationship are prominently covered in the 2005 Cultural Expressions Convention, which, even though not strictly a heritage treaty (as argued in Chapter 5), looks precisely at the issue of safeguarding traditional expressions in light of mass culture and mass media. This instrument relates to cultural heritage in that it protects the fixation of cultural heritage by 'modern means', such as sound and video recordings.[31] The 2005 Convention is in some ways related to its immediate antecessor in UNESCO standard-setting with respect to culture, the ICHC. It takes a markedly distinct approach to cultural expressions, though: while the intangible heritage instrument presents heritage as an entitlement,[32] the former instrument

[28] Blake, Janet, *Commentary on the UNESCO 2003 Convention on the Safeguarding of the Intangible Cultural Heritage* (Institute for Art and Law, 2006), 37.

[29] UNESCO, Endangered Languages, available at: http://www.unesco.org/new/en/culture/themes/endangered-languages/faq-on-endangered-languages/ (last accessed 9 November 2018).

[30] UNESCO, Culture and Development, available at: http://www.unesco.org/new/en/culture/themes/culture-and-development/ (last accessed 9 November 2018).

[31] Brown, Michael F., 'Heritage Trouble: Recent Work on the Protection of Intangible Cultural Property', *International Journal of Cultural Property* 12(1) (2005), 40–61, 47.

[32] Blake (n 28) 35.

takes a more utilitarian perspective, saying that cultural expressions and the heritage aspects they convey are to be protected because they are useful to the development of humankind, though without there being an entitlement to such culture.[33]

Some of the core norms of the Cultural Expressions Convention include: the reference to a clear linkage between culture and development;[34] the need to respect human rights in the implementation of the Convention;[35] the equitable access to cultural expressions;[36] the idea that cultural expressions are regarded as such independently of the means and technologies employed in fixation;[37] and the norm authorizing the use of a 'cultural exception' to free trade norms.[38] The Cultural Expressions Convention puts the connection between heritage and present-day economics at the forefront in a way that no other UNESCO instrument had previously done, and very successfully so. Even if it is a somewhat weak instrument in terms of enforcement, it has generated powerful discourse about the connections among culture, trade, and development, and it is a great success for UNESCO on that basis.

These are some of the main normative successes and achievements of UNESCO in the field of heritage. But, as argued above, to each success there is a corresponding shadow or an unintended consequence, many of which have to do with excluding communities, or compromising the long-term viability of heritage they seek to protect (sometimes both). The following section explores some of those darker sides of heritage law.

8.2 Dark Sides

8.2.1 Mandate creep, the conservation paradigm, and the Authorized Heritage Discourse

If heritage regimes under UNESCO have been extremely successful as modes of global governance and in creating a uniform language for such governance, this success has not come without a price. Two specific issues come to mind, one related to mandate creep, and another to the excessive reliance on heritage experts for the creation and implementation of international heritage law. Mandate creep is not an absolute negative; read from a different perspective, it can be seen as greater efforts to engage in other areas of international law. The coordination of multiple heritage treaties, for instance, would be a good thing. The key problem is the lack of proper coordination, and the appearance of an attempt at colonization of one field by the

[33] For this, and for an analysis of the drafting history of this instrument, see Donders, Yvonne, 'The History of the UNESCO Convention on the Protection and Promotion of the Diversity of Cultural Expressions', in Hildegard Scheider and Peter van den Bossche (eds), *Protection of Cultural Diversity from a European and International Perspective* (Intersentia, 2008), 1–31. See also Bruner, Christopher M., 'Culture, Sovereignty, and Hollywood: UNESCO and the Future of Trade in Cultural Products', *New York University Journal of International Law and Politics* 40(2) (2008), 352–436.

[34] Convention on the Protection and Promotion of the Diversity of Cultural Expressions (adopted 20 October 2005, entry into force 18 March 2007), 2440 UNTS 311, Article 1.

[35] Ibid., Article 2(1). [36] Ibid., Article 2(7). [37] Ibid., Article 4.

[38] Ibid., Article 6.

other. Thus, intrusions into mandates that uncritically pursue political or legal objectives for which the organization has no clear experience are what I consider problematic mandate creep. These incursions into other mandates are also often made at the expense of communities, which makes it even harder for international heritage law to be community-centric.

One important example in this respect is that of the Virunga National Park, in the Democratic Republic of the Congo (DRC). The Virunga Park was inscribed on the World Heritage List in 1979 for its rich biological diversity, including endangered animals like gorillas and hippopotamuses. Because of the ongoing conflict in the DRC, though, it has become a site of presence of rebel forces, internally displaced persons, and the military itself (trying to expel the rebel forces and protect the populations). As a result of the presence of these parties in the park, activities such as logging and poaching have increased quite significantly, threatening the ecological balance there. With a view to remedying the situation, the World Heritage Committee has called for the removal of all armed groups from the park, as well as the halting of all military activities. Most importantly, it has also initiated and funded a project (via the World Heritage Fund discussed in Chapter 7) aiming to strengthen the protection of the park via its rangers, which includes paramilitary training and the provision of equipment to park rangers. While this attitude has been praised for creating a means of mediating conflicting interests (the necessities of conflict on one hand and the need to protect the World Heritage Site on the other),[39] what is in fact happening is that UNESCO (with the World Heritage Committee as its proxy here) is overstepping its mandate and in fact trying to alter the balance of power in an armed conflict. UNESCO is trying to 'backdoor' its involvement in what is ultimately a military matter with implications for heritage. It is a consequence of heritage becoming a central part of conflict (one of the bright sides discussed above), and it is certainly problematic if it happens in this somewhat opaque way. It also affects communities in that at least some of them, in engaging in activities against the state, are in fact turned into criminals by and for UNESCO purposes.

Lack of transparency, or at least the lack of involvement of relevant stakeholders, is a problem within other UNESCO heritage regimes, too. More specifically, by creating a uniform language for heritage governance, UNESCO paid the price of privileging heritage experts over heritage practitioners, holders, or custodians. This phenomenon has been referred to as the 'Authorized Heritage Discourse' (AHD),[40] or the conservation paradigm discussed in Chapter 1. Heritage is defined and governed by philosophies that go back to a specific Euro-American way of imagining the relationship between the past and the present, and a late-modern obsession with vulnerability, uncertainty, and risk.[41] These philosophies, while originating historically for the most part from laypeople, have since been captured by experts, who

[39] Sjöstedt, Britta, 'The Role of Multilateral Environmental Agreements in Armed Conflict: "Green-Keeping" in Virunga Park', *Nordic Journal of International Law* 82(1) (2013), 129–53. While I am a bit more sceptical than Britta Sjösted on the potentials of what she calls 'green-keeping', I rely entirely on her research on this issue, and for that I thank her.

[40] Smith, Laurajane, *Uses of Heritage* (Routledge, 2006).

[41] Harrison (n 12) 8.

are the official spokespeople for what heritage is and what is should mean. The risk of losing our heritage, our memory, is calculated and defined by experts, who make that risk manageable. This is the basic premise behind this book's critique of the conservation paradigm and its exclusionary effects.

The AHD, an integral part of the conservation paradigm, is a self-referential discourse, which engenders a set of consequences, as discussed in Chapters 1 and 3. Mainly, the AHD needs to establish its own reality, and thus create its own boundaries. One of these is the disconnection of heritage from the present and present-day values. The other is that heritage passes on to the near-exclusive domain of experts, who determine its meaning and nature.[42] Even in early efforts to institutionalize heritage, experts assumed a prominent role. For instance, in the US National Parks movement, the figure of the 'park ranger' was the sole interpreter of the material traces of human and natural history, and the only one capable of translating them to visitors. The past and nature thus became separate from the people visiting the parks, and needed to be translated into terms ordinary citizens could understand.[43]

As discussed in Chapter 3, what the AHD and conservation paradigm mean for international law is the transposition of the basic claims and assumptions to the legal-institutional level through UNESCO and the many instruments enacted under its umbrella. Law drafted by the encouragement of experts tends to rely on experts for its own drafting and, consequently, for its implementation, enabling experts to create self-perpetuating mechanisms to ensure their own relevance and the relevance of their espoused views. Importantly, too, the work of experts, while giving them the prerogatives, exempts them from responsibilities, rendering them virtually unaccountable, and their actions not susceptible to challenge.[44] They lay down the rules, but it is up to states and other actors to implement them.

Perhaps the clearest example of the influential role of the conservation paradigm is the 2001 Underwater Cultural Heritage Convention (UCHC). This treaty is purely expert-driven, as discussed in Chapter 3—the main governing body of the UCHC is the Meeting of the State Parties, which has created a Scientific and Technical Advisory Body, composed solely of experts, whose function is to implement the rules annexed to the treaty.[45] These rules further reinforce the exclusivity claim of experts over the body of underwater heritage, by containing elements dedicated to archaeological exploitation of this heritage, and imposing high thresholds of technical knowledge for access to heritage. Even the cultural connections to heritage are to be documented through strict regulations overseeing scientific activities.[46] A recommendation by the Advisory Body on the inclusion of NGOs in the implementation of the UCHC recommends that only NGOs with proven 'competence, expertise and experience' in underwater cultural heritage be allowed to participate,

[42] Ibid., 11–12. [43] Ibid., 104.

[44] Kennedy, David, 'One, Two, Three, Many Legal Orders: Legal Pluralism and the Cosmopolitan Dream', *New York University Review of Law and Social Change* 31(3) (2007), 641–61, 647.

[45] Convention on the Protection of the Underwater Cultural Heritage 2001 (adopted 2 November 2001, entered into force 2 January 2009) 2562 UNTS 3 (UCHC), Article 23.

[46] Rule 6 of the Rules Concerning Activities Directed at Underwater Cultural Heritage, Annex to the Convention on the Protection of the Underwater Cultural Heritage.

thus excluding NGOs who might have grass-roots experience with underwater heritage, but lack expert backing to direct the meanings that can be attributed to underwater heritage.[47]

The preamble of the UCHC mentions 'the public at large' as a party whose cooperation is essential in the protection of this type of heritage, but the actual text of the treaty does not mention the participation of communities or the public, restricting itself to the setting up of means for expert action to protect underwater heritage by conserving it preferably *in situ*, and access by non-expert actors is deemed acceptable only to the extent it is non-intrusive.[48] In this way, underwater heritage is actually frozen and stripped of any possible meaningful cultural connection to local communities. Heritage is to be appreciated from a distance, not to be interacted with, not to be really experienced, but just gazed at. States can claim a stake on underwater cultural heritage by proving cultural, historical or archaeological ties,[49] but it is still the state's prerogative to make the actual claim, and nowhere in the instrument or the recommendations of the Advisory Body is it indicated that communities are to be involved in this process. The view that communities can be connected to their underwater heritage is not as controversial as lawyers would have it, with multiple examples in non-legal literature.[50]

This disconnect between heritage experts and heritage practitioners is perhaps UNESCO's biggest problem in the heritage field, and gives rise to several other problems, one of which is the excessive deference to state sovereignty in the implementation of UNESCO instruments. To that I move next.

8.2.2 A giant on clay feet?

In addition to the many problems of domestic implementation and translation, international mechanisms are also fraught with difficulties. In 2009, China successfully inscribed Tibetan Opera in the Representative List of Intangible Heritage. This inscription can be read as a laudable outreach initiative aimed at including Tibetan culture as part of the national Chinese culture, ultimately giving it legitimacy that is denied in domestic political fora. At the same time, however, a more critical reading indicates that, by inscribing Tibetan cultural manifestations in this list (and consequently in the national inventory), the Chinese government actually asserts control over the cultural manifestation, and the culture as a whole, subordinating its political caveats to tourism promotion and other economic interests, as well as to a larger national Chinese identity, ultimately diminishing the political strength of the

47 Convention on the Protection of the Underwater Cultural Heritage—Scientific and Advisory Body. Recommendation 4/MAB 1, adopted in Cartagena, on 13–15 June 2010. Doc. UCH/10/1.MAB/220/6 REV.

48 UCHC, Article 2.

49 UCHC, Article 11(4).

50 See eg the work of Andrews, Charlotte, 'Community Uses of Maritime Heritage in Bermuda: A Heritage Ethnography with Museum Implications', PhD Thesis (Cambridge University, 2010), available at https://www.repository.cam.ac.uk/handle/1810/236188 (accessed 30 December 2018). Andrews, Charlotte, 'Conceptualising Heritage through the Maritime Lens: A Heritage Ethnography of Maritime Bermuda', *International Journal Of Heritage Studies* 18(4) (2012), 352–68.

Tibetan culture and all political claims of Tibetans.[51] Communities therefore become pawns in territorial states' domestic political agendas (legitimized unwittingly by international processes), and international posturing (superficially showcasing an embrace of multicultural values that is not actually there).

In other words, states ultimately control what is heritage worth protecting at the international level and, that way, they get to exclude heritage that is in any way 'subversive' or contrary to a certain view of national identity the state may be willing to support.[52] It is a fact that states are the main actors of the international legal system, and that international organizations still largely depend on states to implement their mandates, but I suggest that, when it comes to heritage, states (alongside experts, the only non-state actor with any power on the international heritage stage, as discussed in Chapter 3) have too much power in defining what heritage is. This is a significant flaw of the UNESCO heritage system, and one that cannot easily be fixed. Therefore, if UNESCO heritage instruments are incredibly successful in their ratification numbers, that has partly to do with how protective they are of state sovereignty. Thus, international treaties under UNESCO in the field of heritage, rather than creating rights in international law (and thus eroding sovereignty), seem to create cooperation mechanisms that reinforce sovereign prerogatives,[53] often at the expense, directly or indirectly, of communities.

8.2.3 Listing as a 'one-size-fits-all' answer

Another problem with listing is that, however successful it is as a model of awareness-raising, it is often seen as a one-size-fits-all solution, as discussed in Chapter 7. It does not account for different perceptions about the uses of heritage, assuming that heritage is to be made public in all instances, and given broad knowledge, and join a universal pool of the 'cultural commons'. While that is true for the majority of manifestations of heritage, it is not always the case, and the excessive focus on listing seems to prevent sufficient focus being given to alternative solutions, or even to a state in which people may first ask themselves whether that heritage is in fact meant for wide publicity before publicizing it. Because communities are not consulted in the design of safeguarding architecture, they are left with a mechanism (listing) that

[51] See in this regard Silverman, Helaine and Ruggles, D. Fairchild, 'Cultural Heritage and Human Rights', in Helaine Silverman and D. Fairchild Ruggles (eds), *Cultural Heritage and Human Rights* (Springer, 2007), 3–29, 11–12 (using a different example of subordination of the Tibetan culture, involving a road construction project that created a cultural route). A similar situation happens in Myanmar, where identities and manifestations of intangible heritage that are ethnically Burman and Buddhist are given preferential treatment by the government, at the expense of minority groups. On the Burma example, see Philp, Janette, 'The Political Appropriation of Burma's Cultural Heritage and its Implications for Human Rights', in Michele Langfield, William Logan, and Mairead Nic Craith (eds), *Cultural Diversity, Heritage and Human Rights: Intersections in Theory and Practice* (Routledge, 2010), 83–101.

[52] See also Lixinski, Lucas, 'Selecting Heritage: The Interplay of Art, Politics and Identity', *European Journal of International Law* 22(1) (2011), 81–100.

[53] Cf. Francioni, Francesco, 'Beyond State Sovereignty: The Protection of Cultural Heritage as a Shared Interest of Humanity', *Michigan Journal of International Law* 25 (2003–4), 1209–28, 1210 (arguing that international heritage law in fact helps promote a move beyond state sovereignty).

may not be their preferred tool, or, worse, may in fact clash with or negate part of a community's culture.

One example is the possibility of using intellectual property (IP) mechanisms in the field of heritage. While very controversial for its commodifying effects, there are instances in which the use of IP seems ideally suited. More specifically, when religious sentiments are at stake, and the reproduction of heritage would violate notions of the sacred, it is permissible for legal protection to freeze culture, at least for outsiders. Perhaps the most prominent example to help illustrate this point is the Carpets Case[54] which came before Australian courts. In this case, a group of well-known Aboriginal artists, among them Banduk Marika, produced several sacred paintings and exhibited them at the National Gallery of Australia in Canberra. A carpet factory located in Vietnam, which produced carpets for an Australian company called Indofurn, copied one of these paintings from the exhibition catalogue, called 'Djanda and the Sacred Waterhole', painted by Ms. Marika. This painting represents the origin of the world to her community, the Rirratingu clan, of which she was a traditional custodian responsible for the dreaming story. The reproduction and circulation of the painting could have led to her losing her religious rights, and having severe penalties imposed. And the fact that the reproduction of her art would have been walked on was diametrically opposed to the cultural use of the central imagery and underlying knowledge in her work. Indofurn was ordered to pay damages and compensation, as well as remove all carpets from commercialization.

Listing heritage can actively hinder the protection of religious rights in other contexts, too. I have argued elsewhere that, in the event of conflict between religious rights and the protection of listed heritage, heritage values tend to prevail over religious ones, at least inasmuch as heritage is a proxy for secularism and cosmopolitanism, whereas religion can still be seen as a slippery slope towards fundamentalism and division. Thus, privileging religion is incompatible with a world view of peace and dialogue among nations, which international law tends to privilege.[55] That said, often religious views are more central to a community's relationship to their heritage than heritage labels, which privilege state and experts' interests.

Even though the Carpets Case was ultimately successful, it is evidence of how much can be missed by a system that focuses too much on listing. Granted, more recent instruments like the ICHC contain relationship clauses reminding of the existence of other instruments,[56] and even encourage the adoption of measures outside the scope of the treaty itself.[57] But it is still important to remember how much is necessarily missed by foregrounding UNESCO treaties as the principal means of safeguarding heritage.

[54] *M* (deceased) v. Indofurn*. On this case see Janke, Terri, *Minding Culture: Case Studies on Intellectual Property and Traditional Cultural Expressions* (WIPO, 2003).

[55] Lixinski, Lucas, 'Religious Cultural Heritage: The Law and Politics of Conservation, Iconoclasm and Identity', in Glenn Hooper (ed.), *Heritage at the Interface: Interpretation and Identity* (Florida University Press, 2018) 121–35.

[56] Convention for Safeguarding of the Intangible Cultural Heritage 2003 (adopted 17 October 2003, entered into force 20 April 2006) 2368 UNTS 3 (ICHC), Article 3.

[57] Ibid., Article 13.

8.2.4 'Authorized' diversity

Another dark side of the international heritage system is an unintended consequence of the thrust for diversity contained in heritage instruments. That eagerness to promote diversity, when coupled with the dark sides of the conservation paradigm and of excessive deference to state sovereignty noted above, gives rise to the notion that only 'authorized' diversity is worth protecting, and that certain forms of diversity will be excluded, for one reason or another, from heritage protection. Naturally, editing diversity from the outside impacts first and foremost on communities, generating disconnects from and resentment towards heritage processes that can compromise the safeguarding of heritage.

One example is the inscription of the *Uluru–Kata Tjuta* World Heritage Site.[58] Known as the red heart of Australia, Uluru and Kata Tjuta are two geological formations of central importance to the Anangu people's culture and knowledge system. The Uluru–Kata Tjuta Park was originally inscribed on the World Heritage List in 1987, from a nomination file submitted in 1986. This file sought to inscribe the Park as a mixed (natural and cultural) property, but it was ultimately only evaluated by IUCN, who recommended the inscription on account of its natural elements; ICOMOS, responsible for the evaluation of the cultural value of the site, did not submit a report, and the Park was inscribed solely as a natural site. It was only in 1994 that the listing was revised, and the Uluru–Kata Tjuta Park was re-inscribed on the World Heritage List as a cultural landscape, a mixed natural and cultural property.

What this example shows is that a simple oversight by an expert group got to determine what aspect of the Uluru–Kata Tjuta Park was being represented to the world—what was being re-created as World Heritage, the heritage of humankind and part of a world governance project. Culture was excluded from the process and, in this way, only the authorized diversity of the natural value of the formations as geological sites became relevant internationally. Had heritage practitioners been given an opportunity to be present at the UNESCO meeting, this error would surely have been corrected at the start and the Anangu would not have had to wait for seven years to have their cultural worth recognized by UNESCO. Diversity on the list would not have been that authorized by the IUCN (and ICOMOS's silence), but would have been that portrayed by the Anangu themselves.

8.2.5 What version of the right to culture?

The flip side of international heritage law's success in promoting human rights, particularly the right to culture, has to do with what version of human rights is actually

[58] A fuller account of the case is found in Harrison (n 12) 118–27. See also Walliss, Jillian, 'The Right to Land Versus the Right to Landscape: Lessons from Uluru–Kata Tjuta National Park, Australia', in Shelley Egoz, Jala Mkhzoumi, and Gloria Pungetti (eds), *The Right to Landscape: Contesting Landscape and Human Rights* (Routledge, 2011), 153–64; and Greer, Shelley, 'Heritage and Empowerment: Community-Based Indigenous Cultural Heritage in Northern Australia', *International Journal of Heritage Studies* 16(1–2) (2010), 45–58.

promoted, and also with what culture is deemed 'permissible' in this context. The relationship between human rights and heritage suggests that no traditional practice that impinges on universal human rights will be considered heritage for international protection purposes. Illustrative of this notion is that the definition of intangible heritage in the ICH Convention imposes human rights as a limit to what can be considered intangible heritage worth safeguarding.[59]

The objection to intangible heritage that affects human rights is related to the 'invisible asterisk', or the idea that cultural rights, and cultural distinctiveness, will be protected as long as they do not violate other human rights.[60] While the idea of the 'invisible asterisk' (or its critique, to be more precise) seems to lean towards cultural relativism, the invisible asterisk can indeed be a useful tool for communities. More specifically, while at a first glance this limitation may be seen as an obstacle to the protection of culture, it can also be looked at as informing the debate about certain cultural practices as it opens communities, albeit forcefully, to cultural exchange. The colonial imprint is noticeable in this argument to the extent that it suggests communities can be 'civilized' or can 'change their ways' towards more universally acceptable standards based on contact with other groups. However, if one is to advance a position of safeguarding ICH that adds to cultural diversity, it may be permissible to essentialize communities, at least if these communities are willing to open their heritage to the appreciation of the outside world (and that is a question difficult to answer under current heritage listing rules). It is not about imposing a colonial morality or mentality, but rather the non-negotiable core of human rights connected to a culturally sensitive universalist orientation, to which I am aligned. Human rights as a limitation to heritage therefore functions as another stream in the 'cultural flow' that constantly transforms and gives new meanings to heritage. But the imposition of this narrative from the outside is inevitably going to be at odds with (at least some) communities, and needs to be done carefully, via community-driven practices.

Naturally, this 'positive' look at this 'asterisk' must be balanced by the idea that, inevitably, pressures for recognition and international aid can force communities to abandon their practices altogether, without going through any sort of debate as to the actual human rights implications of their practice. But mechanisms on community participation can help address this concern.

These participatory mechanisms are often grounded on individual rights, which is in fact another problem of the relationship between human rights and heritage. International legal discourse around human rights focuses on individual rights for

[59] ICHC: 'Article 2—definitions. [. . .] For the purposes of this Convention, consideration will be given solely to such intangible cultural heritage as is compatible with existing international human rights instruments [. . .]'.

[60] This idea is more fully articulated in Engle, Karen, *The Elusive Promise of Indigenous Development: Culture, Rights, Strategy* (Duke University Press, 2010), 133–7; and Povinelli, Elizabeth A., *The Cunning of Recognition: Indigenous Alterities and the Making of Australian Multiculturalism* (Duke University Press, 2002).

the most part,[61] whereas heritage is practised collectively. While the protection of individuals in international law has many advantages (for one, it gives these individuals the right to contest the practices of the groups within which they were born), there is also an important disenfranchisement that takes place if communities' role in the formation of individual identity is ignored. If individuals are considered only as such, and not also as part of a certain collective entity, they are necessarily in a lesser position to stand up for certain prerogatives. This vision of individual rights reflects the Cold War environment in which UNESCO was set up, and how it went about articulating the connection between culture and identity. This connection was articulated as a matter for individual (Indigenous) artists, who should apply 'his [sic] own creative talent [to] the enrichment of the world and his [sic] own satisfaction and economic benefit'.[62]

8.2.6 Heritage as souvenirs

Finally, the dark side of using heritage as a tool for economic development lies in what precisely one considers to be 'development'. From a certain short-sighted perspective, development translates into economic development and, in the case of heritage, translates almost automatically into using heritage for tourism-attraction purposes. While it is not intrinsically wrong to use heritage for tourism enhancement (provided a minimum threshold of cultural respect for sacred sites and practices has been met), to think of heritage solely as a tool to attract tourists misses the point about the potentials of heritage and the notion of integral development, as discussed in Chapter 5.

This dual role came to the fore in debates about the inscription of the Wayúu normative system on the Representative List of the Intangible Heritage of Humanity.[63] The Wayúu normative system was inscribed on the representative list in November 2010 by Colombia in the domain of 'social customs and ritual', because of its promise of cross-cultural dialogue. The Wayúu are an Indigenous people living in the La Guajira peninsula, between Colombia and Venezuela. The Wayúu normative system revolves around the Pütchipü'üi (the *palabrero*), who is the person 'in charge of administering the words' (in Spanish, *palabras*, or, in Wayúu, pütchikalü).[64] This

[61] A notable exception, as discussed above, is in the Inter-American Court. *Kaliña and Lokono Peoples v. Suriname* (Merits, Reparations, and Costs) Inter-American Court of Human Rights Series C No. 309 (25 November 2015).

[62] UNESCO Doc. UNESCO/Lond/9, 9–10. Cited in Vrdoljak (n 2) 183.

[63] For an in-depth discussion, see Lixinski, Lucas, 'Falling Short: the UNESCO Intangible Cultural Heritage Regime, Indigenous heritage and the UN Declaration on the Rights of Indigenous Peoples', in Sarah Sargent and Jo Samanta (eds), *Indigenous Rights: Changes and Challenges for the 21st Century* (Buckingham University Press 2016), 37–54.

[64] Most of this account is drawn from interviews with *palabreros* available on YouTube. See at: http://www.youtube.com/watch?v=XnWuldfC-0w (first of a three-part series of an interview with a *palabrero*); http://www.youtube.com/watch?v=fojEsmitk8M (interview with a historian specialized in Wayúu history); and http://www.youtube.com/watch?v=V_vM_i4yorA (video prepared to support the UNESCO nomination). Another important source is an audio interview with the *palabrero* Guillermo Ojeda Jayariyu (also coordinator of the main body of *palabreros*, the Junta Mayor Autónoma de Palabreros Wayúu) on the Colombian National Radio's website, highlighting the risks and advantages of inscription on the UNESCO list. See at: http://albaciudad.org/2017/

figure arises historically from a need to resolve disputes within the community, and is a figure of authority. The *palabrero* is chosen on an ad hoc basis, taking into account an individual's social and economic status within the community. It is this status (including social connections) that creates and legitimates the authority of the *palabrero*. Gradually, the administration-of-justice role of the *palabrero* imposed that the *palabrero* proved stronger cultural connections and awareness of how their decisions impact on the social status of the group as a whole (which is connected to knowledge of history and a form of precedent within the community). Elder councils in the communities have a bearing on the activities of *palabreros*. Elder councils are the 'precedent library' from which the *palabrero* draws. The Wayúu normative system collectivizes law, as traditionally the decisions of the *palabrero* have effects not only on the individual who is found guilty of misconduct, but on the individual's entire family or clan (Eirukü).

For the most part, *palabreros* and Wayúu communities showed appreciation for the listing before UNESCO, as it raised the profile of their normative system and their culture, which means increased awareness about their existence, translatable into preservation measures and some degree of recognition. Notably, a Venezuelan *palabrero*, attending a ceremony in Colombia celebrating the UNESCO inscription, stated that the recognition by UNESCO amounted to recognition of the Wayúu nation independently of the boundaries of the two countries over which the Wayúu people is spread (Colombia and Venezuela).[65] The safeguarding plan presented to UNESCO, in this sense, goes beyond the protection of the *palabrero* system alone. The aspirations of the Wayúu with respect to safeguarding under UNESCO encompass measures aimed at the Wayúu language, spirituality, social organization, understanding of territory, and traditional economy.[66] The Colombian Minister of Culture, by contrast, discussing the inscription on the UNESCO list, highlighted the possibilities of exploring the inscription of the Wayúu normative system as a means to promote cultural tourism,[67] which is a peculiar means of exploiting the system, and one which further 'ceremonializes' and 'folklorizes' it. The risk of 'folklorization' was highlighted by Guillermo Ojeda Jayariyu, coordinator of the main body of *palabreros*, the *Junta Mayor Autónoma de Palabreros Wayúu*.[68] In his statement, Ojeda Jayariyu pointed out the negative consequences of 'folklorization' for the survival of the Wayúu culture in the long run.

Even if the listing was generally well received by the Wayúu, there are negative implications resulting from the inscription on the Representative List. If on one hand it may be hailed as a means of enhancing the visibility of the legal system, on the other

03/sistema-normativo-wayuu-preserva-la-armonia-social-desde-el-saber-ancestral/ (last accessed 9 November 2018).

[65] See De la Hoz, José Luis, 'Ministra de Cultura entregó el reconocimiento Patrimonio de la humanidad a los palabreros Wayúu', *El Informador* (30 November 2010), available at http://www.elinformador.com.co/index.php/region-caribe/77-la-guajira/8243-ministra-de-cultura-entrego-el-reconocimiento-patrimonio-de-la-humanidad-a-palabreros-wayuu (accessed 30 October 2018).

[66] See audio interview with the *palabrero* Guillermo Ojeda Jayariyu (n 64).

[67] De la Hoz (n 65).

[68] See audio interview with the *palabrero* Guillermo Ojeda Jayariyu (n 64).

there is a certain risk of 'folklorization' of the legal system. This 'folklorization' would mean not only a potential risk of freezing the legal system in time, but, perhaps more importantly, it turns the system into a 'cultural token'—a cultural performance to be gazed at, but containing no meanings, significance, or practical implications that should be taken to heart. In this way, a mechanism meant to serve communities instrumentalizes them, and turns their heritage into something that can almost be separated from that community, for external consumption.

There are thus many dark sides to international heritage law; but there are also great achievements which can form the basis of a more community-centred and self-aware system of international heritage law, if only lessons are learned from the shadows cast by each of the bright sides, and new light cast on them. Lessons can be learned connecting international heritage law to other forms of international law-making, as well as to other processes and actors. Communities are the central actor that needs to be engaged.

With respect to connections, lessons can be learned about the need for better co-ordination among UNESCO treaties, and some (as yet not fully tested) relationship clauses already in heritage treaties, as discussed in Chapter 1. Further, more connections can be articulated within UNESCO to regimes external to the organization and the field of international heritage law more generally, as suggested in Chapters 5, 6, and 7, but avoiding the trap of mandate creep by UNESCO (or any other institution). Virunga National Park is a perfect example of how the values of international environmental law, discussed in Chapter 6, can be tapped into elsewhere as well to fit heritage in its broader context.

Relatedly, clearer connections to domestic law are also needed, as well as an awareness of what is lost in the translation processes, as discussed particularly in Chapters 2 and 7. It is not sufficient to have the treaties ratified, if the categories are not aligned with the background norms associated, and if the values of international heritage law are not given due weight, as the case involving Brasilia suggests. Better interactions between domestic and international also tell us to be more mindful of how the domestic feeds back into international heritage law, particularly through non-law practices with respect to the conservation paradigm which challenge the uniform languages of heritage in productive ways, as discussed in Chapter 1 and throughout this book. The connection between law and non-law, discussed in particular in Chapters 1 and 2, is a key means through which the values articulated in the system of international heritage law can be made a reality and promote a humanized international heritage law that also brings about lasting peace.

The articulation of values highlights the importance of being aware of the effects of expert rule discussed in Chapter 3, and the need to include communities in international heritage governance. Bringing communities to the table means also shedding light on the difficulties of defining and implementing the value of cultural diversity. It is hard to conceive and implement values of cultural diversity when a non-diverse group of stakeholders is involved. A more effective integration of cultural diversity and human rights values allows us to better identify international heritage law's place in the world's not only legal but also social order, as part of a project of not only governance but also emancipation, as discussed in Chapter 4.

And, as Chapter 5 reminds us, emancipation through heritage cannot be complete without a full exploration of the possibilities of redistribution via heritage.

These bright and dark sides of heritage, thus, help bring to the fore the challenges that lie ahead for the system of international heritage law. More importantly, they also remind us of the stakes of the field, and what it can do not only for culture, but for humanity more broadly.

9
Conclusions

The system of international heritage law does not work to favour communities; rather, it ostensibly focuses on heritage as an end in itself, and, in so doing, privileges expert rule, or the co-option of heritage processes by basic state values such as sovereignty and territoriality. There is nothing surprising about that narrative, though. Expert rule has been a staple of global governance across a number of areas for years, and is in many ways the result of Cold War bipolarity, with technique fashioned as a neutral response to East–West politics. However, the belief in the neutrality of science and technique ignores the possibility that expert classes themselves have interests and that, however well-meaning individual experts and heritage managers are on the ground, there is always the potential for putting the interests of experts above those of other stakeholders. Further, experts are often in the invisible or at least under-regulated or self-regulating private. Sometimes, a search for visibility or reliance on neutral technique may mean experts align their interests with states (who ultimately provide them with funding and legitimacy) and their narratives of heritage, rather than counter-narratives which may in fact be attempts to subvert the state.

States, therefore, benefit from expert rule, even if only indirectly. But they also benefit directly from their positions in UNESCO treaties as still largely quintessential, state-centric ways of designing, enacting, and implementing international law. State sovereignty is key in selecting heritage, determining the narratives around heritage, and attaching heritage to other national political values. In defining heritage, for instance, states time and again have protected their own prerogatives with respect to what heritage is and what it can be used for, and have avoided elements in these definitions that challenge their positions of privilege.

As a result, communities are left out. Communities face a number of challenges in their attempts to gain a seat at the international table. First, international law's exceptions to state sovereignty are usually rights-based narratives; however, communities cannot be easily accommodated in individualistic rights narratives that allow stakeholders such as museums and collectors to have more influence in some areas of international heritage action. That is because they are collectivities, and the rights paradigm has so far advanced relatively little vis-à-vis group or peoples' rights. This reluctance can be partly explained since groups, far more than individuals, can pose an actual challenge to state sovereignty. And that is the second great challenge communities face: their position vis-à-vis states is usually assumed to be one of opposition, rather than cooperation, which creates difficulties in even admitting a

International Heritage Law for Communities. Lucas Lixinski. © Lucas Lixinski 2019. Published 2019 by Oxford University Press.

conversation about community rights in international law. Groups are accommodated, to larger or smaller extents, under a number of states' constitutional or other public law systems, but that always happens well within the confines of the state, with little input from international law.

The third challenge faced by communities in their struggle to be more represented in international decision-making vis-à-vis their heritage is that, at least in theory, communities are *already* represented. Experts and expert organizations, after all, are meant to translate communities' desires with respect to the definition, selection, management, and future of heritage in international fora. Again, while good intentions abound, there is always room for improvement, and a system that sees heritage as an end in itself is less likely to be able to accurately convey community aspirations that largely see heritage as an instrument in the pursuit of broader goals. Translation filters fall short, in sum. And, even for those organizations that have been successful in bringing communities closer to heritage listing processes, their efforts are still largely voluntary, and communities are brought in under someone else's umbrella, playing under someone else's 'stage management' rules, and never in full.

The result of this state of affairs is that the conservation paradigm goes on. It is a paradigm that may see communities as allies in heritage preservation, to be sure, but also sees them as obstacles: the objective of the paradigm is heritage in a pristine and past-oriented state, and not the emancipation or involvement of communities that can mean changes to heritage because of continuing use, or even its replacement with something new that reflects the evolution of a culture. There are multiple initiatives around the world that challenge the conservation paradigm in fundamental ways, such as the Burra Charter. But these initiatives are still to have their effects felt as far as international law is concerned. A mismatch between international heritage law and heritage management and studies partly accounts for the lack of a 'trickle-up' effect. Some of this mismatch can be explained because management largely happens through domestic legal structures, and, in moving from international to domestic, values like the meaning of 'heritage' instead of 'property' can be lost, not to mention that domestic bureaucratic structures do not necessarily map neatly onto UNESCO categories and structures, creating difficulties not only of implementation and effectiveness, but also more fundamentally of conveying international values clearly in domestic settings. State sovereignty again prevails, even if unintentionally.

Efforts to define heritage have made numerous concessions to state sovereignty and avoided interference with harmonizing domestic law. The same reluctance is felt in mapping out stakeholders, which, as Chapter 3 discussed, excludes communities, however defined. The definition of communities is in fact elusive, and bears a certain colonial managerial imprint, but that loaded history is not, in my opinion, a reason not to appropriate the category and use it to give voice to subaltern groups.

The colonial imprint is not limited to the definition of communities, though; rather, it is felt throughout the entire system of international heritage law. From the relationship between market and source nations, to the relationship between international heritage law and time, there is a running thread. Time is manipulated to erase wrongs experienced by communities and other weaker parties, and to maintain the status quo at the time of the negotiation of the relevant treaties. Heritage's potential to redress historical wrongs, and its ability to write and rewrite history, is co-opted by international lawmaking in disingenuous ways, to protect sovereignty, and with the effect of excluding specific stakeholders.

Of course, while much as this book has focused on the system of international heritage law within UNESCO, this field of international law is not immune from influences from other areas, and international law continues to be implemented systemically. In this respect, there is a tension in the fragmentation of international law. On one hand, if we do not pay attention to the five key treaties in their relations to one another, we miss the fact that they should aggregate around common themes like the definition of heritage, the relationship of heritage law to historical wrongs, and the tension between expert rule and inclusiveness. On the other hand, focus too much on the five treaties under UNESCO and how they connect to one another, and we may overlook the connection to other areas of international law and their possible influence, particularly as a means to introduce other values, such as the human dimension, into how we think about international heritage law. Communities somehow fall through the cracks in both these versions (inclusiveness and human dimension failure), underscoring the Westphalian logic of international heritage law, out of step with the reality it seeks to shape.

External influences on international heritage law have mixed effects. Some, like the connection between heritage law and genocide, help articulate the blind spots in heritage law's relationship with time, and the possibilities of international heritage law as a transformative vehicle. Others, like the relationship between heritage and economics, highlight how intentional blind spots in international heritage law can deepen inequalities. More specifically, international heritage instruments have at times excluded, ignored, or outright demonized the possibilities of the economic uses of heritage. A system focused on heritage as an end in itself would do as much, since heritage is a precious and finite public good. However, at the same time, practice shows that economic uses of heritage do not go away; rather, other mechanisms are used, far less friendly to heritage and cultural objectives more broadly. Which is all to say, to exclude themes because they may pose a threat to heritage is not a good strategy. It creates distance and resentment, and moves the conversation elsewhere to fora where heritage is at most a secondary consideration. If heritage law wants to be taken seriously in its overlaps with communities, and other points of connection to the international legal and political order more broadly, scholars and practitioners in the field would be well advised to attempt those connections in the field's own renewed, community-centric terms, rather than wait for them to appear elsewhere.

Not all influences from the external international legal order are negative, though. The enforcement of international heritage law, in the current state of affairs, is not possible internally, and it relies on external venues. Limited experience to date has overall had positive effects in articulating the goals of international heritage law. The encounter between international heritage law and international criminal law, for instance, has led to a more humanized version of international heritage law, it seems. Because international criminal courts (like human rights adjudicatory and quasi-adjudicatory bodies) have to narrate the law and its effects in human terms, the effort by the International Criminal Court of translating international heritage law has led to a very community-centric re-reading of the aims of international heritage treaties, and their role in society. That is a welcome development, but we cannot expect the outcomes of other intersections to be as positive, even when all concerned bodies of law are dedicated to protecting agreeable social goods.

One example is the connection between international heritage law and sustainable development. On paper, very little should go wrong: both concepts, heritage and sustainable development, focus on an international public good; both focus on intergenerational benefits, and the legacy we leave for future generations; both are intent on preservation. However, this encounter seems to amplify the unintended negative consequences of the conservation paradigm. The emphasis on preservation of the past leads to the exclusion of the present, and in doing so compromises the future. That culture and nature are closer than normally assumed helps explain the conservation paradigm, and the enduring influence of scientificism on heritage. To recover the narrative of how nature and culture belong to the same ilk of preservationism helps to understand how heritage excludes certain stakeholders for the benefit of others, or of an undefined 'greater good'. If it is difficult to define a community, it is even harder to define whose greater good is at stake in the conservation paradigm. And yet, international heritage law is far more willing to attempt the latter (unsuccessfully) than the former.

These tensions permeate the implementation and enforcement of international heritage law, and ultimately its effectiveness. Mechanisms built into international heritage treaties fall short of full-blown legal enforcement, but they still come a long way in promoting other objectives of international law. Key among those goals is the enhancement of the visibility of heritage, and its importance for world cultures. Listing is the main means through which this purpose is accomplished, and most treaties under UNESCO can be seen as squarely owing their success to listing mechanisms. But listing only reinforces state sovereignty prerogatives, as well as expert rule, and enshrines the conservation paradigm by essentially conceiving of the values of heritage, and even its appreciation as such, as essentially immutable, thereby also reinforcing a problematic relationship with time, which turns heritage into a static snapshot of culture, rather than a continuing process of engagement with heritage narratives.

Other implementation mechanisms essentially assume listing as a requirement for international attention and protection, and in doing so reinforce listing, as international heritage funds are increasingly used to promote new nominations onto international lists as a key focus, or to safeguard elements already on international lists and at risk of disappearing. Further, funds also reinforce the conservation paradigm by imposing requirements of technical assistance that come from the same international expert groups that, due among other factors to lack of time on the ground, fail to really engage with communities in order to understand the deterioration process, and to plant seeds for sustained conservation in the communities' terms in the future. Further, these processes, like the conservation paradigm and international heritage law more generally, do not seem to admit the possibility that cultural heritage may in fact disappear organically, and that there is nothing fundamentally wrong with said disappearance. A principled preservationist attitude pervades international heritage law, which again causes communities not to be heard, especially when they seek to use their heritage in ways that transform it into something else.

My critical engagement with international heritage law should not be read as meaning that the UNESCO system has no redeeming features—much to the contrary. I believe that most heritage experts are well intentioned and committed, and the same applies to the treaties they have helped put in place, and the international lawyers and other scholars and professionals committed to their success. But there are blind spots which we need to be mindful of.

To every major accomplishment of international heritage law there is a corresponding dark side; an unintended consequence of international heritage law's own success. Is that to say that international heritage law is overall fraught with fundamental problems, with the ultimate consequence being that it should be abandoned, or rebooted? That is not my position.

My intent is first and foremost to generate debate that can lead to a more self-aware international heritage law, one that, rather than blindly relying on the potentials and successes of the field (and there are many), will also consider issues beyond the rather narrow constraints of the law. More specifically, I advocate for a system of international heritage law that can realize its human dimension by including communities more centrally into the identification, safeguarding, and management of heritage in international law. One must not confuse work in the field with work on the problem. There is more to heritage than what international heritage law has been able to accomplish, and I hope this book has pointed to some of those gaps and blind spots.

International heritage law is an important part of international law, and one that certainly has much to contribute to debates on international governance (it is in fact part of international legal governance projects). But, like all of (international) law, once it is placed at the foreground, other issues surrounding heritage, and the possibilities of heritage as a contributor to the emancipatory potentials of international law, are missed. A more self-aware international heritage law, sensitive to its dark sides, unintended consequences, and blind spots, is in a better position to make sure international heritage law fulfills its potential.

This book has highlighted the potentials and pitfalls of international heritage law in its scope and application, and in doing so has provided elements to redefine and reshape the field. The key to that redefinition, I argue, is to include communities more centrally in international heritage processes. Unfiltered by experts. On equal footing with states. A key part of heritage management at the international level as well.

A more community-centred international heritage law is ultimately a better and more sustained way of safeguarding heritage for present and future generations. If communities remain involved with heritage, heritage's future is more easily guaranteed. The exploitation of heritage becomes not a threat, but a means to preserve it, as communities will ensure more of the money related to heritage tourism stays in the community, instead of going to foreign tourism operators, for instance. The listing of heritage can more easily accommodate changing values and perceptions about the worth of heritage. Heritage can change and in doing so ensure the viability of its mandate as a conduit between the past and the future, straddled by the present. Heritage's relationship with the past will be more dynamic, leading to the realization of its potential to define itself in a way that fulfils the promise in the UNESCO Constitution of promoting peace through heritage and culture.

There are a number of ways to bring communities into the international governance of heritage. A preliminary step is closer coordination among heritage mechanisms under UNESCO, not only because this coordination helps expose blind spots, but also because it creates a unified front for communities to access and engage with, and a more coherent interpretation of definitions of heritage that is more in line with communities' aspirations towards their heritage.

Second, communities should be an integral part of the implementation of international heritage law, not only domestically but also internationally. For instance, communities should be allowed to propose elements for inscription on international inventories, so they can define not only their own heritage, but also the terms of engagement with it for themselves and other stakeholders. Relatedly, communities should also be allowed to access international funds directly for the safeguarding of heritage, as, being closer to the situation on the ground, they are likely to have a better sense of how these funds are to be expended. At the very least, buy-in from communities for any conservation or safeguarding initiative is key to its enduring success, as past experience documented in this book shows.

Related to listing processes, communities should also be allowed to ask for changes to the assessments of values of listed heritage. I argue that in general those statements of values should be reassessed periodically, and, when they are, they should include those stakeholders closer to the communities. Again, many expert organizations, most notably the IUCN, already engage communities in the assessment of sites for inscription on the World Heritage List. But the practice should be universal, and mandatory. Further, as shown in this book, listing has many problematic effects, such as the hierarchies of heritage it creates, which are not necessarily in line with a notion of inclusiveness in heritage. But they are also very efficient means of promoting greater visibility of heritage around the world, and, if treated as more example-compiling than value-creating enterprises, some of the hierarchies and commodifying effects can be minimized.

Underlying all of these initiatives is the issue of control over heritage. And control is at its strongest, from a legal sense, when property titling is involved. But, as argued above, property here takes on a more socially-aware and -responsible connotation, in which collective interests are a key part of the very core of property, rather than a disturbance of a near-absolute right. In this version of property, communities still get to control the meanings and uses of their property in the first instance, but they also negotiate with other stakeholders on an equal plane, as opposed to the current situation, in which they are at a disadvantage vis-à-vis states and expert groups.

The reintroduction of property as a category in international heritage law reapproximates the latter to domestic frameworks, therefore rendering it less far-fetched. It also creates an imperative for more engagement with the economics of heritage within international heritage law. Attempts to ignore, demonize, or even criminalize the market have failed, and thus international heritage law is no longer in a position to keep ignoring economics. Rather, it must assert its presence and role in these conversations.

This reassertion of UNESCO's role may involve the amplification of mechanisms for the implementation and enforcement not just of the economics of international heritage law, but also in other respects, currently lacking. In spite of understandable concerns about the excessive proliferation of international (particularly judicial) bodies, they may be a necessary step for UNESCO to engage with the effects of international heritage law beyond the protection and perpetuation of the conservation paradigm. Surely communities are entitled to expect that they be given standing to seek the implementation and enforcement of international heritage law and the values associated therewith in international fora. UNESCO should create the means to enable this standing, ideally through adjustments to the structure of its existing bodies that may not even require amendments to the treaties, instead of having to always rely on versions of international law filtered by other bodies, or creating another treaty that is likely to cause confusion and generate resistance.

None of these suggestions does away with current structures entirely; they are simply meant to further their mandates in light of the current state of international heritage law in UNESCO's eighth decade of operation. After all, decisions on how to prioritize funding distribution still need to be made, as well as on what heritage is listed, and how it is safeguarded. But communities should be an integral part of these 'stage management' processes as well, instead of being filtered or tokenistic members of international heritage governance. Only then can we speak of a system of international heritage law having a clear mandate to realize its potential for promoting peace and human emancipation through culture.

References

Abu-Khafajah, Shatha and Rababeh, Shaher, 'The Silence of Meanings in Conventional Approaches to Cultural Heritage in Jordan: The Exclusion of Contexts and the Marginalisation of the Intangible', in Michelle L. Stefano, Peter Davis, and Gerard Corsane (eds), *Safeguarding Intangible Cultural Heritage* (Boydell Press, 2012), 71–83.

Address by Mr René Maheu, Director-General of the United Nations Educational, Scientific and Cultural Organization (UNESCO), at the opening of the meeting of the Special Committee of Governmental Experts to prepare a draft Convention and a draft Recommendation to Member States concerning the protection of monuments, groups of buildings and sites (4 April 1972).

Affolder, Natasha, 'Mining and the World Heritage Convention: Democratic Legitimacy and Treaty Compliance', *Pace Environmental Law Review* 24(1) (2007), 35–66.

Ahmed, Mohsen Al Attar, Aylwin, Nicole S., and Coombe, Rosemary J., 'Indigenous Cultural Heritage Rights in International Human Rights Law', in Catherine Bell and Robert Patterson (eds), *Protection of First Nations' Cultural Heritage: Laws, Policy and Reform* (University of British Columbia Press, 2009), 311–42.

Aikawa-Faure, Noriko, 'From the Proclamation of Masterpieces to the Convention for the Safeguarding of Intangible Cultural Heritage', in Laurajane Smith and Natsuko Agakawa (eds), *Intangible Heritage* (Routledge, 2009), 1–44.

Amestoy, Victoria Ateca, 'Demand for Cultural Heritage', in Ilde Rizzo and Anna Mignosa (eds), *Handbook on the Economics of Cultural Heritage* (Edward Elgar, 2013), 89–110.

Anderson, Jane E., *Law, Knowledge, Culture: The Production of Indigenous Knowledge in Intellectual Property Law* (Edward Elgar, 2009).

Andrews, Charlotte, 'Community Uses of Maritime Heritage in Bermuda: A Heritage Ethnography with Museum Implications'. PhD thesis (Cambridge University, 2010), available at https://www.repository.cam.ac.uk/handle/1810/236188 (accessed 30 December 2018).

Andrews, Charlotte, 'Conceptualising Heritage through the Maritime Lens: A Heritage Ethnography of Maritime Bermuda', *International Journal of Heritage Studies* 18(4) (2012), 352–68.

Anghie, Antony, *Imperialism, Sovereignty and the Making of International Law* (Cambridge University Press, 2007).

Anglin, Raechel, 'The World Heritage List: Bridging the Cultural Property Nationalism–Internationalism Divide', *Yale Journal of Law & the Humanities* 20(2) (2008), 241–75.

Appiah, Kwame Anthony, 'Whose Culture is It?', in James Cuno (ed.), *Whose Culture? The Promise of Museums and the Debate over Antiquities* (Princeton University Press, 2009), 71–86.

Arnold, Bettina and Hassmann, Henning, 'Archaeology in Nazi Germany: The Legacy of the Faustian Bargain', in Philip L. Kohl and Clare Fawcett (eds), *Nationalism, Politics, and the Practice of Archaeology* (Cambridge University Press, 1995), 70–81.

Arnold, Bettina, 'Justifying Genocide: Archaeology and the Construction of Difference', in Alex Laban Hinton (ed.), *Annihilating Difference: The Anthropology of Genocide* (University of California Press, 2002), 95–116.

Ashworth, Gregory J., 'Heritage and Local Development: A Reluctant Relationship', in Ilde Rizzo and Anna Mignosa (eds), *Handbook on the Economics of Cultural Heritage* (Edward Elgar, 2013), 367–85.

Ashworth, Gregory J., 'Heritage and Economic Development: Selling the Unsellable', *Heritage & Society* 7(1) (2014), 3–17.

Audi, Alan, 'A Semiotics of Cultural Property Argument', *International Journal of Cultural Property* 14 (2007), 131–67.

Aykan, Bahar, 'How Participatory is Participatory Heritage Management? The Politics of Safeguarding the Alevi *Semah* Ritual as Intangible Heritage', *International Journal of Cultural Property* 20 (2013), 381–405.

Bainton, Nicholas A., Ballard, Chris, Gillespie, Kirsty, and Hall, Nicholas, 'Stepping Stones Across the Lihir Islands: Developing Cultural Heritage Management in the Context of a Gold-Mining Operation', *International Journal of Cultural Property* 18 (2011), 81–110.

Banerjee, S. B., 'Who Sustains Whose Development? Sustainable Development and the Reinvention of Nature', *Organization Studies* 24(1) (2003) 143–80.

Barton, Gregory A., *Empire Forestry and the Origins of Environmentalism* (Cambridge University Press, 2002).

Becker Lorca, Arnulf, *Mestizo International Law: A Global Intellectual History 1842–1933* (Cambridge University Press, 2014).

Bedate, Ana, Herrero, Luis César, and Sanz, José Ángel, 'Economic Valuation of the Cultural Heritage: Application to Four Case Studies in Spain', *Journal of Cultural Heritage* 5 (2004), 101–11.

Bell, Jonathan S., 'The Politics of Preservation: Privileging One Heritage over Another', *International Journal of Cultural Property* 20 (2013), 431–50.

Bendix, Regina, 'Héritage et patrimoine: de leurs proximités sémantiques et de leurs implications', in Chiara Bortolotto (ed.), *Le Patrimoine Culturel Immaterial: Enjeux d'une Nouvelle Catégorie* (Éditions de la Maison des sciences de l'homme, 2011), 99–121.

Bevan, Robert, *The Destruction of Memory: Architecture at War* (Reaktion Books, 2nd edn, 2016).

Bicskei, Marianna, Bizer, Kilian, and Gubaydullina, Zulia, 'Protection of Cultural Goods—Economics of Identity', *International Journal of Cultural Property* 19 (2012), 97–118.

Biondi, Andrea, 'The Legal Protection of Traditional Commercial Activities: Two Decisions of the Italian Constitutional Court', *International Journal of Cultural Property* 4(1) (1995), 129–36.

Bivar, Venus, 'History for Sale: The International Art Market and the Nation State', *International Journal of Cultural Property* 13 (2006), 259–83.

Blake, Janet, 'On Defining the Cultural Heritage', *International and Comparative Law Quarterly* 49 (2000), 61–85.

Blake, Janet, *Developing a New Standard-Setting Instrument for the Safeguarding of Intangible Cultural Heritage: Elements for Consideration* (UNESCO Publishing, 2001).

Blake, Janet, *Commentary on the UNESCO 2003 Convention on the Safeguarding of the Intangible Cultural Heritage* (Institute for Art and Law, 2006).

Blake, Janet, 'UNESCO's 2003 Convention on Intangible Cultural Heritage: The Implications of Community Involvement in "Safeguarding"', in Laurajane Smith and Natsuko Akagawa (eds), *Intangible Heritage: Key issues in cultural heritage* (Routledge, 2009), 45–74.

Blake, Janet, 'Taking a Human Rights Approach to Cultural Heritage Protection', *Heritage & Society* 4(2) (2011), 199–238.

Blake, Janet, *International Cultural Heritage Law* (Oxford University Press, 2015).

Blake, Janet, 'The Impact of UNESCO's 2003 Convention on National Policy-Making: Developing a New Heritage Protection Paradigm?', in Michelle L. Stefano and Peter Davis (eds), *The Routledge Companion to Intangible Cultural Heritage* (Routledge, 2017).

Boardman, Sir John, 'Archaeologists, Collectors, and Museums', in James Cuno (ed.), *Whose Culture? The Promise of Museums and the Debate over Antiquities* (Princeton University Press, 2009), 107–24.

Boer, Ben, 'Solomon Islands: Condensed Version of Legal Review', in Ben Boer (ed.), *Environmental Law in the South Pacific: Consolidated Report of the Reviews of Environmental Law in the Cook Islands, Federated States of Micronesia, Kingdom of Tonga, Republic of the Marshall Islands and Solomon Islands* (IUCN, 1996), 189–241.

Boer, Ben, 'Article 3: Identification and Delineation of World Heritage Properties', in Francesco Francioni and Federico Lenzerini (eds), *The 1972 World Heritage Convention: A Commentary* (Oxford University Press, 2008), 85–103.

Boer, Ben and Wiffen, Graeme, *Heritage Law in Australia* (Oxford University Press, 2006).

Bonet, Lluís, 'Heritage Tourism', in Ilde Rizzo and Anna Mignosa (eds), *Handbook on the Economics of Cultural Heritage* (Edward Elgar, 2013), 386–401.

Bortolotto, Chiara, 'Introduction: Le trouble du patrimoine culturel immatériel', in Chiara Bortolotto (ed.), *Le patrimoine culturel immatériel* (Éditions de la Maison des sciences de l'homme, 2011), 21–43.

Boswell, Christina, *The Political Uses of Expert Knowledge—Immigration Policy and Social Research* (Cambridge University Press, 2009).

Bowden, Brett, *The Empire of Civilization: The Evolution of an Imperial Idea* (University of Chicago Press, 2014).

Bowen, John R., 'Culture, Genocide, and a Public Anthropology', in Alex Laban Hinton (ed.), *Annihilating Difference: The Anthropology of Genocide* (University of California Press, 2002), 382–96.

Bowitz, Einar and Ibenholt, Karin, 'Economic Impacts of Cultural Heritage—Research and Perspectives', *Journal of Cultural Heritage* 10 (2009), 1–8.

Boyd, Willard L., 'Museums as Centers of Cultural Understanding', in John Henry Merryman (ed.), *Imperialism, Art and Restitution* (Cambridge University Press, 2006), 47–64.

Braverman, Irus, *Wild Life: The Institution of Nature* (Stanford University Press, 2015).

Brichet, Robert, 'Study on the Legal Provisions Required for Ensuring the Protection of the Monumental Heritage', presented at the Meeting of Experts to co-ordinate, with a view to their international adoption, principles and scientific, technical and legal criteria which would make it possible to establish an effective system for the protection of monuments and sites, SHC/CS/27/5, of 26 January 1968.

Brooks, Graham, 'Communicating Heritage: A UNWTO Handbook for the Tourism Sector', paper presented at the 55th Meeting of the UNWTO Commission for Europe and Seminar on Tourism on World Heritage Sites: Challenges and Opportunities, available at http://europe.unwto.org/event/55th-meeting-unwto-commission-europe-and-seminar-tourism-world-heritage-sites-challenges-and-o (accessed 30 October 2017).

Brown, Michael F., 'Heritage Trouble: Recent Work on the Protection of Intangible Cultural Property', *International Journal of Cultural Property* 12(1) (2005), 40–61.

Brown, Michael F., 'Exhibiting Indigenous Heritage in the Age of Cultural Property', in James Cuno (ed.), *Whose Culture? The Promise of Museums and the Debate over Antiquities* (Princeton University Press, 2009), 145–64.

Brumann, Christophe and Berliner, David, 'Introduction. UNESCO World Heritage—Grounded?', in Christophe Brumann and David Berliner (eds), *World Heritage on the Ground—Ethnographic Perspectives* (Berghahn, 2016), 1–34.

Bruner, Christopher M., 'Culture, Sovereignty, and Hollywood: UNESCO and the Future of Trade in Cultural Products', *New York University Journal of International Law and Politics* 40(2) (2008), 352–436.

Burström, Mats, 'More than a Sensitive Ear: What to Expect of a Professional Expert', in John Schofield (ed.), *Who Needs Experts? Counter-mapping Cultural Heritage* (Ashgate, 2014), 101–12.

Callon, Michel, Lascounes, Pierre, Barthe, Yannick, and Burchell, Graham, *Acting in an Uncertain World: An Essay of Technical Democracy* (MIT Press, 2011). Discussed in Rodney Harrison, *Heritage: Critical Approaches* (Routledge, 2013), 223–25.

Cameron, Christina and Rössler, Mechtild, *Many Voices, One Vision: The Early Years of the World Heritage Convention* (Ashgate, 2013).

Campbell, Peter B., 'The Illicit Antiquities Trade as a Transnational Criminal Network: Characterizing and Anticipating Trafficking of Cultural Heritage', *International Journal of Cultural Property* 20 (2013), 113–53.

Carducci, Guido, 'Articles 4–7', in Francesco Francioni (ed.), *The 1972 World Heritage Convention: A Commentary* (Oxford University Press, 2008), 103–45.

Carman, John, *Against Cultural Property: Archaeology, Heritage and Ownership* (Duckworth, 2005).

Carman, John and Sørensen, Marie-Louise Stig, 'Heritage Studies: An Outline', in Marie-Louise Stig Sørensen and John Carman (eds), *Heritage Studies: Methods and Approaches* (Routledge, 2009), 11–28.

Carozza, Paolo G., 'Subsidiarity as a Structural Principle of International Human Rights Law', *American Journal of International Law* 97 (2003), 38–79.

Carreiro Carril, Beatriz, *La Diversidad Cultural en el Derecho InternacionalLa Convención de la UNESCO* (Iustel, 2011).

Casaly, Paige, 'Al Mahdi before the ICC: Cultural Property and World Heritage in International Criminal Law', *Journal of International Criminal Justice* 14(5) (2016), 1199–220.

Castañer, Xavier, 'Management Challenges of Cultural Heritage Organizations', in Ilde Rizzo and Anna Mignosa (eds), *Handbook on the Economics of Cultural Heritage* (Edward Elgar, 2013), 209–30.

Chainoglou, Kalliopi, 'The Protection of Intangible Cultural Heritage in Armed Conflict: Dissolving the Boundaries Between the Existing Legal Regimes?', *Santander Art and Culture Law Review*, 2/2017(3) (2017), 109–34.

Chang, Grace and Kim, Kathleen, 'Reconceptualizing Approaches to Human Trafficking: New Directions and Perspectives from the Field(s)', *Stanford Journal of Civil Rights & Civil Liberties* 3 (2007), 317–44.

Chechi, Alessandro, 'Plurality and Coordination of Dispute Settlement Methods in the Field of Cultural Heritage', in Francesco Francioni and James Gordley (eds), *Enforcing International Cultural Heritage Law* (Oxford University Press, 2013), 177–205.

Chechi, Alessandro, *The Settlement of International Cultural Heritage Disputes* (Oxford University Press, 2014).

Chimni, B. S., *International Law and World Order: A Critique of Contemporary Approaches* (Cambridge University Press, 2nd edn 2017).

Chirikure, Shadreck, Manyanga, Munyaradzi, Ndoro, Webber, and Pwiti, Gilbert, 'Unfulfilled Promises? Heritage Management and Community Participation at some of Africa's Cultural Heritage Sites', *International Journal of Heritage Studies* 16(1–2) (2010), 30–44.

Choi, Andy S. et al., 'Economic Valuation of Cultural Heritage Sites: A Choice Modeling Approach', *Tourism Management* 31 (2010), 213–20.

Claesson, Stefan, 'The Value and Valuation of Maritime Cultural Heritage', *International Journal of Cultural Property* 18 (2011), 61–80.

Coggins, Clemency Chase, 'A Licit International Traffic in Ancient Art: Let There Be Light!', *International Journal of Cultural Property* 4(1) (1995), 61–80.

Colbert, François, 'The Marketing of Heritage Venues or Destinations', in Ilde Rizzo and Anna Mignosa (eds), *Handbook on the Economics of Cultural Heritage* (Edward Elgar, 2013), 231–48.

Collins, John, 'The Sounds of Tradition: Arbitrariness and Agency in a Brazilian Cultural Heritage Center', *Ethnos: Journal of Anthropology* 72(3) (2007), 383–407.

Committee on Economic, Social and Cultural Rights, General comment No. 21—Right of everyone to take part in cultural life (Art. 15, para. 1(a), of the International Covenant on Economic, Social and Cultural Rights). UN Doc. E/C.12/GC/21 (21 December 2009).

Convention on the Protection of the Underwater Cultural Heritage—Scientific and Advisory Body. Recommendation 4 / MAB 1, adopted at the first meeting in Cartagena, Spain, on 13–15 June 2010. Doc. UCH/10/1.MAB/220/6 REV.

Coombe, Rosemary J., and Baird, Melissa F., 'The Limits of Heritage: Corporate Interests and Cultural Rights on Resource Frontiers', in William Logan, Máiréad Nic Craith, and Ullrich Kockel (eds), *A Companion to Heritage Studies* (John Wiley and Sons, 2015), 337–54.

Coombe, Rosemary J. and Weiss, Lidsaw M., 'Neoliberalism, Heritage Regimes, and Cultural Rights', in Lynn Meskell (ed.), *Global Heritage: A Reader* (Wiley-Blackwell, 2015), 43–69.

Corsane, Gerard (ed.), *Heritage, Museums and Galleries: An Introductory Reader* (Routledge, 2005).

Crooke, Elizabeth, 'The Politics of Community Heritage: Motivations, Authority and Control', *International Journal of Heritage Studies* 16(1–2) (2010), 16–29.

Cruz, Jasmine T., 'The Economics of Heritage', *Business World* (27 December 2012).

Cuno, James, 'View from the Universal Museum', in John Henry Merryman (ed.), *Imperialism, Art and Restitution* (Cambridge University Press, 2006), 15–36.

Cuno, James, *Who Owns Antiquity? Museums and the Battle over Our Ancient Heritage* (Princeton University Press, 2008).

Cuno, James, 'Acknowledgements', in James Cuno (ed.), *Whose Culture? The Promise of Museums and the Debate over Antiquities* (Princeton University Press, 2009), ix.

d'Ossat, G. De Angelis, 'The Scientific Concepts on Which the Protection and Presentation of Monuments and Sites is Based', paper presented at the Meeting of Experts to co-ordinate with a view to their international adoption, the principles and scientific, technical and legal criteria which would make is [sic] possible to establish an effective system for the protection of monuments and sites (January 1968). SXC/CS/27/3.

Dagan, Hanoch, *Property Values and Institutions* (Oxford University Press, 2011).

Dailoo, Shabnam Inanloo and Pannekoek, Frits, 'Nature and Culture: A New World Heritage Context', *International Journal of Cultural Property* 15 (2008), 25–47.

de L'Estoile, Benoit, 'Rationalizing Colonial Domination? Anthropology and Native Policy in French-Ruled Africa', in Benoit de L'Estoile, Federico Neiburg, and Lygia Sigaud (eds), *Empires, Nations, and Natives: Anthropology and State-Making* (Duke University Press, 2005), 30–57.

de L'Estoile, Benoit, Neiburg, Federico, and Sigaud, Lygia, 'Introduction: Anthropology and the Government of "Natives," a Comparative Approach', in Benoit de L'Estoile, Federico Neiburg, and Lygia Sigaud (eds), *Empires, Nations, and Natives: Anthropology and State-Making* (Duke University Press, 2005), 1–29.

De la Hoz, José Luis, 'Ministra de Cultura entregó el reconocimiento Patrimonio de la humanidad a los palabreros Wayúu', *El Informador* (30 November 2010), available at http://www.elinformador.com.co/index.php/region-caribe/77-la-guajira/8243-ministra-de-cultura-entrego-el-reconocimiento-patrimonio-de-la-humanidad-a-palabreros-wayuu (accessed 30 October 2018).

de la Torre, Marta, 'Values and Heritage Conservation', *Heritage & Society* 60(2) (2013), 155–66.

de Magalhães, Marta, 'Exotic Objects, Uncanny Encounters: Anthropological Knowledge, Tourism and Challenges of Representing a World Heritage Site', in Stephanie Koerner and Ian Russell (eds), *Unquiet Pasts: Risk Society, Lived Cultural Heritage, Re-designing Reflexivity* (Ashgate, 2010), 223–37.

de Miguel Asensio, Pedro A., 'Transnational Contracts Concerning the Commercial Exploitation of Intangible Cultural Heritage', in Tullio Scovazzi, Benedetta Ubertazzi, and Lauso Zagato (eds), *Il Patrimonio Culturale Intangibile nelle Sue Diverse Dimensioni* (Giuffrè Editore, 2012), 93–126.

de Montebello, Philippe, 'And What do You Propose Should be Done with Those Objects?', in James Cuno (ed.), *Whose Culture? The Promise of Museums and the Debate over Antiquities* (Princeton University Press, 2009), 55–70.

de Nordenflycht, J., 'El Culto Postmoderno a los Monumentos: Patrimonio Local en Contexto Global', paper presented at the International Council on Monuments and Sites 13th General Assembly and Scientific Symposium, Madrid, 1–5 December 2002, available at http://www.international.icomos.org/madrid2002/actas/177.pdf (accessed 30 October 2017).

Defensoría del Pueblo del Ecuador, *Informe Temático: El Pueblo Afrodescendiente en Ecuador* (2012).

Deloumeaux, Lydia, 'Current Challenges in Cultural Statistics: A Focus on Heritage', in Ilde Rizzo and Anna Mignosa (eds), *Handbook on the Economics of Cultural Heritage* (Edward Elgar, 2013), 187–206.

Deuchar, Stephen, 'Sense and Sensitivity: Appraising the *Titanic*', *International Journal of Heritage Studies* 2(4) (1996), 212–21.

Donders, Yvonne, 'The History of the UNESCO Convention on the Protection and Promotion of the Diversity of Cultural Expressions', in Hildegard Scheider and Peter van den Bossche (eds), *Protection of Cultural Diversity from a European and International Perspective* (Intersentia, 2008), 1–31.

dos Santos, Paula Assunção and Müller, Elaine, 'When ICH Takes Hold of the Local Reality in Brazil: Notes from the Brazilian State of Pernambuco', in Michelle L. Stefano, Peter Davis, and Gerard Corsane (eds), *Safeguarding Intangible Cultural Heritage* (Boydell Press, 2012), 213–22.

Draft Report of the Special Committee of Governmental Experts to prepare a draft Recommendation on means of prohibiting and preventing the illicit export, import and sale of cultural property, 13–24 April 1964. IEIS/DR/91, 24 April 1964.

Droit, Roger-Pol, *Humanity in the making: Overview of the Intellectual History of UNESCO 1945–2005* (UNESCO Publishing, 2005).

Droit, Roger-Pol, 'Lieux Communs', in François Barret-Ducrocq (ed.), *Communauté* (Éditions UNESCO, 2006), 230–5.

Dromgoole, Sarah, *Underwater Cultural Heritage and International Law* (Cambridge University Press, 2013).

Du Cros, Hillary, *Tourism and Intangible Cultural Heritage* (UNWTO, 2012).

Dunaway, David K., 'The World's Non-Physical Heritage', paper prepared for the Consultation of Experts to Define the Noechin-Physical Heritage (27–30 November 1984). CLT-84/CONF.603/COL (1 September 1984).

Durbach, Andrea and Lixinski, Lucas (eds), *Heritage, Culture and Rights Challenging Legal Discourses* (Hart, 2017).

Durney, Mark, 'Reevaluating Art Crime's Famous Figures', *International Journal of Cultural Property* 20 (2013), 221–32.

Eggert, Paul, *Securing the Past: Conservation in Art, Architecture and Literature* (Cambridge University Press, 2009).

Elsorady, Dalia A., 'The Economic Value of Heritage Properties in Alexandria, Egypt', *International Journal of Heritage Studies* 20(2) (2014), 107–22.

Engle, Karen, *The Elusive Promise of Indigenous Development: Culture, Rights, Strategy* (Duke University Press, 2010).

Engle, Karen, 'Self-Critique, (Anti) Politics and Criminalization: Reflections on the History and Trajectory of the Human Rights Movement', in J. M. Beneyto and D. Kennedy (eds), *New Approaches to International Law: The European and the American Experiences* (TMC Asser Press, 2012), 41–73.

Engle, Karen, 'Anti-Impunity and the Turn to Criminal Law in Human Rights', *Cornell Law Review* 100(5) (2015), 1070–127.

Escobar, Arturo, 'Construction Nature: Elements for a Poststructural Political Ecology' in R. Peet and M. Watts (eds), *Liberation Ecologies: Environment, Development, Social Movements* (Routledge, 1996), 46–68.

Escobar, Arturo, *Territories of Difference: Place, Movements, Life, Redes* (Duke University Press, 2008).

Eslava, Luis, *Local Space, Global Life: The Everyday Operation of International Law and Development* (Cambridge University Press, 2015).

Fagan, Brian M., *The Rape of the Nile: Tomb Robbers, Tourists, and Archaeologists in Egypt* (Westview, 2004).

Fairclough, Graham, 'What Was Wrong with Dufton? Reflections on Counter-Mapping: Self, Alterity and Community', in John Schofield (ed.), *Who Needs Experts? Counter-mapping Cultural Heritage* (Ashgate, 2014), 241–8.

Fakhri, Michael, 'The WTO, Self-Determination and Multi-Jurisdictional Sovereignty', *AJIL Unbound* (2015).

Fechner, Frank C., 'The Fundamental Aims of Cultural Property Law', *International Journal of Cultural Property* 7(2) (1998), 376–94.

Felch, Jason and Frammolino, Ralph, *Chasing Aphrodite: The Hunt for Looted Antiquities at the World's Richest Museum* (Houghton Mifflin Harcourt, 2011).

Final Report of the Meeting of Experts to Draw Up a Future Programme Concerning the Non-Physical Heritage. CLT-84/CONF.603/COL.2, of 31 May 1985.

Fincham, Derek, 'A Coordinated Legal and Policy Approach to Undiscovered Antiquities: Adapting the Cultural Heritage Policy of England and Wales to Other Nations of Origin', *International Journal of Cultural Property* 15 (2008), 347–70.

Fincham, Derek, 'Social Norms and Illicit Cultural Heritage', in Francesco Francioni and James Gordley (eds), *Enforcing International Cultural Heritage Law* (Oxford University Press, 2013), 206–27.

Fish, Allison, 'The Commodification and Exchange of Knowledge in the Case of Transnational Yoga', *International Journal of Cultural Property* 13 (2006), 189–206.

Fishman, Joseph P., 'Locating the International Interest in Intranational Cultural Heritage Disputes', *The Yale Journal of International Law* 35 (2010), 347–404.

Fitschen, Thomas, 'Licit International Art Trade in Times of Armed Conflict?', *International Journal of Cultural Property* 5(1) (1996), 127–32.

Form ICH-01 (2016)—Urgent Safeguarding List.

Form ICH-02 (2016)—Representative List. Explanatory Note.

Forrest, Craig, *International Law and the Protection of Cultural Heritage* (Routledge, 2010).

Foucault, Michel, *Les Mots et les Choses: Une Archeologie des Sciences Humaines* (Gallimard, 1966).

Foucault, Michel, *The Archaeology of Knowledge* (trans. A. M. Sheridan Smith) (Routledge, 1972).

Fournier, Laurent-Sébastien, 'La Tarasque métamorphosée', in Chiara Bortolotto (ed), *Le Patrimoine Culturel Immatériel* (Éditions de la Maison des sciences de l'homme, 2011), 149–66.

Francioni, Francesco, 'Beyond State Sovereignty: The Protection of Cultural Heritage as a Shared Interest of Humanity', *Michigan Journal of International Law* 25 (2003–4), 1209–28.

Francioni, Francesco, 'A Dynamic Evolution of Concept and Scope: From Cultural Property to Cultural Heritage', in Abdulqawi A. Yusuf (ed.), *Standard-setting in UNESCO: Normative Action in Education, Science and Culture* (Martinus Nijhoff, 2007), 221–36.

Francioni, Francesco, 'Au-delà des traités: l'émergence d'un nouveau droit coutumier pour la protection du patrimoine culturel', *Revue Internationale de Droit International Public* 111 (2007), 19–41.

Francioni, Francesco (ed.), *The 1972 World Heritage Convention: A Commentary.* (Oxford University Press, 2008).

Francioni, Francesco, 'Cultural Property-International Law', *Max Planck Encyclopedia of Public International Law* (Oxford University Press, 2008).

Francioni, Francesco, 'The Human Dimension of International Cultural Heritage Law: An Introduction', *European Journal of International Law,* 22(1) (2011), 9–16.

Francioni, Francesco, 'Public and Private in the International Protection of Global Cultural Goods', *The European Journal of International Law* 23(3) (2012), 719–30.

Francioni, Francesco, 'Plurality and Interaction of Legal Orders in the Enforcement of Cultural Heritage Law', in Francesco Francioni and James Gordley (eds), *Enforcing International Cultural Heritage Law* (Oxford University Press, 2013), 9–21.

Francioni, Francesco and Lenzerini, Federico, 'The Destruction of the Buddhas of Bamiyan and International Law', *European Journal of International Law* 14(4) (2003), 619–51.

Francioni, Francesco and Lenzerini, Federico, 'The Obligation to Prevent and Avoid Destruction of Cultural Heritage: From Bamiyan to Iraq', in Barbara T. Hoffman (ed.), *Art and Cultural Heritage: Law, Policy and Practice* (Cambridge University Press, 2006), 28–41.

Francioni, Francesco and Gordley, James (eds), *Enforcing International Cultural Heritage Law* (Oxford University Press, 2013).

Francioni, Francesco and Gordley, James, 'Introduction', in Francesco Francioni and James Gordley (eds), *Enforcing International Cultural Heritage Law* (Oxford University Press, 2013), 1–5.

Francioni, Francesco and Lixinski, Lucas, 'Opening the Toolbox of International Human Rights Law in the Safeguarding of Cultural Heritage', in Andrea Durbach and Lucas Lixinski (eds), *Heritage, Culture and Rights Challenging Legal Discourses* (Hart, 2017), 11–34.

Frey, Bruno S., 'Evaluating Cultural Property: The Economic Approach', *International Journal of Cultural Property* 6(2) (1997), 231–46.

Frey, Bruno S. and Steiner, Lasse, 'World Heritage List', in Ilde Rizzo and Anna Mignosa (eds), *Handbook on the Economics of Cultural Heritage* (Edward Elgar, 2013), 171–86.

Frigo, Manlio, 'Cultural Property V Cultural Heritage: A "Battle of Concepts" in International Law?', *International Review of the Red Cross* 86(854) (2004), 367–78.

Fumaroli, Marc, 'Le Lien Culturel?', in François Barret-Ducrocq (ed), *Communauté* (Éditions UNESCO, 2006), 33–9.

Funari, Pedro Paulo A., 'Book Review: John Carman, *Against Cultural Property: Archaeology, Heritage and Ownership*'. *International Journal of Cultural Property* 15 (2008), 97–9.

Gardner, Maggie, 'UNESCO to Recommend a New Approach for Protecting Historic Cities: Bringing Technocracy to the People?', *Cultural Heritage & Arts Review* (Summer 2011), 17–21.

Gauthier, Antoine, *Confessions d'un Gestionnaire: Les Possibilités et les Choix Liés au Patrimoine Immatériel à L'Échelle Nationale* (2014).

Geirmar, Haidy and Tilley, Christopher, 'Negotiating Materiality: International and Local Museum Practices at the Vanuatu Cultural Centre and National Museum', *Oceania* 73(3) (2003), 170–88.

Gerstenblith, Patty, 'Enforcement by Domestic Courts: Criminal Law and Forfeiture in the Recovery of Cultural Objects', in Francesco Francioni and James Gordley (eds), *Enforcing International Cultural Heritage Law* (Oxford University Press, 2013), 150–74.

Giblin, John Daniel, 'Decolonial Challenges and Post-Genocide Archaeological Politics in Rwanda', *Public Archaeology* 11(3) (2012), 123–43.

Giblin, John Daniel, 'Post-Conflict Heritage: Symbolic Healing and Cultural Renewal', *International Journal of Heritage Studies* 20(5) (2014), 500–18.

Gilman, Derek, *The Idea of Cultural Heritage* (Cambridge University Press, 2010).

Ginsburgh, Victor and Mairesse, François, 'Issues in the International Market for Cultural Heritage', in Ilde Rizzo and Anna Mignosa (eds), *Handbook on the Economics of Cultural Heritage* (Edward Elgar, 2013), 151–70.

Godden, Lee, 'Preserving Natural Heritage: Nature as Other', *Melbourne University Law Review* 22 (1998), 719–42.

Golder, Ben and Fitzpatrick, Peter, 'The Laws of Michel Foucault', in Ben Golder and Peter Fitzpatrick (eds), *Foucault's Law* (Routledge, 2010), xi–xxvi.

Goldstone, Patricia, *Making the World Safe for Tourism* (Yale University Press, 2001).

Goodman, Simon, *The Orpheus Clock: The Search for My Family's Art Treasures Stolen by the Nazis* (Scribe, 2015).

Government of the Solomon Islands, *Nomination of East Rennell, Solomon Islands, for Inclusion in the World Heritage List—Natural Sites*, File Name 854 (June 1997).

Graham, Gael M., 'Protection and Reversion of Cultural Property: Issues of Definition and Justification', *The International Lawyer* 21(3) (1987), 755–93.

Greer, Shelley, 'Heritage and Empowerment: Community-Based Indigenous Cultural Heritage in Northern Australia', *International Journal of Heritage Studies* 16(1–2) (2010), 45–58.

Greffe, Xavier, 'Is Heritage an Asset or a Liability?', *Journal of Cultural Heritage* 5 (2004), 301–9.

Grenet, Sylvie and Hottin, Christian, 'Avant-propos: Un livre politique', in Chiara Bortolotto (ed.), *Le Patrimoine Culturel Immatériel* (Éditions de la Maison des sciences de l'homme, 2011), 9–19.

Hafstein, Valdimar Tr., 'Célébrer les differences, renforcer la conformité', in Chiara Bortolotto (ed.), *Le Patrimoine Culturel Immatériel* (Éditions de la Maison des sciences de l'homme, 2011), 75–97.

Hagen, Joshua, 'Historic Preservation in Nazi Germany: Practices, Patterns, and Politics', in Glenn Hooper (ed.), *Heritage at the Interface: Interpretation and Identity* (University Press of Florida, 2018) 56–71.

Hall, C. Michael, Mitchell, Ian, and Keelan, Ngawini, 'Maori Culture and Heritage Tourism in New Zealand', *Journal of Cultural Geography* 12(2) (1992), 115–28.

Hall, Melanie, 'Introduction', in Melanie Hall (ed.), *Towards World Heritage: International Origins of the Preservation Movement 1870–1930* (Ashgate, 2011), 1–19.

Halman, Talat, 'From Global Pillage to Pillars of Collaboration', in John Henry Merryman, *Imperialism, Art and Restitution* (Cambridge University Press, 2006), 37–46.

Harcourt, Bernard E., 'Neoliberal Penality: A Brief Genealogy', *Theoretical Criminology* 14(1) (2010), 74–92.

Harrison, Rodney, 'The Politics of Heritage', in Rodney Harrison (ed.), *Understanding the Politics of Heritage* (Manchester University Press, 2010), 154–96.

Harrison, Rodney, *Heritage: Critical Approaches* (Routledge, 2013).

Harrison, Rodney and Likman, Audrey, 'Critical Approaches to Heritage', in Rodney Harrison (ed.), *Understanding the Politics of Heritage* (Manchester University Press, 2010), 48–80.

Harvey, David C., 'Heritage Pasts and Heritage Presents: Temporality, Meaning and the Scope of Heritage Studies', *International Journal of Heritage Studies* 7(4) (2001), 319–38.

Harvey, Simon, *Smuggling: Seven Centuries of Contraband* (Reaktion Books, 2016).

Hemming, Steve and Rigney, Daryle, 'Decentring the New Protectors: Transforming Aboriginal Heritage in South Australia', *International Journal of Heritage Studies* 16(1–2) (2010), 90–106.

Henckaerts, Jean-Marie, 'New Rules for the Protection of Cultural Property in Armed Conflict: The Significance of the Second Protocol to the 1954 Hague Convention for the Protection of Cultural Property in the Event of Armed Conflict', in María Teresa Dutli (ed.), *Protection of Cultural Property in the Event of Armed Conflict* (International Committee of the Red Cross, 2002), 27–55.

Henson, Don, 'The Academy and the Public', in Stephanie Koerner and Ian Russell (eds), *Unquiet Pasts: Risk Society, Lived Cultural Heritage, Re-designing Reflexivity* (Ashgate, 2010), 209–22.

Hiebert, Fredrik and Cambon, Pierre (eds), *Afghanistan: Hidden Treasures from the National Museum, Kabul* (National Geographic Society, 2008).

Hinton, Alexander Laban, 'The Dark Side of Modernity: Toward and Anthropology of Genocide', in Alexander Laban Hinton (ed.), *Annihilating Difference: The Anthropology of Genocide* (University of California Press, 2002), 1–40.

Hladík, Jan, 'UNESCO's Activities for the Implementation and Promotion of the 1954 Hague Convention for the Protection of Cultural Property in the Event of Armed Conflict and its two Protocols', in María Teresa Dutli (ed.), *Protection of Cultural Property in the Event of Armed Conflict* (International Committee of the Red Cross, 2002), 57–77.

Hobsbawm, Eric, 'Introduction: Inventing Traditions', in Eric Hobsbawm and Terence Ranger (eds), *The Invention of Tradition* (Cambridge University Press, 1982), 1–14.

Holtorf, Cornelius and Kristensen, Troels Myrup, 'Heritage Erasure: Rethinking 'Protection' and 'Preservation'', *International Journal of Heritage Studies* 21(4) (2015), 313–17.

I Diplomatic Conference on the Second Protocol to the Hague Convention for the Protection of Cultural Property in the Event of Armed Conflict. The Hague, 15–26 March 1999. Summary Report. Paris, June 1999.

Ickerodt, Ulf, 'The Social and Political Significance of Prehistoric Archaeology in Modern and Post-modern Societies', in Stephanie Koerner and Ian Russell (eds), *Unquiet Pasts: Risk Society, Lived Cultural Heritage, Re-designing Reflexivity* (Ashgate, 2010), 81–98.

ICOMOS Australia, *Practice Note: The Burra Charter and Archaeological Practice* (2013).

Intergovernmental Committee for the Safeguarding of the Intangible Cultural Heritage, First Extraordinary Session (Chengdu, China, 23–27 May 2007), Discussion on the Implementation of Article 18 of the Convention for the Safeguarding of the Intangible Cultural Heritage, Doc.ITH/07/1.EXT.COM/CONF.207/11 (20 April 2007).

Intergovernmental Committee for the Safeguarding of the Intangible Cultural Heritage, Note by the Office of International Standards and Legal Affairs on the Incorporation of Masterpieces into the Representative List under Article 31 of the Convention for the Safeguarding of the Intangible Cultural Heritage. Doc.ITH/07/2.COM/CONF.208/14 (23 July 2007).

Intergovernmental Committee for the Safeguarding of the Intangible Cultural Heritage, Second Session (Tokyo, Japan, 3–7 September 2007), Preliminary Draft Directives for Implementing Article 18 of the Convention for the Safeguarding of the Intangible Cultural Heritage, Doc.ITH/07/2.COM/CONF.208/12 (30 July 2007).

Intergovernmental Committee for the Safeguarding of the Intangible Cultural Heritage, Report of the Rapporteur of the subsidiary body on the modalities for the participation of communities or their representatives, practitioners, experts, centers of expertise and research institutes in the implementation of the Convention, Second Extraordinary Session (Sofia, Bulgaria, 18–22 February 2008). Doc. ITH/08/2.EXT.COM/CONF.201/INF.4 (12 February 2008).

Intergovernmental Committee for the Safeguarding of the Intangible Cultural Heritage, Report of the Rapporteur of the subsidiary body on the modalities for the participation of communities or their representatives, practitioners, experts, centers of expertise and research institutes in the implementation of the Convention, presented at the Second Extraordinary Session (Sofia, Bulgaria, 18–22 February 2008). Doc. ITH/08/2.EXT.COM/CONF.201/INF.4, of 12 February 2008. Annex 1.

Intergovernmental Committee for the Safeguarding of the Intangible Cultural Heritage, Second Extraordinary Session (Sofia, Bulgaria, 18–22 February 2008), Decision 2.EXT.COM 17 (Report of the Intergovernmental Committee for the Safeguarding of the Intangible Cultural Heritage on its activities between the first and second sessions of the General Assembly of the States Parties to the Convention).

Intergovernmental Committee for the Safeguarding of the Intangible Cultural Heritage, Draft Amendments to the Operational Directives on safeguarding, commercialization and sustainable development, Doc. ITH/13/8.COM/13.a (11 October 2013). Annex.

Intergovernmental Committee for the Safeguarding of the Intangible Cultural Heritage, Tenth Session (Windhoek, Namibia, 30 November–4 December 2015), Draft Plan for the Use of the Resources of the Intangible Cultural Heritage Fund in 2016–2017, Doc. ITH/15/10.COM/8 (2 November 2015).

Intergovernmental Conference on the Protection of Cultural Property in the Event of Armed Conflict, Observations concerning the Draft Convention for the Protection of Cultural

Property in the Event of Armed Conflict. The Hague, 21 April–12 May 1954. CBC/4 (15 February 1954).

Intergovernmental Conference on the Protection of Cultural Property in the Event of Armed Conflict, Observations concerning the Draft Convention for the Protection of Cultural Property in the Event of Armed Conflict. The Hague, 21 April–12 May 1954. CBC/4 Add. (16 April 1954).

International Instruments on the Prevention and Coverage of Risks to Movable Cultural Property. Final report prepared under Article 10.3 of the Rules of Procedure concerning Recommendations to Member States and International Conventions covered by the terms of Article IV, paragraph 4, of the Constitution. CC-78/WS/9, 20 March 1978. Annex I—Analytical study of the general observations and comments made by Member States on the preliminary report and the first draft recommendation (Document CC-77/WS/45).

Jakubowski, Andrzej, 'Articles 25–28: Intangible Cultural Heritage Fund', in Janet Blake and Lucas Lixinski (eds), *The 2003 Intangible Cultural Heritage Convention—A Commentary* (Oxford University Press, forthcoming) (manuscript on file, cited with permission).

Janke, Terri, *Minding Culture: Case Studies on Intellectual Property and Traditional Cultural Expressions* (WIPO, 2003).

Jenkins, Tiffany, *Keeping their Marbles: How the Treasures of the Past Ended Up in Museums... and Why They Should Stay There* (Oxford University Press, 2016).

Johannot-Gradis, Christiane, 'Protecting the Past for the Future: How Does Law Protect Tangible and Intangible Cultural Heritage in Armed Conflict?', *International Review of the Red Cross* 97(900) (2015), 1253–75.

Johns, Fleur, 'Global Governance through the Pairing of List and Algorithm', *Environment and Planning D: Society and Space* 34(1) (2015), 126–49.

Joyner, Christopher C, 'Legal Implications of the Concept of the Common Heritage of Mankind', *International and Comparative Law Quarterly* 35 (1986), 190–9.

Kapoor, Ilan, *The Postcolonial Politics of Development* (Routledge, 2008).

Kato, Kumi, 'Prayers for the Whales: Spirituality and Ethics of a Former Whaling Community—Intangible Cultural Heritage for Sustainability', *International Journal of Cultural Property* 14 (2007), 283–313.

Kaye, Lawrence M., 'The Recovery of Stolen Cultural Property: A Practitioner's View—War Stories and Morality Tales', *Villanova Sports & Entertainment Law Journal* 5(1) (1998), 5–17.

Kearney, Amanda, 'Intangible Cultural Heritage: Global Awareness and Local Interest', in Laurajane Smith and Natsuko Akagawa (eds), *Intangible Heritage* (Routledge 2009), 209–26.

Keitumetse, S. O., 'Sustainable Development and Cultural Heritage Management in Botswana: Towards Sustainable Communities', *Sustainable Development* 19(1) (2011), 49–59.

Kelly, John D. and Kaplan, Martha, *Represented Communities: Fiji and World Decolonization* (University of Chicago Press, 2001).

Kennedy, David, 'Challenging Expert Rule: The Politics of Global Governance', *Sydney Law Review* 27 (2005), 5–28.

Kennedy, David, *The Dark Sides of Virtue: Reassessing International Humanitarianism* (Princeton University Press, 2005).

Kennedy, David, *Of War and Law* (Princeton University Press, 2006).

Kennedy, David, 'One, Two, Three, Many Legal Orders: Legal Pluralism and the Cosmopolitan Dream', *New York University Review of Law and Social Change* 31(3) (2007), 641–61.

Kennedy, David, 'Some Caution about Property Rights as a Recipe for Economic Development', *Accounting, Economics and Law* 1 (2011), 1–62.

Kennedy, David, *A World of Struggle: How Power, Law and Expertise Shape Global Political Economy* (Princeton University Press, 2016).

Kennedy, Duncan, 'Form and Substance in Private Law Adjudication', *Harvard Law Review* 89 (1976), 1685–778.

Kennedy, Duncan, 'A Semiotics of Legal Argument', *Syracuse Law Review* 42 (1991), 75–116.

Keough, Elizabeth Betsy, 'Heritage in Peril: A Critique of UNESCO's World Heritage Program', *Washington University Global Studies Law Review* 10(3) (2011), 593–615.

Kersel, Morag and Chesson, Meredith, 'Not the Usual Suspects. New Directions in Community Archaeology', *SAA Record* 11(4) (2011), 43–6.

Klamer, Arjo, Mignosa, Anna, and Petrova, Lyudmila, 'Cultural Heritage Policies: A Comparative Perspective', in Ilde Rizzo and Anna Mignosa (eds), *Handbook on the Economics of Cultural Heritage* (Edward Elgar, 2013), 37–86.

Klamer, Arjo and Zuidhof, Peter-Wim, 'The Values of Cultural Heritage: Merging Economic and Cultural Appraisals', in *Economics and Heritage Conservation—A Meeting Organized by the Getty Conservation Institute, December 1998* (J. Paul Getty Trust, 1998), 23–58.

Koerner, Stephanie, 'Contextualizing Contradictory Trends of Globalisation Risk Society', in Stephanie Koerner and Ian Russell (eds), *Unquiet Pasts: Risk Society, Lived Cultural Heritage, Re-designing Reflexivity* (Ashgate, 2010), 11–31.

Koerner, Stephanie, 'Revisiting the Dewey-Lippman (1925–7) Debate, Faro and Expertise in the Humanities', in John Schofield (ed.), *Who Needs Experts? Counter-mapping Cultural Heritage* (Ashgate, 2014), 13–42.

Kohl, Philip L. and Fawcett, Clare (eds), *Nationalism, Politics, and the Practice of Archaeology* (Cambridge University Press, 1995).

Kono, Toshiyuki, 'UNESCO and Intangible Cultural Heritage from the Viewpoint of Sustainable Development' in A. Yusuf (ed.), *Standard-Setting in UNESCO Volume 1: Normative Action in Education, Science and Culture* (UNESCO Publishing and Martinus Nijhoff, 2007), 237–65.

Koskenniemi, Martti, *From Apology to Utopia: The Structure of International Legal Argument* (Cambridge University Press, 2006).

Krus, Anna, 'Heritage—Function—Economy: Three Perspectives on Values in Estate Management', in Mikko Mälkki, Raine Mäntysalo, and Kaisa Schmidt-Thomé (eds), *Economics and Built Heritage—Towards New European Initiatives* (Helsinki University of Technology, 2008), 71–90.

Kunich, John Charles, 'World Heritage in Danger in the Hotspots', *Indiana Law Journal* 78(2) (2003), 619–58.

Kurin, Richard, 'Safeguarding Intangible Cultural Heritage: Key Factors in Implementing the 2003 Convention', *International Journal of Intangible Heritage* 2 (2007), 10–15.

Kuruk, Paul, 'Cultural Heritage, Traditional Knowledge and Indigenous Rights: An Analysis of the Convention for the Safeguarding of Intangible Cultural Heritage', *Macquarie Journal of International and Comparative Environmental Law* 1(1) (2004), 111–34.

Kuzmarov, Betina, 'The Coherence of the Concept of Cultural Property: A Critical Examination', *International Journal of Cultural Property* 20 (2013), 233–56.

Labadi, Sophia, 'World Heritage, Authenticity and Post-Authenticity', in Sophia Labadi and Colin Long (eds), *Heritage and Globalisation* (Routledge, 2010), 66–84.

Landorf, C., 'Managing for Sustainable Tourism: A Review of Six Cultural World Heritage Sites', *Journal of Sustainable Tourism* 17(1) (2009), 53–70.

Laves, Walter H. C. and Thomson, Charles A., *UNESCO: Purpose, Progress, Prospects* (Indiana University Press, 1957).

Lee, Kelsey, 'A House Divided: Divergent Approaches to Sex Trafficking in International Law', *Temp. Int'l & Comp. L. J.* 30 (2015), 383–414.

Leiboff, Marett, 'Clashing Things', *Griffith Law Review* 10(2) (2001), 294–316.

Lélé, S. M., 'Sustainable Development: A Critical Review', *World Development* 19(6) (1991), 607–21.

Lemaistre, Anne and Lenzerini, Federico, 'Articles 19–26: International Assistance', in Francesco Francioni (ed.), *The 1972 World Heritage Convention: A Commentary* (Oxford University Press, 2008), 305–24.

Lenzerini, Federico, 'Articles 15–16: World Heritage Fund', in Francesco Francioni (ed.), *The 1972 World Heritage Convention: A Commentary* (Oxford University Press, 2008), 269–88.

Lenzerini, Federico, 'The Role of International and Mixed International Criminal Courts in the Enforcement of International Norms Concerning the Protection of Cultural Heritage', in Francesco Francioni and James Gordley (eds), *Enforcing International Cultural Heritage Law* (Oxford University Press, 2013), 40–64.

Lenzerini, Federico, *The Culturalization of Human Rights Law* (Oxford University Press, 2014).

Lévi-Strauss, Claude, *Anthropologie Structurale Deux* (Plon, 1973).

Lima, Antonio Carlos de Souza, 'Indigenism in Brazil: The International Migration of State Policies', in Benoit de L'Estoile, Federico Neiburg, and Lygia Sigaud (eds), *Empires, Nations, and Natives: Anthropology and State-Making* (Duke University Press, 2005), 197–222.

Lixinski, Lucas, 'Selecting Heritage: The Interplay of Art, Politics and Identity', *European Journal of International Law* 22(1) (2011), 81–100.

Lixinski, Lucas, Bordin, Fernando Lusa, and Schmitz, Maite de Souza, 'Identity Beyond Borders: International Cultural Heritage Law and the Temple of Preah Vihear Dispute', *ILSA Quarterly* 20(1) (2011), 30–7.

Lixinski, Lucas, '*Luci e Ombre*: The Bright and Dark Sides of International Heritage Law', *Italian Yearbook of International Law* 22 (2012), 133–53.

Lixinski, Lucas, 'International Cultural Heritage Regimes, International Law and the Politics of Expertise', *International Journal of Cultural Property* 20(4) (2013), 407–29.

Lixinski, Lucas, *Intangible Cultural Heritage in International Law* (Oxford University Press, 2013).

Lixinski, Lucas, 'A Tale of Two Heritages: Claims of Ownership over Intangible Cultural Heritage and the Myth of "Authenticity"', *Transnational Dispute Management* 11(2) (2014).

Lixinski, Lucas, 'Environment and War: Lessons from Cultural Heritage Law', in Rosemary Rayfuse (ed.), *War and the Environment: New Approaches to Protecting the Environment in Relation to Armed Conflict* (Martinus Nijhoff, 2014), 157–77.

Lixinski, Lucas, 'Heritage for Whom? Individuals' and Communities' Roles in International Cultural Heritage Law', in Federico Lenzerini and Ana Filipa Vrdoljak (eds), *International Law for Common Goods—Normative Perspectives on Human Rights, Culture and Nature* (Hart, 2014), 193–213.

Lixinski, Lucas, 'Sustainable Development in International Heritage Law: Embracing a Backwards Look for the Sake of Forwardness?', *Australian Yearbook of International Law* 32 (2015), 65–86.

Lixinski, Lucas, 'Heritage Listing as a Tool for Advocacy: The Possibilities for Dissent, Contestation and Emancipation in International Law through International Cultural Heritage Law', *Asian Journal of International Law* 5(2) (2015), 387–409.

Lixinski, Lucas, 'Between Orthodoxy and Heterodoxy: the Troubled Relationships between Heritage Studies and Heritage Law', *International Journal of Heritage Studies* 21(3) (2015), 203–14.

Lixinski, Lucas, 'Cultural Heritage Law and Transitional Justice: Lessons from South Africa', *International Journal of Transitional Justice* 9(2) (2015), 278–96.

Lixinski, Lucas, 'Falling Short: the UNESCO Intangible Cultural Heritage Regime, Indigenous Heritage and the UN Declaration on the Rights of Indigenous Peoples', in Sarah Sargent and Jo Samanta (eds), *Indigenous Rights: Changes and Challenges for the 21st Century* (Buckingham University Press, 2016), 37–54.

Lixinski, Lucas, 'Moral, Legal and Archaeological Relics of the Past: Portrayals of International Cultural Heritage Law in Cinema', *London Review of International Law* 4(3) (2016) 421–37.

Lixinski, Lucas, 'ESIL—International Human Rights Law Symposium: International Human Rights Law and International Cultural Heritage Law: Cooperation, Conflict or Cooption?' *EJIL: Talk!* (12 February 2016), available at http://www.ejiltalk.org/esil-international-human-rights-law-symposium-international-human-rights-law-and-international-cultural-heritage-law-cooperation-conflict-or-cooption/ (accessed 30 October 2017).

Lixinski, Lucas, 'Heritage Listing as Self-Determination', in Andrea Durbach and Lucas Lixinski (eds), *Heritage, Culture and Rights: Challenging Legal Discourses* (Hart, 2017), 227–50.

Lixinski, Lucas, 'Intangible Heritage Economics and the Law: Listing, Commodification and Market Alienation', in Natsuko Akagawa and Laurajane Smith (eds), *Safeguarding Intangible Heritage: Practices and Politics* (Routledge 2018), 54–67.

Lixinski, Lucas, 'Religious Cultural Heritage: The Law and Politics of Conservation, Iconoclasm and Identity', in Glenn Hooper (ed.), *Heritage at the Interface: Interpretation and Identity* (Florida University Press, 2018) 121–35.

Lixinski, Lucas and Buckingham, Louise, 'Propertization, Safeguarding and the Cultural Commons: The Turf Wars of Intangible Cultural Heritage and Traditional Cultural Expressions', in Valentina Vadi and Bruno de Witte (eds), *Culture and International Economic Law* (Routledge, 2015), 160–74.

Lixinski, Lucas and Schreiber, Lara, 'The Limits of Framing in International Law: The Shortcomings of International Heritage Protection in the Isis Conflicts', *RUMLAE Research Paper No. 17-4* (2017).

Lixinski, Lucas and Tzevelekos, Vassilis, 'The Strained, Elusive and Wide-Ranging Relationship between International Cultural Heritage Law and the Law of State Responsibility: From Collective Enforcement to Concurrent Responsibility', in Alessandro Chechi and Marc-Andre Renold (eds), *Cultural Heritage Law and Ethics: Mapping Recent Developments* (Schulthess, 2017) 7–43.

Lixinski, Lucas and Williams, Sarah, 'Enforcing International Heritage Law through Criminal Prosecution: the ICC's important—but limited—contribution' (manuscript on file, cited with permission).

Long, Darrin Lee, 'Cultural Heritage Management in Post-Colonial Polities: *Not* the Heritage of the Other', *International Journal of Heritage Studies* 6(4) (2000), 317–22.

Lostal, Marina, *International Cultural Heritage Law in Armed Conflict: Case-Studies of Syria, Libya, Mali, the Invasion of Iraq, and the Buddhas of Bamiyan* (Cambridge University Press, 2017).

Loulanski, Tolina, 'Revising the Concept for Cultural Heritage: The Argument for a Functional Approach', *International Journal of Cultural Property* 13 (2006), 207–33.

Lowenthal, David, *The Heritage Crusade and the Spoils of History* (Cambridge University Press, 1998).

Lowenthal, David, 'Natural and Cultural Heritage', *International Journal of Heritage Studies* 11(1) (2005), 81–92.

Lowenthal, David, 'Why Sanctions Seldom Work: Reflections on Cultural Property Internationalism', *International Journal of Cultural Property* 12 (2005), 393–423.

Lumley, Robert, 'The Debate on Heritage Reviewed', in Gerard Corsane (ed.), *Heritage Museums and Galleries: An Introductory Reader* (Routledge, 2005), 15–25.

McCann, Anthony et al., 'The 1989 Recommendation Ten Years On: Towards a Critical Analysis', in Peter Seitel (ed.), *Safeguarding Traditional Culture: A Global Assessment* (Smithsonian Institution, 2001), 57–64.

MacGregor, Neil, 'To Shape the Citizens of "That Great City, the World"', in James Cuno (ed.), *Whose Culture? The Promise of Museums and the Debate over Antiquities* (Princeton University Press, 2009), 39–54.

Mainetti, Vittorio, 'De Nuremberg à La Haye: L'Émergence des Crimes Contre la Culture et la Pratique des Tribunaux Internationaux', in Vincent Négri (ed), *Le Patrimoine Culturel, Cible des Conflits Armés: De la Guerre Espagnole aux Guerres du 21e Siécle* (Bruylant, 2014), 151–82.

Martinell Sempere, Alfons and Funollet Obiols, Urgell, 'Derechos Culturales y Desarrollo: Una Propuesta de Análisis de Sus Impactos', in Alfons Martinell Sempere (ed.), *Impactos de la Dimensión Cultural en el Desarrollo* (Documenta Universitaria, 2013), 17–52.

Mansuri, Ghazala and Rao, Vijayendra, 'Community-Based and -Driven Development: A Critical Review', *World Bank Research Observer* 19(1) (2004), 1–39.

Mason, Randall, 'Economics and Heritage Conservation: Concepts, Values, and Agendas for Research', in *Economics and Heritage Conservation – A Meeting Organized by the Getty Conservation Institute, December 1998* (J. Paul Getty Trust, 1998), 2–18.

Mason, Randall, 'Conference Reports: Economics and Heritage Conservation: Concepts, Values and Agendas for Research, Getty Conservation Institute, Los Angeles (December 8–11, 1998)', *International Journal of Cultural Property* 8(2) (1999), 550–62.

Mason, Randall, 'Assessing Values in Conservation Planning: Methodological Issues and Choices', in Marta de la Torre (ed.), *Assessing the Values of Cultural Heritage: Research Report* (J. Paul Getty Trust, 2002), 5–30.

Mason, Randall, 'Economics and Historic Preservation: A Guide and Review of the Literature', *Brookings Institution Metropolitan Policy Program Discussion Paper* (2005), 11–18.

Mason, Randall, 'Be Interested and Beware: Joining Economic Valuation and Heritage Conservation', *International Journal of Heritage Studies* 14(4) (2008), 303–18.

Matsuda, David, 'The Ethics of Archaeology, Subsistence Digging, and Artifact Looting in Latin America: Point, Muted Counterpoint', *International Journal of Cultural Property* 7(1) (1998), 87–97.

Maurel, Chloé, *La pensée et la action de l'UNESCO dans le domaine de la culture. 1946–1974*, Mémoire (Université Paris I, 2001).

Mazzanti, Massimiliano, 'Cultural Heritage as Multi-Dimensional, Multi-Value and Multi-Attribute Economic Good: Toward a New Framework for Economic Analysis and Valuation', *Journal of Socio-Economics* 31 (2002), 529–58.

Mazzanti, Massimiliano, 'Valuing Cultural Heritage in a Multi-Attribute Framework: Microeconomic Perspectives and Policy Implications', *Journal of Socio-Economics* 32 (2003), 549–69.

Means of Prohibiting the Illicit Import, Export and Sale of Cultural Property. Preliminary report prepared in accordance with Article 10.1 of the rules of procedure concerning the recommendations to Member States and International Conventions covered by the terms of Article IV, paragraph 4, of the Constitution. UNESCO/CUA/123 (15 July 1963).

Means of Prohibiting the Illicit Import, Export and Sale of Cultural Property. Preliminary report prepared in accordance with Article 10.1 of the rules of procedure concerning the recommendations to Member States and International Conventions covered by the terms of Article IV, paragraph 4, of the Constitution. UNESCO/CUA/123, 15 July 1963. Annex II—Secretariat's Response.

Means of Prohibiting the Illicit Import, Export and Sale of Cultural Property. Preliminary report prepared in accordance with Article 10.1 of the rules of procedure concerning the recommendations to Member States and International Conventions covered by the terms of Article IV, paragraph 4, of the Constitution. UNESCO/CUA/123, of 15 July 1963. Annex I—Replies to circular letter CL/1667 and document UNESCO/CUA/123, received from Member States by 10 February 1964.

Means of prohibiting and preventing the illicit import, export and transfer of ownership of cultural property—Preliminary report prepared in compliance with Article 10.1 of the rules of procedure concerning Recommendations to Member States and International Conventions covered by the terms of Article IV, paragraph 4, of the Constitution. SHC/MD/3 (8 August 1969).

Mebratu, D, 'Sustainability and Sustainable Development: Historical and Conceptual Review', *Environmental Impact Assessment Review* 18 (1998), 496–503.

Meeting of Experts to co-ordinate, with a view to their international adoption, principles and scientific, technical and legal criteria applicable to the protection of cultural property, monuments and sites, Final Report (31 December 1968). SHC/CS/27/8.

Mégret, Frédéric, 'The Case for Collective Reparations before the International Criminal Court', in Jo-Anne M. Wemmers (ed.), *Reparation for Victims of Crimes against Humanity: The Healing Role of Reparation* (2014).

Mégret, Frédéric, 'The Anxieties of International Criminal Justice', *Leiden Journal of International Law* 29(1) (2015), 197–221.

Meller, H., 'Taking it to the Next Level: The Internationalization of Domestic Norms and Intangible Cultural Heritage', *Gnovis: A Journal of Communication, Culture, and Technology* 10(3) (2010) available at http://www.gnovisjournal.org/2010/08/26/taking-it-next-level-internationalization-domestic-norms-and-intangible-cultural-heritage/ (accessed 30 October 2017).

Merryman, John Henry, 'Thinking about the Elgin Marbles', *Michigan Law Review* 83 (1984–5), 1881–923.

Merryman, John Henry, 'Two Ways of Thinking about Cultural Property', *American Journal of International Law* 80(4) (1986), 831–53.

Merryman, John Henry, 'A Licit International Trade in Cultural Objects', *International Journal of Cultural Property* 4(1) (1995), 13–60.

Merryman, John Henry, 'The Free International Movement of Cultural Property', *NYU Journal of International Law and Politics* 31 (1998), 1–14.

Merryman, John Henry, 'Cultural Property, International Trade and Human Rights', *Cardozo Arts & Entertainment Law Journal* 19 (2001), 51–68.

Merryman, John Henry, 'Cultural Property Internationalism', *International Journal of Cultural Property* 12(1) (2005), 11–39.

Merryman, John Henry, 'Whither the Elgin Marbles?', in John Henry Merryman (ed.), *Imperialism, Art and Restitution* (Cambridge University Press, 2006), 98–113.

Merryman, John Henry, *Thinking About the Elgin Marbles: Critical Essays on Cultural Property, Art and Law* (2nd edn, Alphen aan den Rijn, 2009).

Merryman, John Henry, 'The Nation and the Object', in James Cuno (ed.), *Whose Culture? The Promise of Museums and the Debate over Antiquities* (Princeton University Press, 2009), 183–208.

Meskell, Lynn, 'UNESCO and the Fate of the World Heritage Indigenous Peoples Council of Experts (WHIPCOE)', *International Journal of Cultural Property* 20 (2013), 155–74.

Meskell, Lynn, *A Future in Ruins: UNESCO, World Heritage, and the Dream of Peace* (Oxford University Press, 2018).

Meskell, Lynn, Liuzza, Claudia, Berrtacchini, Enrico, and Saccone, Donatella, 'Multilateralism and UNESCO World Heritage: Decision-Making, States Parties and Political Processes', *International Journal of Heritage Studies* 21(5) (2015), 423–40.

Messender, Phyllis Mauch (ed.), *The Ethics of Collecting Cultural Property: Whose Culture? Whose Property?* (University of New Mexico Press, 1991).

Miele, Chris, 'Heritage and its Communities: Reflections on the English Experience in the Nineteenth and Twentieth Centuries', in Melanie Hall (ed.), *Towards World Heritage: International Origins of the Preservation Movement 1870–1930* (Ashgate, 2011), 155–79.

Miller, Barbara D., 'Heritage Management Inside Out and Upside Down: Questioning Outsider and Top-Down Approaches', *Heritage Management* 2(1) (2009), 5–10.

Morss, John R., *International Law as the Law of Collectives: Toward a Law of People* (Ashgate, 2013).

Mourato, Susana and Mazzanti, Massimiliano, 'Economic Valuation of Cultural Heritage: Evidence and Prospects', in Marta de la Torre (ed.), *Assessing the Values of Cultural Heritage: Research Report* (J. Paul Getty Trust, 2002), 51–76.

Muir Watt, Horatia, 'Private International Law beyond the Schism', *Transnational Legal Theory* 2(3) (2011), 347–427.

Munjeri, Dawson, 'Following the Length and Breadth of the Roots: Some Dimensions of Intangible Heritage', in Laurajane Smith and Natsuko Akagawa (eds), *Intangible Heritage* (Routledge, 2009), 207–42.

Murphy, J. David, 'The People's Republic of China and the Illicit Trade in Cultural Property: Is the Embargo Approach the Answer?', *International Journal of Cultural Property* 3(2) (1994), 227–42.

Musi, Maja, 'The International Heritage Doctrine and the Management of Heritage in Sarajevo, Bosnia and Herzegovina: the Case of the Commission to Preserve National Monuments', *International Journal of Heritage Studies* 20(1) (2014), 54–71.

Nafziger, James A. R., 'The 1970 UNESCO Convention: Insights, Circumspections, and Outlooks', in Jorge A. Sánchez Cordero (ed.), *La Convención de la UNESCO de 1970: Sus Nuevos Desafíos* (2014) 211–28.

Nafziger, James A. R., 'The UNESCO Convention on the Protection of the Underwater Cultural Heritage: Its Growing Influence', *Journal of Maritime Law & Commerce* 49(3) (2018) 371–400.

Nafziger, James A. R., and Scovazzi, Tullio (eds), *The Cultural Heritage of Mankind* (Martinus Nijhoff, 2008).

Nicholas, Lynn H., *The Rape of Europa: The Fate of Europe's Treasures in the Third Reich and the Second World War* (Vintage, 1995).

Nollkaemper, André, 'International Adjudication of Global Public Goods: The Intersection of Substance and Procedure', *European Journal of International Law* 23(3) (2012), 769–91.

Noonan, Douglas S., 'Market Effects of Historic Preservation', in Ilde Rizzo and Anna Mignosa (eds), *Handbook on the Economics of Cultural Heritage* (Edward Elgar, 2013), 344–63.

Novic, Elisa, *The Concept of Cultural Genocide: An International Law Perspective* (Oxford University Press, 2016).

O'Hagan, John and McAndrew, Clare, 'Restricting International Trade in the Artistic Patrimony: Economic Rationale and Policy Instruments', *International Journal of Cultural Property* 10(1) (2001), 32–54.

O'Keefe, Patrick J., '"Commercial Exploitation': Its Prohibition in the UNESCO Convention on Protection of the Underwater Cultural Heritage 2001 and Other Instruments', *Art, Antiquity & Law* 18(2) (2013), 129–48.

O'Keefe, Roger, 'World Cultural Heritage Obligations to the International Community as a Whole?' *International and Comparative Law Quarterly* 53 (2004), 189–209.

O'Keefe, Roger, *The Protection of Cultural Property in Armed Conflict* (Cambridge University Press, 2006).

O'Keeffe, Tadhg, 'Who Would Believe Experts? Interrogating the Discourses of Archaeologists and Interest Groups in Two Recent Heritage Disputes in Ireland', in John Schofield (ed.), *Who Needs Experts? Counter-mapping Cultural Heritage* (Ashgate, 2014), 113–32.

O'Neill, Kevin Lewis, 'Anthropology and Genocide', in Donald Bloxham and A. Dirk Moses (eds), *The Oxford Handbook of Genocide Studies* (Oxford University Press, 2010), 182–96.

Olsson, Krister, 'The Value of Preservation: Analysis of the Decision-making Processes in Urban Heritage Management, in Mikko Mälkki, Raine Mäntysalo, and Kaisa Schmidt-Thomé (eds), *Economics and Built Heritage—Towards New European Initiatives* (Helsinki University of Technology, 2008), 113–29.

Olwig, Kenneth Robert, '"Time out of Mind"–"Mind out of Time": Custom Versus Tradition in Environmental Heritage Research and Interpretation', *International Journal of Heritage Studies* 7(4) (2001), 339–54.

Orbaşlı, Aylin, 'Nara+20: a Theory and Practice Perspective', *Heritage & Society* 8(2) (2015), 178–88.

Orford, Anne (ed.), *International Law and Its Others* (Cambridge University Press, 2006).

Overton, J. and Purdie, N., 'Think Local, Act Global? Reflections on Sustainable Development in the Pacific Islands', *Development Bulletin* 41 (1997), 37–9.

Owen, David I., 'Censoring Knowledge: The Case for the Publication of Unprovenanced Cuneiform Tablets', in James Cuno (ed.), *Whose Culture? The Promise of Museums and the Debate over Antiquities* (Princeton University Press, 2009), 125–42.

Pagiola, Stefano, 'Economic Analysis of Investments in Cultural Heritage: Insights from Environmental Economics', *World Bank Staff Paper* (World Bank, 1996).

Pahuja, Sundhya, *Decolonising International Law: Development, Economic Growth and the Politics of Universality* (Cambridge University Press, 2011).

Patchett, Lynne, 'Articles 17–18: Activities to Support the World Heritage Fund', in Francesco Francioni (ed.), *The 1972 World Heritage Convention: A Commentary* (Oxford University Press, 2008), 289–304.

Paterson, Robert K., 'The "Curse of the London Nataraja"', *International Journal of Cultural Property* 5(2) (1996), 330–8.

Paterson, Robert K. and Telesetsky, Anastasia, 'Heritage Inc.: A Mini-Symposium on Heritage Protection and Private Actors. Held at the Faculty of Law, University of British Columbia, Vancouver, Canada, 16 March 2012', *International Journal of Cultural Property* 19 (2012), 549–71.

Peacock, Alan and Rizzo, Ilde, *The Heritage Game: Economics, Policy and Practice* (Oxford University Press, 2008).

Pearson, Christopher E. M., *Designing UNESCO: Art, Architecture and International Politics at Mid-Century* (Ashgate, 2010).

Perkin, Corinne, 'Beyond the Rhetoric: Negotiating the Politics and Realizing the Potential of Community-Driven Heritage Engagement', *International Journal of Heritage Studies* 16(1–2) (2010), 107–22.

Perrone, Nicolás M., 'The International Investment Regime and Local Populations: Are the Weakest Voices Unheard?', *Transnational Legal Theory* 7(3) (2016), 1–23.

Philp, Janette, 'The Political Appropriation of Burma's Cultural Heritage and its Implications for Human Rights', in Michele Langfield, William Logan, and Mairead Nic Craith (eds), *Cultural Diversity, Heritage and Human Rights: Intersections in Theory and Practice* (Routledge, 2010), 83–101.

Posner, Eric A., 'The International Protection of Cultural Property: Some Skeptical Observations', *Chicago Public Law and Legal Theory Working Paper No. 141* (2006), available at http://ssrn.com/abstract_id=946778.

Poulos, Ioannis, 'Moving Beyond a Values-Based Approach to Heritage Conservation', *Conservation and Management of Archaeological Sites* 12(2) (2010), 170–85.

Povinelli, Elizabeth A., 'The Cunning of Recognition: Real Being and Aboriginal Recognition in Settler Australia', *Australian Feminist Law Journal* 11 (1998), 3–27.

Povinelli, Elizabeth A., *The Cunning of Recognition: Indigenous Alterities and the Making of Australian Multiculturalism* (Duke University Press, 2002).

Prott, Lyndel V., 'The International Movement of Cultural Objects', *International Journal of Cultural Property* 12 (2005), 225–48.

Prott, Lyndel V., 'UNESCO International Framework for the Protection of the Cultural Heritage', in James A. R. Nafziger and Ann M. Nicgorski (eds), *Cultural Heritage Issues: The Legacy of Conquest, Colonization and Commerce* (Martinus Nijhoff, 2009), 257–85.

Prott, Lyndel V. and O'Keefe, Patrick J., '"Cultural Heritage" or "Cultural Property"?', *International Journal of Cultural Property* 1 (1992), 307–20.

Ranger, Terence, 'The Invention of Tradition in Colonial Africa', in Eric Hobsbawm and Terence Ranger (eds), *The Invention of Tradition* (Cambridge University Press, 1982), 211–62.

Rao, Kishore, 'Remarks by Kishore Rao, Director of the UNESCO World Heritage Center', at the 55th Meeting of the UNWTO Commission for Europe and Seminar on Tourism on World Heritage Sites: Challenges and Opportunities, available at http://europe.unwto.org/event/55th-meeting-unwto-commission-europe-and-seminar-tourism-world-heritage-sites-challenges-and-o (accessed 30 October 2017).

Rapoport Delegation on Afro-Ecuadorian Land Rights, *Forgotten Territories, Unrealized Rights: Rural Afro-Ecuadorians and their Fight for Land, Equality, and Security* (2009), 34–5, available at https://law.utexas.edu/wp-content/uploads/sites/31/2016/02/ecuador-eng.pdf (accessed 30 October 2017).

Redgwell, Catherine, 'Article 2—Definition of Natural Heritage', in Francesco Francioni and Federico Lenzerini (eds), *The 1972 World Heritage Convention: A Commentary* (Oxford University Press, 2008), 63–84.

Reid, Andrew, 'Cattle, Identity and Genocide in the African Great Lakes Region', *Archaeology International* 4 (2000), 35–8.

Report of the fourth meeting of governmental experts on the draft Convention on the protection of the underwater cultural heritage (26 March–6 April 2001). CLT-2001/CONF.203/INF.3.

Report of the meeting of governmental experts on the draft convention for the protection of the underwater cultural heritage (29 June–2 July 1998). CLT-98/CONF.202/7.

Report of the World Heritage Committee, 22nd sess., WHC-98/CONF.203/18 (30 November–5 December 1998).

Resource Management Objectives and Guidelines for East Rennell, Solomon Islands, File Name 854 (June 1997), attachment 1 8 [4.4].

Robertson, Iain J. M., 'Introduction: Heritage from Below', in Iain J. M. Robertson (ed.), *Heritage from Below* (Ashgate, 2012), 1–27.

Robinson, Daniel F., *Biodiversity, Access and Benefit-Sharing: Global Case Studies* (Routledge, 2015).

Robinson, J., 'Squaring the Circle? Some Thoughts on the Idea of Sustainable Development', *Ecological Economics* 48 (2004), 369–84.

Rodríguez-Uribe, N. and Rodríguez-Uribe, D., 'Emerging Indigenous Voices: Safeguarding Intangible Heritage in Colombia and the Reaffirmation of Cultural Rights' in R. Amoêda, S Lira, and C. Pinheiro (eds), *Heritage 2012: Proceedings of the 3rd International Conference on Heritage and Sustainable Development* (Green Lines Institute, 2012), 1469–79.

Roodt, Christa, *Private International Law, Art and Cultural Heritage* (Edward Elgar, 2015).

Ruijgrok, E. C M., 'The Three Economic Values of Cultural Heritage: A Case Study in the Netherlands', *Journal of Cultural Heritage* 7 (2006), 206–13.

Rypkema, Donovan D., 'Heritage and Development: The Role of Public–Private Partnerships', in Mikko Mälkki, Raine Mäntysalo. and Kaisa Schmidt-Thomé (eds), *Economics and Built Heritage—Towards New European Initiatives* (Helsinki University of Technology, 2008), 131–50.

Sandholtz, Wayne, *Prohibiting Plunder: How Norms Change* (Oxford University Press, 2007).

Saunders, David, Chairman's message about the new Guidelines, attached to The Australia ICOMOS *Guidelines for the Conservation of Places of Cultural Significance* ('Burra Charter') (1979).

Sax, Joseph L., 'Heritage Preservation as a Public Duty: The Abbé Grégoire and the Origins of an Idea', *Michigan Law Review* 88(5) (1990), 1142–69.

Sax, Joseph L., *Playing Darts with a Rembrandt: Public and Private Interests in Cultural Treasures* (University of Michigan Press, 1999).

Schaap, Andrew, 'Political Reconciliation Through a Struggle for Recognition', *Social & Legal Studies* 13(4) (2004), 523–40.

Schofield, John, 'Heritage Expertise and the Everyday: Citizens and Authority in the Twenty-First Century', in John Schofield (ed.), *Who Needs Experts? Counter-mapping Cultural Heritage* (Ashgate, 2014), 1–11.

Seaman, Bruce A., 'The Role of the Private Sector in Cultural Heritage', in Ilde Rizzo and Anna Mignosa (eds), *Handbook on the Economics of Cultural Heritage* (Edward Elgar, 2013), 111–28.

Segall, Anna, 'Protecting Culture in Practice: The Unique Role of UNESCO', *International Humanitarian Law Magazine* 2 (2016), 8.

Shapiro, Daniel, 'Opinion: Legal Issues in the Trade of Antiquities', *International Journal of Cultural Property* 3(2) (1994), 365–95.

Shapiro-Phim, Toni, 'Dance, Music, and the Nature of Terror in Democratic Kampuchea', in Alexander Laban Hinton (ed.), *Annihilating Difference: The Anthropology of Genocide* (University of California Press, 2002), 179–93.

Shepherd, Robert J. and Yu, Larry, *Heritage Management, Tourism, and Governance in China: Managing the Past to Serve the Present* (Springer, 2013).

Shipley, Robert, 'Heritage Designation and Property Values: Is There an Effect?', *International Journal of Heritage Studies* 6(1) (2000), 83–100.

Shipley, R. and Snyder, M., 'The Role of Heritage Conservation Districts in Achieving Community Economic Development Goals', *International Journal of Heritage Studies* 19(3) (2013), 304–21.

Shyllon, Folarin, 'Cultural Heritage Legislation and Management in Nigeria', *International Journal of Cultural Property* 5(2) (1996), 235–68.

Siehr, Kurt, 'The Protection of Cultural Heritage and International Commerce', *International Journal of Cultural Property* 6(2) (1997), 304–25.

Silverman, Helaine and Ruggles, D. Fairchild, 'Cultural Heritage and Human Rights', in Helaine Silverman and D. Fairchild Ruggles (eds), *Cultural Heritage and Human Rights* (Springer, 2007), 3–29.

Sjöstedt, Britta, 'The Role of Multilateral Environmental Agreements in Armed Conflict: "Green-Keeping" in Virunga Park', *Nordic Journal of International Law* 82(1) (2013), 129–53.

Smith, A., 'East Rennell World Heritage Site: Misunderstandings, Inconsistencies and Opportunities in the Implementation of the World Heritage Convention in the Pacific Islands', *International Journal of Heritage Studies* 17 (2011), 592–607.

Smith, A. and Turk, C., 'Customary Systems of Management and World Heritage in the Pacific Islands' in S. Brockwell, S. O'Connor, and D. Byrne (eds), *Transcending the Nature–Culture Divide in Cultural Heritage: Views from the Asia-Pacific Region* (ANU E-Press, 2013), 23–34.

Smith, Laurajane, *Uses of Heritage* (Routledge, 2006).

Smith, Laurajane, 'Editorial', *International Journal of Heritage Studies* 18(6) (2012), 533–40.

Smith, Laurajane, 'Theorizing Museum and Heritage Visiting', in *The International Handbooks of Museum Studies*, vol. 3 (Wiley, 2015), 459–84.

Sneddon, C., Howarth, R. B., and Norgaard, R. B., 'Sustainable Development in a Post-Brundtland World', *Ecological Economics* 57 (2006), 253–68.

Soderland, Hilary A., 'The History of Heritage: A Method in Analyzing Legislative Historiography', in Marie-Louise Stig Sørensen and John Carman (eds), *Heritage Studies: Methods and Approaches* (Routledge, 2009), 55–84.

Sprankling, John G., *The International Law of Property* (Oxford University Press, 2014).

Stanziola, Javier, 'Modelling the Heritage World: Economic, Legal and Political Considerations', *International Journal of Heritage Studies* 4(3–4) (1998), 168–76.

Starrenburg, Sophie H., 'Effectively Protecting Cultural Heritage: Incorporating Cultural Genocide into the International Legal Definition of Genocide', BA thesis (Leiden University, 2014).

Stovel, Herb, 'Effective Use of Authenticity and Integrity as World Heritage Qualifying Conditions', *City & Time* 2(3) (2007), 21–36.

Strati, Anastasia, *Draft Convention on the Protection of Underwater Cultural Heritage—A Commentary prepared for UNESCO* (CLT-99/WS/8, April 1999).

Swenson, Astrid, 'The Law's Delay? Preservation Legislation in France, Germany and England, 1970–1994', in Melanie Hall (ed.), *Towards World Heritage: International Origins of the Preservation Movement 1870–1930* (Ashgate, 2011), 139–54.

Taylor, Christopher C., *Sacrifice as Terror: The Rwandan Genocide of 1994* (Berg, 1999).

Technical and Legal Aspects of the Preparation of International Regulations to Prevent the Illicit Import, Export and Sale of Cultural Property, UNESCO/CUA/115, of 14 April 1962.

Telesetsky, Anastasia and Nafziger, James A. R., 'Toward a Broader Concept of the Intangible Cultural Heritage', *Transnational Dispute Management* 11(2) (2014) 1–16.

Tharoor, Ishaan, 'Timbuktu's Destruction: Why Islamists Are Wrecking Mali's Cultural Heritage', *Time* World 2 July 2012, available at http://world.time.com/2012/07/02/timbuktus-destruction-why-islamists-are-wrecking-malis-cultural-heritage/ (accessed 30 October 2017).

The Bernard and Audre Rapoport Center for Human Rights and Justice, *Afro-Descendant Land Rights Project*, available at https://law.utexas.edu/humanrights/project-type/afro-descendants/ (accessed 30 October 2017).

Third Meeting of Governmental Experts to consider the draft Convention on the Protection of the Underwater Cultural Heritage. Synoptic Report of comments on the Draft Convention on the Protection of the Underwater Cultural Heritage made by Member States of UNESCO (April 2000). CLT-2000/CONF.201/3.

Thomas, David Hurst, 'Finders Keepers and Deep American History: Some Lessons in Dispute Resolution', in John Henry Merryman (ed.), *Imperialism, Art and Restitution* (Cambridge University Press, 2006), 218–53.

Thompson, Erin L., *Possession: The Curious History of Private Collectors from Antiquity to the Present* (Yale University Press, 2016).

Thornton, Sarah, *Seven Days in the Art World* (W. W. Norton & Company, 2008).

Throsby, David, 'Cultural Capital and Sustainability Concepts in the Economics of Cultural Heritage', in Marta de la Torre (ed.), *Assessing the Values of Cultural Heritage: Research Report* (J. Paul Getty Trust, 2002), 101–17.

Throsby, David, 'Regional Aspects of Heritage Economics: Analytical and Policy Issues', *Australasian Journal of Regional Studies* 13(1) (2007), 21–30.

Toman, Jiří, *Cultural Property in War: Improvement in Protection—Commentary on the 1999 Second Protocol to the Hague Convention of 1954 for the Protection of Cultural Property in the Event of Armed Conflict* (UNESCO Publishing, 2009).

Tornatore, Jean-Louis, 'Du patrimoine ethnologique au patrimoine culturel immatériel: suivre la voie politique de l'immatérialité culturelle', in Chiara Bortolotto (ed), *Le Patrimoine Culturel Immatériel* (Éditions de la Maison des sciences de l'homme 2011), 213–27.

Trindade, Ivonei Souza, *Caso Pavle Strugar: Um Estudo sobre a Proteção de Bens Culturais em Caso de Conflito Armado* (Casa de Autores, 2016).

Tythacott, Louise, 'Book Review: *Heritage Management, Tourism, and Governance in China: Managing the Past to Serve the Present*, by Robert J. Shepher and Larry Yu. *International Journal of Heritage Studies* 21(8) (2015), 842–3.

Ubertazzi, Benedetta, 'The Territorial Condition for the Inscription of Elements on the UNESCO Lists of Intangible Cultural Heritage', in Nicolas Adell, Regina F. Bendix, Chiara Bortolotto, and Markus Tauschek (eds), *Between Imagined Communities and Communities of Practice: Participation, Territory and the Making of Heritage* (Universitätsverlag Göttingen, 2015), 111–22.

Ulph, Janet, 'Criminal Offenses Affecting the Trade in Art and Antiquities', in Janet Ulph and Ian Smith (eds), *The Illicit Trade in Art and Antiquities: International Recovery and Criminal and Civil Liability* (Hart, 2012), 78–146.

Ulph, Janet and Smith, Ian, *The Illicit Trade in Art and Antiquities: International Recovery and Criminal and Civil Liability* (Hart, 2012).

Underkuffler, Laura S., *The Idea of Property: Its Meaning and Power* (Oxford University Press, 2003).

UNESCO Archives, *Protection des bien culturels*, Folder 069:7, Parts I–IV.

'UNESCO Director-General Deplores Destruction of Ancient Aleppo Markets, a World Heritage Site', available at http://whc.unesco.org/en/news/940 (accessed 30 October 2017).

UNESCO Executive Board, *Feasibility Study for the drafting of a new instrument for the protection of the underwater cultural heritage* (23 March 1995). 146 EX/27.

UNESCO Executive Board, *Possible International Instrument for the Protection of Monuments and Sites of Universal Value* (22 April 1970), 84 EX/14.

UNESCO Executive Board, *Report on the preliminary study on the advisability of regulating internationally, through a new standard-setting instrument, the protection of traditional culture and folklore.* 161 EX/15, of 16 May 2001.

UNESCO General Conference, 16th Session. *Item 19 of the Provisional Agenda—Draft convention on the means of prohibiting and preventing the illicit import, export and transfer of ownership of cultural property*, 16 C/17, 13 July 1970. Annex II—Report of the Special Committee of Governmental Experts to examine the draft convention on the means of prohibiting and preventing the illicit import, export and transfer of ownership of cultural property.

UNESCO General Conference, *Draft Convention for the Protection of the World Cultural and Natural Heritage and Draft Recommendation Concerning the Protection, at National Level, of the Cultural and Natural Heritage* (15 June 1972), 17 C/18.

UNESCO General Conference, *Report by the Director-General on action taken concerning the desirability of preparing an international instrument for the protection of the underwater cultural heritage*, of 5 August 1997. Annex I—Summary report of the meeting of experts for the protection of underwater cultural heritage (22-24 May 1996). 29 C/22.

UNESCO Intergovernmental Committee for the Safeguarding of the Intangible Cultural Heritage, *Decisions—Marimba music, traditional chants and dances from the Colombia South Pacific region and Esmeraldas Province of Ecuador*, 10th sess., Decision 10.COM 10.b.13, ITH/15/10.COM/Decisions (30 November–4 December 2015).

UNESCO Intergovernmental Committee for the Safeguarding of the Intangible Cultural Heritage, *Decisions*, 5th sess., Decision 5.COM 6.8, ITH/10/5.COM/CONF.202/ Decisions (15–19 November 2010).

UNESCO Intergovernmental Committee for the Safeguarding of the Intangible Cultural Heritage, *Nomination File for Inscription on the Representative List of the Intangible Cultural Heritage in 2010*, 5th sess., Document No 00436 (November 2010).

UNESCO Intergovernmental Committee for the Safeguarding of the Intangible Cultural Heritage, *Nomination File for Inscription on the Representative List of the Intangible Cultural Heritage in 2015*, 10th sess., Document No 01099 (November 2015).

UNESCO Intergovernmental Committee for the Safeguarding of the Intangible Cultural Heritage, *Decisions*, 10th sess., Decision 10.COM 10.b.13, ITH/15/10.COM/Decisions (30 November–4 December 2015).

UNESCO World Heritage Centre, *Sustainable Tourism—UNESCO World Heritage and Sustainable Tourism Programme*, available at http://whc.unesco.org/en/tourism/ (accessed 30 October 2017).

UNESCO World Heritage Centre, *World Heritage Lists*, available at http://whc.unesco.org/en/list/ (accessed 30 October 2017).

UNESCO World Heritage Committee, *Decision: East Rennell (Solomon Island) (N 854)*, 37 COM 7B.14, 37th sess., WHC-13/37.COM/20 (16–27 June 2013).

UNESCO, 'Address by Mr Koïchiro Matsuura, Director-General of the United Nations Educational, Scientific and Cultural Organization (UNESCO), on the occasion of the International Round Table: "*Intangible Cultural Heritage: Working Definitions*"'. DG/2001/33 (14 March 2001).

UNESCO, 'UNESCO supports a project of preservation for the Tuol Sleng Genocide Museum premises and its archives to keep alive the memory of Cambodian history', available at http://www.unesco.org/new/en/culture/themes/museums/museum-projects/archive/unesco-supports-a-project-of-preservation-for-the-tuol-sleng-genocide-museum-premises-and-its-archives-to-keep-alive-the-memory-of-cambodian-history/ (accessed 29 October, 2017).

UNESCO, *Culture and Development*, available at http://www.unesco.org/new/en/culture/themes/culture-and-development/ (last accessed 9 February 2017).

UNESCO, *Endangered Languages*, available at http://www.unesco.org/new/en/culture/themes/endangered-languages/faq-on-endangered-languages/ (accessed 30 January 2019).

UNESCO, Intergovernmental Committee for the Safeguarding of the Intangible Cultural Heritage, Nomination for Inscription on the Representative List in 2009 (Reference No. 00225)—The Dragon Boat Festival.

UNESCO, *International Coordination Committee for the Safeguarding of the Cultural Heritage of Iraq*, available at http://whc.unesco.org/en/activities/181/ (accessed 27 October 2017).

UNESCO, *International Round Table: 'Intangible Cultural Heritage—Working Definitions'*, meeting held in Turin, Italy, on 14–17 March 2001.

UNESCO, *Preparation of a preliminary draft International Convention on the Intangible Cultural Heritage, Meeting of the 'Restricted Drafting Group' (RDG) in Paris, 20–22 March 2002—Outline Work Plan.*

UNESCO, *Report on the Expert Meeting on Criteria for Inscription on the Lists Established by the 2003 Convention for the Safeguarding of the Intangible Cultural Heritage* (Paris, 5–6 December 2005).

UNESCO, *State of Conservation (SOC) Report: East Rennell (Solomon Islands)* (2013) UNESCO World Heritage Centre, available at http://whc.unesco.org/en/soc/1876 (accessed 30 October 2017).

UNESCO, *UNESCO reiterates call for unity and coordination to protect Syrian Cultural Heritage*, available at http://whc.unesco.org/en/news/1475 (accessed 27 October 2017).

UNESCO, *World Heritage List: East Rennell*, UNESCO World Heritage Centre, available at http://whc.unesco.org/en/list/854 (accessed 30 October 2017).

United Nations, *Framework of Analysis for Atrocity Crimes: A Tool for Prevention* (2014).

United Nations Human Rights Council, *Final report of the study on indigenous peoples and the right to participate in decision-making—Report of the Expert Mechanism on the Rights of Indigenous Peoples*, UN Doc. A/HRC/18/42 (17 August 2011).

UNWTO, *Conclusions & Highlights of the 6th UNWTO International Meeting on Silk Road Tourism* (Dunhuang, Gansu, 1–3 August 2013), available at http://silkroad.unwto.org/event/meeting-information-6th-unwto-international-meeting-silk-road-tourism (accessed 30 October 2017).

UNWTO, *History*, available at http://www2.unwto.org/content/history-0 (accessed 30 October 2017).

UNWTO, *UNWTO & the UN System*, available at http://icr.unwto.org/content/unwto-un-system (accessed 30 October 2017).

UNWTO, *Who We Are*, available at http://www2.unwto.org/content/who-we-are-0 (accessed 30 October 2017).

UNWTO, *Why Tourism?*, available at http://www2.unwto.org/content/why-tourism (accessed 30 October 2017).

Vadi, Valentina, *Cultural Heritage in International Investment Law and Arbitration* (Cambridge University Press, 2014).

Vadi, Valentina, 'Cultural Heritage in International Economic Law', in Valentina Vadi and Bruno de Witte (eds), *Culture and International Economic Law* (Routledge, 2015), 53–71.

Van Damme, Isabelle, 'Treaty Interpretation by the WTO Appellate Body', *European Journal of International Law* 21(3) (2010), 605–48.

van der Haagen, J. K., 'The Part Played by UNESCO in the Preservation of the Cultural Heritage of Mankind and in the Development of Museums', speech delivered at an Archaeological Congress organized by the League of Arab States. WS/018.68, January 1958.

van der Walt, A. J., *Property in the Margins* (Hart, 2009).

van Meijl, Toon, 'Pacific Discourses about Cultural Heritage and Its Protection: An Introduction', *International Journal of Cultural Property* 16 (2009), 221–32.

Vaughan, D. R., 'The Cultural Heritage: An Approach to Analyzing Income and Employment Effects', *Journal of Cultural Economics* 8(2) (1984), 1–36.

Vives, Alberto Abello and Candela, Dina, 'La Cultura en la Superación de la Pobreza', in Alfons Martinell Sempere (ed.), *Impactos de la Dimensión Cultural en el Desarrollo* (Documenta Universitaria, 2013), 53–100.

Voon, Tania, *Cultural Products and the World Trade Organization* (Cambridge University Press, 2007).

Vrdoljak, Ana Filipa, *International Law, Museums and the Return of Cultural Objects* (Cambridge University Press, 2006).

Vrdoljak, Ana Filipa, 'Article 13: World Heritage Committee and International Assistance', in Francesco Francioni (ed.), *The 1972 World Heritage Convention: A Commentary* (Oxford University Press, 2008), 219–41.

Vrdoljak, Ana Filipa, 'Cultural Heritage in Human Rights and Humanitarian Law', in Ben-Naftali Orna (ed.), *International Humanitarian Law and International Human Rights Law* (Oxford University Press, 2011), 250–302.

Vrdoljak, Ana Filipa, 'Genocide and Restitution: Ensuring Each Group's Contribution to Humanity', *European Journal of International Law* 22(1) (2011), 17–47.

Vrdoljak, Ana Filipa, 'Human Rights and Cultural Heritage in International Law', in F. Lenzerini and A. F. Vrdoljak (eds), *International Law for Common Goods: Normative Perspectives on Human Rights, Culture and Nature* (Hart, 2014), 139–74.

Vrdoljak, Ana Filipa, 'Cultural Heritage in Human Rights and Humanitarian Law'(January 2009), working paper available at http://works.bepress.com/ana_filipa_vrdoljak/15 (accessed 29 October 2017).

Vrdoljak, Ana Filipa, 'Cultural Heritage, Human Rights and the Privatisation of War', in Andrea Durbach and Lucas Lixinski (eds), *Heritage, Culture and Rights—Challenging Legal Discourses* (Hart, 2017), 61–90.

Vrdoljak, Ana Filipa, 'Introductory Note to *Prosecutor v Ahmad Al Faqi Al Mahdi* (Int'l Crim Ct)', 57 *ILM* 17 (2018).

Waelde, Charlotte, Cummings, Catherine, Pavis, Mathilde, and Enright, Helena (eds), *Research Handbook on Contemporary Intangible Cultural Heritage: Law and Heritage* (Edward Elgar, 2018).

Wai-Yin, Chan and Shu-Yun, Ma, 'Heritage Preservation and Sustainability of China's Development', *Sustainable Development* 12 (2004), 15–31.

Walker, Dominic, 'Local World Heritage: Relocating Expertise in World Heritage Management', in John Schofield (ed.), *Who Needs Experts? Counter-mapping Cultural Heritage* (Ashgate, 2014), 181–201.

Walliss, Jillian, 'The Right to Land Versus the Right to Landscape: Lessons from Uluru–Kata Tjuta National Park, Australia', in Shelley Egoz, Jala Mkhzoumi, and Gloria Pungetti (eds), *The Right to Landscape: Contesting Landscape and Human Rights* (Routledge, 2011), 153–64.

Wangkeo, Kanchana, 'Monumental Challenges: The Lawfulness of Destroying Cultural Heritage During Peacetime', 28 *Yale Journal of International Law* (2003) 183–274.

Waterton, Emma, 'Whose Sense of Place? Reconciling Archaeological Perspectives with Community Values: Cultural Landscapes in England', *International Journal of Heritage Studies* 11(4) (2005), 309–25.

Waterton, Emma and Smith, Laurajane, *Heritage, Communities and Archaeology* (Bristol Classical Press, 2009).

Waterton, Emma and Smith, Laurajane, 'The Recognition and Misrecognition of Community Heritage', *International Journal of Heritage Studies* 16(1–2) (2010), 4–15.

Waterton, Emma and Watson, Steve, *The Semiotics of Heritage Tourism* (Channel View Publications, 2014).

Watson, Irene, *Aboriginal Peoples, Colonialism and International Law: Raw Law* (Routledge, 2015).

Watson, Steve and Waterton, Emma, 'Editorial: Heritage and Community Engagement', *International Journal of Heritage Studies* 16(1–2) (2010), 1–3.

Watt, James C. Y., 'Antiquities and the Importance—and Limitations—of Archaeological Context', in James Cuno (ed.), *Whose Culture? The Promise of Museums and the Debate over Antiquities* (Princeton University Press, 2009), 89–106.

Weber, Florence, 'Vichy France and the End of Scientific Folklore (1937–1954)', in Benoit de L'Estoile, Federico Neiburg, and Lygia Sigaud (eds), *Empires, Nations, and Natives: Anthropology and State-Making* (Duke University Press, 2005), 88–107.

Weihe, Hugo Keith, 'Licit International Traffic in Cultural Objects for Art's Sake', *International Journal of Cultural Property* 4(1) (1995), 81–90.

Wells, Clare, *The 'Politicisation' of United Nations Specialised Agencies? UNESCO, the UN and the Politics of Knowledge 1945–82*, PhD thesis (Trinity College Dublin, 1984).

Whitby-Last, K., 'Article 1: Cultural Landscapes', in Francesco Francioni and Federico Lenzerini (eds), *The 1972 World Heritage Convention: A Commentary* (Oxford University Press, 2008), 51–63.

Winter, Michael and Gasson, Ruth, 'Pilgrimage and Tourism: Cathedral Visiting in Contemporary England', *International Journal of Heritage Studies* 2(3) (1996), 172–82.

Winter, Tim, 'Angkor Meets *Tomb Raider*: Setting the Scene', *International Journal of Heritage Studies* 8(4) (2002), 323–36.

Wolferstan, Sarah, 'Ethnography of a "Humble Expert": Experiencing Faro', in John Schofield (ed.), *Who Needs Experts? Counter-mapping Cultural Heritage* (Ashgate, 2014), 43–53.

World Commission on Environment and Development, *Our Common Future: Report of the World Commission on Environment and Development*, UN GAOR, 42nd sess., UN Doc A/42/427 (4 August 1987).

World Heritage Committee, Decisions Adopted by the 27th Session of the World Heritage Committee in 2003, Decision 27 COM 8C.43; UNESCO, *Cultural Landscape and Archaeological Remains of the Bamiyan Valley*, available at http://whc.unesco.org/en/list/208 (accessed 30 October 2017).

World Heritage Committee, *Old Bridge Area of the Old City of Mostar*, available at http://whc.unesco.org/en/list/946 (accessed 30 October 2017).

Worsley, Lucy, 'Changing Notions of Authenticity: Presenting a Castle Over Four Centuries', *International Journal of Heritage Studies* 10(2) (2004), 129–49.

Wright, Nancy E., and Collins-Gearing, Brooke, 'The Rhetoric of Benevolence as an Impediment to the Protection of Indigenous Cultural Rights: A Study of Australian Literature and Law', *Journal of Australian Studies* 29(85) (2005), 57–68.

Xifaras, Mikhail, *La Propriété: Etude de Philosophie du Droit* (Presses Universitaires de France, 2004).

Young, Linda, 'Globalisation, Culture and Museums: A Review of Theory', *International Journal of Heritage Studies* 5(1) (1999), 6–15.

Yusin, Jennifer, 'The Itinerary of Commemoration in the Kigali Memorial Centre: On Trauma, Time and Difference', *Culture, Theory and Critique* 57(3) (2015), 338–56.

Yusuf, Abdulqawi A., 'Article 1—Definition of Cultural Heritage', in Francesco Francioni and Federico Lenzerini (eds), *The 1972 World Heritage Convention: A Commentary* (Oxford University Press, 2008), 23–50.

Zachwatowicz, J., *Scientific and Technical Rules for Protection Operations*, report presented at the Meeting of Experts to co-ordinate with a view to their international adoption, the principles and scientific, technical and legal criteria which would make it possible to establish an effective system for the protection of monuments and sites. SHC/CS/27/4, of 31 January 1968.

Zan, Luca, 'Economic Discourse and Heritage Conservation: Towards and Ethnography of Administrations', *Heritage & Society* 6(2) (2013), 167–84.

Index

For the benefit of digital users, indexed terms that span two pages (e.g., 52–53) may, on occasion, appear on only one of those pages.